久保帯人

"Hi, it's me, Nancy.♡ I live inside the refrigerator at Tite's house.♡ I think the series will already be over in *Weekly Shonen Jump* by the time you read this, but thanks for buying volume 2.♡ You're so wonderful.♡ It makes me want to put tooth marks all over your body.♡ Oh no, I'm running out of space. Okay then, 'bye."♡

-Tite Kubo, 2000

Tite Kubo is best known as the creator of the smash hit *SHONEN JUMP* manga series *Bleach*, which began serialization in *Weekly Shonen Jump* in 2001. *ZOMBIEPOWDER.*, his debut series, began serialization in 1999.

**ZOMBIEPOWDER. VOL. 2**
**The SHONEN JUMP Manga Edition**

STORY AND ART BY
TITE KUBO

Translation/Akira Watanabe
Touch-up Art & Lettering/Stephen Dutro
Design/Sean Lee
Editor/Jason Thompson

Managing Editor/Frances E. Wall
Editorial Director/Elizabeth Kawasaki
VP & Editor in Chief/Yumi Hoashi
Sr. Director of Acquisitions/Rika Inouye
Sr. VP of Marketing/Liza Coppola
Exec. VP of Sales & Marketing/John Easum
Publisher/Hyoe Narita

Published by VIZ Media, LLC
P.O. Box 77010
San Francisco, CA 94107

SHONEN JUMP Manga Edition
10 9 8 7 6 5 4 3 2 1
First printing, December 2006

www.viz.com

THE WORLD'S
MOST POPULAR MANGA

www.shonenjump.com

# ZOMBIEPOWDER.

### Vol. 2
### CAN'T KISS THE RING (OF THE DEAD)

### Story & Art by
### Tite Kubo

*Words don't exist so that we can tell the truth; they exist so that
we can conceal the truth.*

# TERS

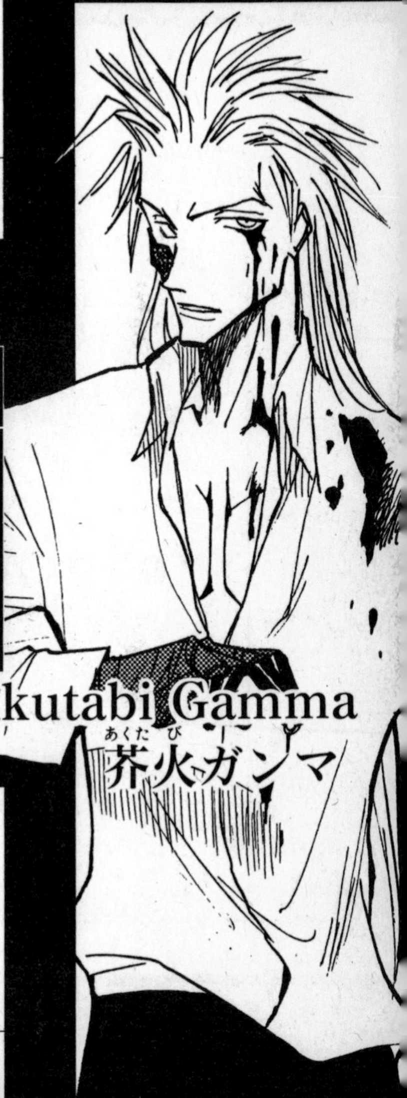

**Akutabi Gamma**
芥火ガンマ

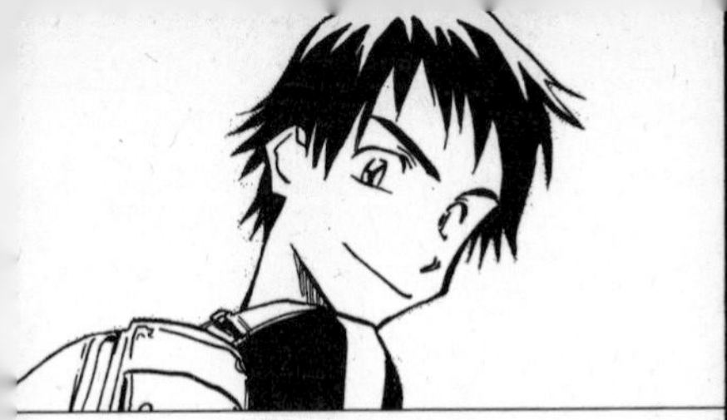

**Elwood**
エルウッド

## R Y

Elwood, a young boy roped into a life of crime, is rescued by Gamma, a Powder Hunter with a black metal arm and a mysterious past. Together with Gamma's partner, the gunman C.T. Smith, they infiltrate the headquarters of a bandit gang to steak one of the all-powerful Rings. In a life-or-death battle, Gamma defeats Calder, the leader of the bandits!

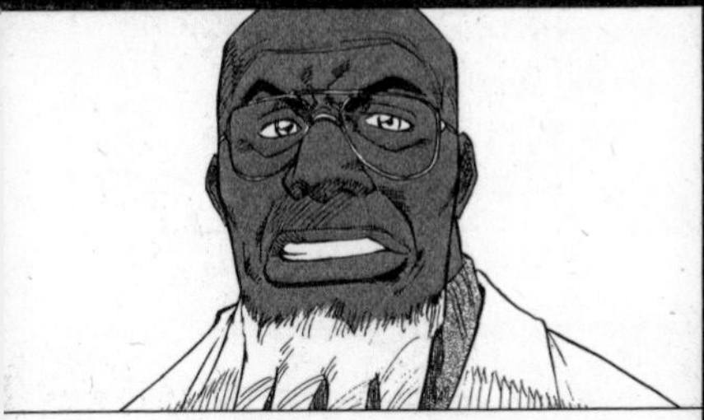

**Roscoe**
ロスコー

# TERS

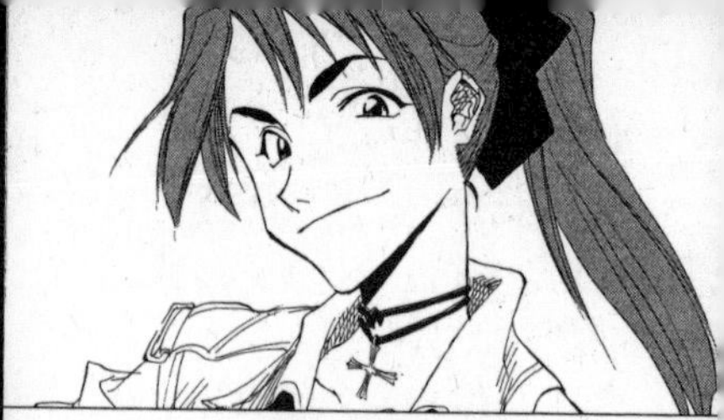

**Wolfina**
ウルフィーナ

## S T O

The Rings of the Dead: the world's only source of "Zombie Powder," a substance said to be able to raise the dead and give the living eternal life. In the badlands of blood and smoke, no one is more feared than the "Powder Hunters," those reckless souls willing to risk their own lives in pursuit of the dream of immortality.

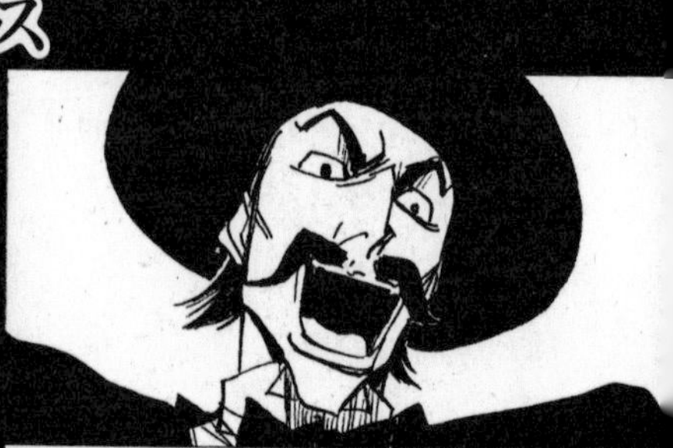

**Balmunk**
バルムンク

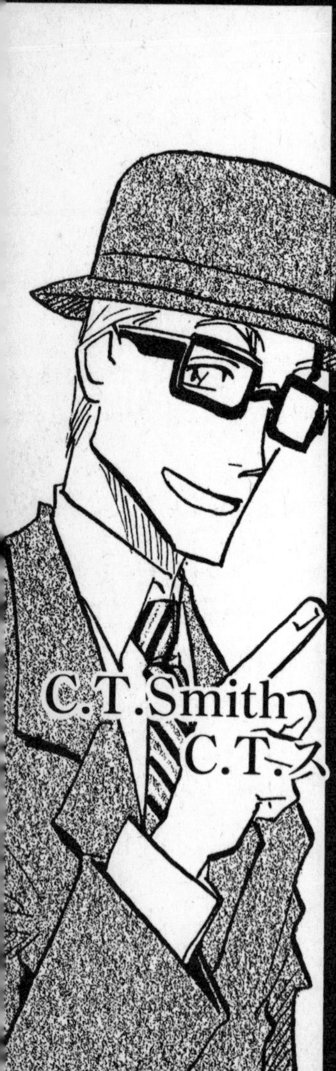
C.T.Smith
C.T.スミス

# ZOMBIEPOWDER.
## Vol. 2
### CAN'T KISS THE RING (OF THE DEAD)

## CONTENTS

Track 8: Search and Bangaway 7

Track 9: Tripod of Justice 28

Track 10: Wolfina (Has No Lips to Tell You) 47

Track 11: Rocker & Mystic 67

Track 12: Ring of the Dead (My Love Will Eat You Up) 85

Track 13: The Evergreen Birdcage 103

Track 14: Killer Circus 125

Ultra Unholy Hearted Machine 145

# Track 8: Search & Bangaway

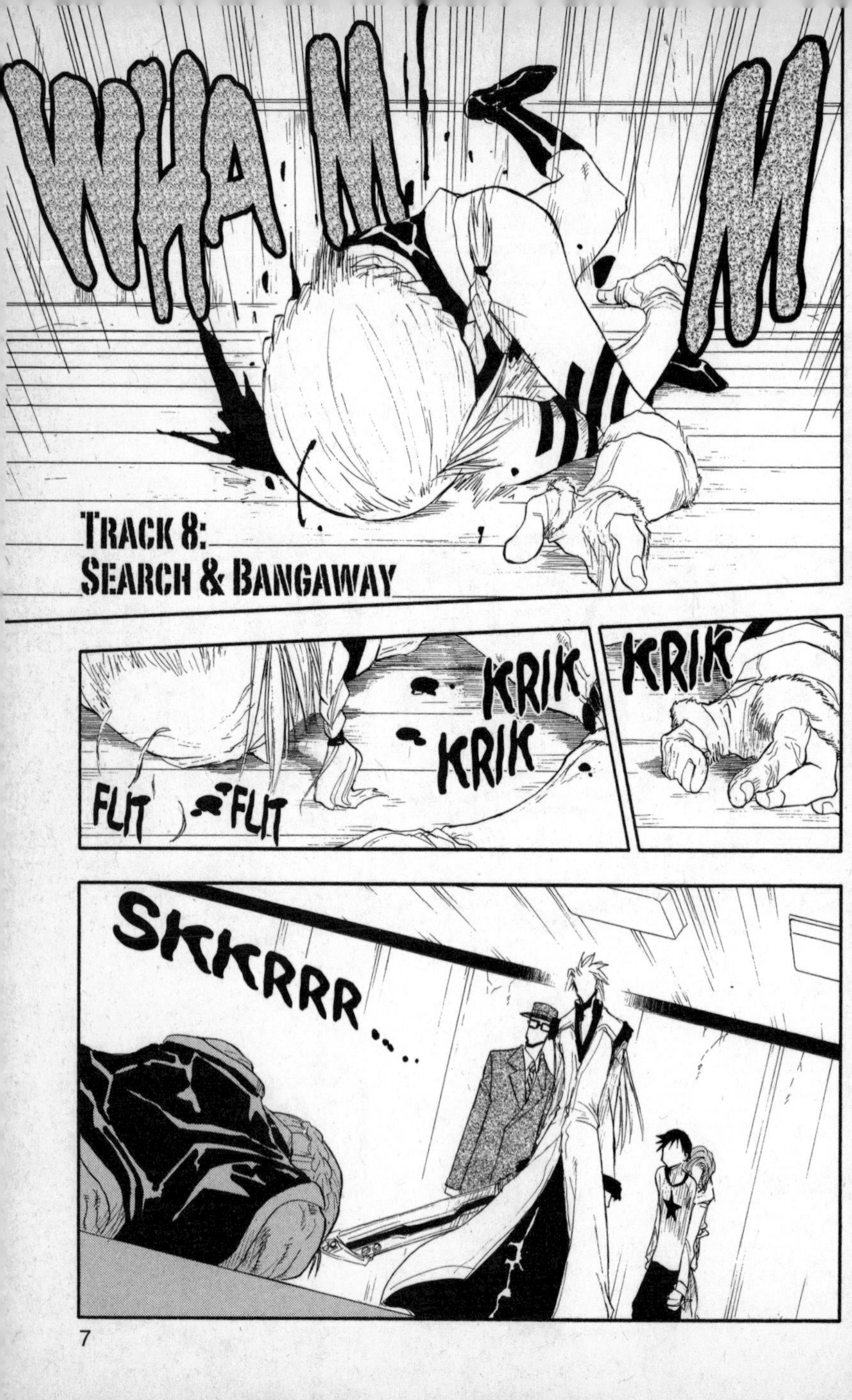
WHAMM
KRIK
KRIK
KRIK
FLIT
FLIT
SKKRRR.....

# ZOMBIEPOWDER.

## TRACK 8: SEARCH & BANGAWAY

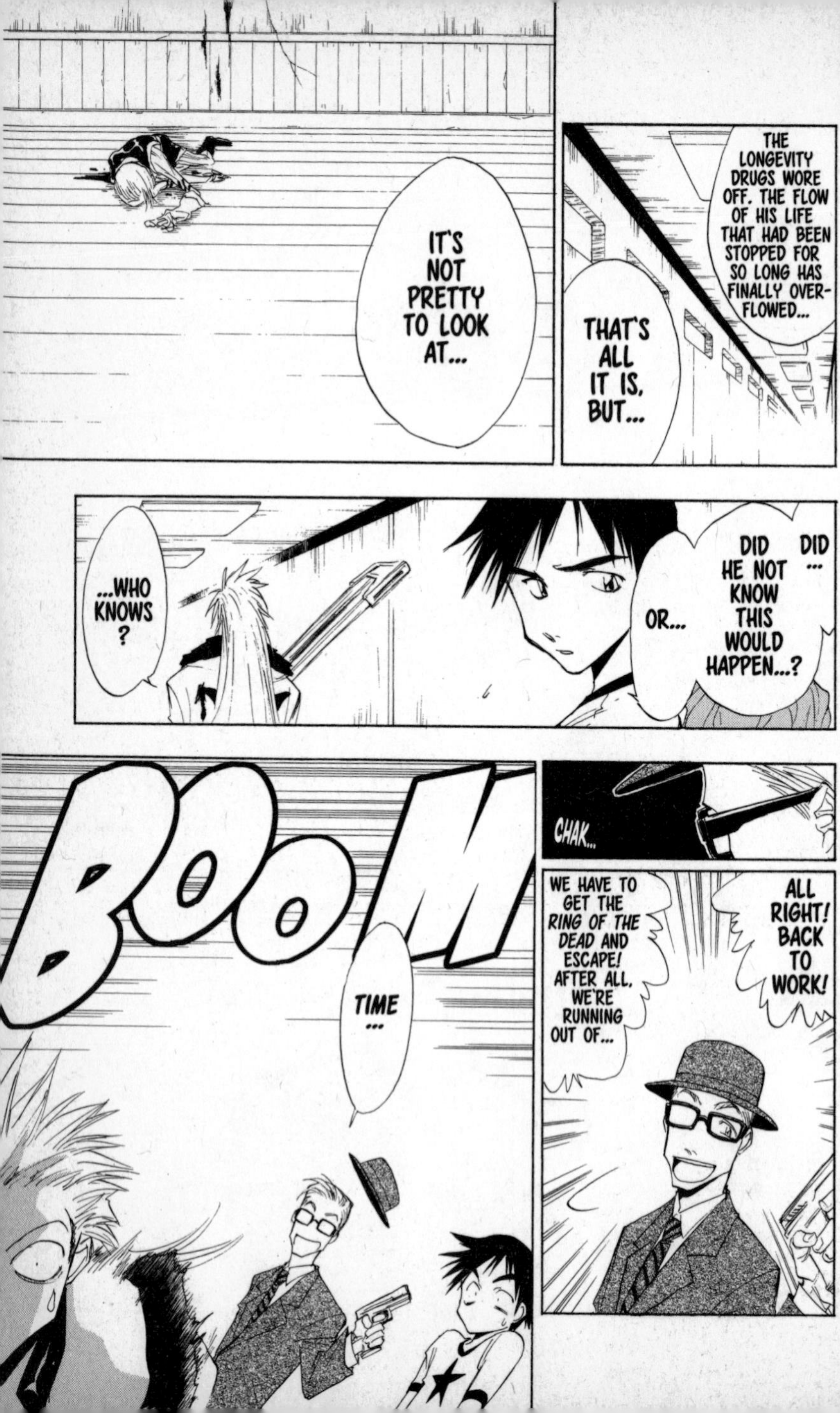
THE LONGEVITY DRUGS WORE OFF. THE FLOW OF HIS LIFE THAT HAD BEEN STOPPED FOR SO LONG HAS FINALLY OVER-FLOWED...
THAT'S ALL IT IS, BUT...
IT'S NOT PRETTY TO LOOK AT...
DID...
DID HE NOT KNOW THIS WOULD HAPPEN...?
OR...
...WHO KNOWS?
CHAK...
ALL RIGHT! BACK TO WORK!
WE HAVE TO GET THE RING OF THE DEAD AND ESCAPE! AFTER ALL, WE'RE RUNNING OUT OF...
TIME...
BOOM

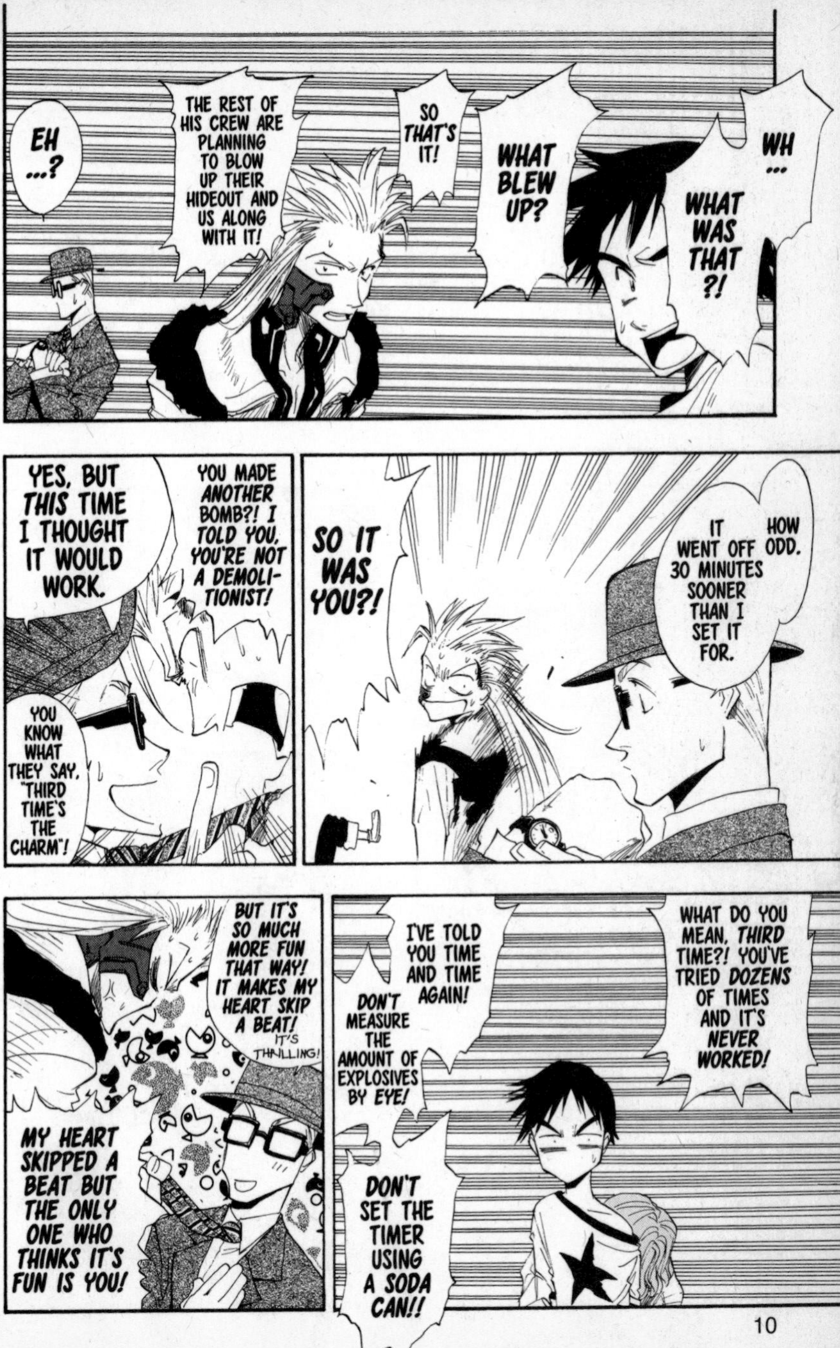
WH ... WHAT WAS THAT?!
WHAT BLEW UP?
SO THAT'S IT!
THE REST OF HIS CREW ARE PLANNING TO BLOW UP THEIR HIDEOUT AND US ALONG WITH IT!
EH ...?
HOW ODD.
IT WENT OFF 30 MINUTES SOONER THAN I SET IT FOR.
SO IT WAS YOU?!
YOU MADE ANOTHER BOMB?! I TOLD YOU, YOU'RE NOT A DEMOLITIONIST!
YES, BUT THIS TIME I THOUGHT IT WOULD WORK.
YOU KNOW WHAT THEY SAY, "THIRD TIME'S THE CHARM"!
WHAT DO YOU MEAN, THIRD TIME?! YOU'VE TRIED DOZENS OF TIMES AND IT'S NEVER WORKED!
I'VE TOLD YOU TIME AND TIME AGAIN!
DON'T MEASURE THE AMOUNT OF EXPLOSIVES BY EYE!
DON'T SET THE TIMER USING A SODA CAN!!
BUT IT'S SO MUCH MORE FUN THAT WAY! IT MAKES MY HEART SKIP A BEAT!
IT'S THRILLING!
MY HEART SKIPPED A BEAT BUT THE ONLY ONE WHO THINKS IT'S FUN IS YOU!

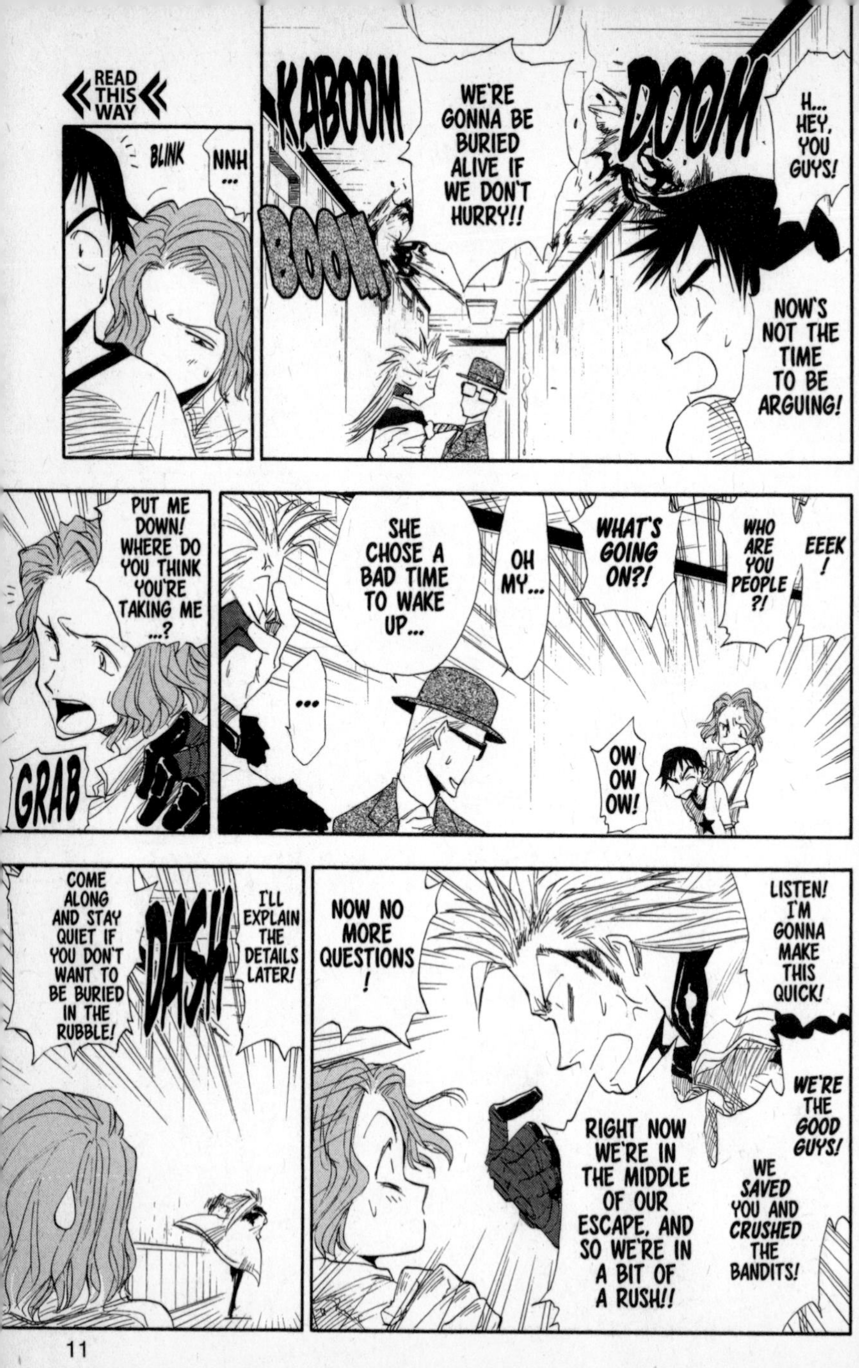
READ THIS WAY
H... HEY, YOU GUYS!
NOW'S NOT THE TIME TO BE ARGUING!
DOOM
WE'RE GONNA BE BURIED ALIVE IF WE DON'T HURRY!!
KABOOM
BOOM
NNH ...
BLINK
EEEK!
WHO ARE YOU PEOPLE?!
WHAT'S GOING ON?!
OH MY...
SHE CHOSE A BAD TIME TO WAKE UP...
...
OW OW OW!
PUT ME DOWN! WHERE DO YOU THINK YOU'RE TAKING ME ...?
GRAB
LISTEN! I'M GONNA MAKE THIS QUICK!
NOW NO MORE QUESTIONS!
WE'RE THE GOOD GUYS!
WE SAVED YOU AND CRUSHED THE BANDITS!
RIGHT NOW WE'RE IN THE MIDDLE OF OUR ESCAPE, AND SO WE'RE IN A BIT OF A RUSH!!
I'LL EXPLAIN THE DETAILS LATER!
DASH
COME ALONG AND STAY QUIET IF YOU DON'T WANT TO BE BURIED IN THE RUBBLE!

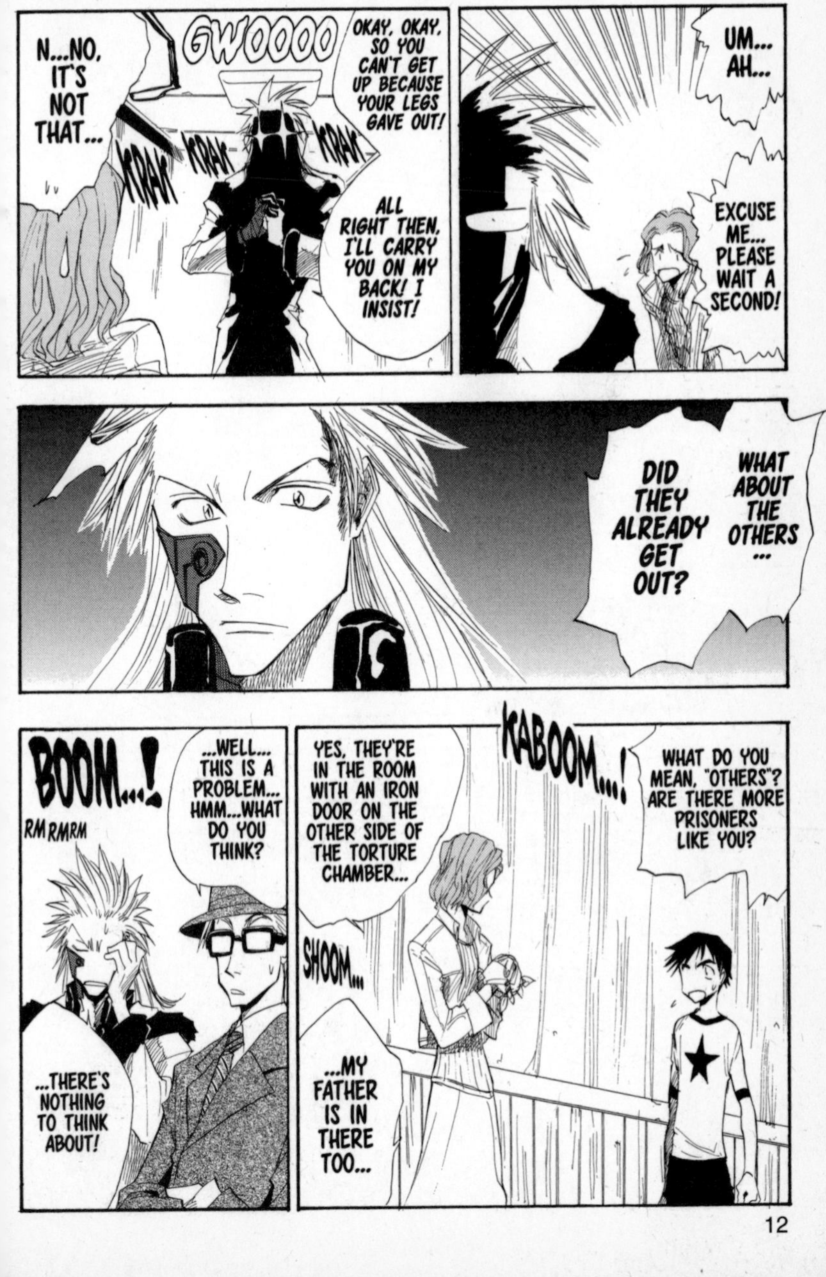
UM... AH...
EXCUSE ME... PLEASE WAIT A SECOND!
GWOOOO
OKAY, OKAY, SO YOU CAN'T GET UP BECAUSE YOUR LEGS GAVE OUT!
KRAK
KRAK
KRAK
ALL RIGHT THEN, I'LL CARRY YOU ON MY BACK! I INSIST!
N...NO, IT'S NOT THAT...
WHAT ABOUT THE OTHERS...
DID THEY ALREADY GET OUT?
KABOOM...!
WHAT DO YOU MEAN, "OTHERS"? ARE THERE MORE PRISONERS LIKE YOU?
YES, THEY'RE IN THE ROOM WITH AN IRON DOOR ON THE OTHER SIDE OF THE TORTURE CHAMBER...
SHOOM...
...MY FATHER IS IN THERE TOO...
BOOM...!
...WELL... THIS IS A PROBLEM... HMM...WHAT DO YOU THINK?
RM RMRM
...THERE'S NOTHING TO THINK ABOUT!

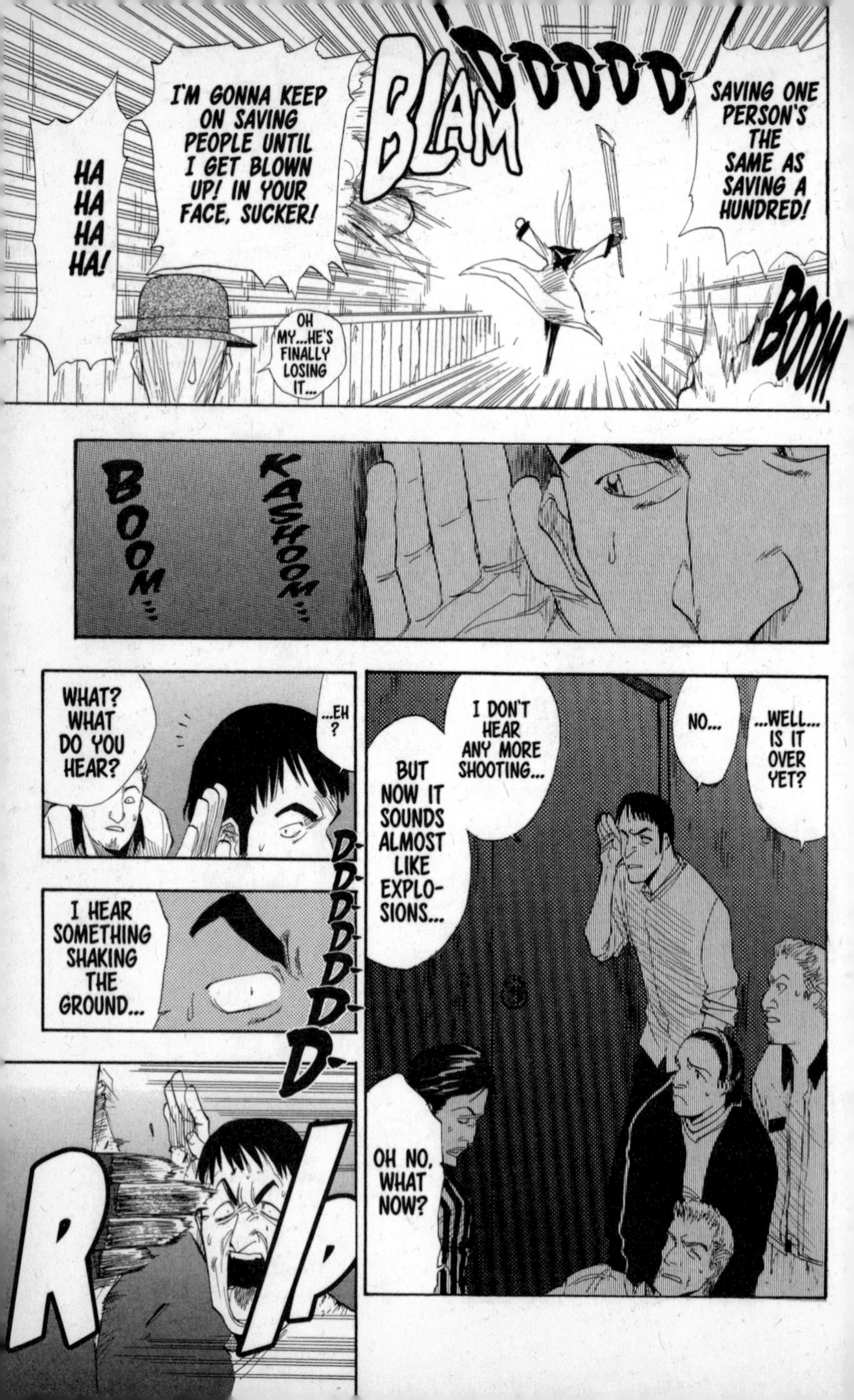
SAVING ONE PERSON'S THE SAME AS SAVING A HUNDRED!
BOOM
BLAM
BDDDDDD
I'M GONNA KEEP ON SAVING PEOPLE UNTIL I GET BLOWN UP! IN YOUR FACE, SUCKER!
HA HA HA HA!
OH MY...HE'S FINALLY LOSING IT...
KASHOOM...
BOOM...
...WELL... IS IT OVER YET?
NO...
I DON'T HEAR ANY MORE SHOOTING...
BUT NOW IT SOUNDS ALMOST LIKE EXPLOSIONS...
OH NO, WHAT NOW?
...EH?
WHAT? WHAT DO YOU HEAR?
I HEAR SOMETHING SHAKING THE GROUND...
DDDDDDD
RIP

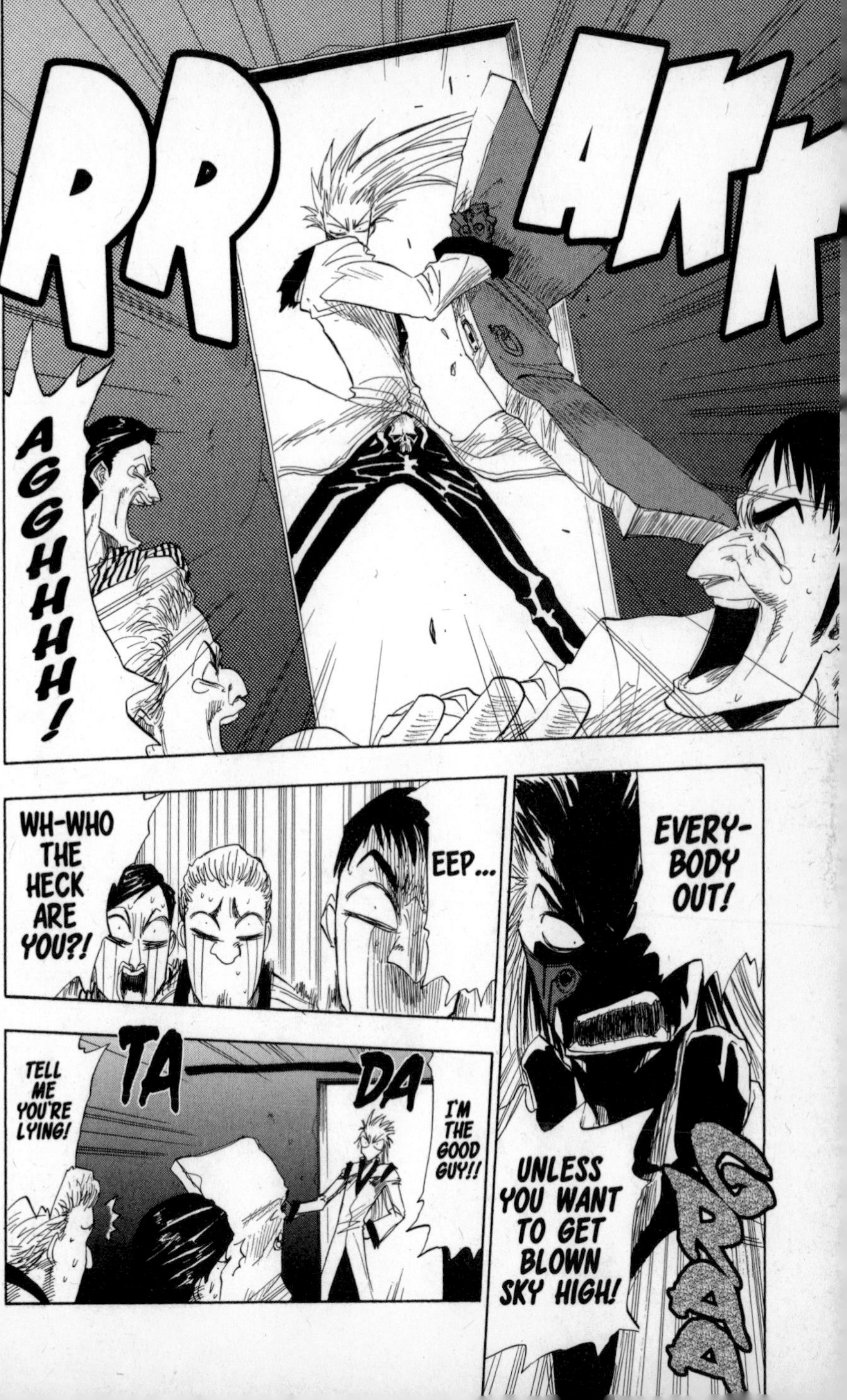
RR
AKK
AGGHHHHHH!
EVERY-BODY OUT!
UNLESS YOU WANT TO GET BLOWN SKY HIGH!
GRAAA
EEP...
WH-WHO THE HECK ARE YOU?!
TA—DA
I'M THE GOOD GUY!!
TELL ME YOU'RE LYING!

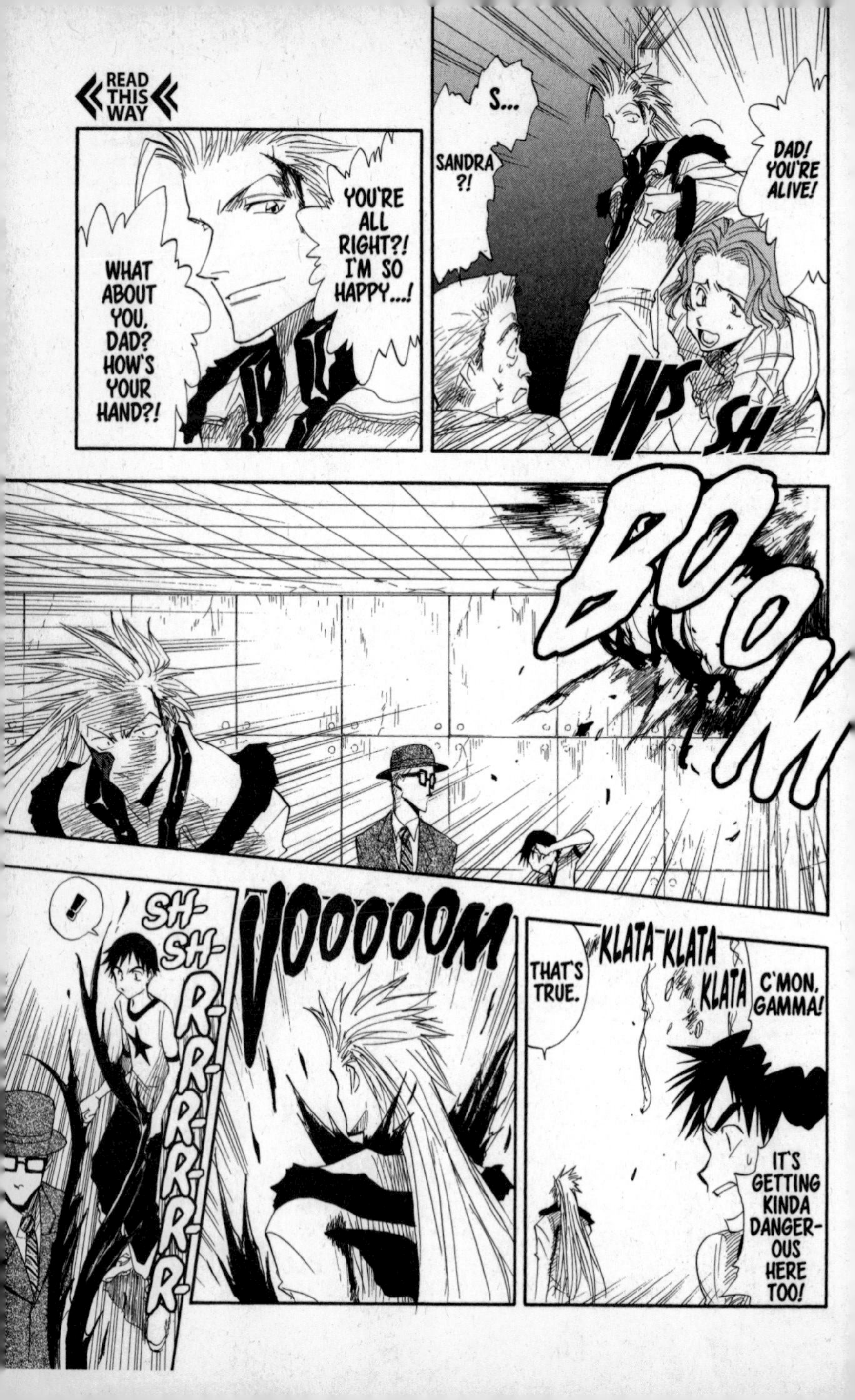
READ THIS WAY
DAD! YOU'RE ALIVE!
S...
SANDRA?!
WSSH
YOU'RE ALL RIGHT?! I'M SO HAPPY...!
WHAT ABOUT YOU, DAD? HOW'S YOUR HAND?!
BOOM
KLATA KLATA KLATA
C'MON, GAMMA!
IT'S GETTING KINDA DANGER-OUS HERE TOO!
THAT'S TRUE.
VOOOOOM
SH-SH-RRRRRR-
!

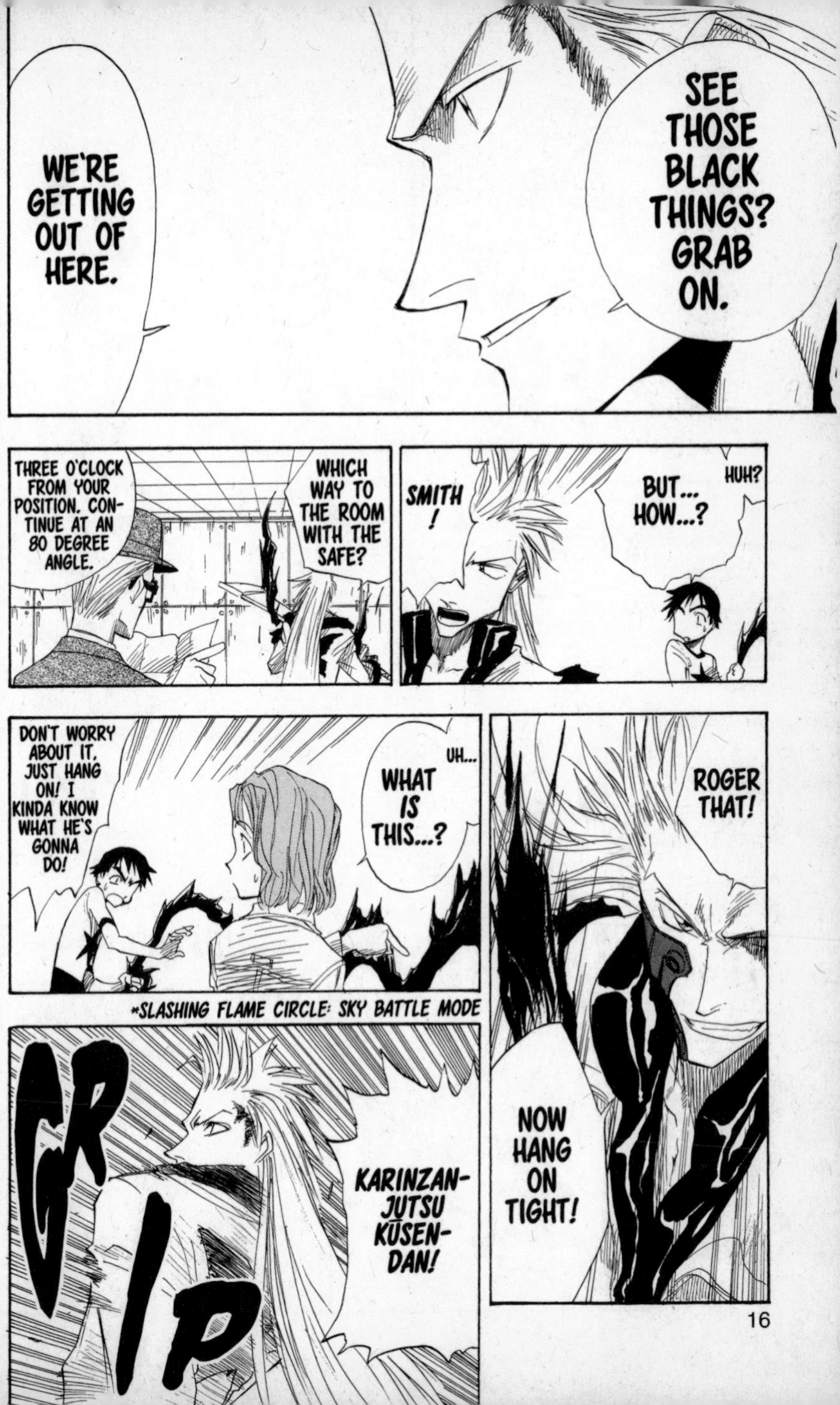
SEE THOSE BLACK THINGS? GRAB ON.
WE'RE GETTING OUT OF HERE.
HUH?
BUT... HOW...?
SMITH!
WHICH WAY TO THE ROOM WITH THE SAFE?
THREE O'CLOCK FROM YOUR POSITION. CONTINUE AT AN 80 DEGREE ANGLE.
ROGER THAT!
NOW HANG ON TIGHT!
UH...
WHAT IS THIS...?
DON'T WORRY ABOUT IT, JUST HANG ON! I KINDA KNOW WHAT HE'S GONNA DO!
*SLASHING FLAME CIRCLE: SKY BATTLE MODE
KARINZAN-JUTSU KŪSEN-DAN!
GRIP

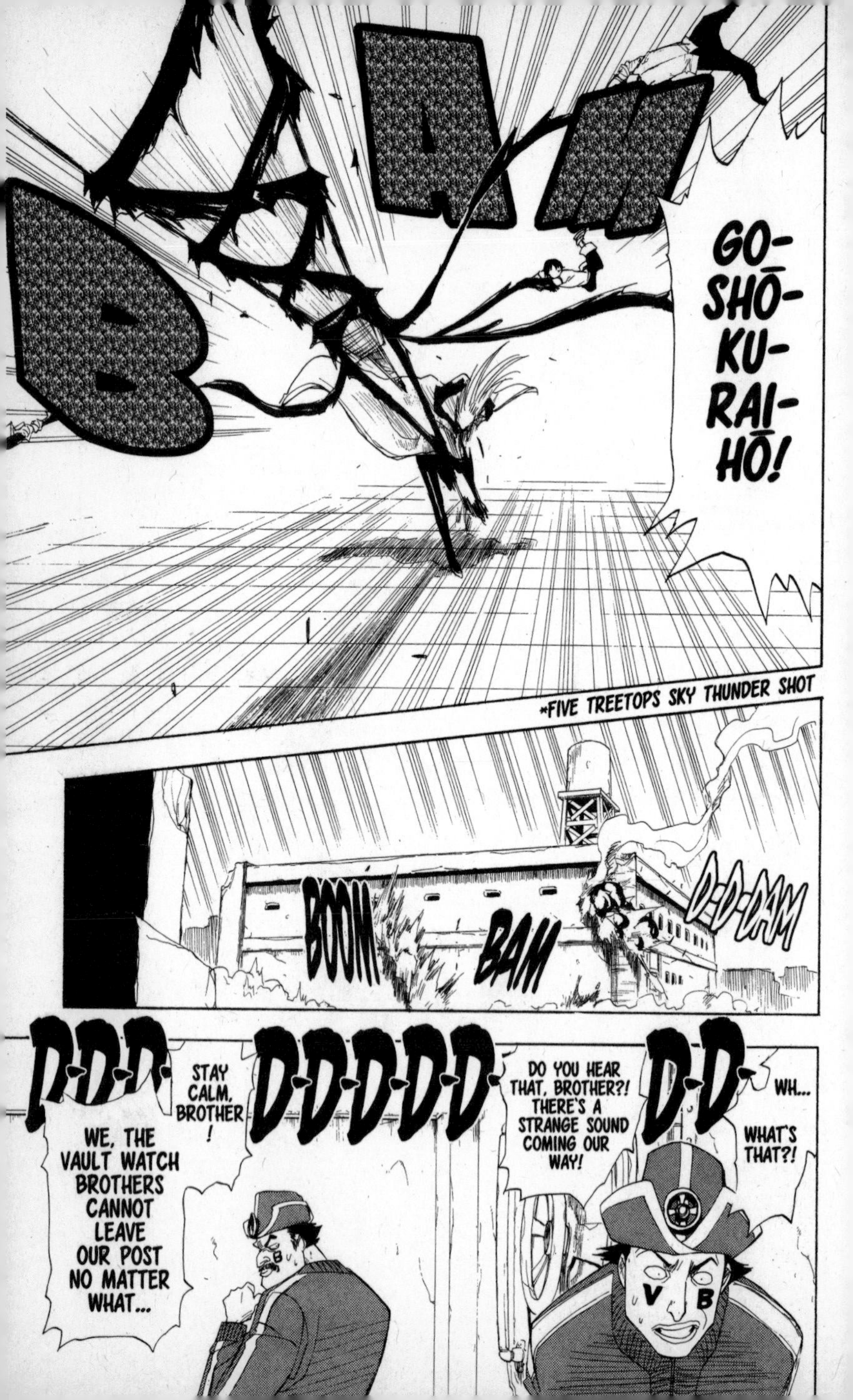
GO-SHŌ-KU-RAI-HŌ!
BAM
*FIVE TREETOPS SKY THUNDER SHOT
D-D-DAM
BAM
BOOM
D-D-
WH...
WHAT'S THAT?!
DO YOU HEAR THAT, BROTHER?! THERE'S A STRANGE SOUND COMING OUR WAY!
D-D-D-D-D-
STAY CALM, BROTHER!
D-D-D-
WE, THE VAULT WATCH BROTHERS CANNOT LEAVE OUR POST NO MATTER WHAT...
V B

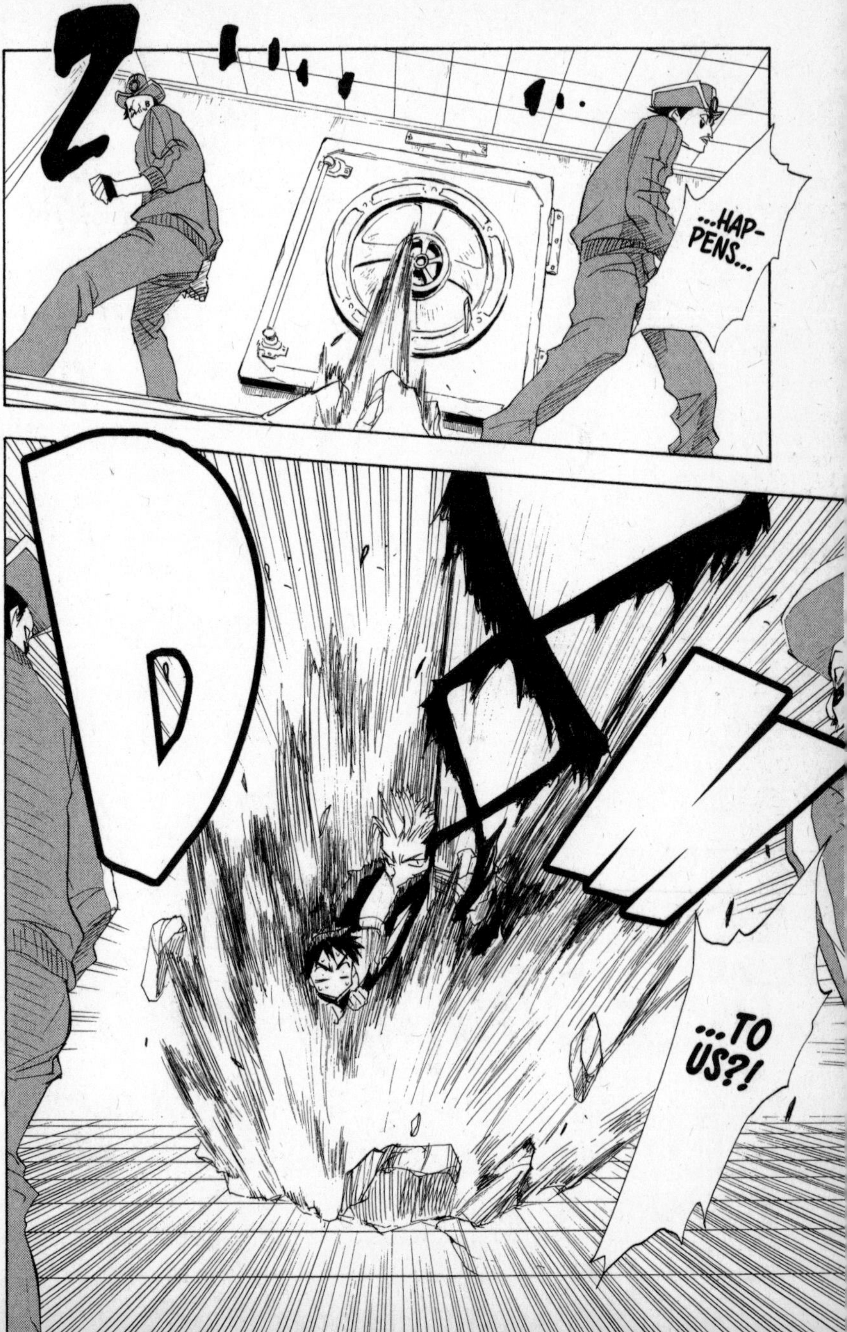
...HAP-
PENS...
...TO
US?!

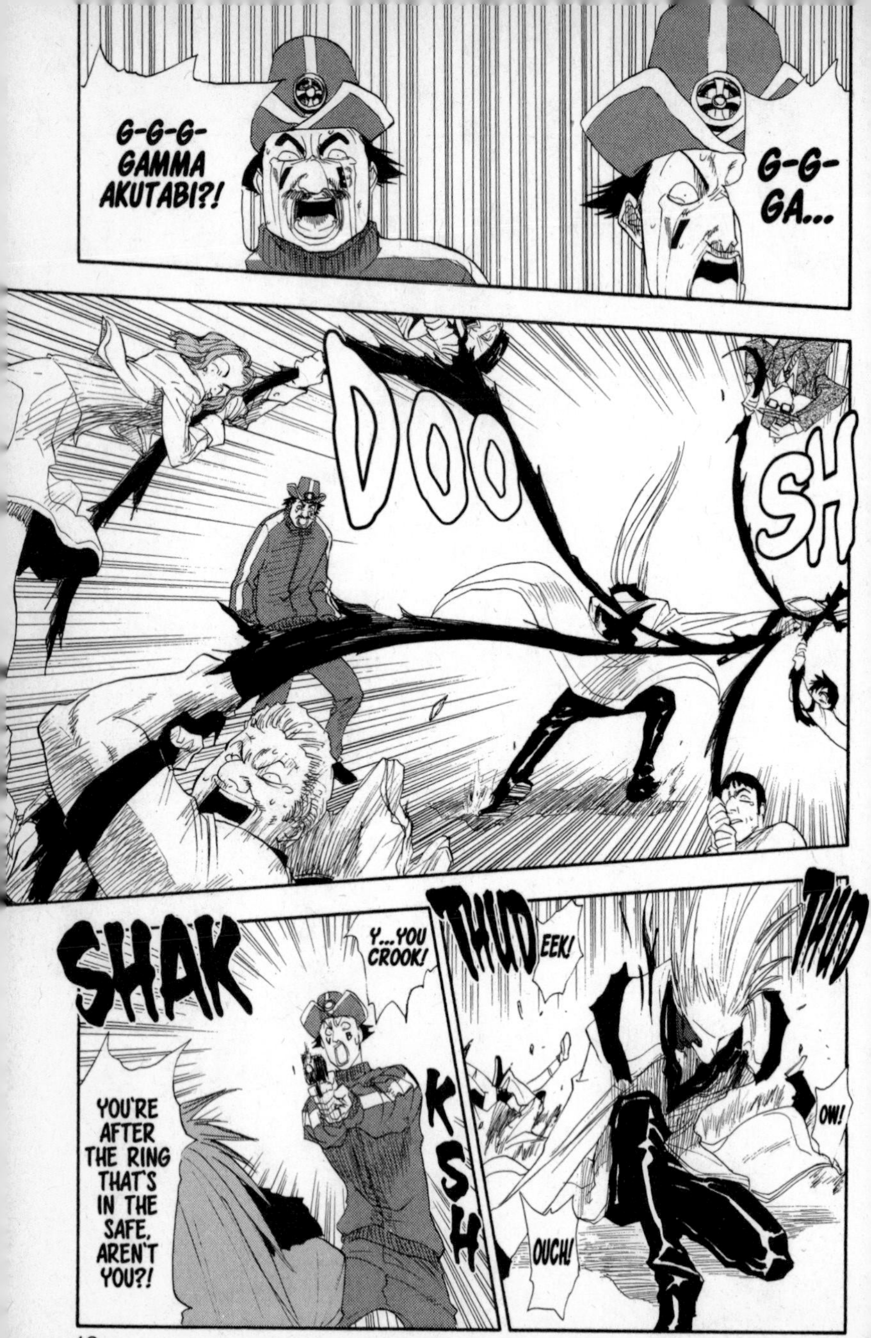
G-G-G-GA...
G-G-G-GAMMA AKUTABI?!
DOOSH
THUD
OW!
EEK!
THUD
OUCH!
Y...YOU CROOK!
SHAK
KSHSH
YOU'RE AFTER THE RING THAT'S IN THE SAFE, AREN'T YOU?!

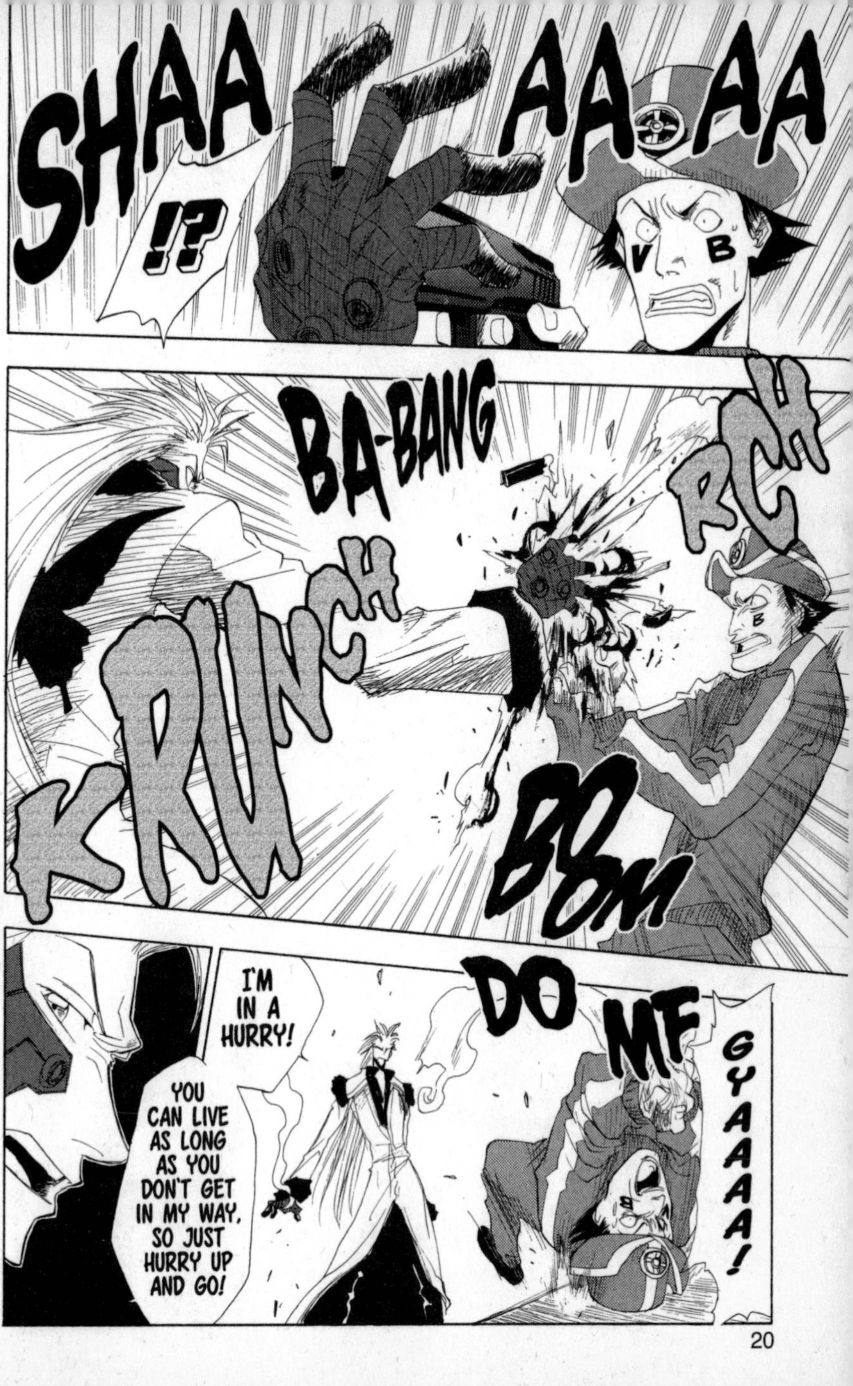
SHAA AA AA
!?
RCH
BA-BANG
KRUNCH
BOOM
DOMF
GYAAAAA!
I'M IN A HURRY!
YOU CAN LIVE AS LONG AS YOU DON'T GET IN MY WAY, SO JUST HURRY UP AND GO!

READ THIS WAY

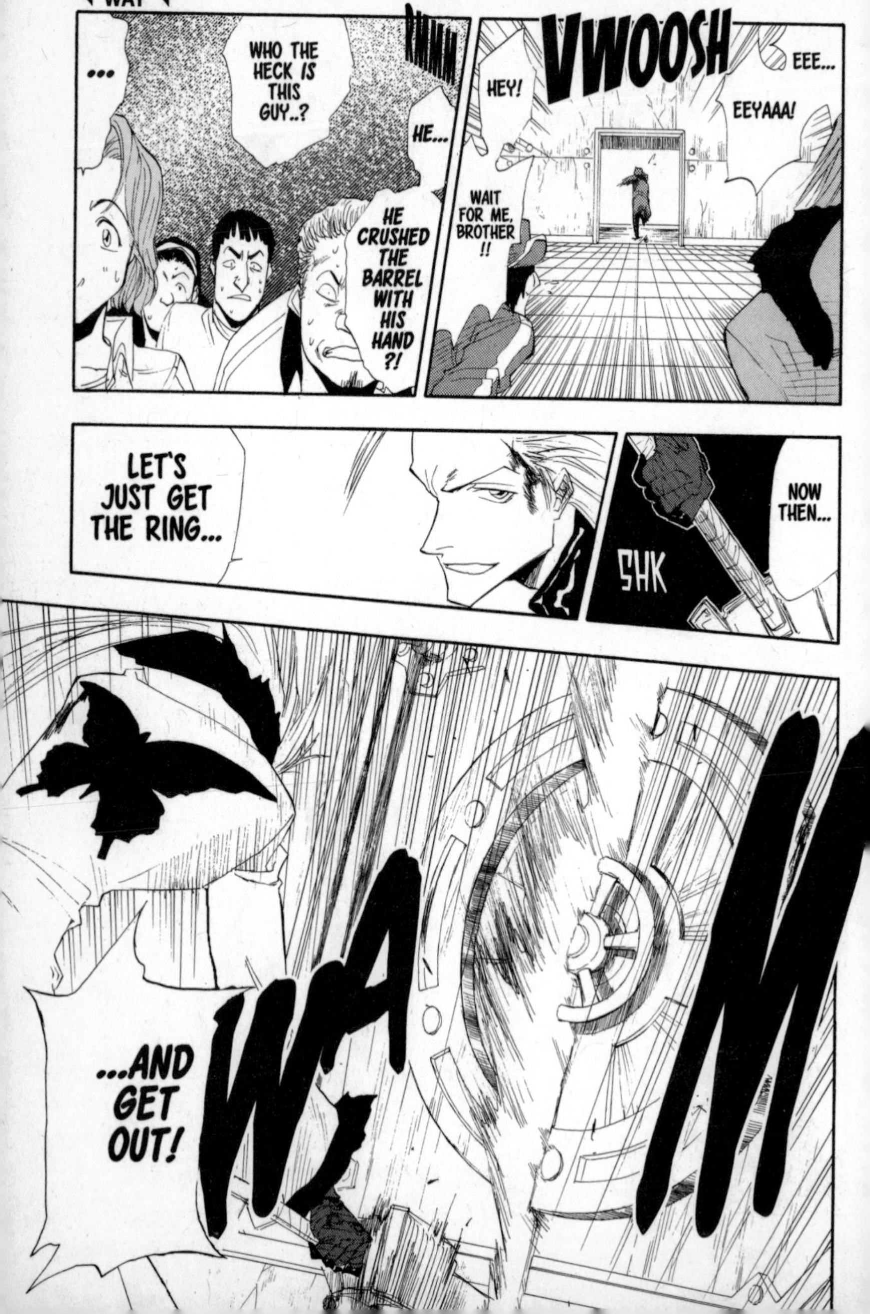
VWOOSH
EEE...
EEYAAA!
HEY!
WAIT FOR ME, BROTHER !!
RMMM
HE...
HE CRUSHED THE BARREL WITH HIS HAND ?!
WHO THE HECK IS THIS GUY..?
...
NOW THEN...
SHK
LET'S JUST GET THE RING...
WAM
...AND GET OUT!

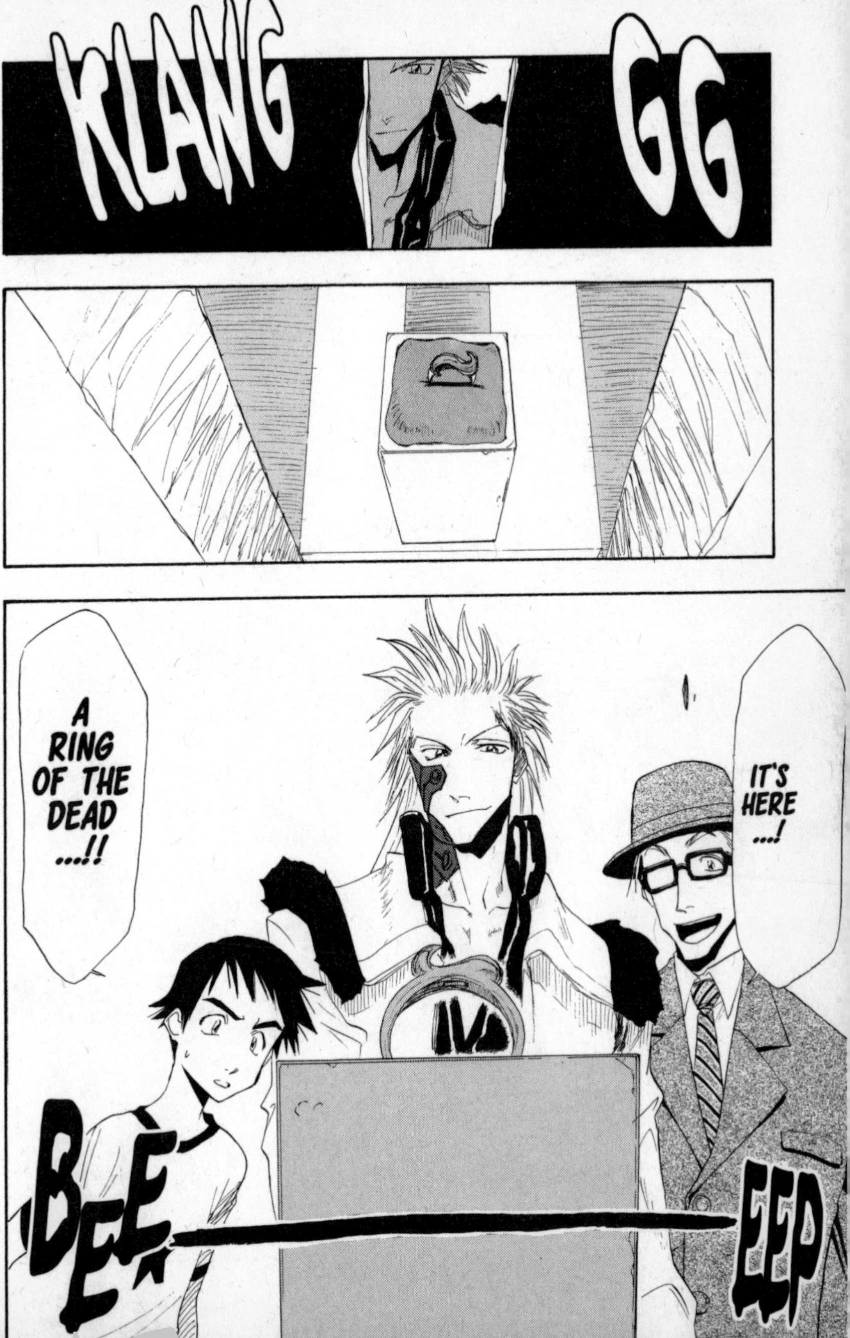
KLANG
GG
IT'S HERE ...!
A RING OF THE DEAD ...!!
BEEE
EEP

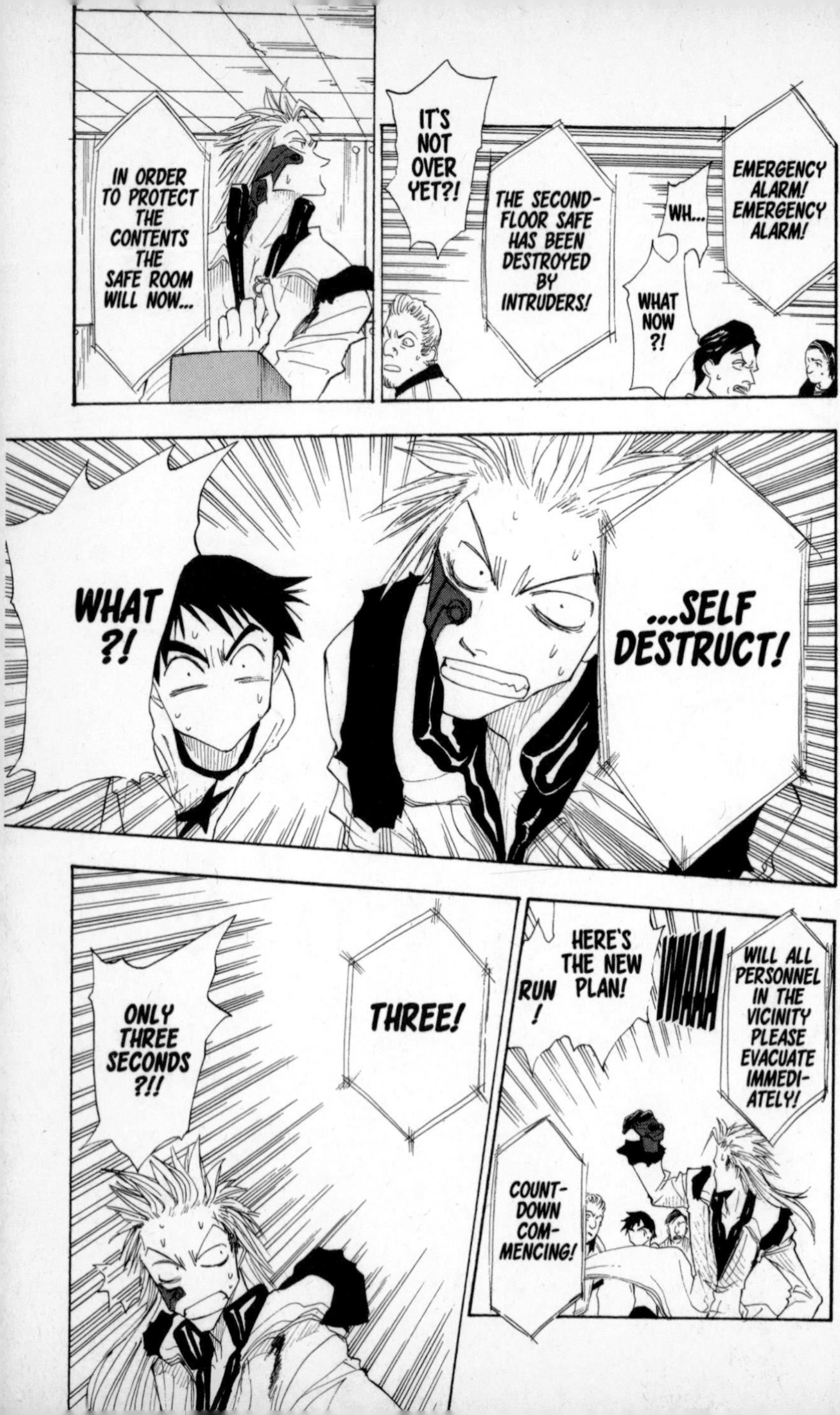
EMERGENCY ALARM! EMERGENCY ALARM!
WH...
WHAT NOW?!
THE SECOND-FLOOR SAFE HAS BEEN DESTROYED BY INTRUDERS!
IT'S NOT OVER YET?!
IN ORDER TO PROTECT THE CONTENTS THE SAFE ROOM WILL NOW...
...SELF DESTRUCT!
WHAT?!
WILL ALL PERSONNEL IN THE VICINITY PLEASE EVACUATE IMMEDIATELY!
WAAAA
HERE'S THE NEW PLAN!
RUN!
COUNT-DOWN COM-MENCING!
THREE!
ONLY THREE SECONDS?!!

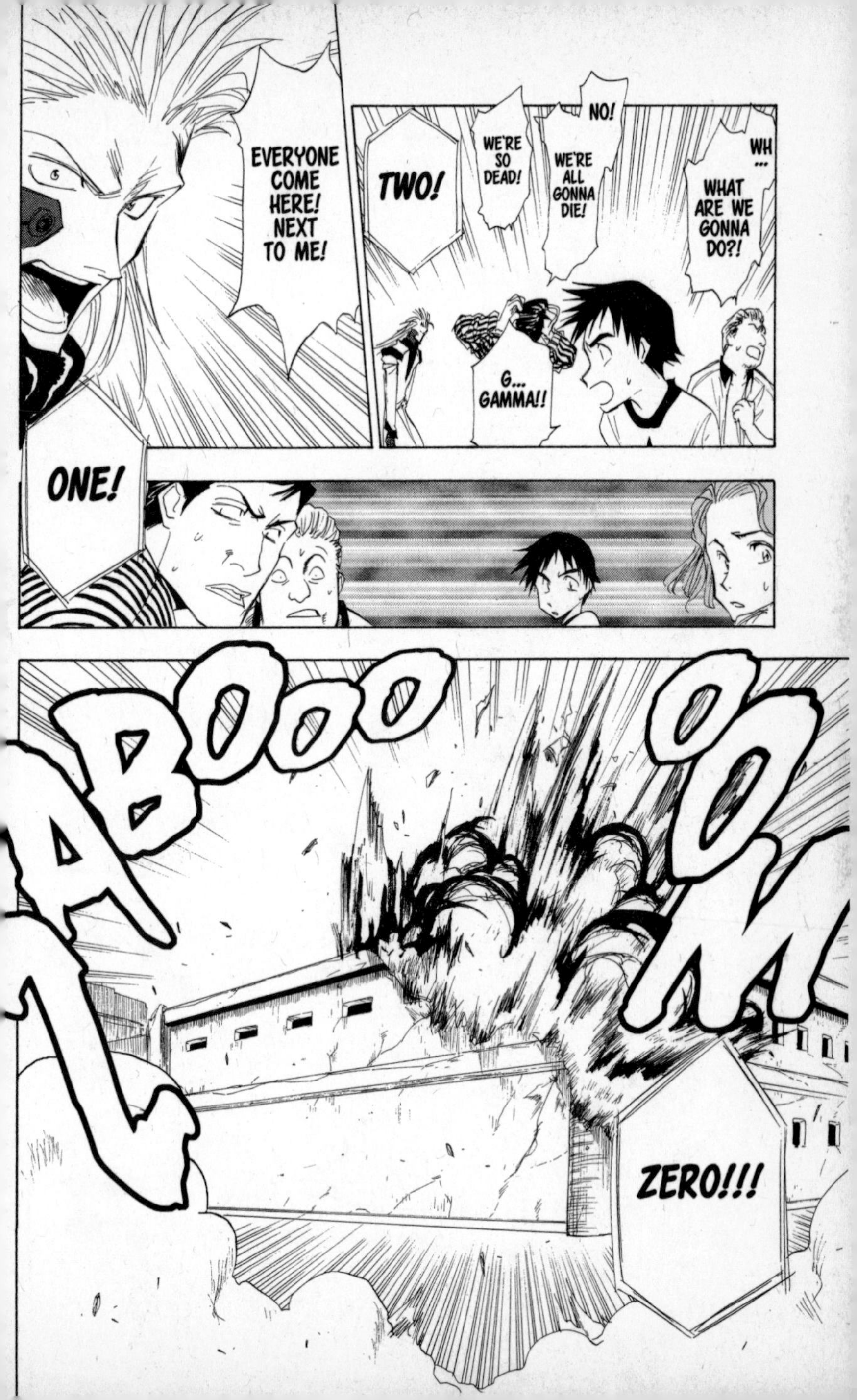
WH... WHAT ARE WE GONNA DO?!
NO!
WE'RE ALL GONNA DIE!
WE'RE SO DEAD!
TWO!
G... GAMMA!!
EVERYONE COME HERE! NEXT TO ME!
ONE!
BOOOOOOM
ZERO!!!

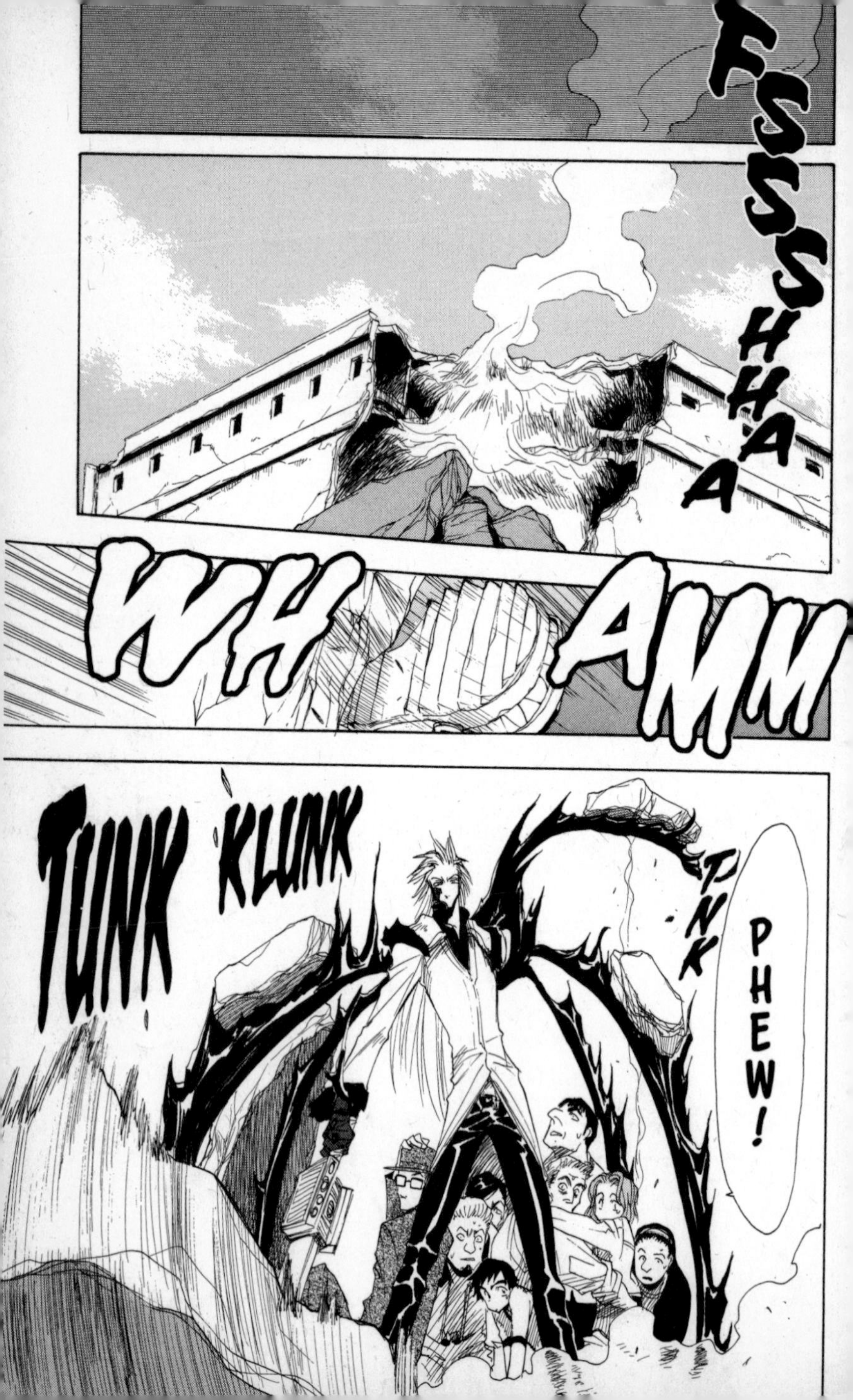
FSSSHHAA
WHAMM
PHEW!
TINK
KLUNK
TUNK!

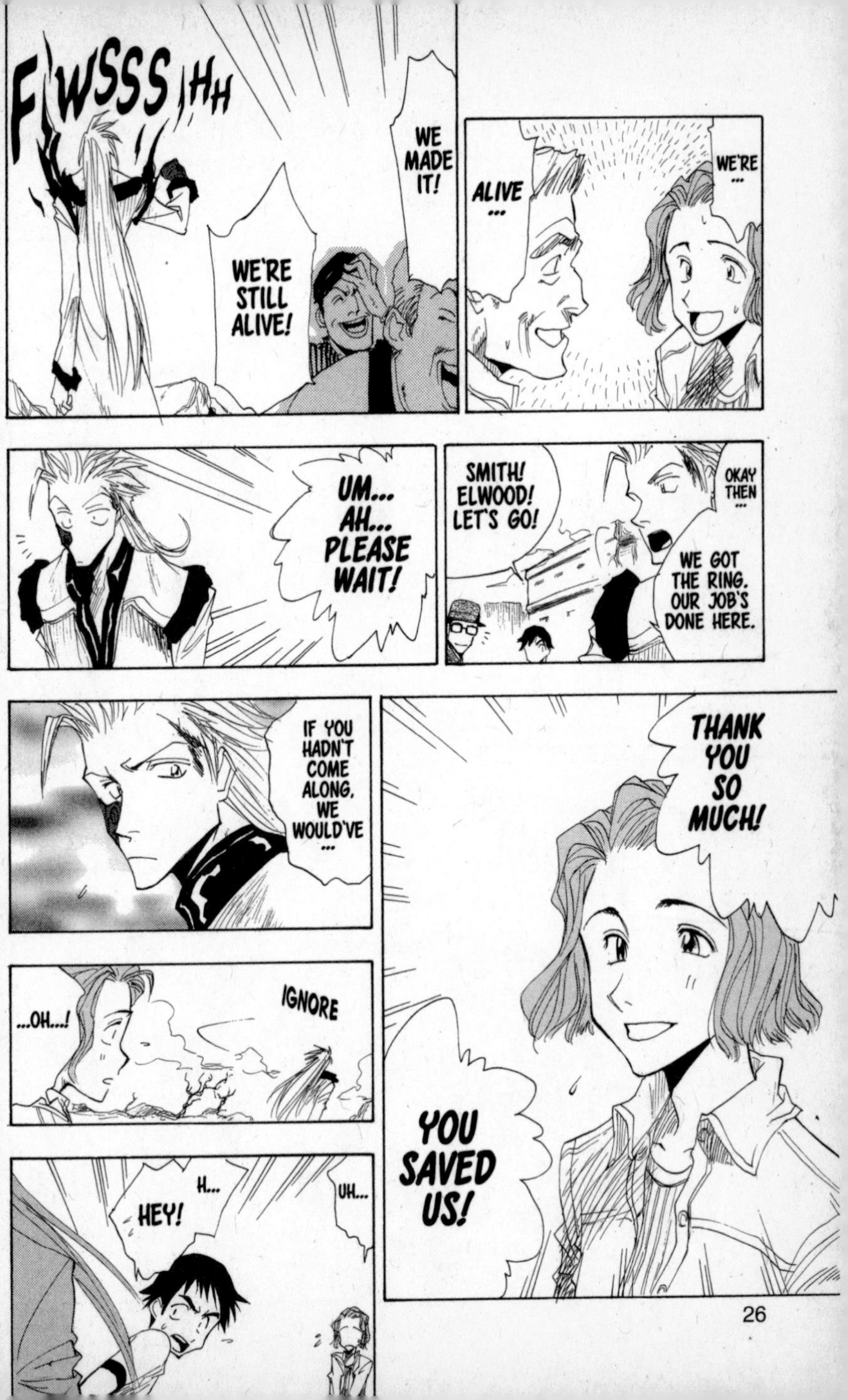
WE'RE ...
ALIVE ...
WE MADE IT!
WE'RE STILL ALIVE!
FWSSSHH
OKAY THEN ...
WE GOT THE RING. OUR JOB'S DONE HERE.
SMITH! ELWOOD! LET'S GO!
UM... AH... PLEASE WAIT!
THANK YOU SO MUCH!
YOU SAVED US!
IF YOU HADN'T COME ALONG, WE WOULD'VE ...
IGNORE
...OH...!
UH...
H... HEY!

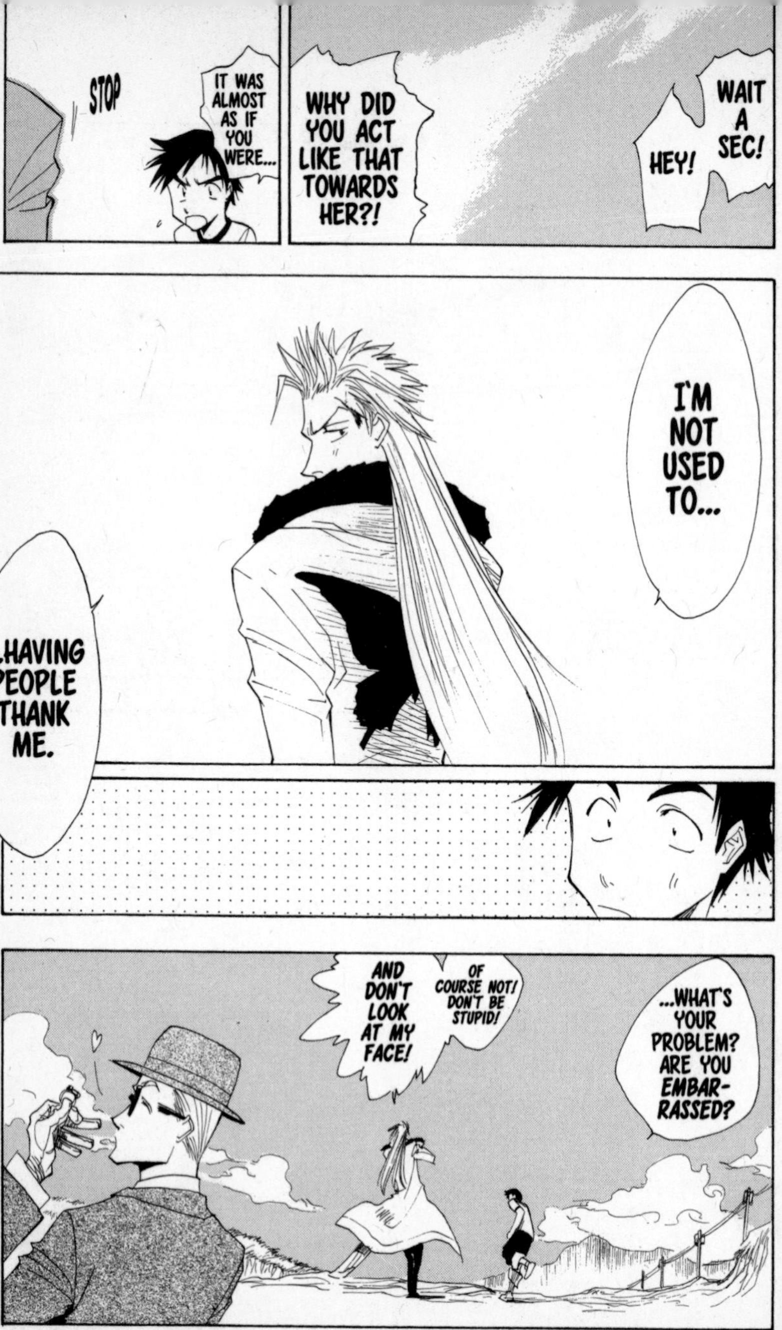
HEY! WAIT A SEC!
WHY DID YOU ACT LIKE THAT TOWARDS HER?!
IT WAS ALMOST AS IF YOU WERE...
STOP
I'M NOT USED TO...
...HAVING PEOPLE THANK ME.
...WHAT'S YOUR PROBLEM? ARE YOU EMBARRASSED?
OF COURSE NOT! DON'T BE STUPID!
AND DON'T LOOK AT MY FACE!

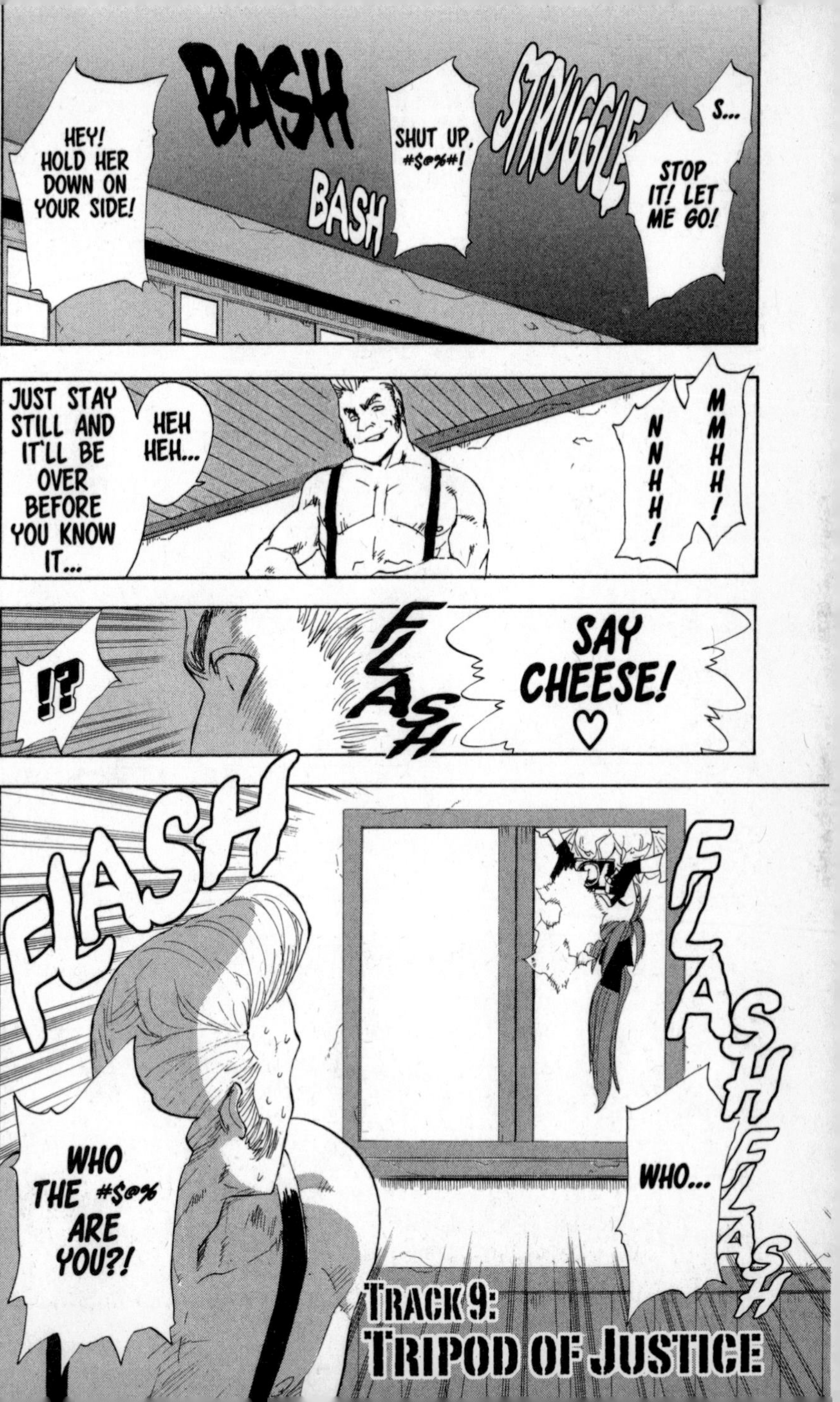
S... STOP IT! LET ME GO!
STRUGGLE
SHUT UP, #$@%#!
BASH
BASH
HEY! HOLD HER DOWN ON YOUR SIDE!
MMHH!
NNHH!
HEH HEH...
JUST STAY STILL AND IT'LL BE OVER BEFORE YOU KNOW IT...
SAY CHEESE! ♡
FLASH
!?
FLASH
FLASH
WHO...
TRACK 9: TRIPOD OF JUSTICE
FLASH
WHO THE #$@% ARE YOU?!

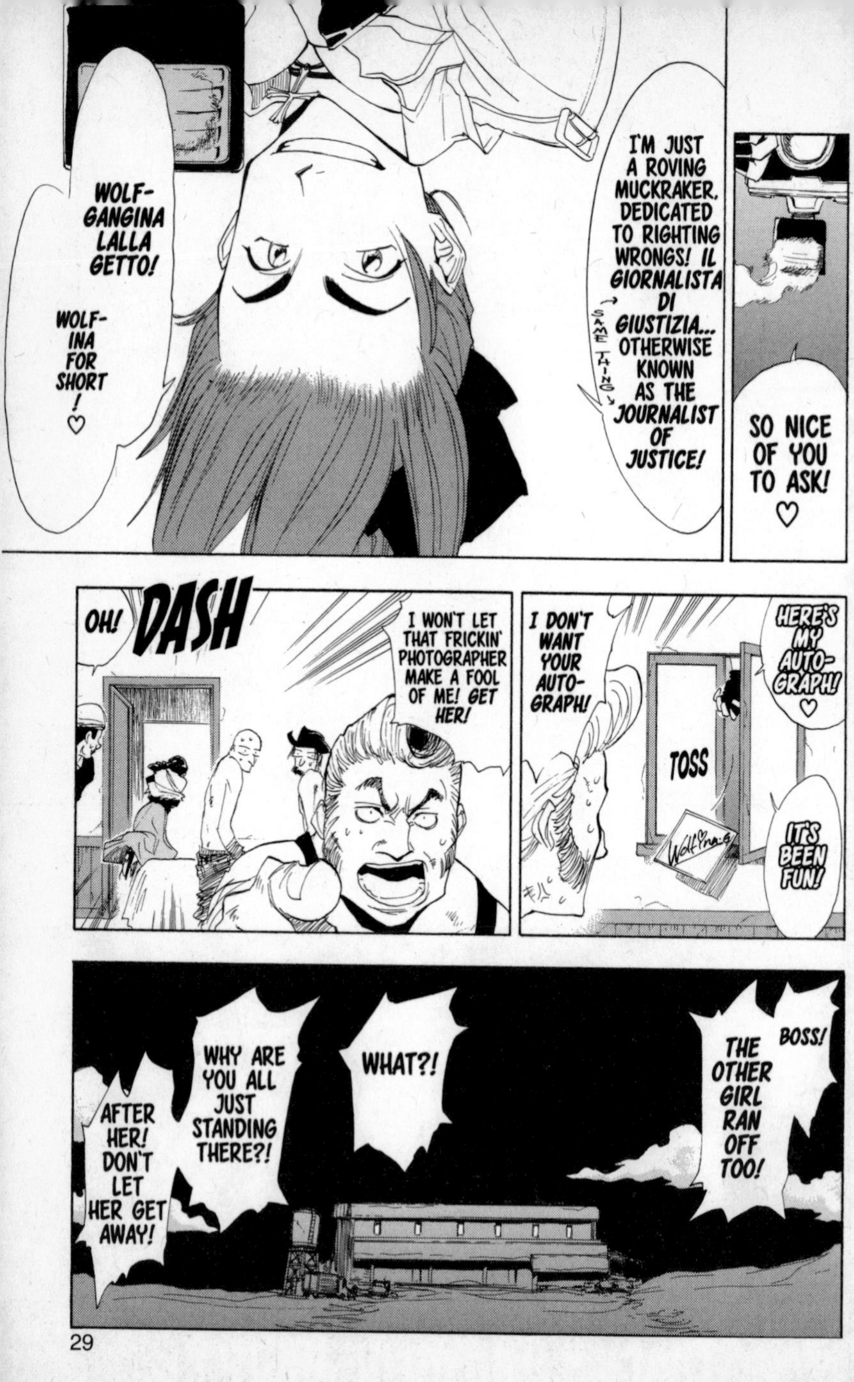
SO NICE OF YOU TO ASK! ♡
I'M JUST A ROVING MUCKRAKER, DEDICATED TO RIGHTING WRONGS! IL GIORNALISTA DI GIUSTIZIA... OTHERWISE KNOWN AS THE JOURNALIST OF JUSTICE!
SAME THING
WOLF-GANGINA LALLA GETTO!
WOLF-INA FOR SHORT! ♡
HERE'S MY AUTO-GRAPH! ♡
IT'S BEEN FUN!
TOSS
I DON'T WANT YOUR AUTO-GRAPH!
I WON'T LET THAT FRICKIN' PHOTOGRAPHER MAKE A FOOL OF ME! GET HER!
DASH
OH!
BOSS!
THE OTHER GIRL RAN OFF TOO!
WHAT?!
WHY ARE YOU ALL JUST STANDING THERE?!
AFTER HER! DON'T LET HER GET AWAY!

# TRACK 9: TRIPOD OF JUSTICE

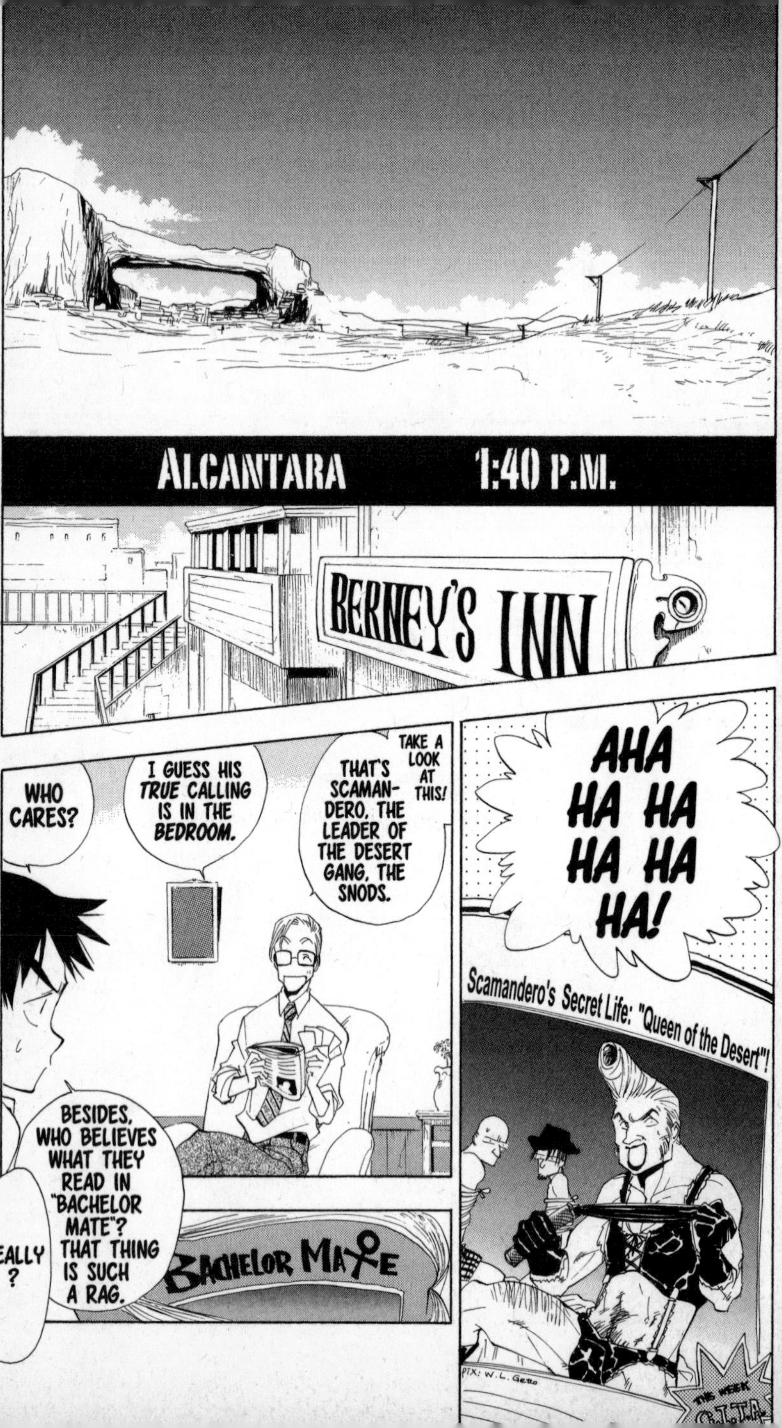
ALCANTARA 1:40 P.M.
BERNEY'S INN
AHA HA HA HA HA HA!
Scamandero's Secret Life: "Queen of the Desert"!
PTX: W.L. Getto
TAKE A LOOK AT THIS!
THAT'S SCAMANDERO, THE LEADER OF THE DESERT GANG, THE SNODS.
I GUESS HIS *TRUE* CALLING IS IN THE *BEDROOM.*
WHO CARES?
BESIDES, WHO BELIEVES WHAT THEY READ IN "BACHELOR MATE"? THAT THING IS SUCH A RAG.
REALLY?
BACHELOR MATE

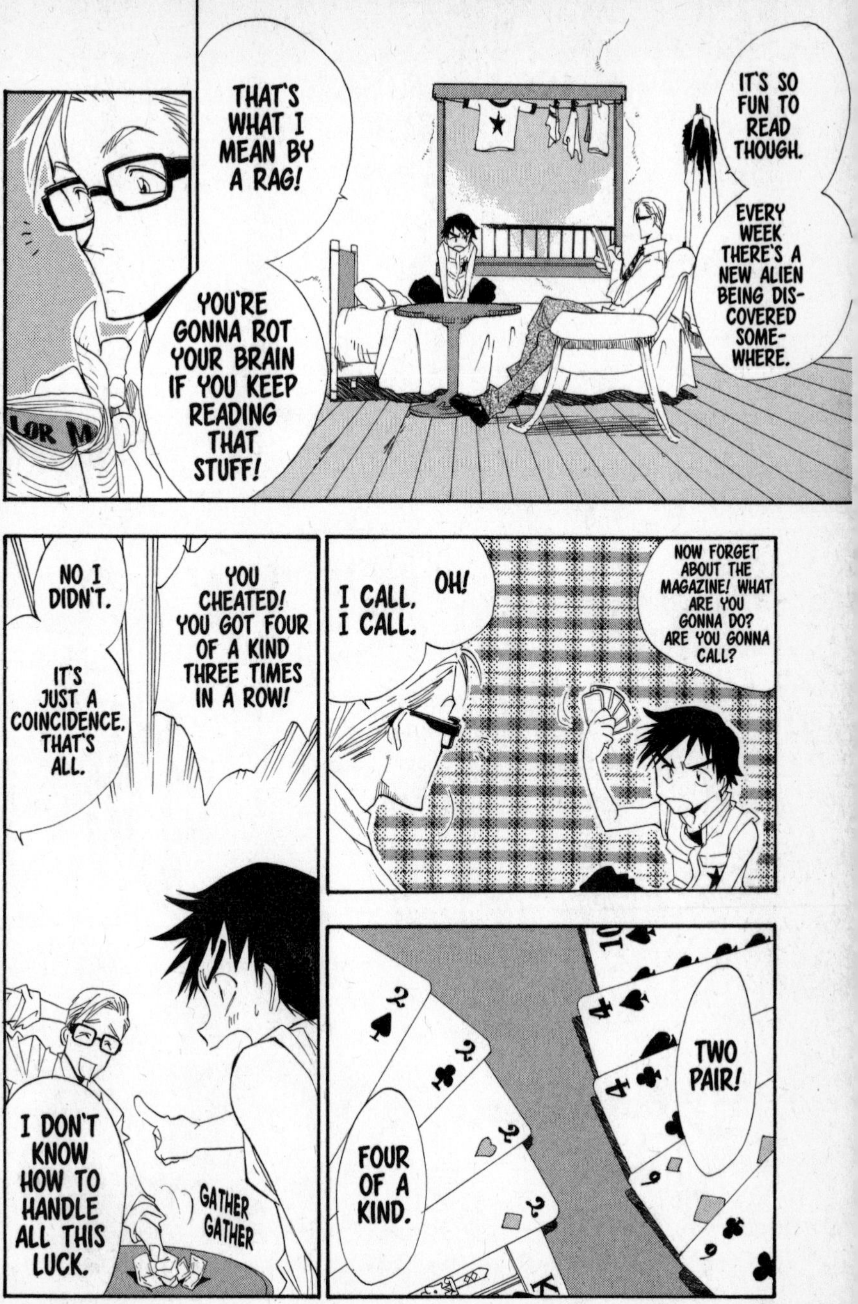
IT'S SO FUN TO READ THOUGH.
EVERY WEEK THERE'S A NEW ALIEN BEING DIS-COVERED SOME-WHERE.
THAT'S WHAT I MEAN BY A RAG!
YOU'RE GONNA ROT YOUR BRAIN IF YOU KEEP READING THAT STUFF!
NOW FORGET ABOUT THE MAGAZINE! WHAT ARE YOU GONNA DO? ARE YOU GONNA CALL?
OH!
I CALL, I CALL.
TWO PAIR!
FOUR OF A KIND.
YOU CHEATED! YOU GOT FOUR OF A KIND THREE TIMES IN A ROW!
NO I DIDN'T.
IT'S JUST A COINCIDENCE, THAT'S ALL.
I DON'T KNOW HOW TO HANDLE ALL THIS LUCK.
GATHER GATHER

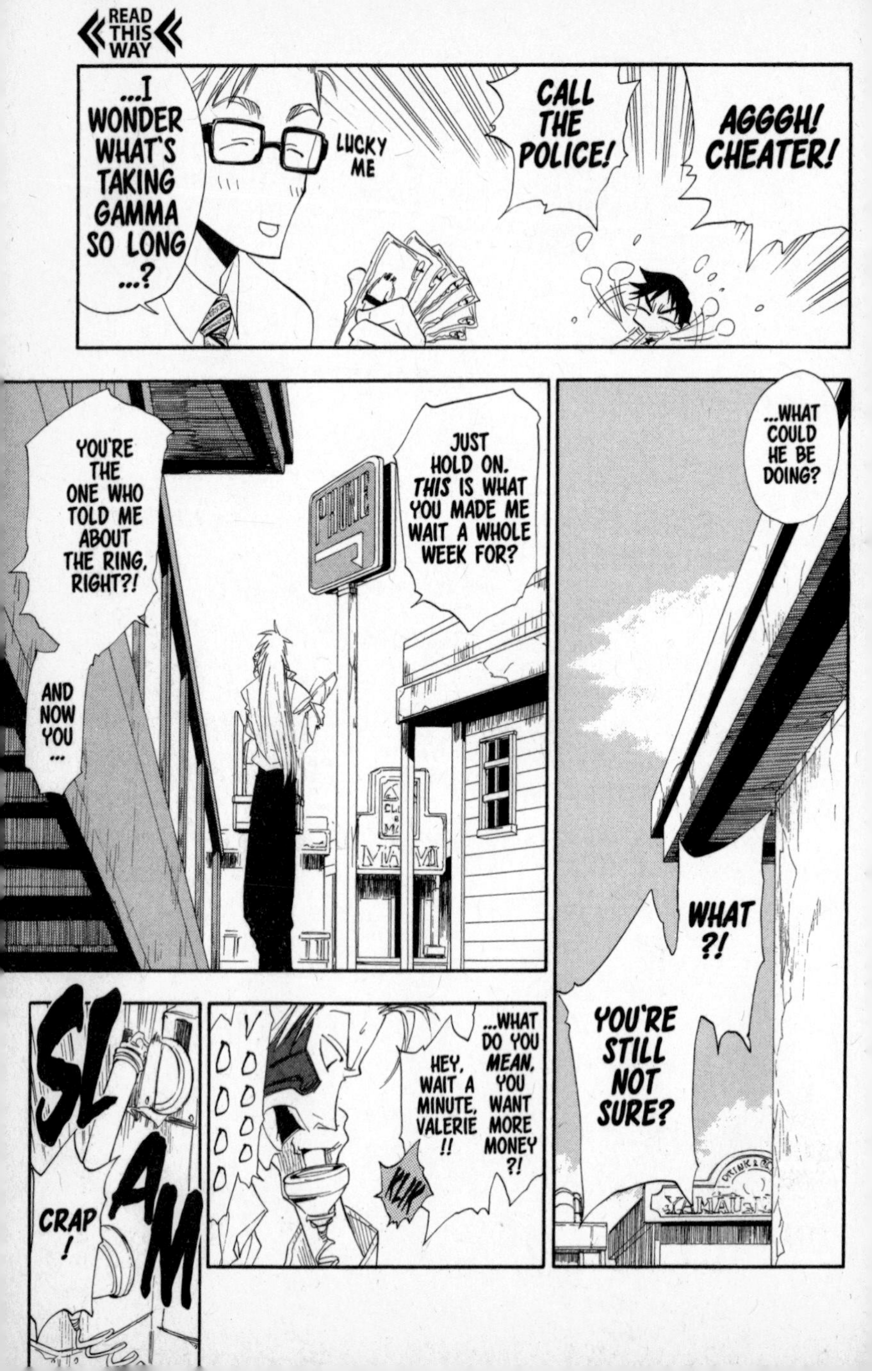
READ THIS WAY
AGGGH! CHEATER!
CALL THE POLICE!
LUCKY ME
...I WONDER WHAT'S TAKING GAMMA SO LONG ...?
...WHAT COULD HE BE DOING?
WHAT ?!
YOU'RE STILL NOT SURE?
JUST HOLD ON. *THIS* IS WHAT YOU MADE ME WAIT A WHOLE WEEK FOR?
YOU'RE THE ONE WHO TOLD ME ABOUT THE RING, RIGHT?!
AND NOW YOU ...
...WHAT DO YOU *MEAN*, YOU WANT MORE MONEY ?!
HEY, WAIT A MINUTE, VALERIE !!
KLIK
SLAM
CRAP !

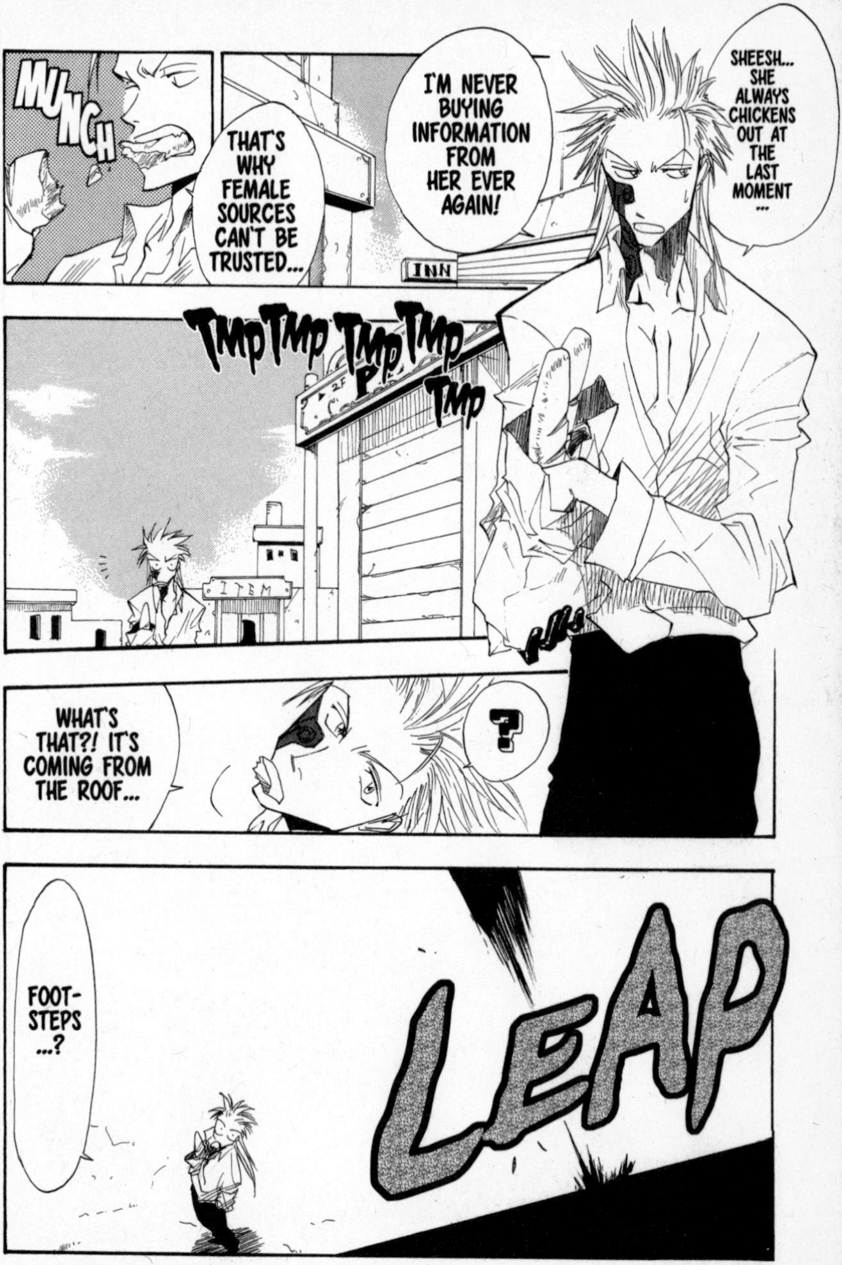
SHEESH... SHE ALWAYS CHICKENS OUT AT THE LAST MOMENT...
I'M NEVER BUYING INFORMATION FROM HER EVER AGAIN!
INN
THAT'S WHY FEMALE SOURCES CAN'T BE TRUSTED...
MUNCH
TMP TMP TMP TMP TMP
ITEM
?
WHAT'S THAT?! IT'S COMING FROM THE ROOF...
LEAP
FOOT-STEPS...?

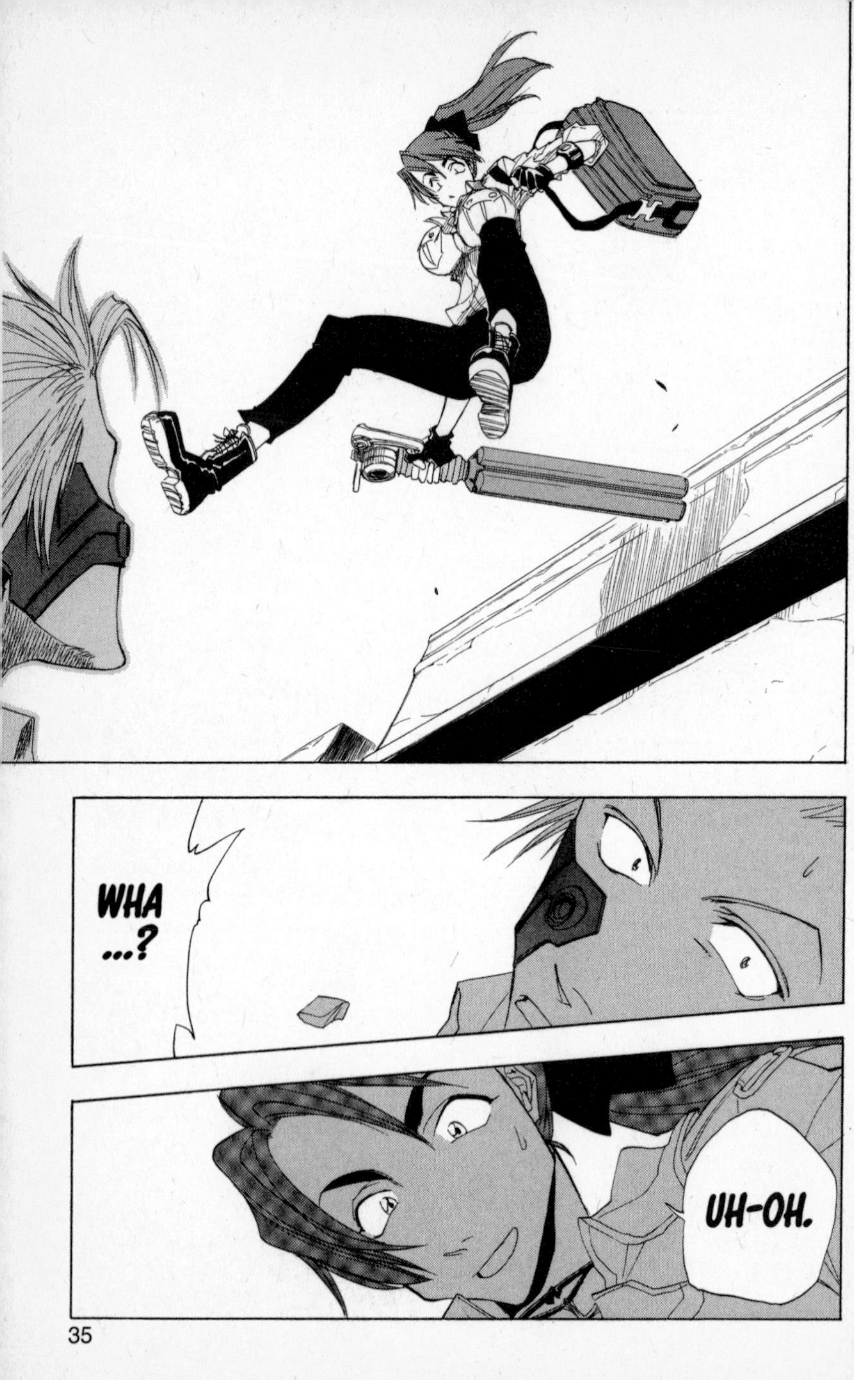
WHA ...?
UH-OH.

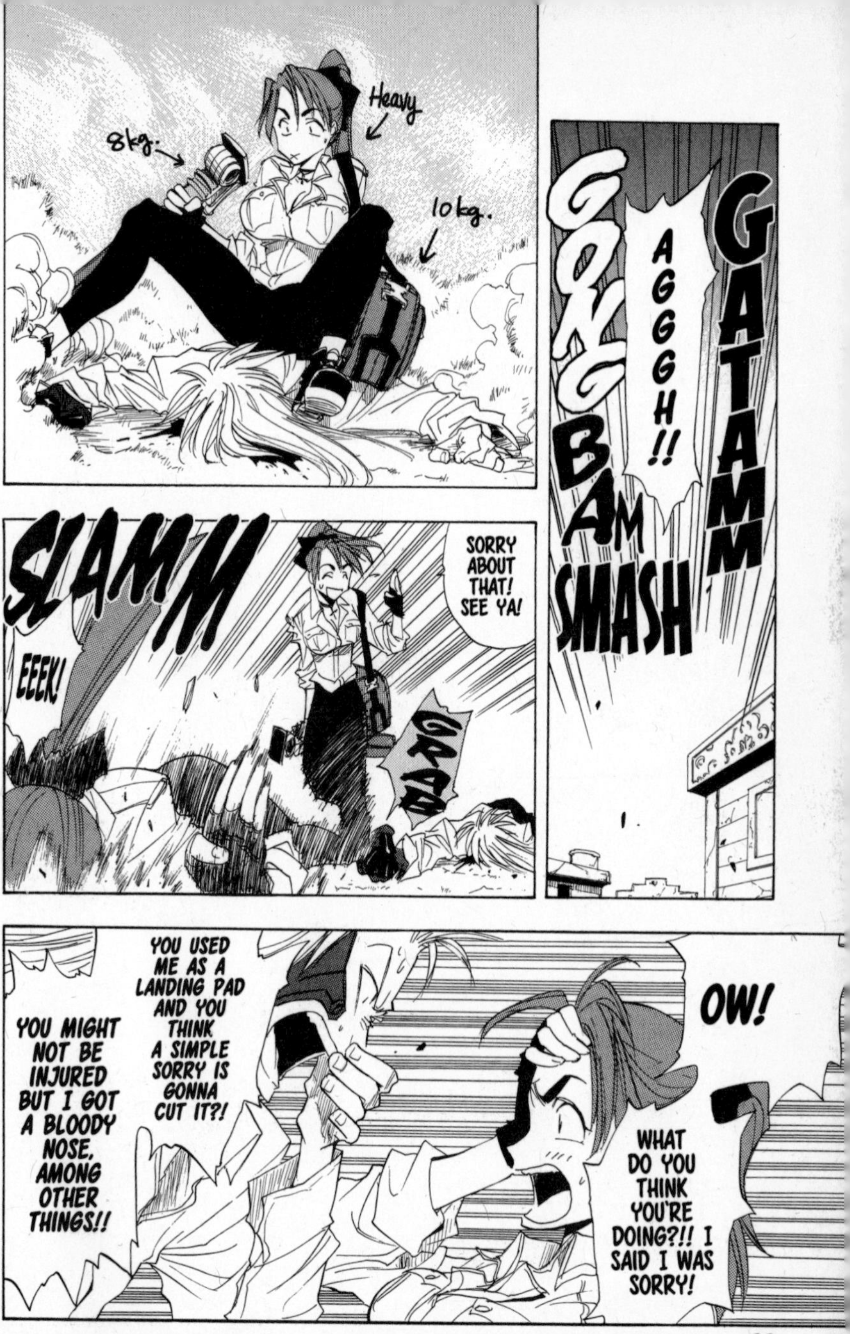
GATAMM
AGGGH!!
GONG
BAM
SMASH
Heavy
8kg.
10kg.
SORRY ABOUT THAT! SEE YA!
SLAMM
GRAB
EEEK!
OW!
WHAT DO YOU THINK YOU'RE DOING?!! I SAID I WAS SORRY!
YOU USED ME AS A LANDING PAD AND YOU THINK A SIMPLE SORRY IS GONNA CUT IT?!
YOU MIGHT NOT BE INJURED BUT I GOT A BLOODY NOSE, AMONG OTHER THINGS!!

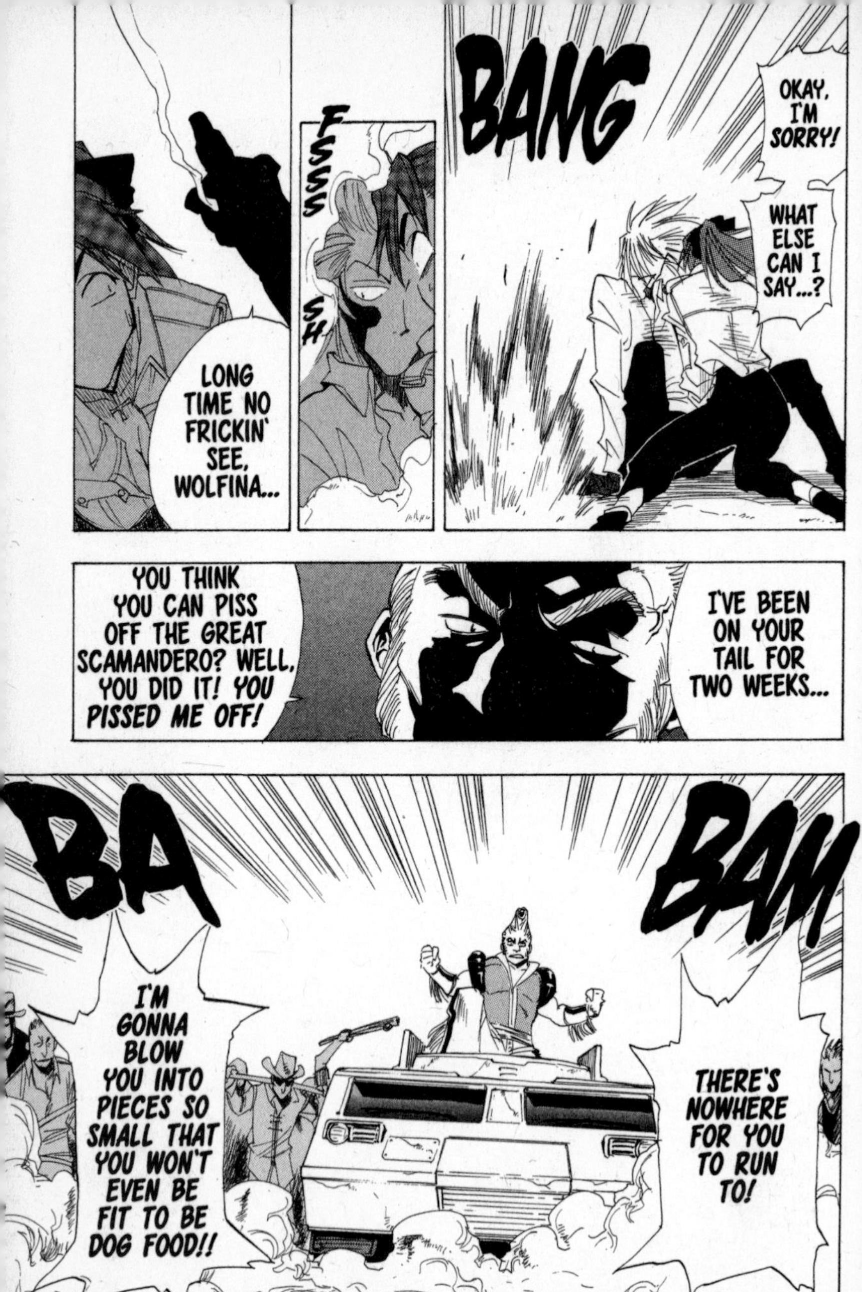
BANG
OKAY, I'M SORRY!
WHAT ELSE CAN I SAY...?
FSSSSH
LONG TIME NO FRICKIN' SEE, WOLFINA...
I'VE BEEN ON YOUR TAIL FOR TWO WEEKS...
YOU THINK YOU CAN PISS OFF THE GREAT SCAMANDERO? WELL, YOU DID IT! YOU PISSED ME OFF!
BA BAM
THERE'S NOWHERE FOR YOU TO RUN TO!
I'M GONNA BLOW YOU INTO PIECES SO SMALL THAT YOU WON'T EVEN BE FIT TO BE DOG FOOD!!

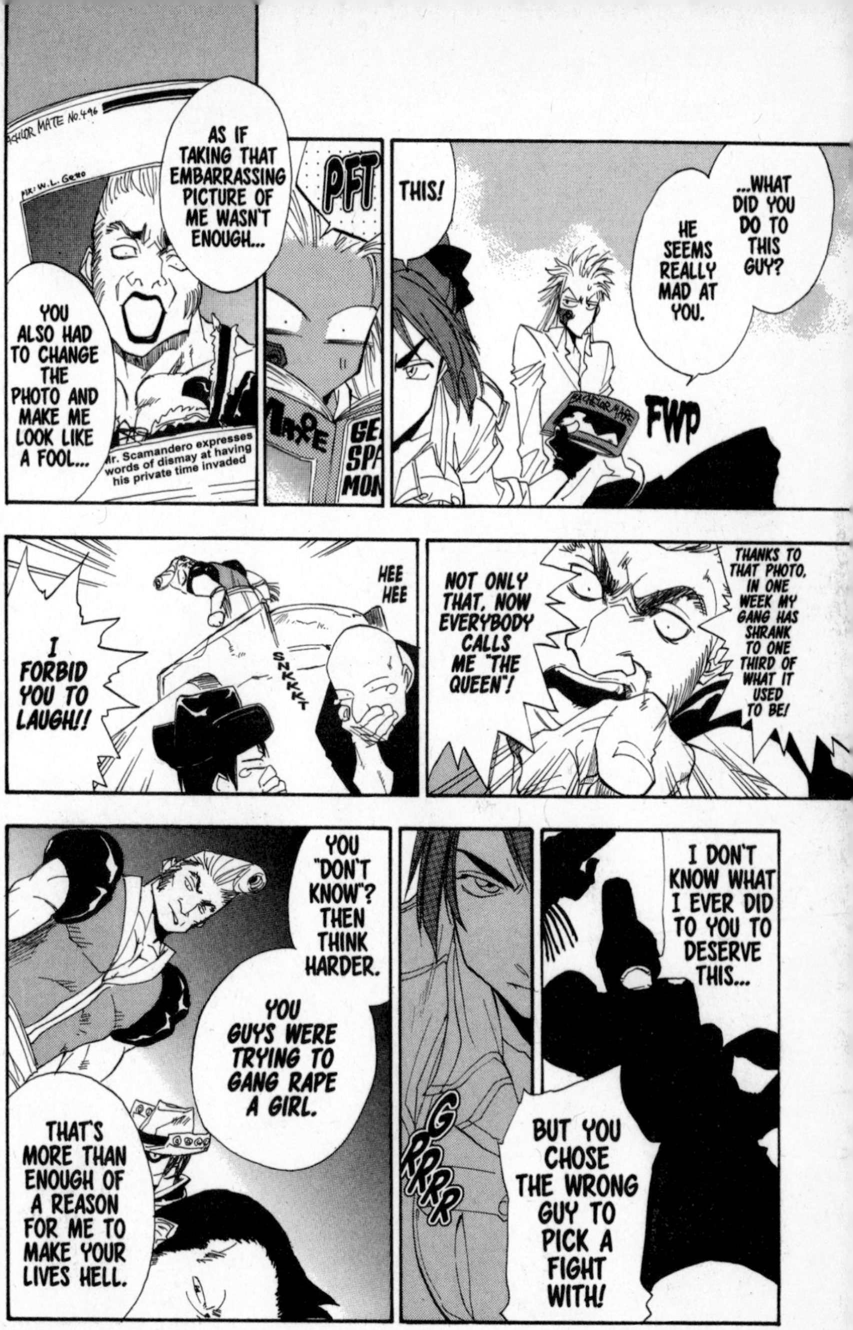
...WHAT DID YOU DO TO THIS GUY?
HE SEEMS REALLY MAD AT YOU.
THIS!
FWP
BACHELOR MATE
PFT
MATE
GE SPA MON
ACHELOR MATE No.496
Mr. W. L. Getto
AS IF TAKING THAT EMBARRASSING PICTURE OF ME WASN'T ENOUGH...
YOU ALSO HAD TO CHANGE THE PHOTO AND MAKE ME LOOK LIKE A FOOL...
Mr. Scamandero expresses words of dismay at having his private time invaded
THANKS TO THAT PHOTO, IN ONE WEEK MY GANG HAS SHRANK TO ONE THIRD OF WHAT IT USED TO BE!
NOT ONLY THAT, NOW EVERYBODY CALLS ME "THE QUEEN"!
HEE HEE
SNKKKT
I FORBID YOU TO LAUGH!!
I DON'T KNOW WHAT I EVER DID TO YOU TO DESERVE THIS...
BUT YOU CHOSE THE WRONG GUY TO PICK A FIGHT WITH!
GRRRR
YOU "DON'T KNOW"? THEN THINK HARDER.
YOU GUYS WERE TRYING TO GANG RAPE A GIRL.
THAT'S MORE THAN ENOUGH OF A REASON FOR ME TO MAKE YOUR LIVES HELL.

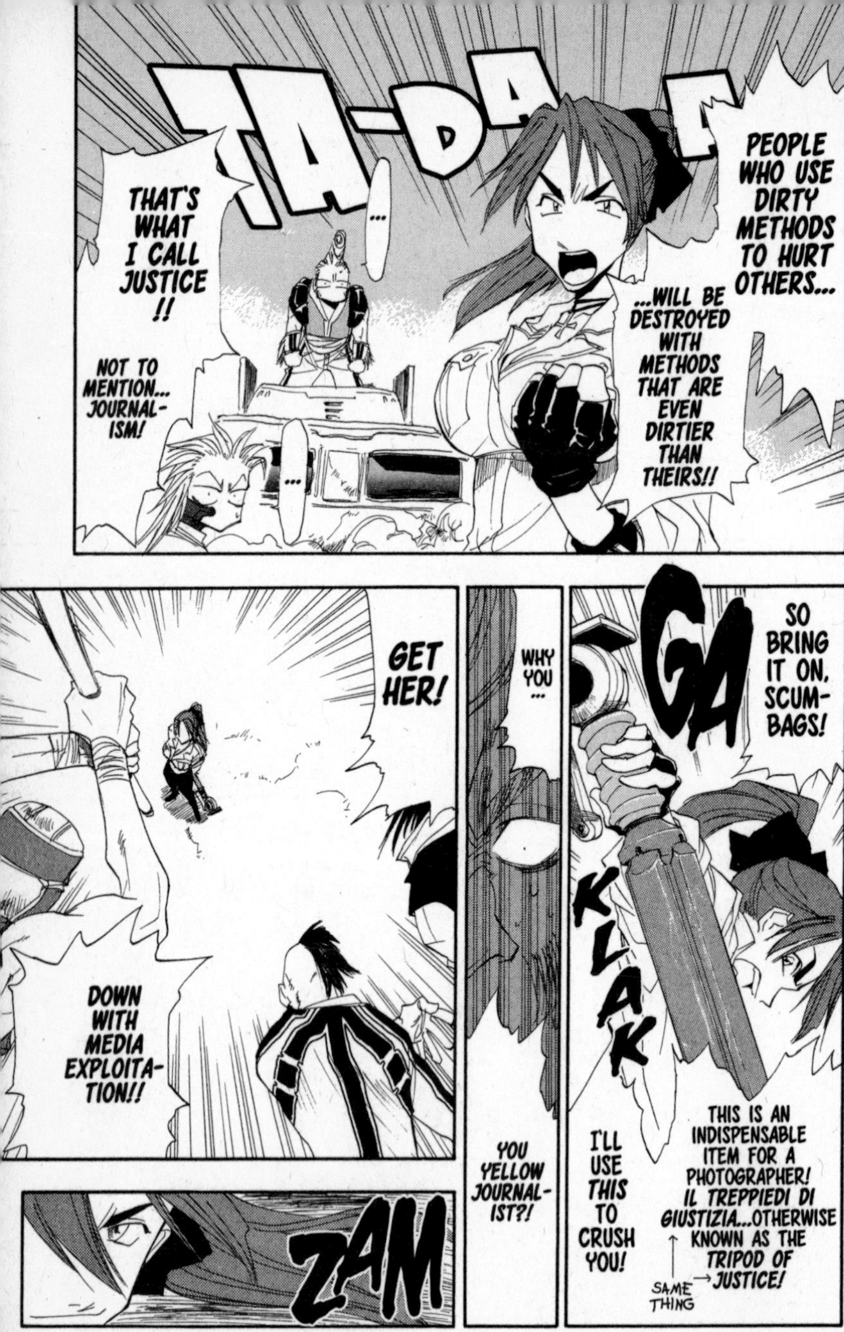
TA-DA
PEOPLE WHO USE DIRTY METHODS TO HURT OTHERS...
...WILL BE DESTROYED WITH METHODS THAT ARE EVEN DIRTIER THAN THEIRS!!
...
THAT'S WHAT I CALL JUSTICE !!
NOT TO MENTION... JOURNAL-ISM!
...
GA
SO BRING IT ON, SCUM-BAGS!
KLAK
THIS IS AN INDISPENSABLE ITEM FOR A PHOTOGRAPHER! IL TREPPIEDI DI GIUSTIZIA...OTHERWISE KNOWN AS THE TRIPOD OF JUSTICE!
SAME THING
I'LL USE THIS TO CRUSH YOU!
WHY YOU ...
YOU YELLOW JOURNAL-IST?!
GET HER!
DOWN WITH MEDIA EXPLOITA-TION!!
ZAM

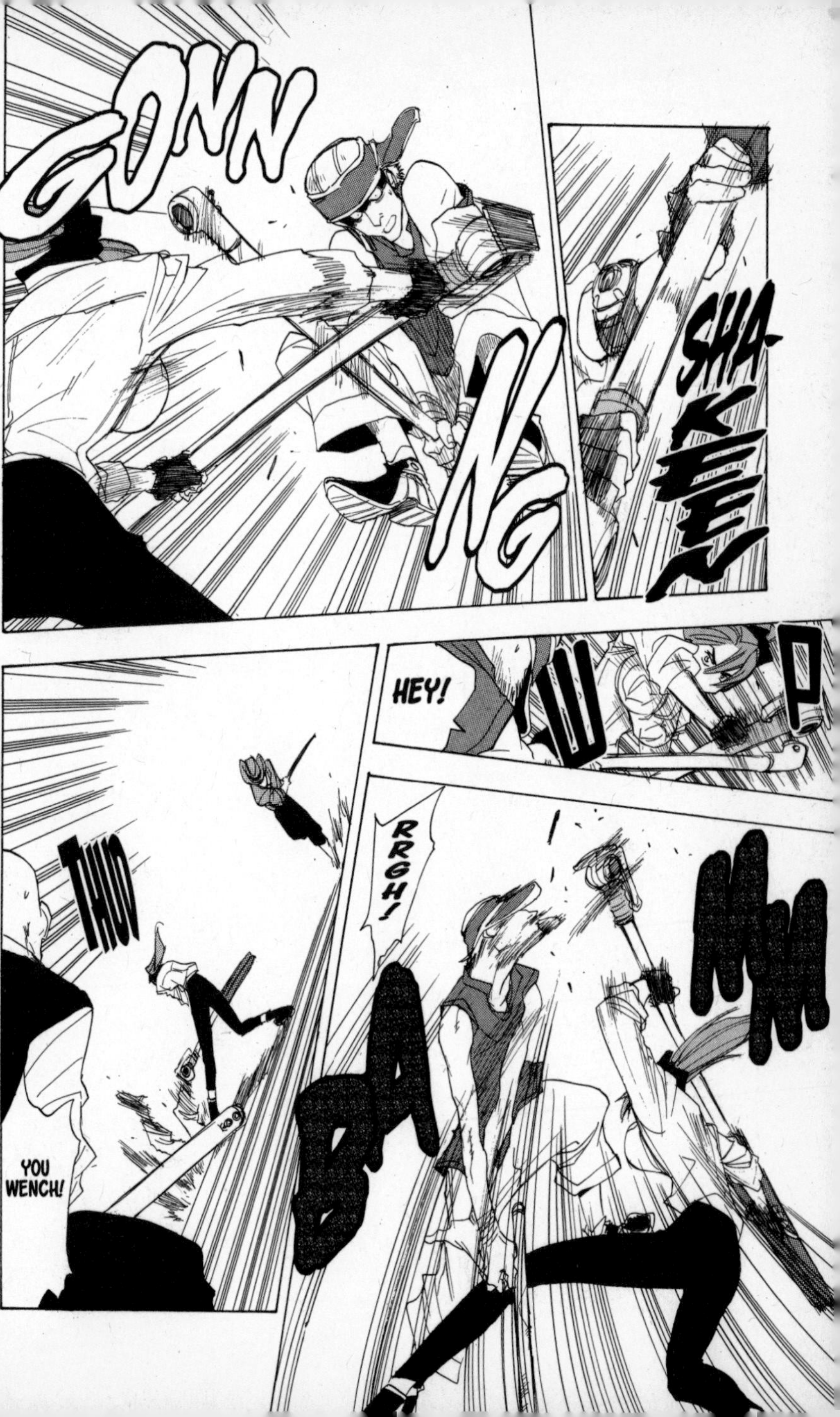
SHA-
KEEN
GONN
NG
HEY!
P
U
RRGH!
NNM
BA
THUD
YOU WENCH!

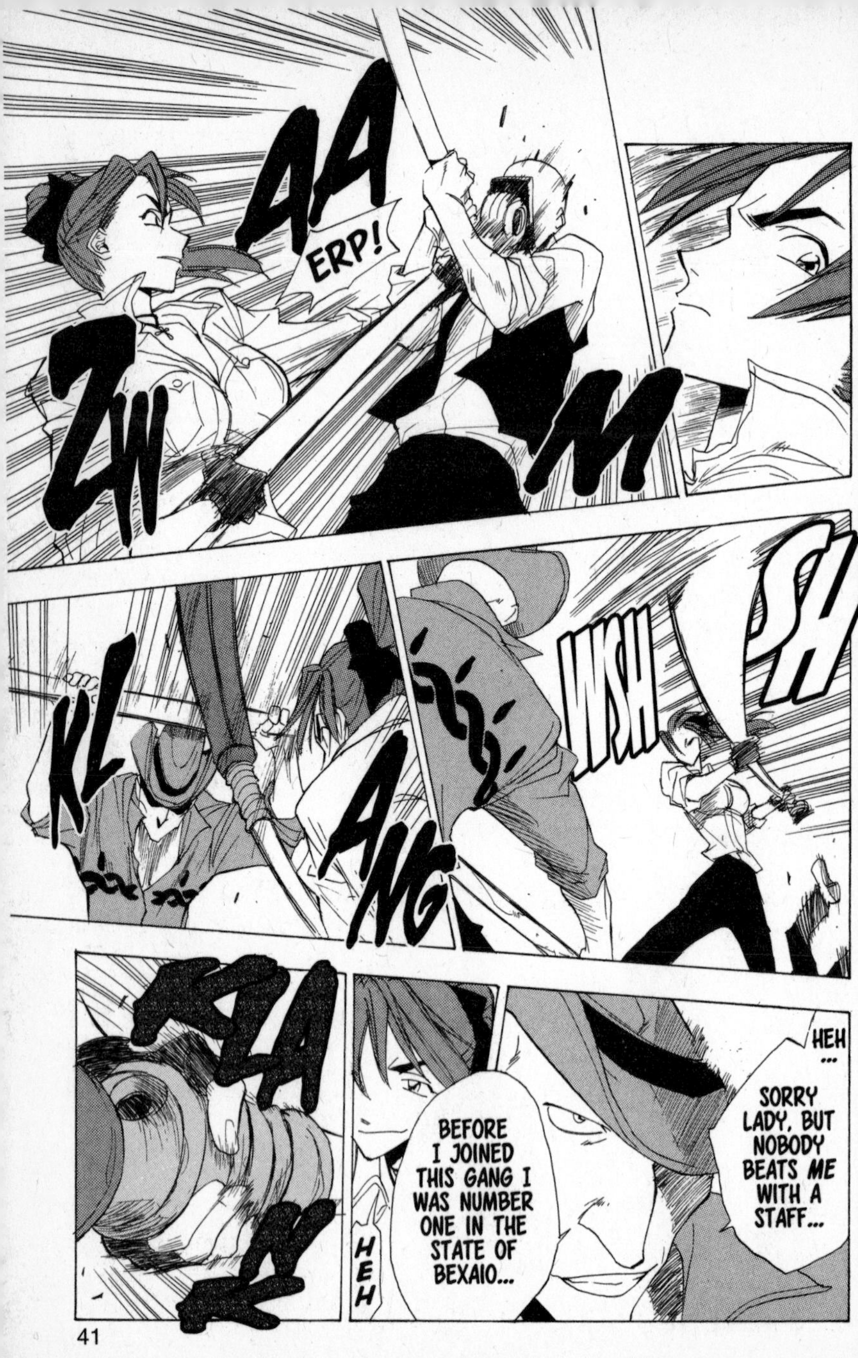
AA
ERP!
ZW
M
SH
WSH
KL
ANG
HEH ...
SORRY LADY, BUT NOBODY BEATS ME WITH A STAFF...
BEFORE I JOINED THIS GANG I WAS NUMBER ONE IN THE STATE OF BEXAIO...
HEH HEH

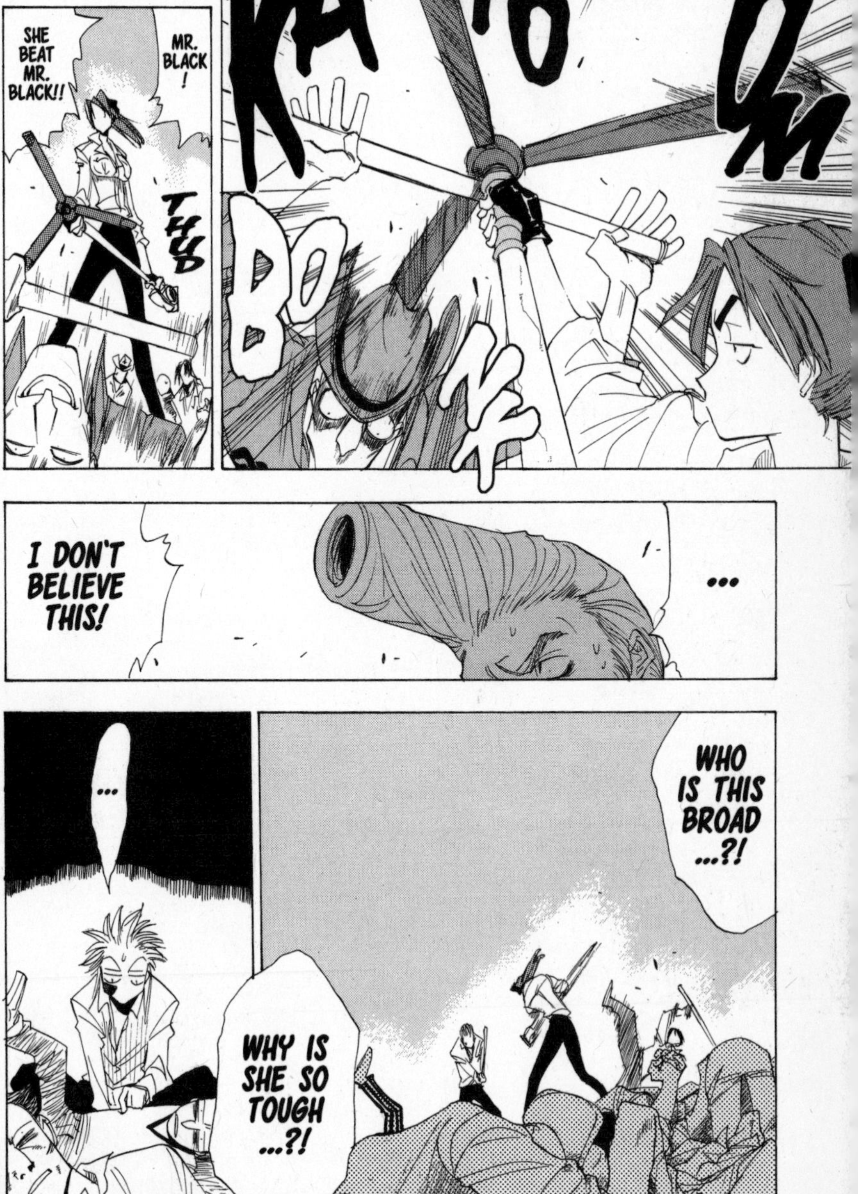
KAFOOM
BONK
MR. BLACK!
SHE BEAT MR. BLACK!!
THUD
...
I DON'T BELIEVE THIS!
WHO IS THIS BROAD ...?!
WHY IS SHE SO TOUGH ...?!
...

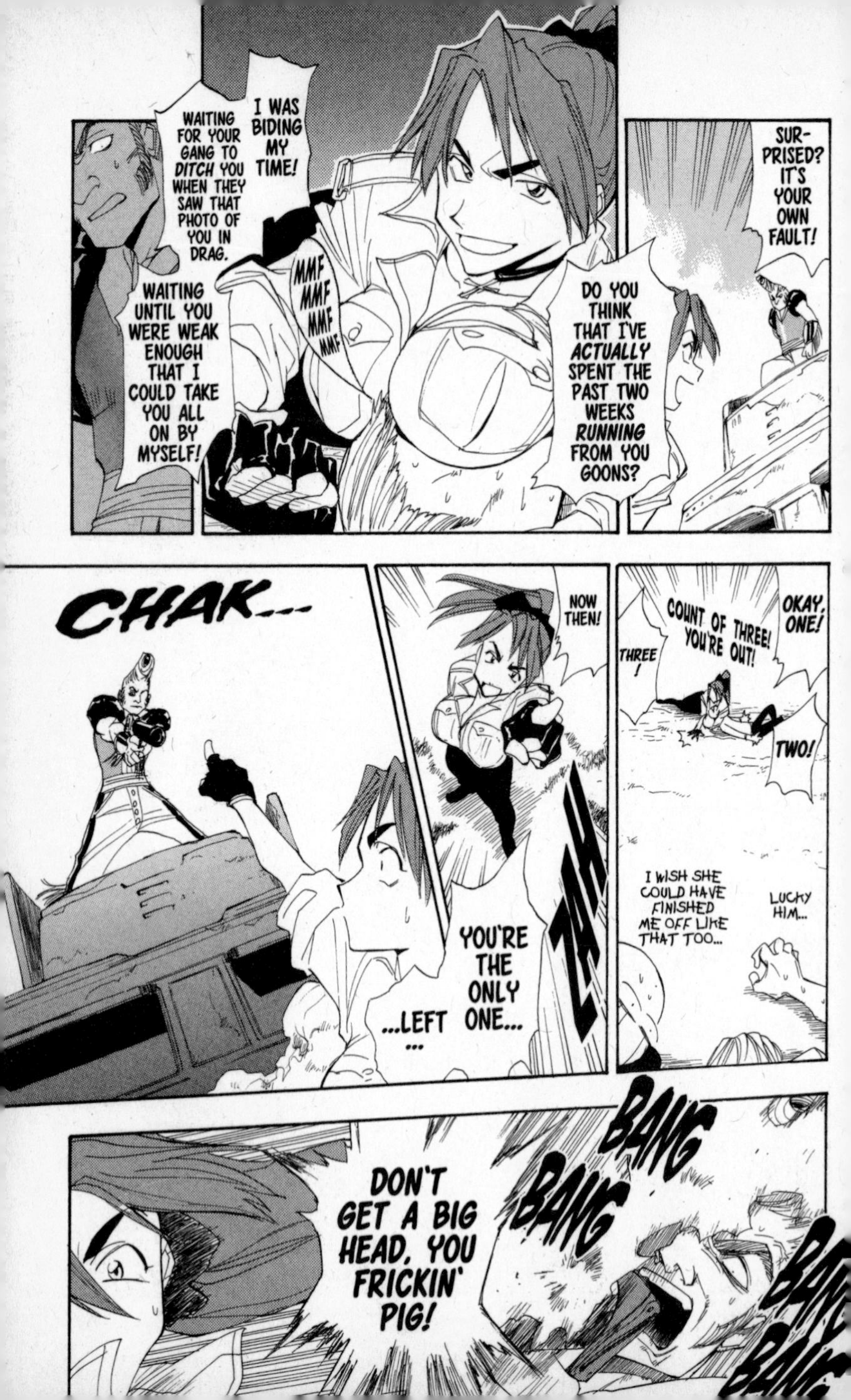
SUR-PRISED? IT'S YOUR OWN FAULT!
DO YOU THINK THAT I'VE *ACTUALLY* SPENT THE PAST TWO WEEKS *RUNNING* FROM YOU GOONS?
MMF MMF MMF MMF
I WAS BIDING MY TIME!
WAITING FOR YOUR GANG TO *DITCH* YOU WHEN THEY SAW THAT PHOTO OF YOU IN DRAG.
WAITING UNTIL YOU WERE WEAK ENOUGH THAT I COULD TAKE YOU ALL ON BY MYSELF!
OKAY, ONE!
COUNT OF THREE! YOU'RE OUT!
TWO!
THREE!
LUCKY HIM...
I WISH SHE COULD HAVE FINISHED ME OFF LIKE THAT TOO...
NOW THEN!
ZAH
YOU'RE THE ONLY ONE...
...LEFT...
CHAK...
BANG
BANG BANG
DON'T GET A BIG HEAD, YOU FRICKIN' PIG!

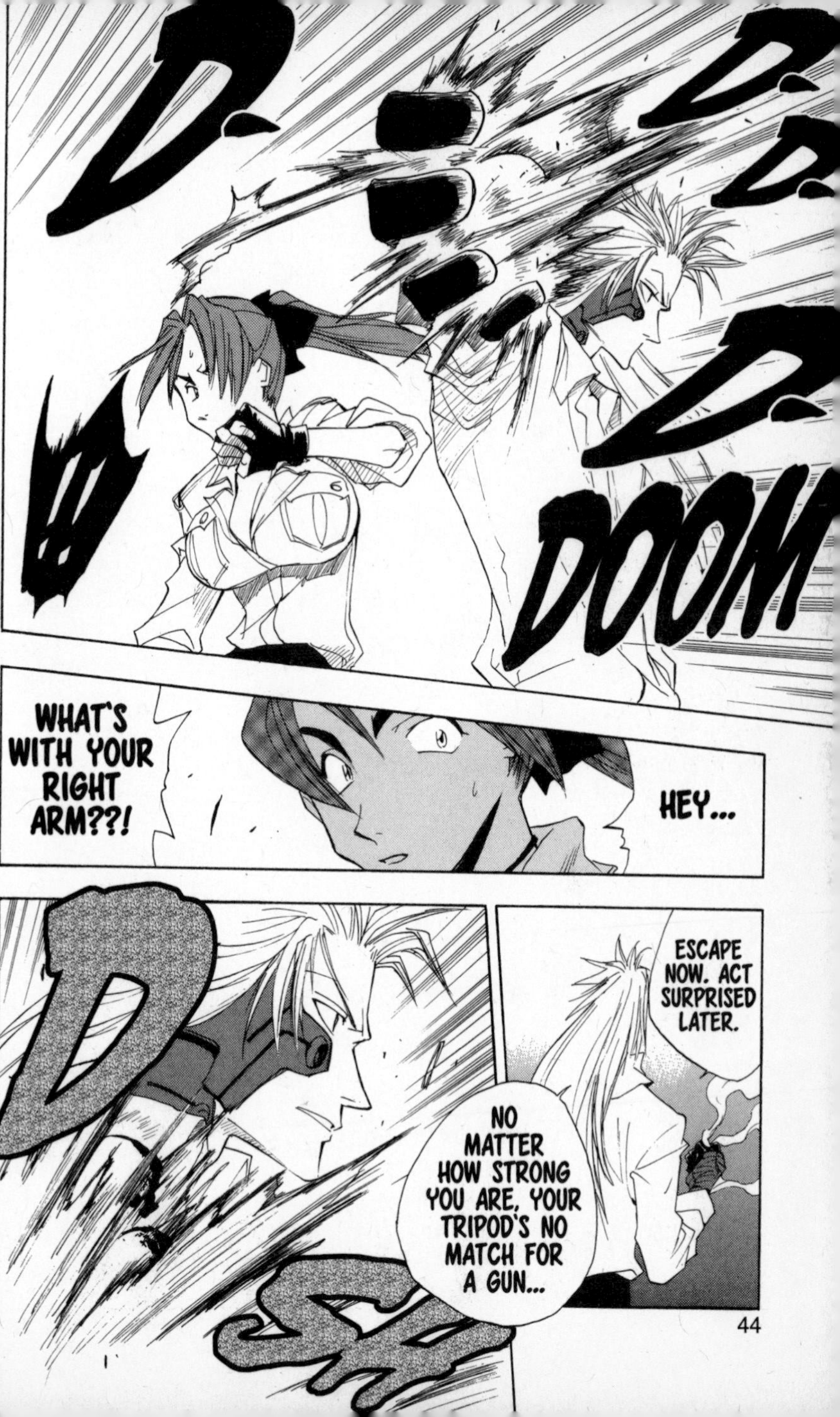
D-D-D-DOOM
D-
!!
HEY...
WHAT'S WITH YOUR RIGHT ARM??!
ESCAPE NOW. ACT SURPRISED LATER.
NO MATTER HOW STRONG YOU ARE, YOUR TRIPOD'S NO MATCH FOR A GUN...
D
SH

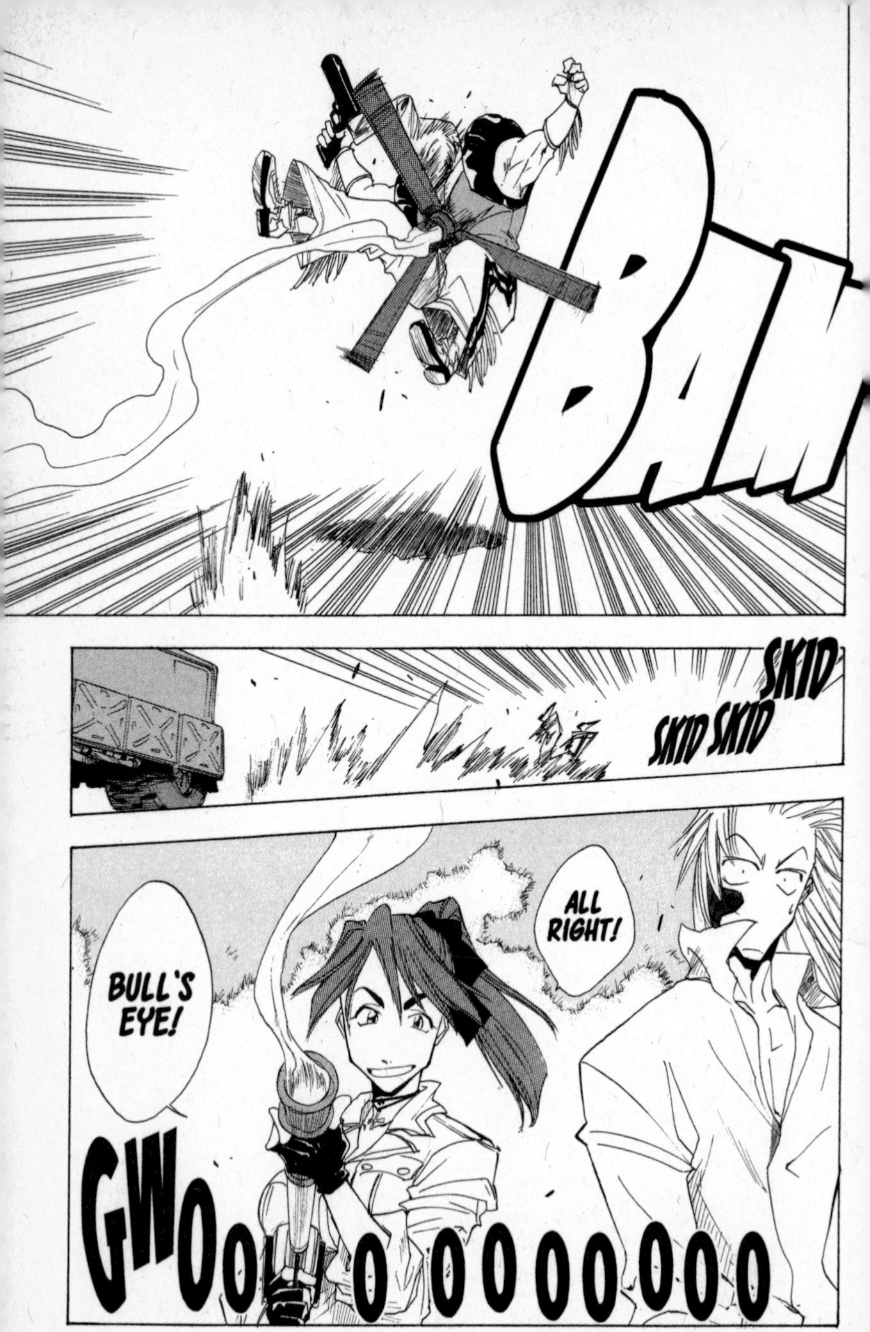
BAM
SKID
SKID SKID
ALL RIGHT!
BULL'S EYE!
GWOOOOOOOOOOOO

# B-side NAKED MONKEYS 6.

## Wolfgangina Lalla Getto
### ウルフギャンギーナ・ララ・ジェット

Height: 171 cm
Weight: 56 kg
Date of Birth: March 31
Age: 18
Blood Type: O(+)
Hometown:
Ciudad Iglesias, Bexaio
Academic Career:
Arthur Marques No. 2 Elementary
School. Dropped out of
St. Bernadetta Girls' School.

A journalist from Shuder Doigrecias in the state of Bexaio. Although she makes a living by exposing the evils of society, her basic belief is that there are more good people than bad in the world. Therefore, she doesn't assume that someone's a villain unless she sees them do something evil with her own eyes. Her flashy looks and "big sister" person-

ality made her queen of the campus during her girls' school days. Her favorite food is her mother's tomato and chicken risotto. She hates eels and roller coasters. Her favorite watches, which she always wears, are Mileil Turgot's "S.R.B." (Self Respecting Bouncers) series and z-chro's "Master of Adventure." By the way, her bust size is a 40-inch (101 cm) H cup.

# Track 10: Wolfina (Has No Lips To Tell You)

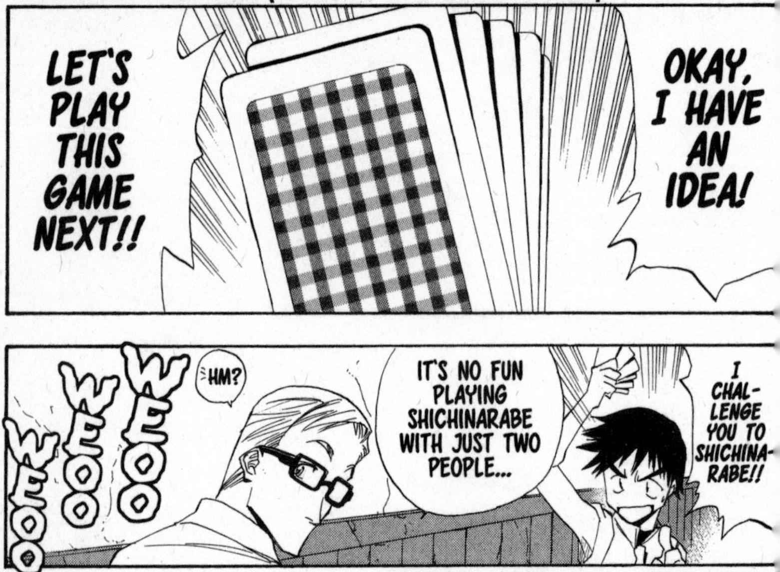
OKAY, I HAVE AN IDEA!
LET'S PLAY THIS GAME NEXT!!
I CHAL-LENGE YOU TO SHICHINA-RABE!!
IT'S NO FUN PLAYING SHICHINARABE WITH JUST TWO PEOPLE...
HM?
WEOO WEOO WEOO

*SHICHINARABE = "SEVEN IN A ROW," A JAPANESE CARD GAME

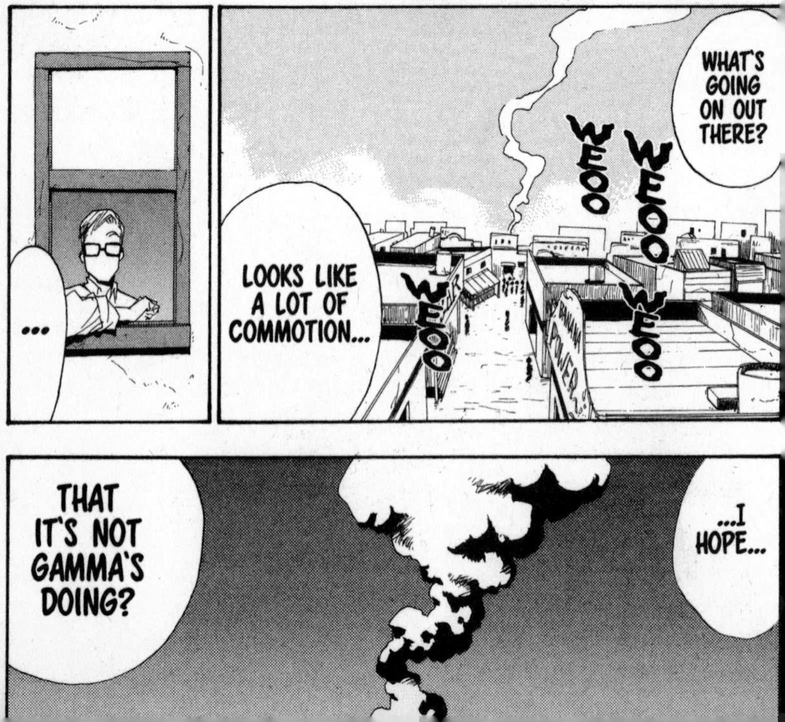
WHAT'S GOING ON OUT THERE?
WEOO WEOO WEOO WEOO
LOOKS LIKE A LOT OF COMMOTION...
...
...I HOPE...
THAT IT'S NOT GAMMA'S DOING?

# ZOMBIEPOWDER.

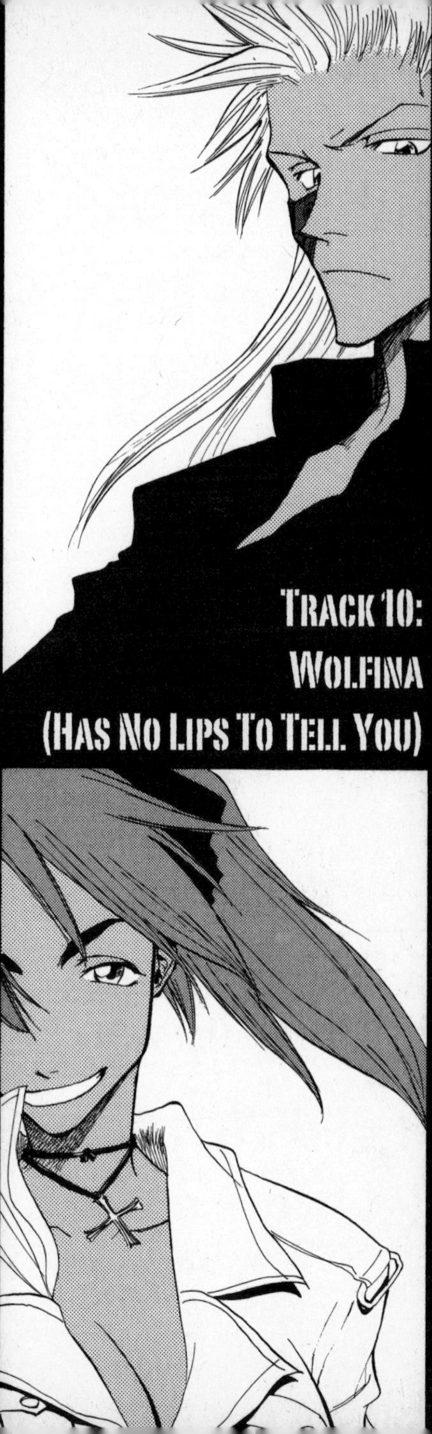

## TRACK 10: WOLFINA (HAS NO LIPS TO TELL YOU)

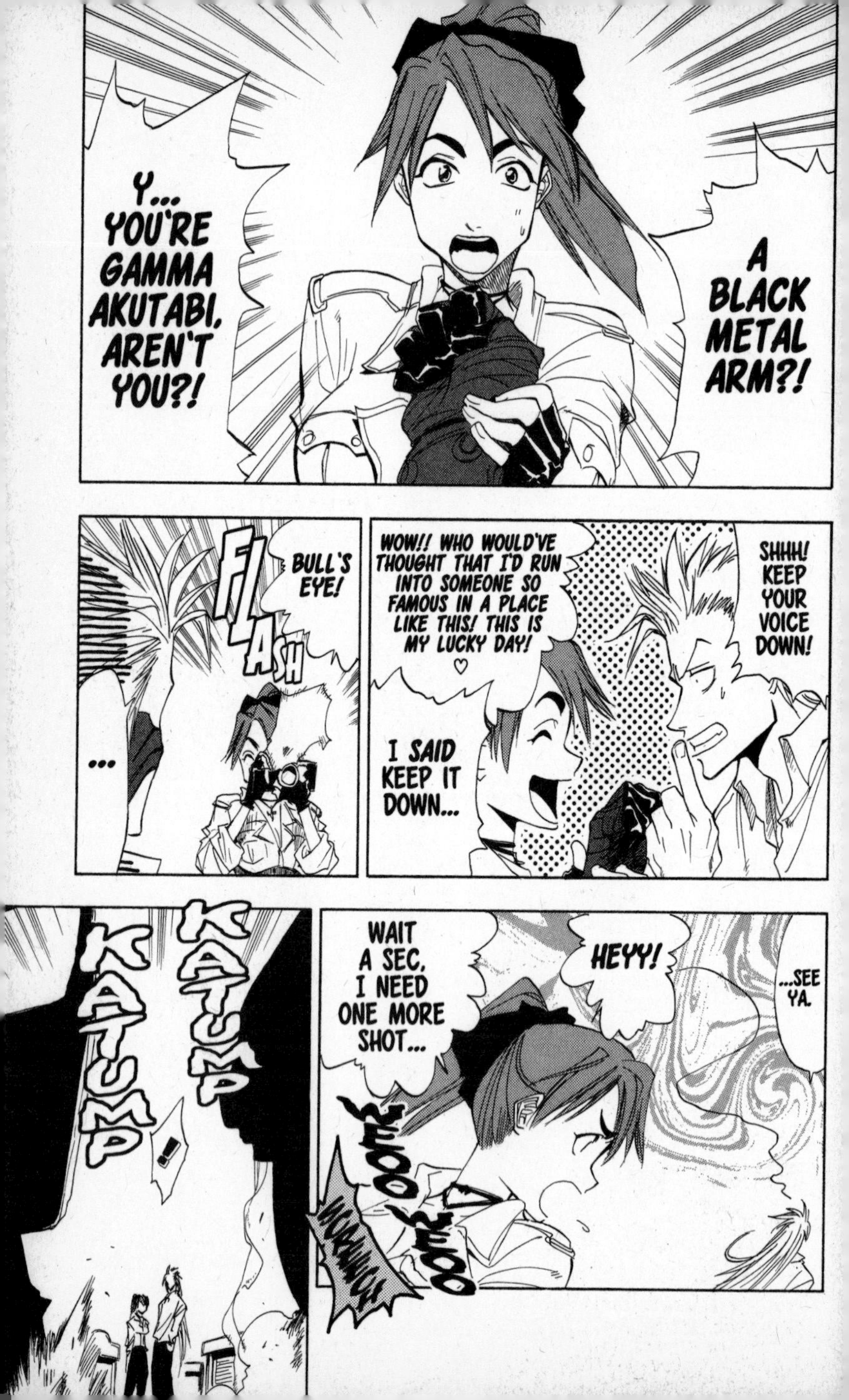
A BLACK METAL ARM?!
Y... YOU'RE GAMMA AKUTABI, AREN'T YOU?!
SHHH! KEEP YOUR VOICE DOWN!
WOW!! WHO WOULD'VE THOUGHT THAT I'D RUN INTO SOMEONE SO FAMOUS IN A PLACE LIKE THIS! THIS IS MY LUCKY DAY! ♡
I SAID KEEP IT DOWN...
BULL'S EYE!
FLASH
...
...SEE YA.
HEYY!
WAIT A SEC, I NEED ONE MORE SHOT...
WEOOO WEOOO
KATUMP
KATUMP
!

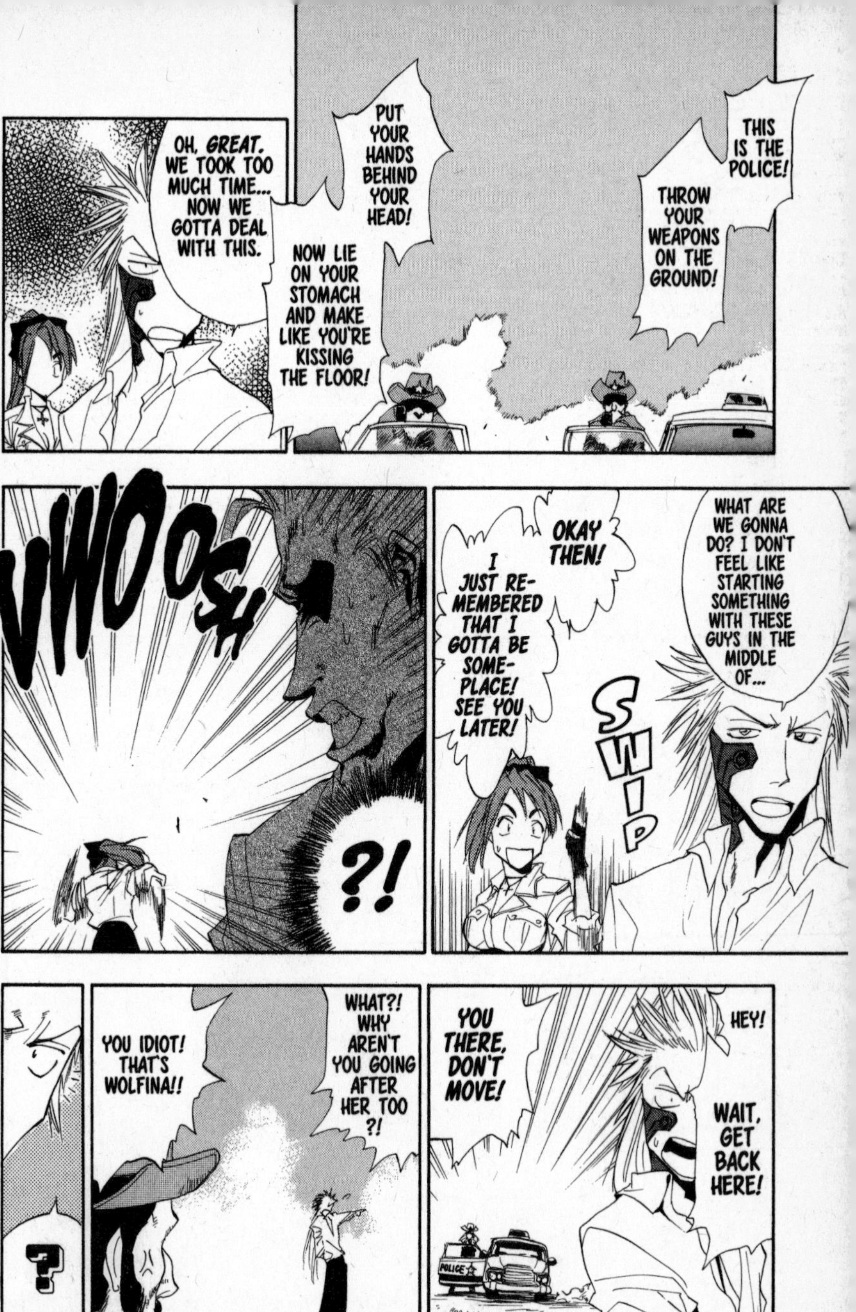
THIS IS THE POLICE!
THROW YOUR WEAPONS ON THE GROUND!
PUT YOUR HANDS BEHIND YOUR HEAD!
NOW LIE ON YOUR STOMACH AND MAKE LIKE YOU'RE KISSING THE FLOOR!
OH, GREAT. WE TOOK TOO MUCH TIME... NOW WE GOTTA DEAL WITH THIS.
WHAT ARE WE GONNA DO? I DON'T FEEL LIKE STARTING SOMETHING WITH THESE GUYS IN THE MIDDLE OF...
OKAY THEN!
I JUST RE-MEMBERED THAT I GOTTA BE SOME-PLACE! SEE YOU LATER!
SWIP
VWOOSH
?!
HEY!
WAIT, GET BACK HERE!
YOU THERE, DON'T MOVE!
POLICE
WHAT?! WHY AREN'T YOU GOING AFTER HER TOO?!
YOU IDIOT! THAT'S WOLFINA!!
?

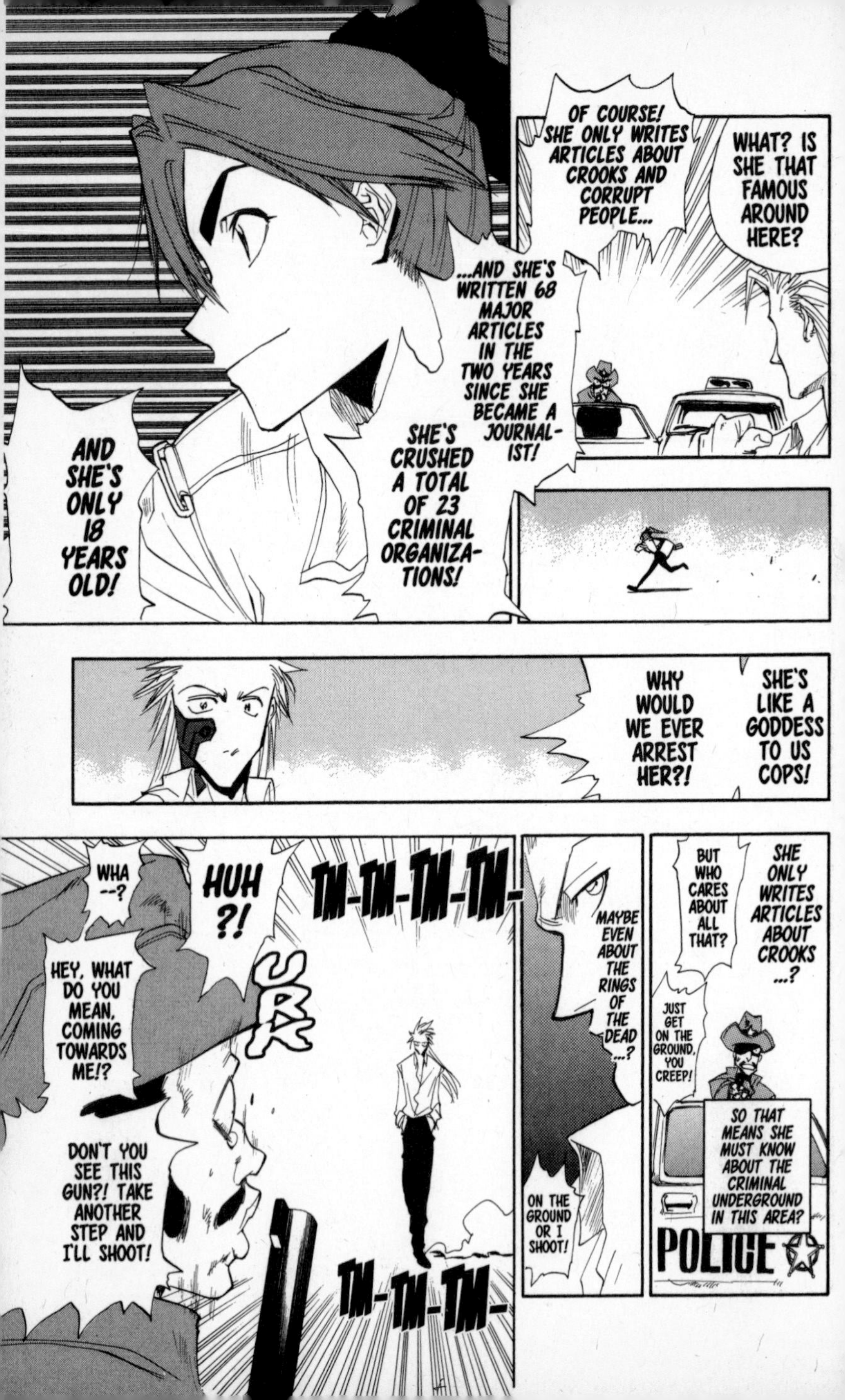
WHAT? IS SHE THAT FAMOUS AROUND HERE?
OF COURSE! SHE ONLY WRITES ARTICLES ABOUT CROOKS AND CORRUPT PEOPLE...
...AND SHE'S WRITTEN 68 MAJOR ARTICLES IN THE TWO YEARS SINCE SHE BECAME A JOURNALIST!
SHE'S CRUSHED A TOTAL OF 23 CRIMINAL ORGANIZATIONS!
AND SHE'S ONLY 18 YEARS OLD!
SHE'S LIKE A GODDESS TO US COPS!
WHY WOULD WE EVER ARREST HER?!
SHE ONLY WRITES ARTICLES ABOUT CROOKS...?
BUT WHO CARES ABOUT ALL THAT?
JUST GET ON THE GROUND, YOU CREEP!
SO THAT MEANS SHE MUST KNOW ABOUT THE CRIMINAL UNDERGROUND IN THIS AREA?
POLICE
MAYBE EVEN ABOUT THE RINGS OF THE DEAD...?
ON THE GROUND OR I SHOOT!
TM-TM-TM-TM-
HUH?!
WHA--?
URK
HEY, WHAT DO YOU MEAN, COMING TOWARDS ME!?
DON'T YOU SEE THIS GUN?! TAKE ANOTHER STEP AND I'LL SHOOT!
TM-TM-TM-

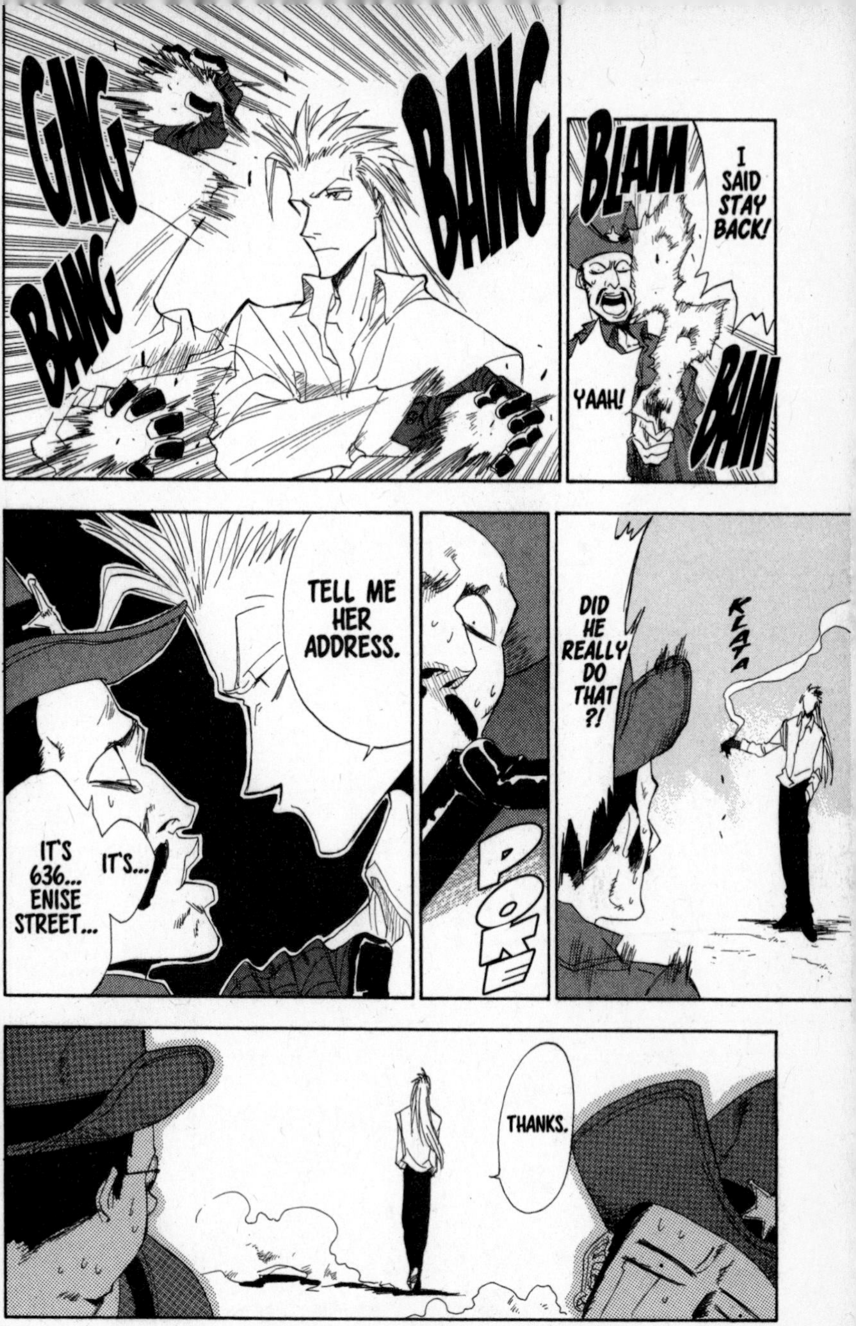
I SAID STAY BACK!
BLAM
BAM
YAAH!
BANG
GING
BANG
KLATA
DID HE REALLY DO THAT?!
POKE
TELL ME HER ADDRESS.
IT'S...
IT'S 636... ENISE STREET...
THANKS.

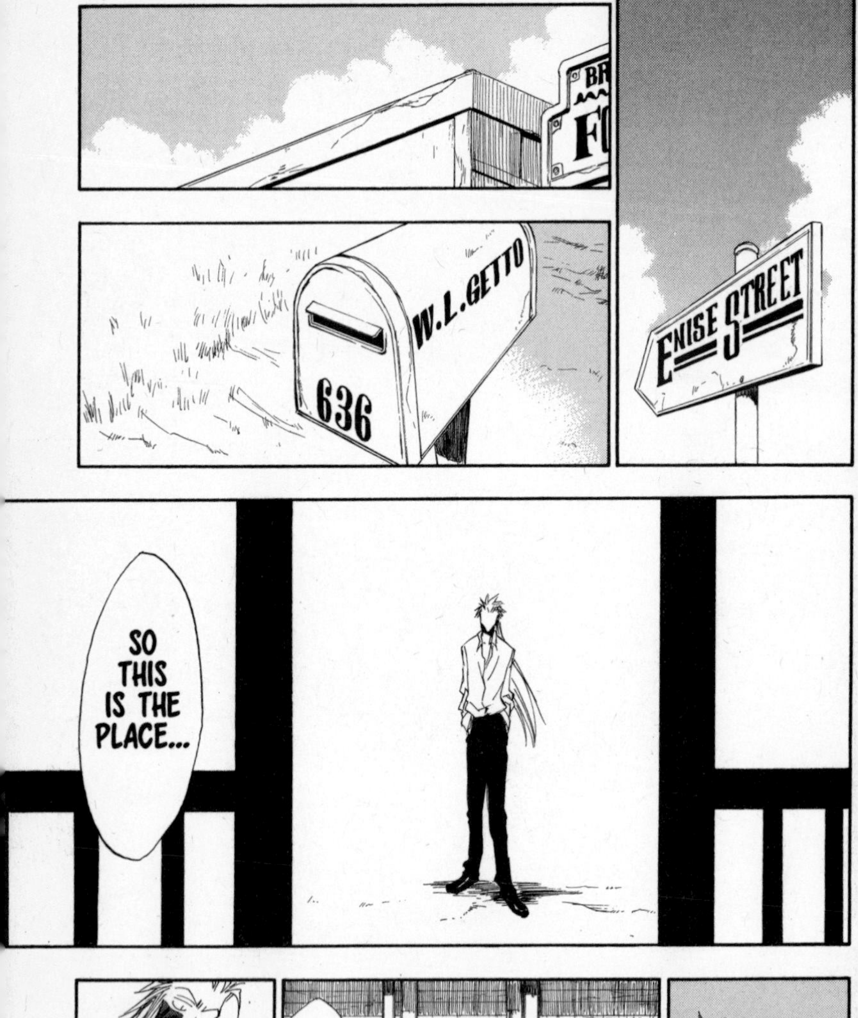
ENISE STREET
BR
FO
W.L.GETTO
636
SO THIS IS THE PLACE...
KNOCK KNOCK
•••
KLAK
...HUH? MAYBE SHE'S NOT HOME YET...

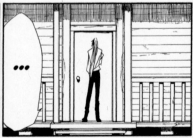

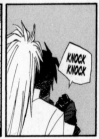

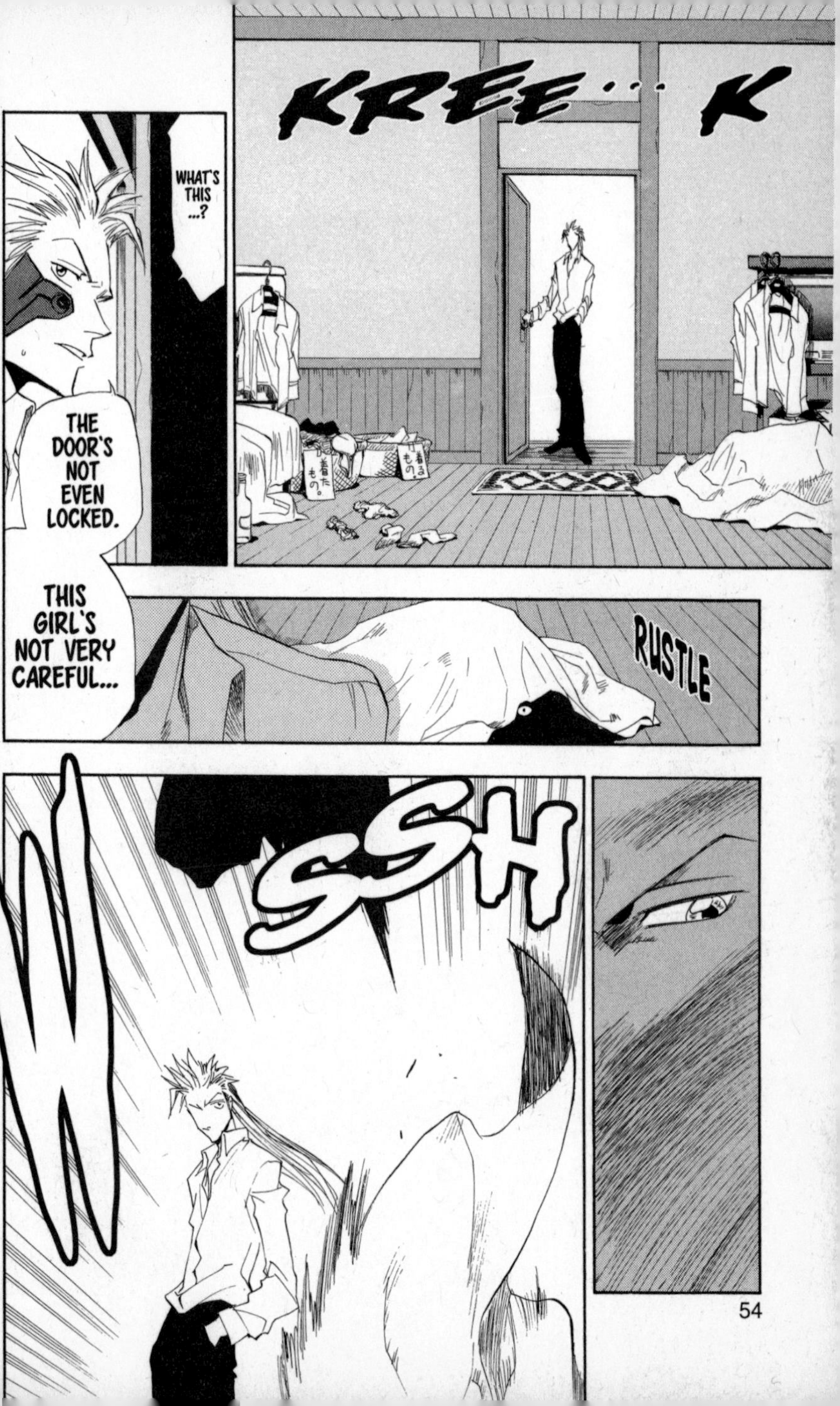
KREE...K
着るもの
着たもの。
WHAT'S THIS ...?
THE DOOR'S NOT EVEN LOCKED.
THIS GIRL'S NOT VERY CAREFUL...
RUSTLE
SSH

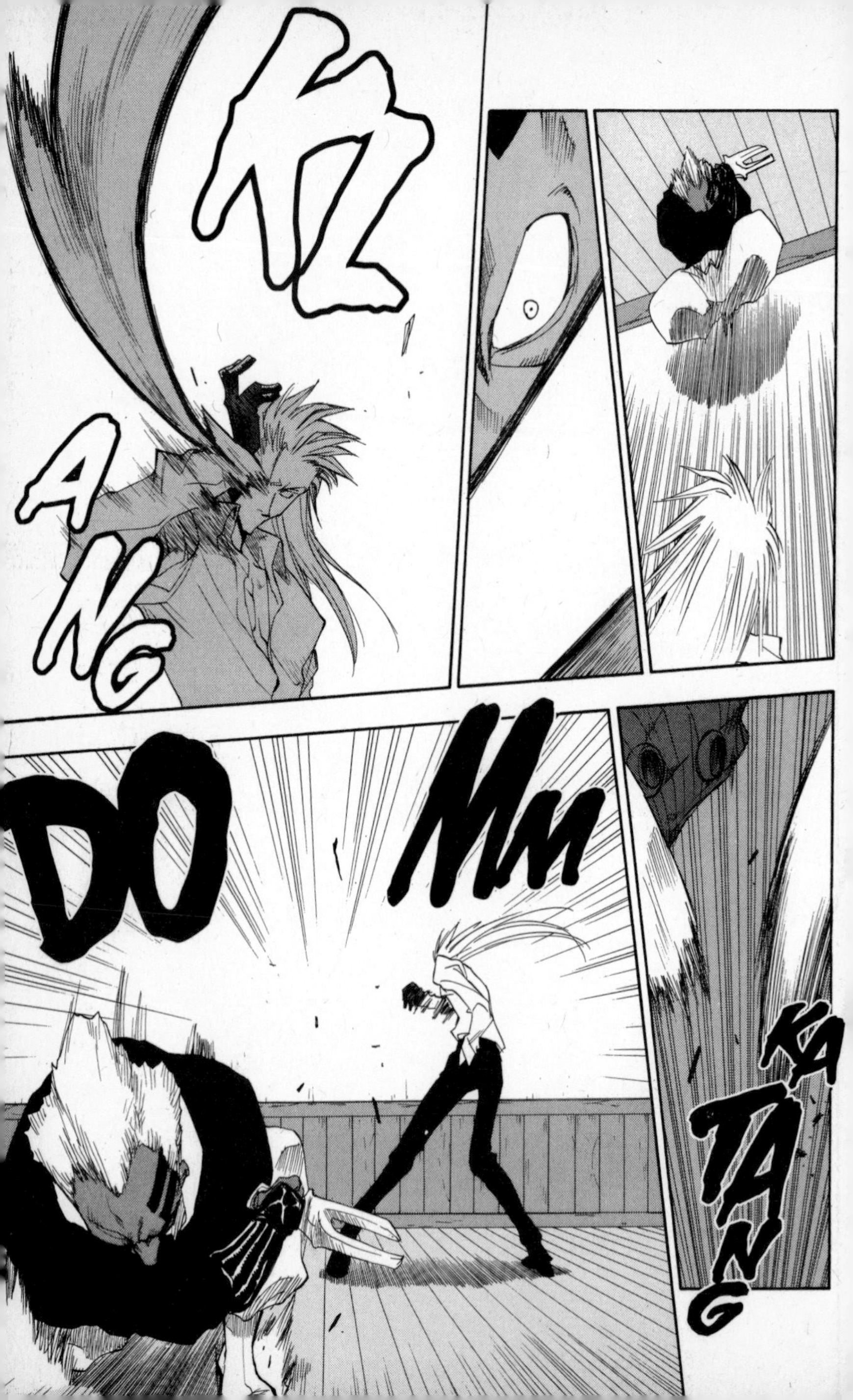
ANG
KATANG
DO
MM

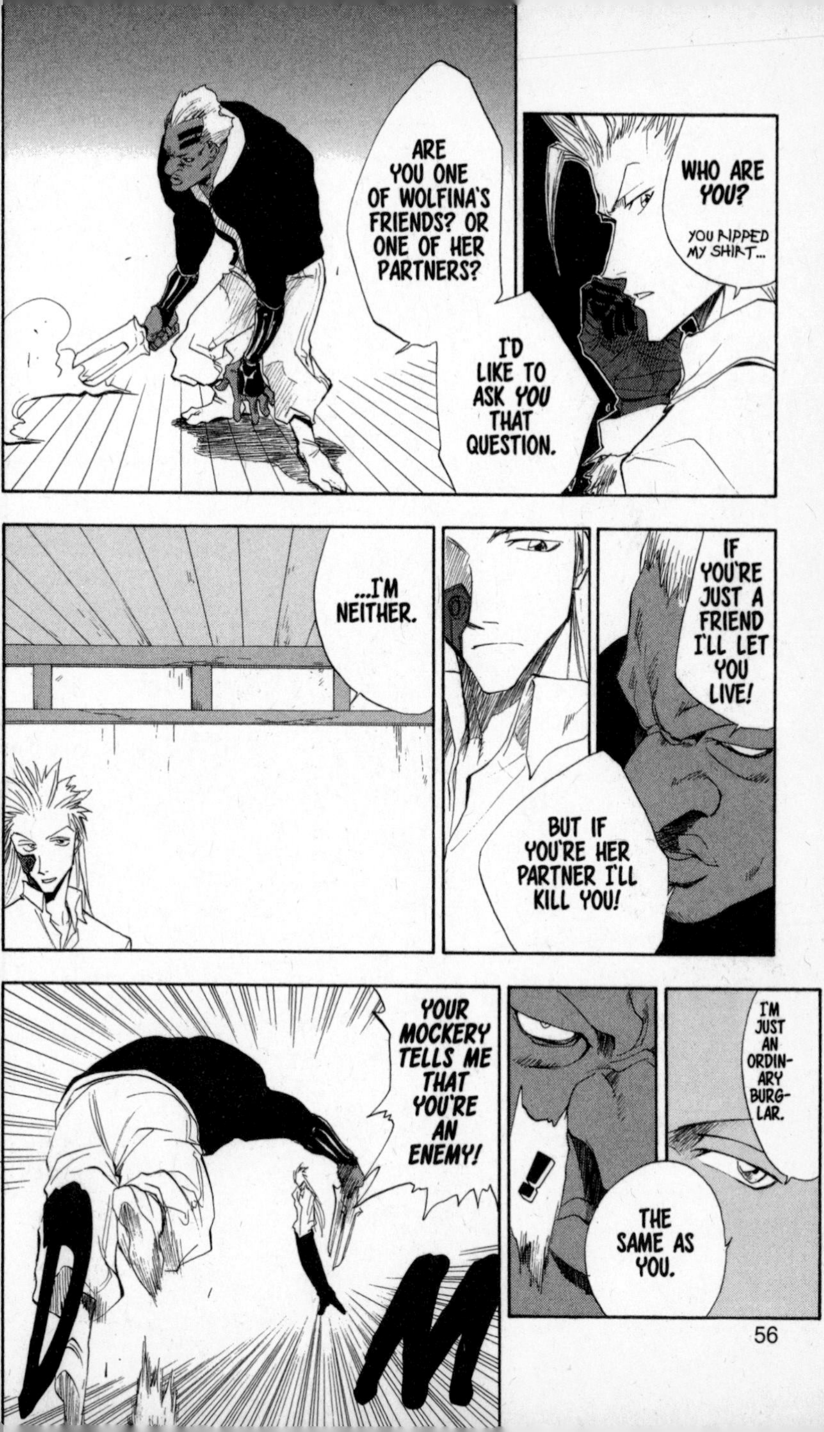
WHO ARE YOU?
YOU RIPPED MY SHIRT...
I'D LIKE TO ASK YOU THAT QUESTION.
ARE YOU ONE OF WOLFINA'S FRIENDS? OR ONE OF HER PARTNERS?
IF YOU'RE JUST A FRIEND I'LL LET YOU LIVE!
BUT IF YOU'RE HER PARTNER I'LL KILL YOU!
...I'M NEITHER.
I'M JUST AN ORDIN-ARY BURG-LAR.
THE SAME AS YOU.
!
YOUR MOCKERY TELLS ME THAT YOU'RE AN ENEMY!

READ THIS WAY

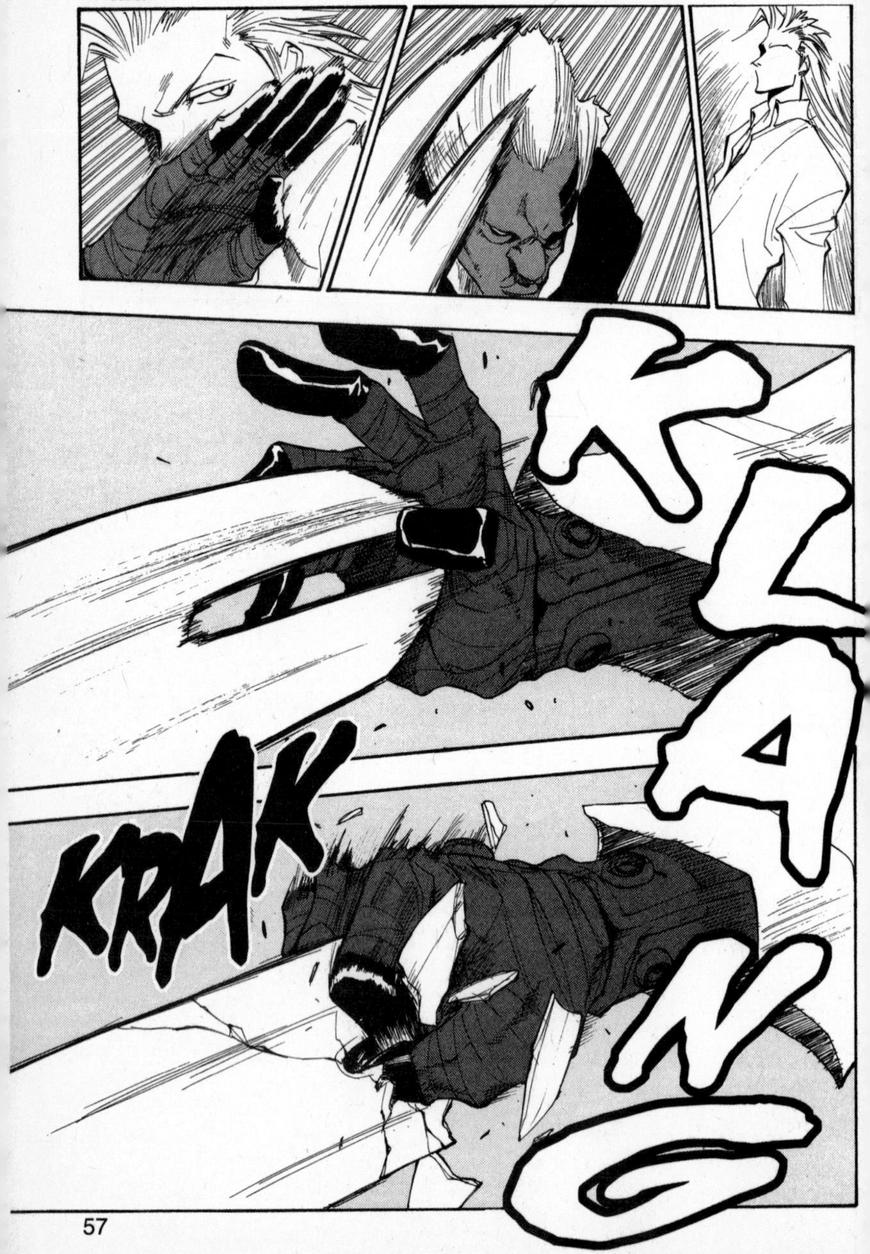
KLANG
KRAK

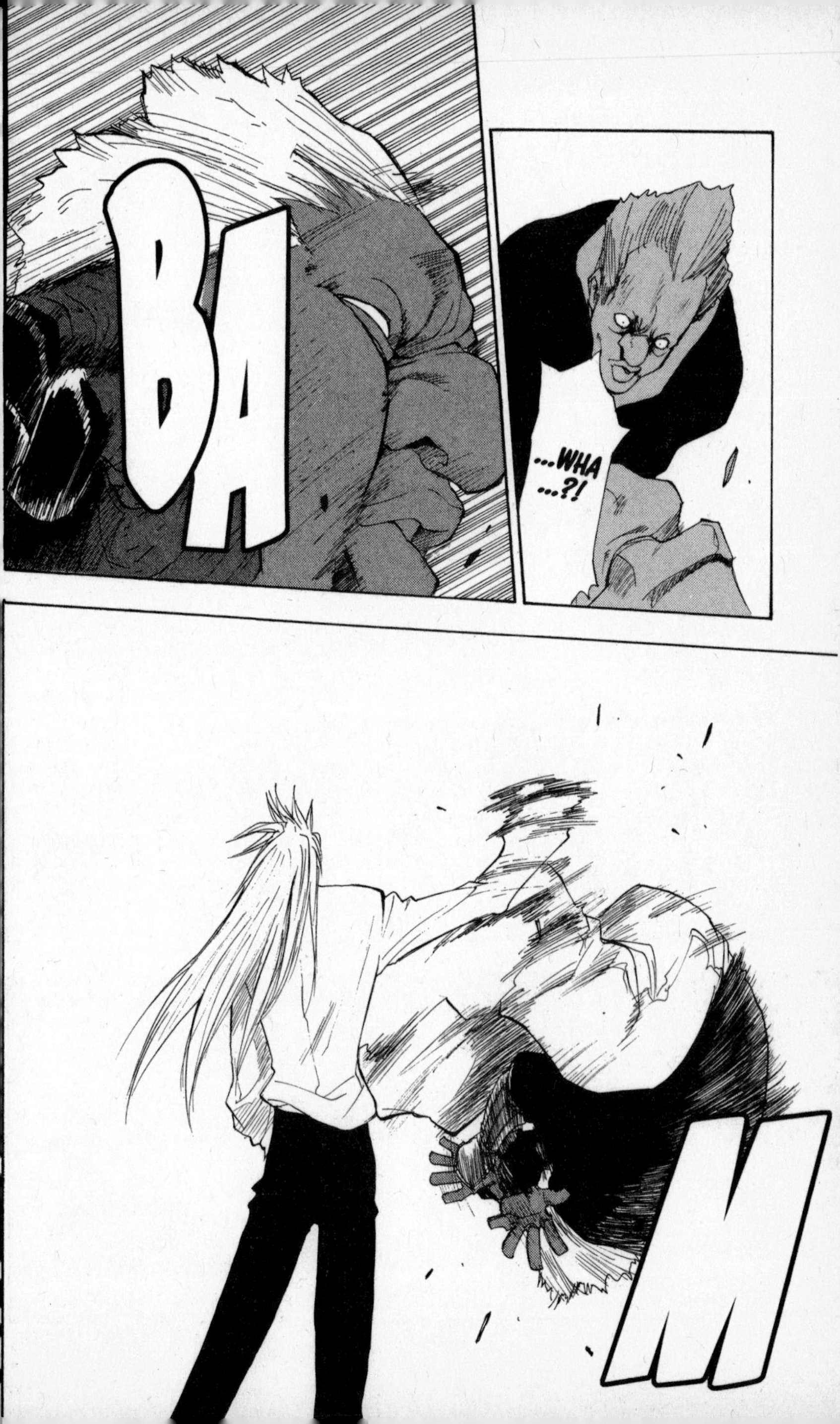
...WHA ...?!
BA
M

READ THIS WAY

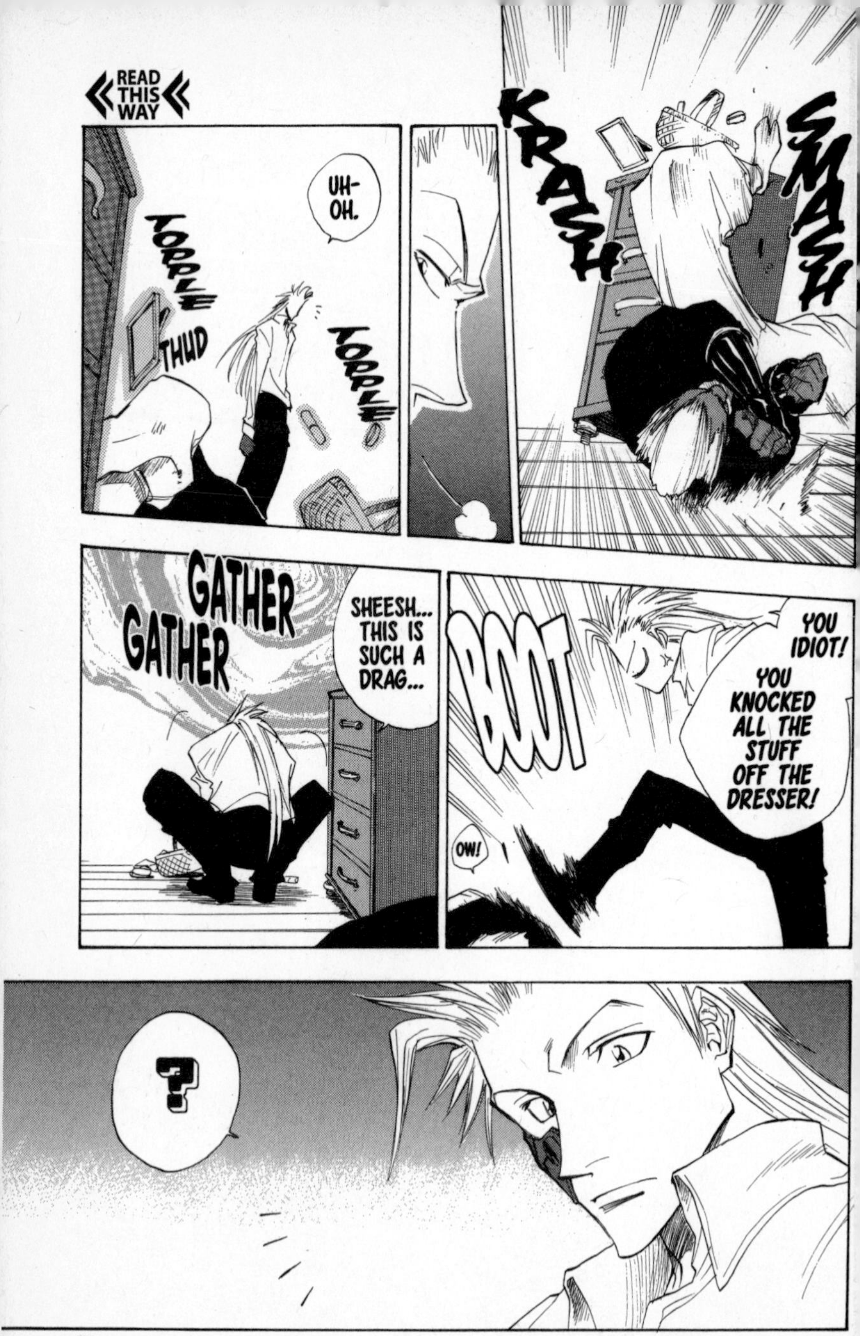
SMASH
KRASH
UH-OH.
TOPPLE
TOPPLE
THUD
YOU IDIOT! YOU KNOCKED ALL THE STUFF OFF THE DRESSER!
BOOT
OW!
SHEESH... THIS IS SUCH A DRAG...
GATHER
GATHER
?

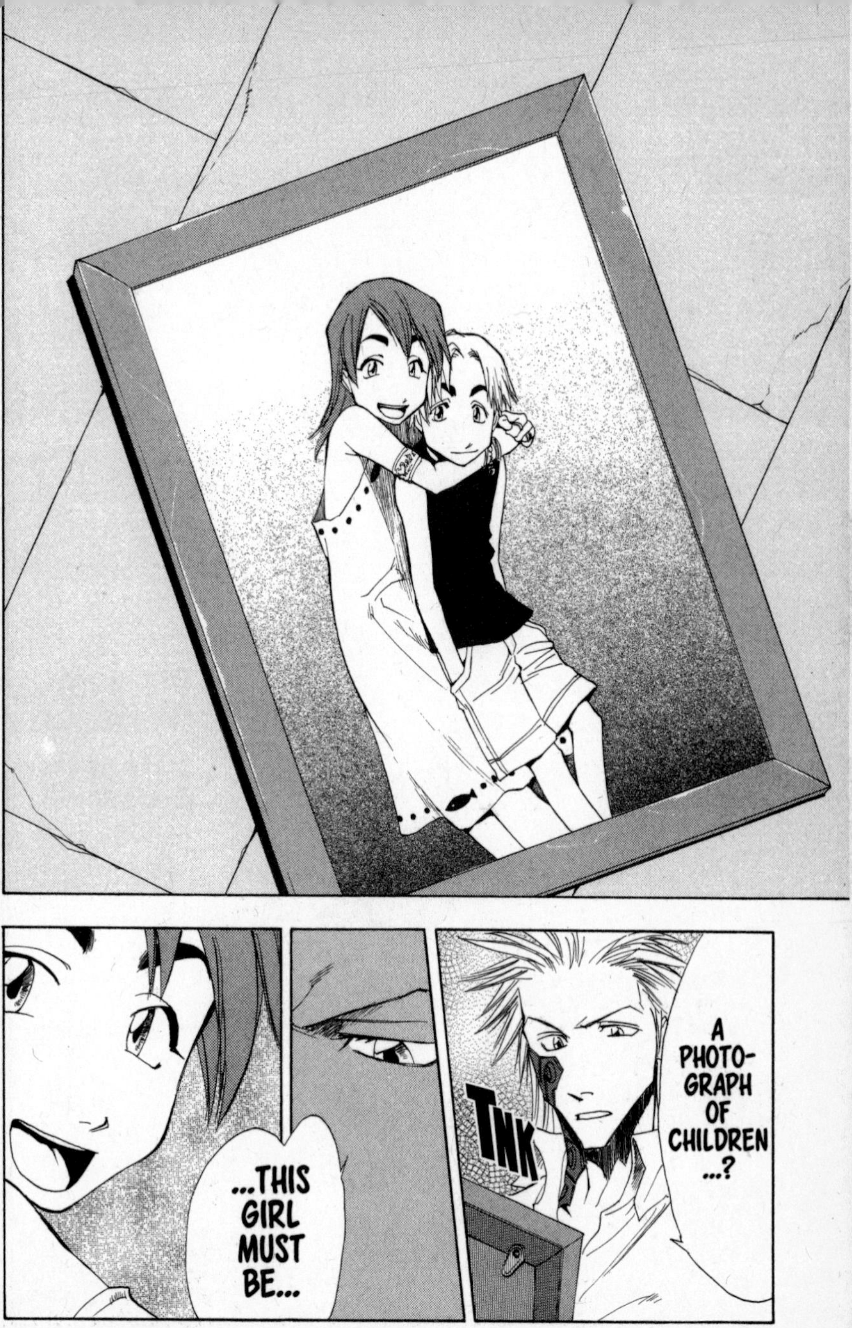
A PHOTOGRAPH OF CHILDREN ...?
TNK
...THIS GIRL MUST BE...

READ THIS WAY

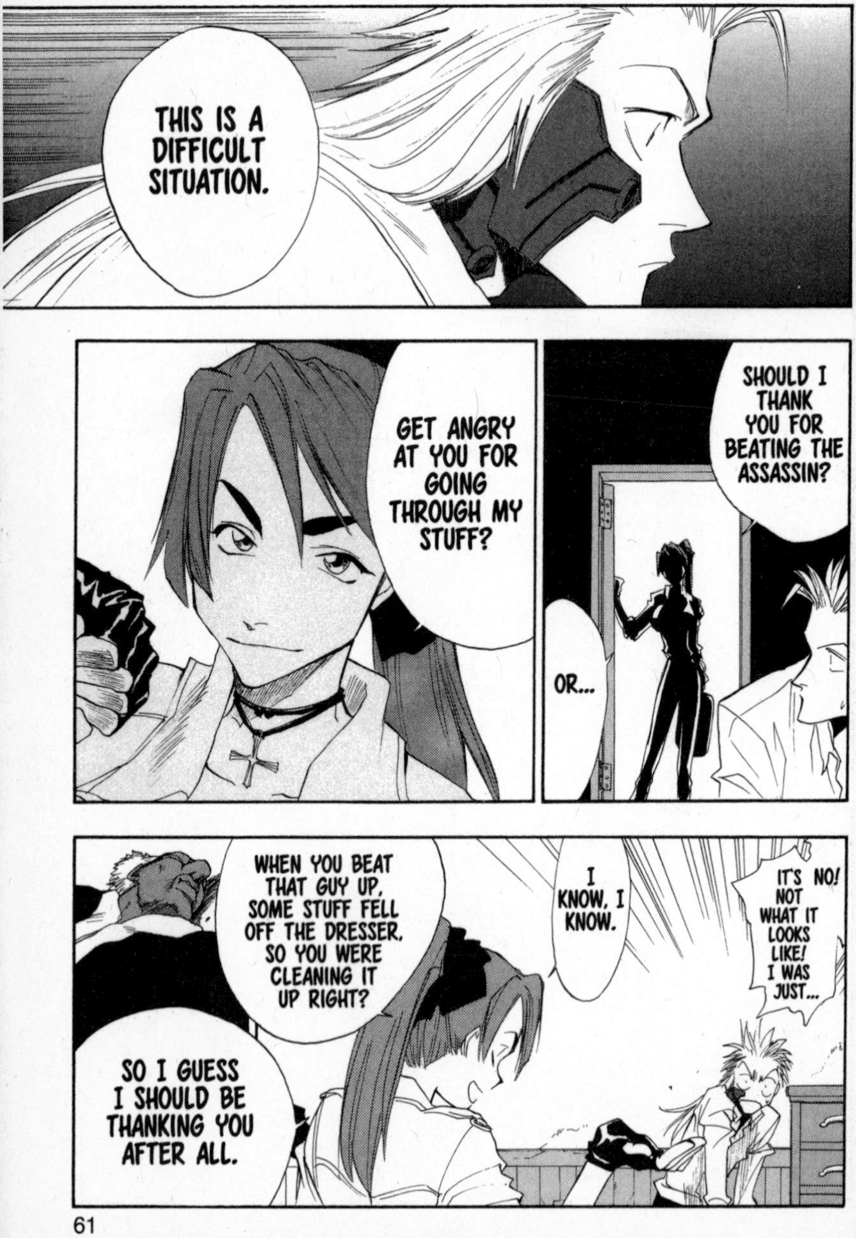
THIS IS A DIFFICULT SITUATION.
SHOULD I THANK YOU FOR BEATING THE ASSASSIN?
OR...
GET ANGRY AT YOU FOR GOING THROUGH MY STUFF?
NO!
IT'S NOT WHAT IT LOOKS LIKE! I WAS JUST...
I KNOW, I KNOW.
WHEN YOU BEAT THAT GUY UP, SOME STUFF FELL OFF THE DRESSER, SO YOU WERE CLEANING IT UP RIGHT?
SO I GUESS I SHOULD BE THANKING YOU AFTER ALL.

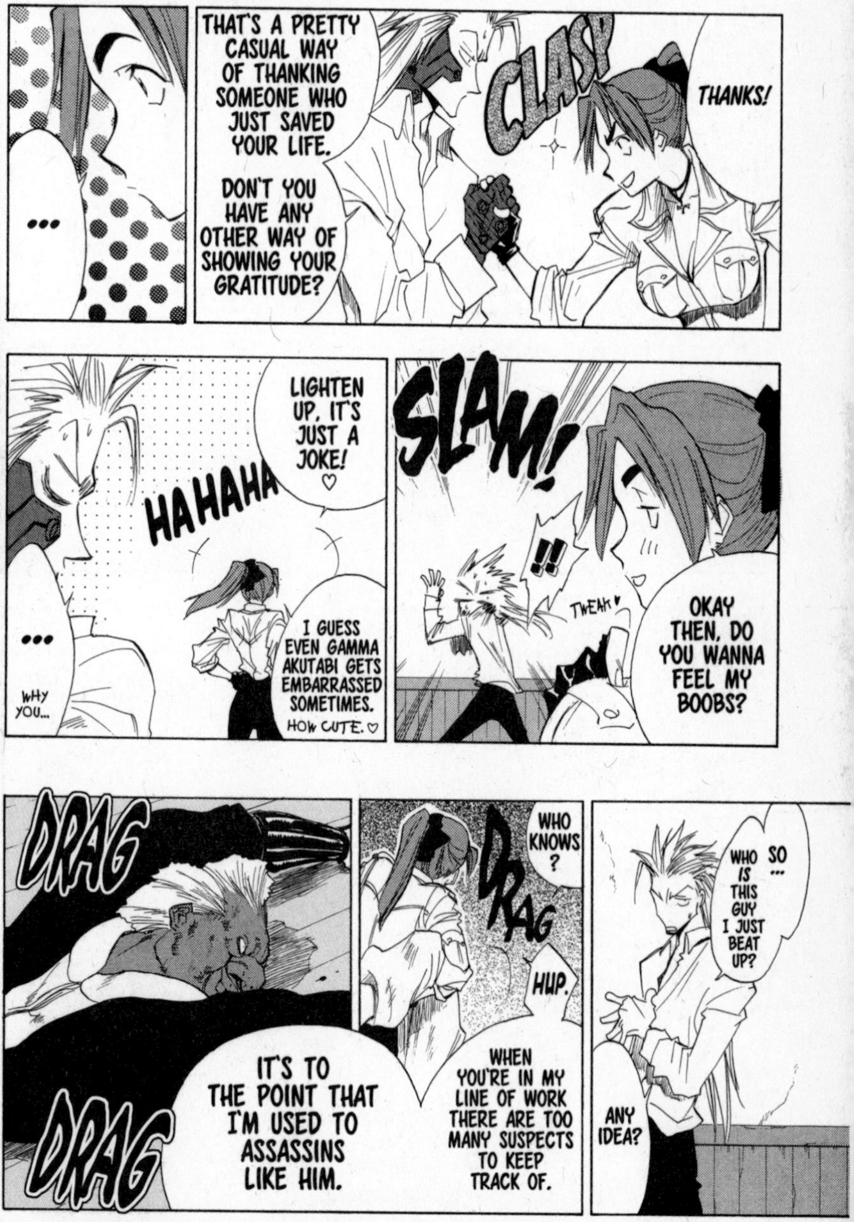
THANKS!
CLASP
THAT'S A PRETTY CASUAL WAY OF THANKING SOMEONE WHO JUST SAVED YOUR LIFE.
DON'T YOU HAVE ANY OTHER WAY OF SHOWING YOUR GRATITUDE?
...
OKAY THEN, DO YOU WANNA FEEL MY BOOBS?
TWEAK
SLAM!
!!
LIGHTEN UP, IT'S JUST A JOKE! ♡
HAHAHA
I GUESS EVEN GAMMA AKUTABI GETS EMBARRASSED SOMETIMES.
HOW CUTE. ♡
...
WHY YOU...
SO... WHO IS THIS GUY I JUST BEAT UP?
ANY IDEA?
WHO KNOWS?
DRAG
HUP.
WHEN YOU'RE IN MY LINE OF WORK THERE ARE TOO MANY SUSPECTS TO KEEP TRACK OF.
DRAG
DRAG
IT'S TO THE POINT THAT I'M USED TO ASSASSINS LIKE HIM.

READ THIS WAY

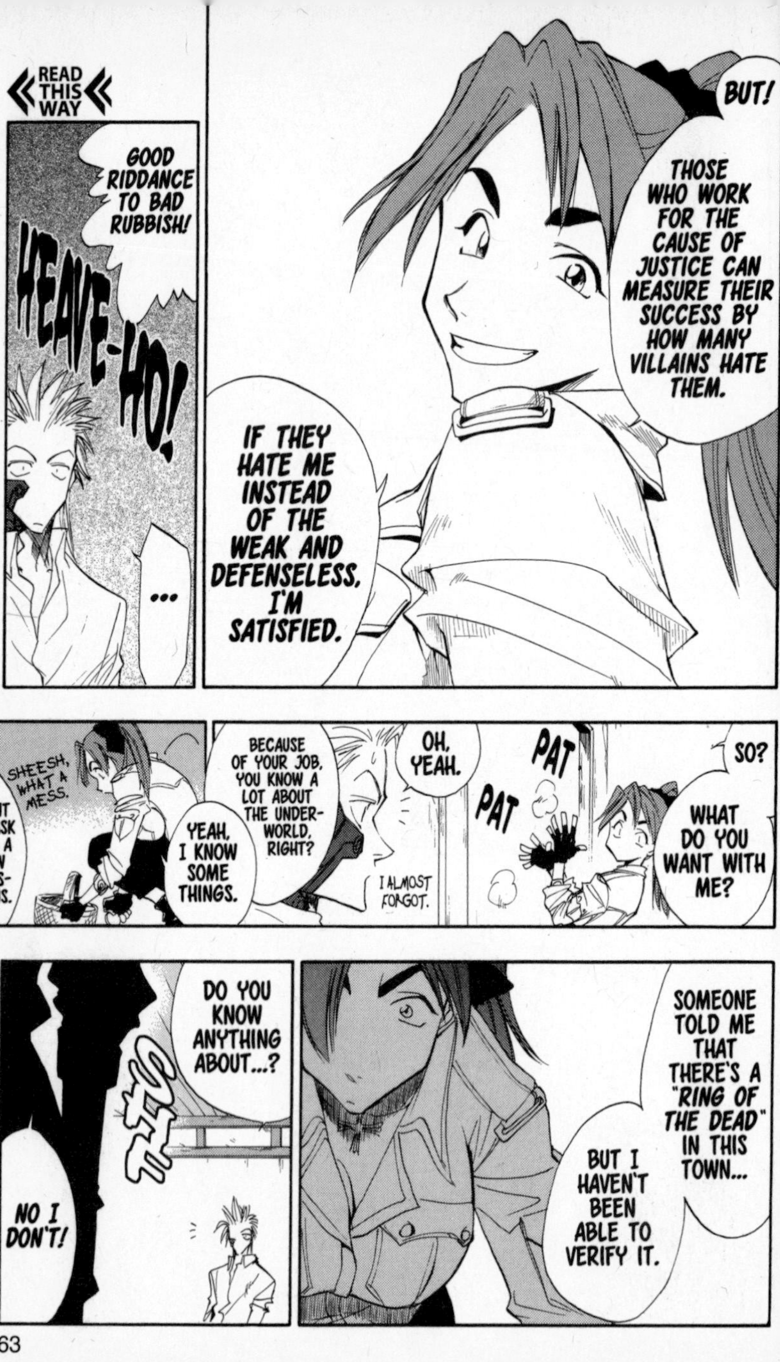

BUT!
THOSE WHO WORK FOR THE CAUSE OF JUSTICE CAN MEASURE THEIR SUCCESS BY HOW MANY VILLAINS HATE THEM.
IF THEY HATE ME INSTEAD OF THE WEAK AND DEFENSELESS, I'M SATISFIED.
GOOD RIDDANCE TO BAD RUBBISH!
HEAVE-HO!
...
SO?
WHAT DO YOU WANT WITH ME?
PAT
PAT
OH, YEAH.
I ALMOST FORGOT.
BECAUSE OF YOUR JOB, YOU KNOW A LOT ABOUT THE UNDER-WORLD, RIGHT?
YEAH, I KNOW SOME THINGS.
SHEESH, WHAT A MESS.
I WANT TO ASK YOU A FEW QUES-TIONS.
SOMEONE TOLD ME THAT THERE'S A "RING OF THE DEAD" IN THIS TOWN...
BUT I HAVEN'T BEEN ABLE TO VERIFY IT.
DO YOU KNOW ANYTHING ABOUT...?
NO I DON'T!

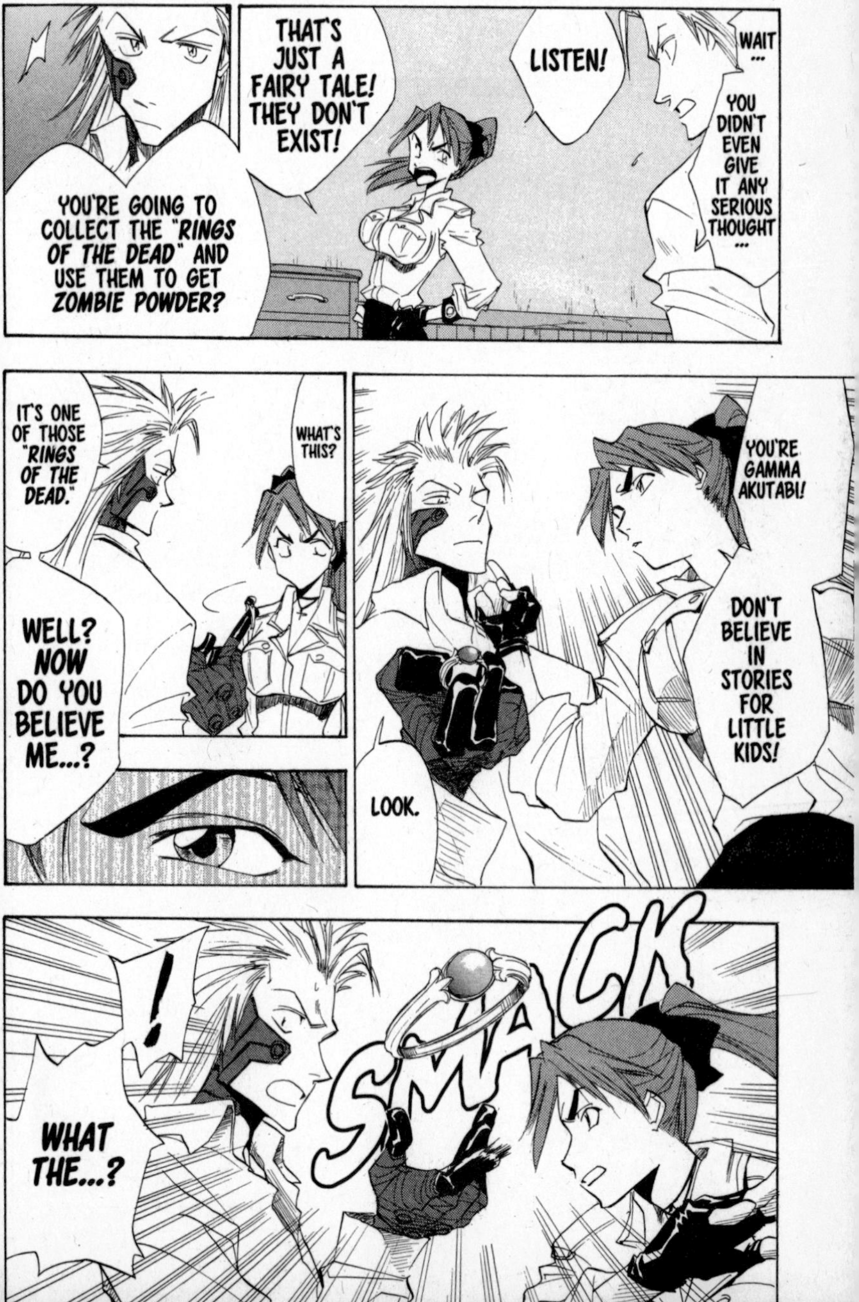
WAIT...
YOU DIDN'T EVEN GIVE IT ANY SERIOUS THOUGHT...
LISTEN!
THAT'S JUST A FAIRY TALE! THEY DON'T EXIST!
YOU'RE GOING TO COLLECT THE "RINGS OF THE DEAD" AND USE THEM TO GET ZOMBIE POWDER?
YOU'RE GAMMA AKUTABI!
DON'T BELIEVE IN STORIES FOR LITTLE KIDS!
LOOK.
WHAT'S THIS?
IT'S ONE OF THOSE "RINGS OF THE DEAD."
WELL? NOW DO YOU BELIEVE ME...?
SMACK
!
WHAT THE...?

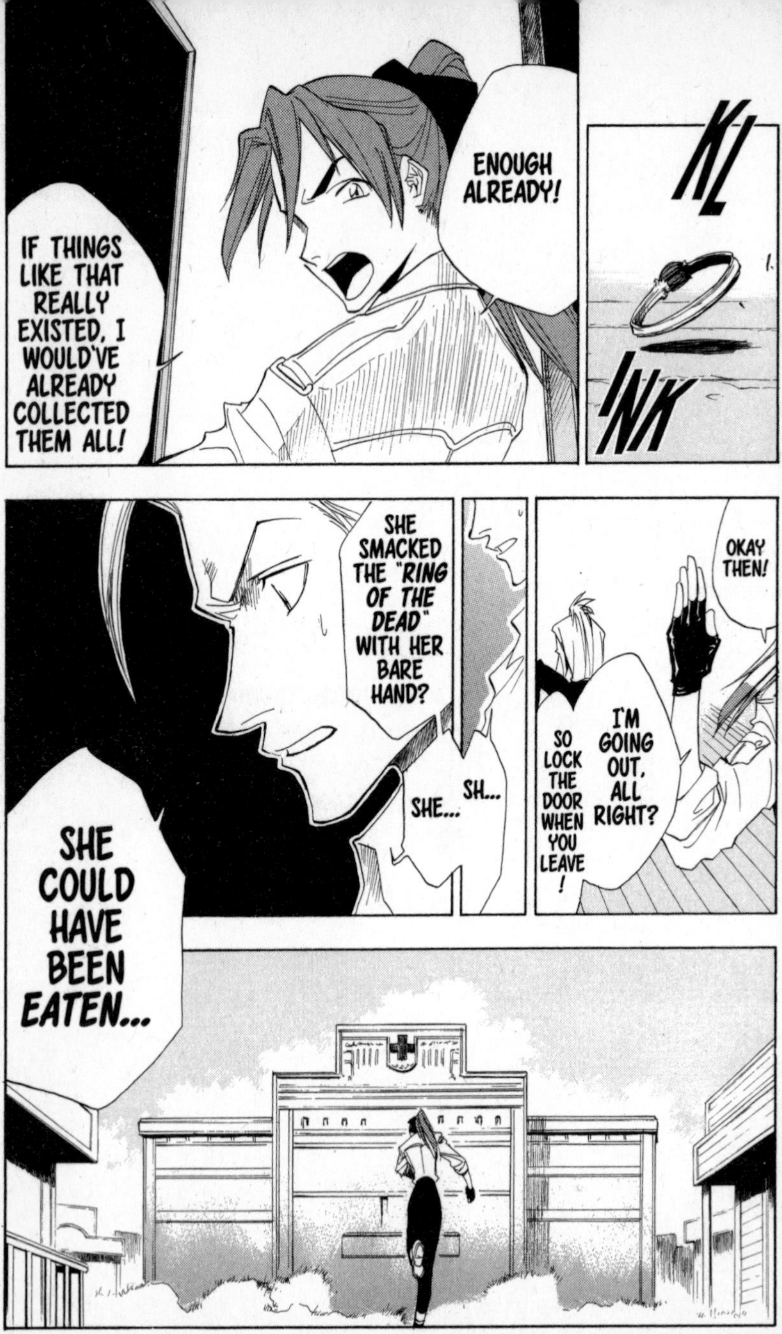
KLINK
ENOUGH ALREADY!
IF THINGS LIKE THAT REALLY EXISTED, I WOULD'VE ALREADY COLLECTED THEM ALL!
OKAY THEN!
I'M GOING OUT, ALL RIGHT?
SO LOCK THE DOOR WHEN YOU LEAVE!
SH...
SHE...
SHE SMACKED THE "RING OF THE DEAD" WITH HER BARE HAND?
SHE COULD HAVE BEEN EATEN...

# B-side NAKED MONKEYS 7.

## Emilio Lufas Getto
### エミリオ・ルーファス・ジェット

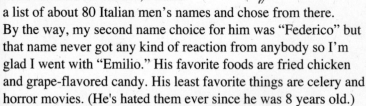

Height: 173 cm
Weight: 54 kg
Date of Birth: September 24
Age: 16
Blood Type: AO(+)

Wolfina's younger brother.
It was tough thinking up a
name for him. In the end, I made
a list of about 80 Italian men's names and chose from there.
By the way, my second name choice for him was "Federico" but
that name never got any kind of reaction from anybody so I'm
glad I went with "Emilio." His favorite foods are fried chicken
and grape-flavored candy. His least favorite things are celery and
horror movies. (He's hated them ever since he was 8 years old.)

## Domenico Alfred Roscoe
### ドメニコ・アルフレッド・ロスコー

Height: 176 cm
Weight: 87 kg
Date of Birth: August 9
Age: 59
Blood Type: AB
Hometown:
Dergit City, Wister

From Dergit City in the state of Wister. Roscoe is a doctor
who currently resides in Alcantara. He has a wife, Judith, and
a daughter, Ellen. He loves peanuts and hot dogs and has a third
degree black belt in Judo.

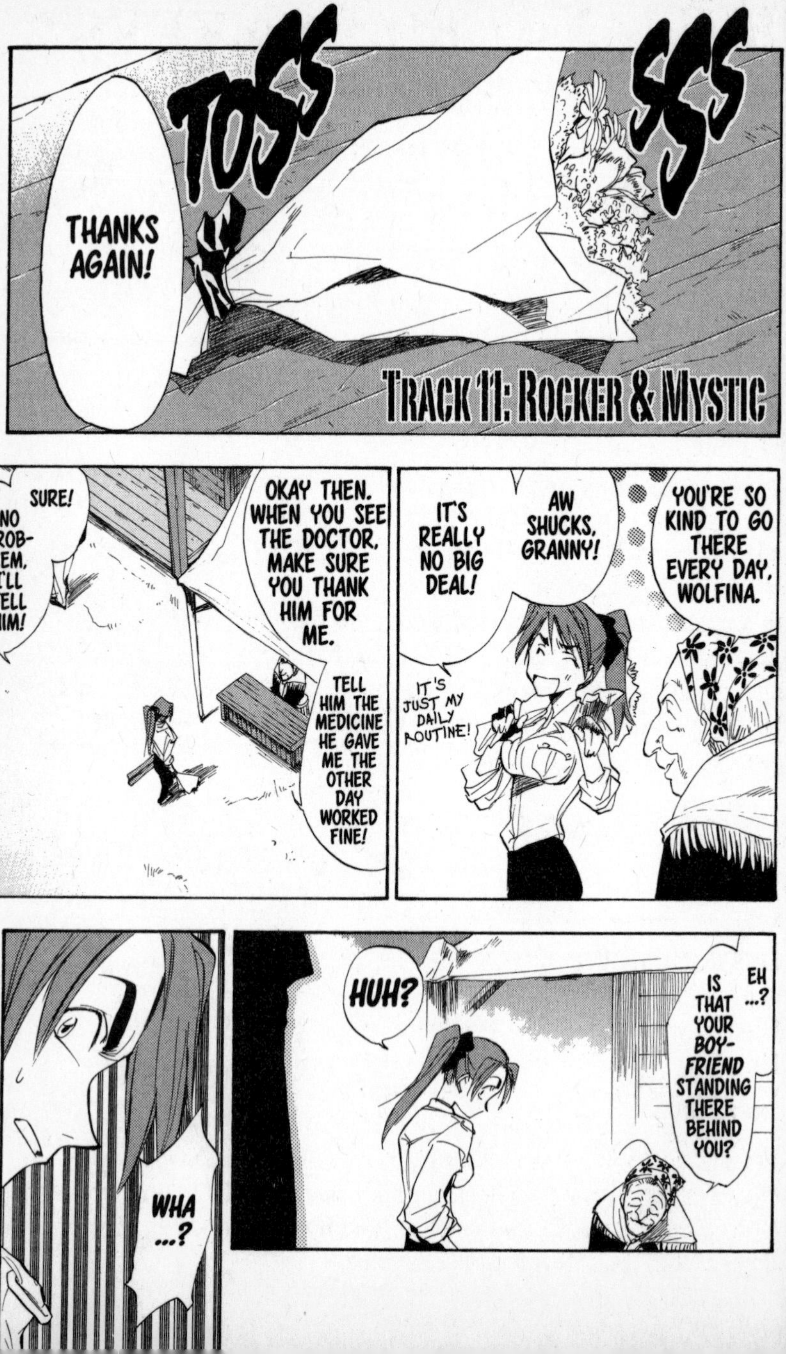
SSS
TOSS
THANKS AGAIN!
TRACK 11: ROCKER & MYSTIC
YOU'RE SO KIND TO GO THERE EVERY DAY, WOLFINA.
AW SHUCKS, GRANNY!
IT'S REALLY NO BIG DEAL!
IT'S JUST MY DAILY ROUTINE!
OKAY THEN. WHEN YOU SEE THE DOCTOR, MAKE SURE YOU THANK HIM FOR ME.
TELL HIM THE MEDICINE HE GAVE ME THE OTHER DAY WORKED FINE!
SURE! NO PROB-LEM, I'LL TELL HIM!
EH ...?
IS THAT YOUR BOY-FRIEND STANDING THERE BEHIND YOU?
HUH?
WHA ...?

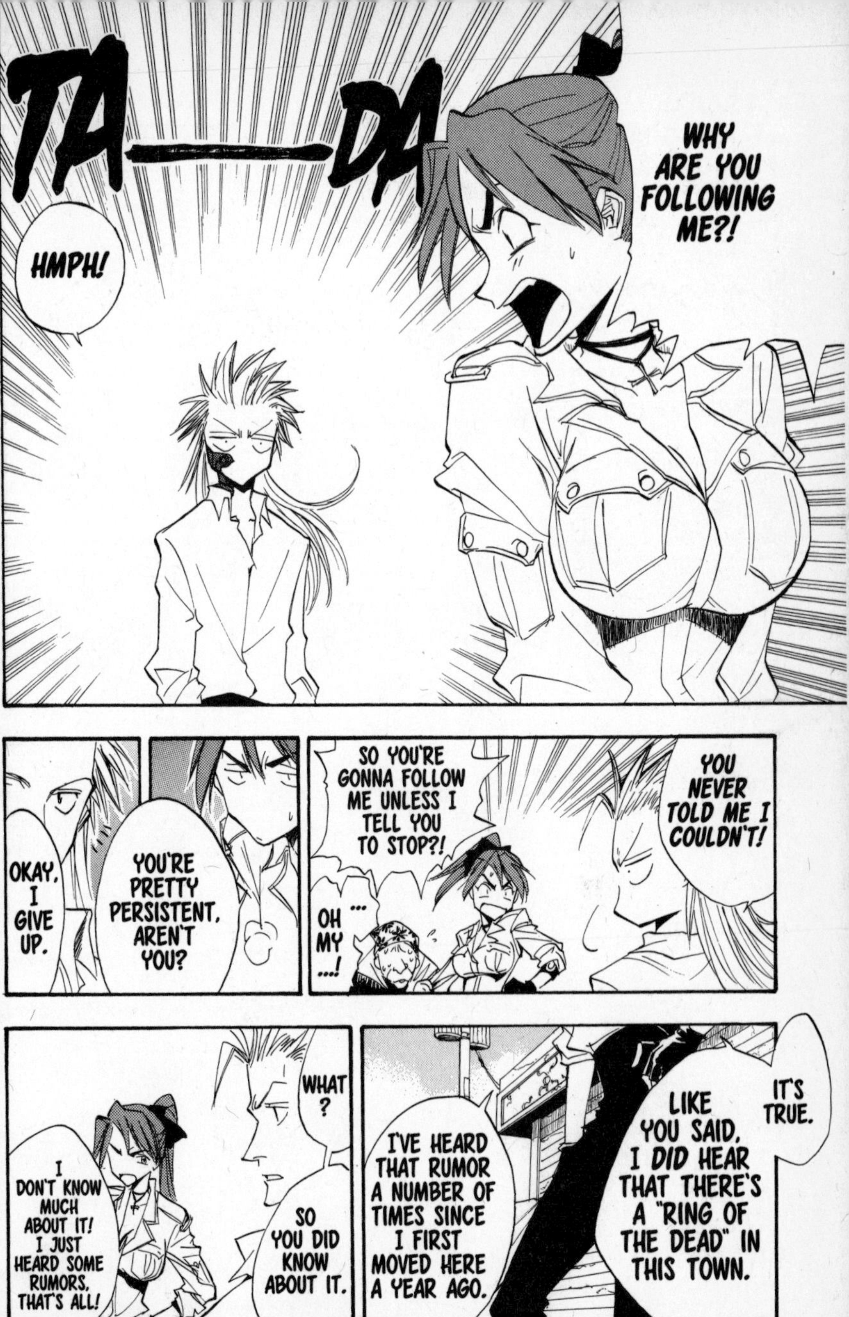
TA——DA
WHY ARE YOU FOLLOWING ME?!
HMPH!
YOU NEVER TOLD ME I COULDN'T!
SO YOU'RE GONNA FOLLOW ME UNLESS I TELL YOU TO STOP?!
...
OH MY ...!
YOU'RE PRETTY PERSISTENT, AREN'T YOU?
OKAY, I GIVE UP.
IT'S TRUE.
LIKE YOU SAID, I *DID* HEAR THAT THERE'S A "RING OF THE DEAD" IN THIS TOWN.
I'VE HEARD THAT RUMOR A NUMBER OF TIMES SINCE I FIRST MOVED HERE A YEAR AGO.
WHAT?
SO YOU DID KNOW ABOUT IT.
I DON'T KNOW MUCH ABOUT IT! I JUST HEARD SOME RUMORS, THAT'S ALL!

READ THIS WAY

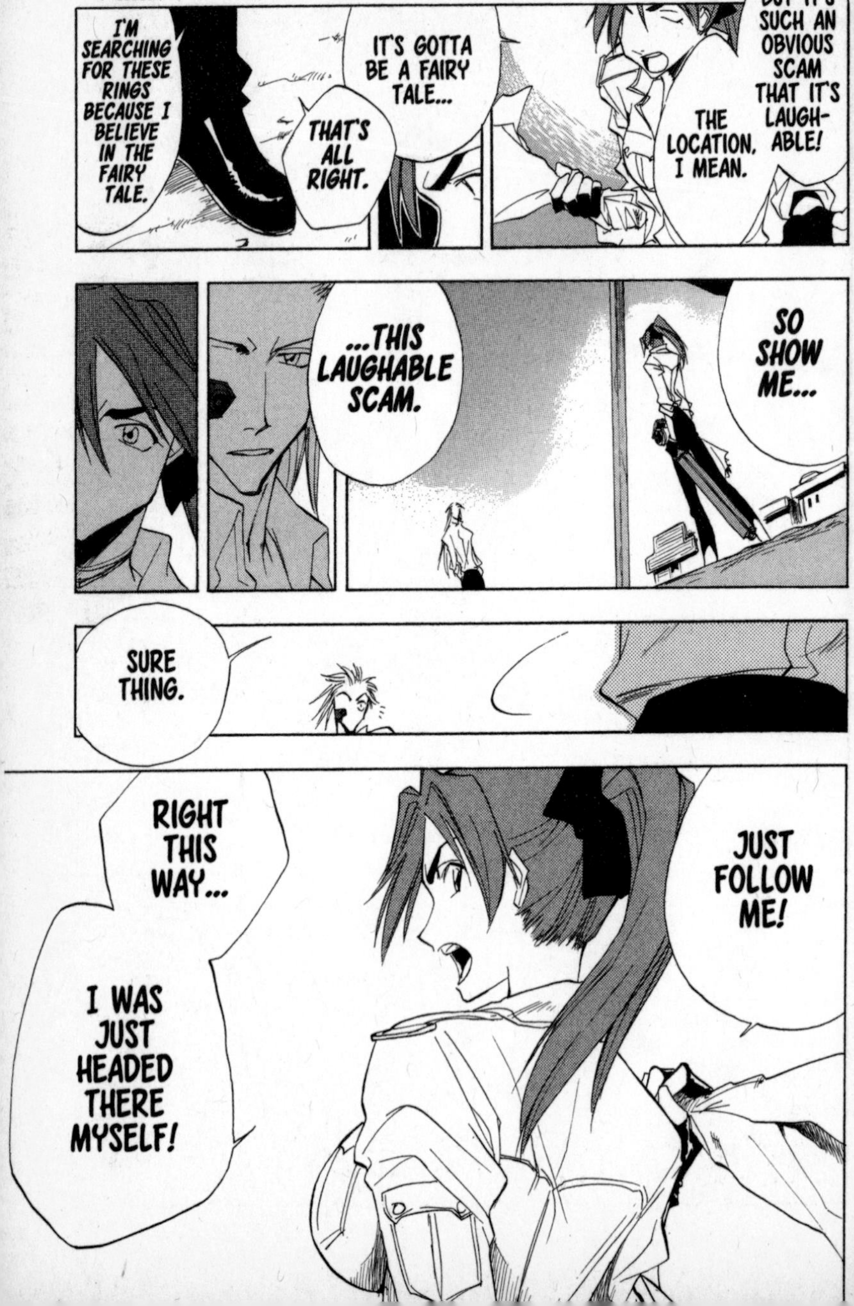
BUT IT'S SUCH AN OBVIOUS SCAM THAT IT'S LAUGHABLE!
THE LOCATION, I MEAN.
IT'S GOTTA BE A FAIRY TALE...
THAT'S ALL RIGHT.
I'M SEARCHING FOR THESE RINGS BECAUSE I BELIEVE IN THE FAIRY TALE.
SO SHOW ME...
...THIS LAUGHABLE SCAM.
SURE THING.
JUST FOLLOW ME!
RIGHT THIS WAY...
I WAS JUST HEADED THERE MYSELF!

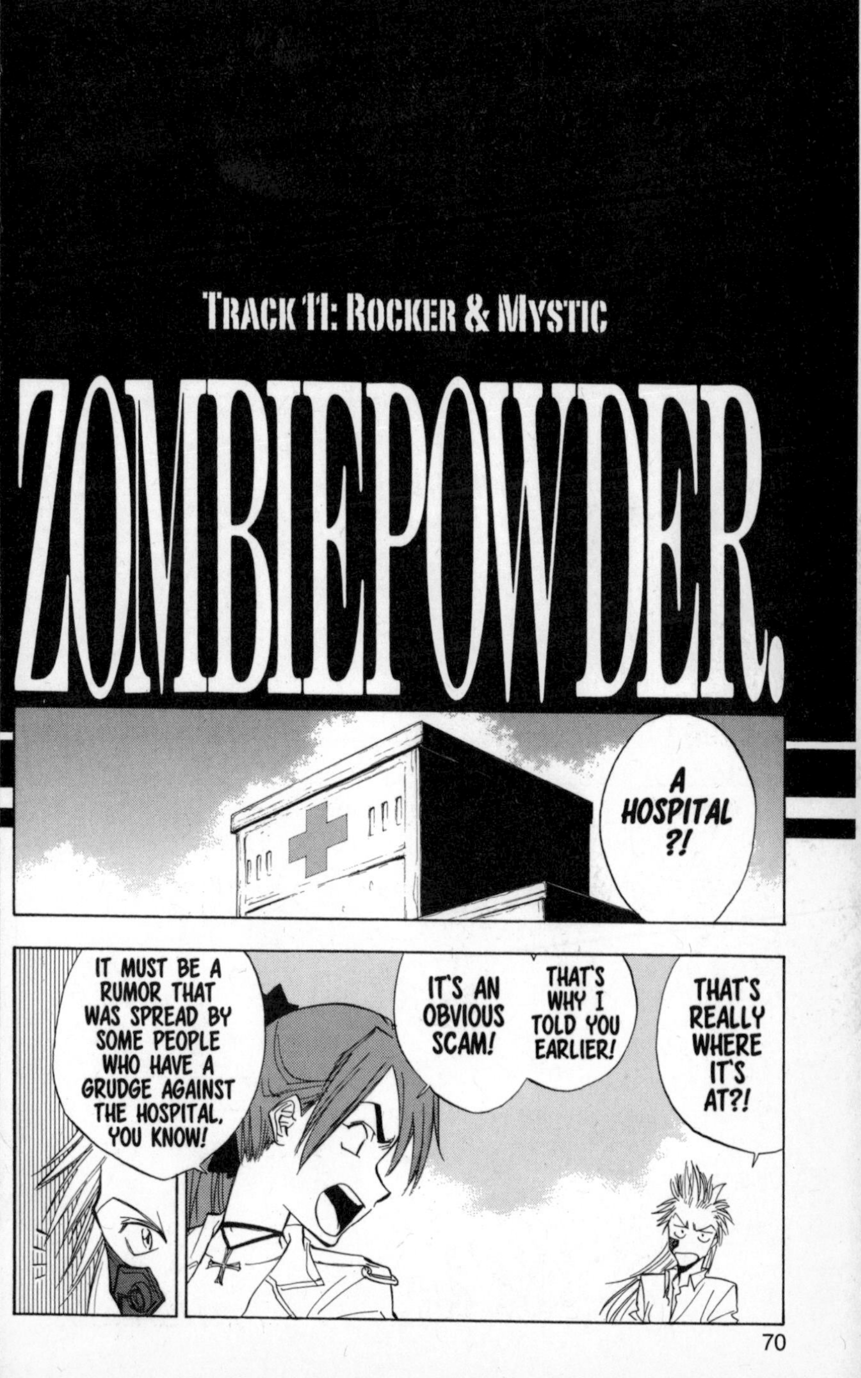
TRACK 11: ROCKER & MYSTIC
ZOMBIEPOWDER.
A HOSPITAL ?!
THAT'S REALLY WHERE IT'S AT?!
THAT'S WHY I TOLD YOU EARLIER!
IT'S AN OBVIOUS SCAM!
IT MUST BE A RUMOR THAT WAS SPREAD BY SOME PEOPLE WHO HAVE A GRUDGE AGAINST THE HOSPITAL, YOU KNOW!

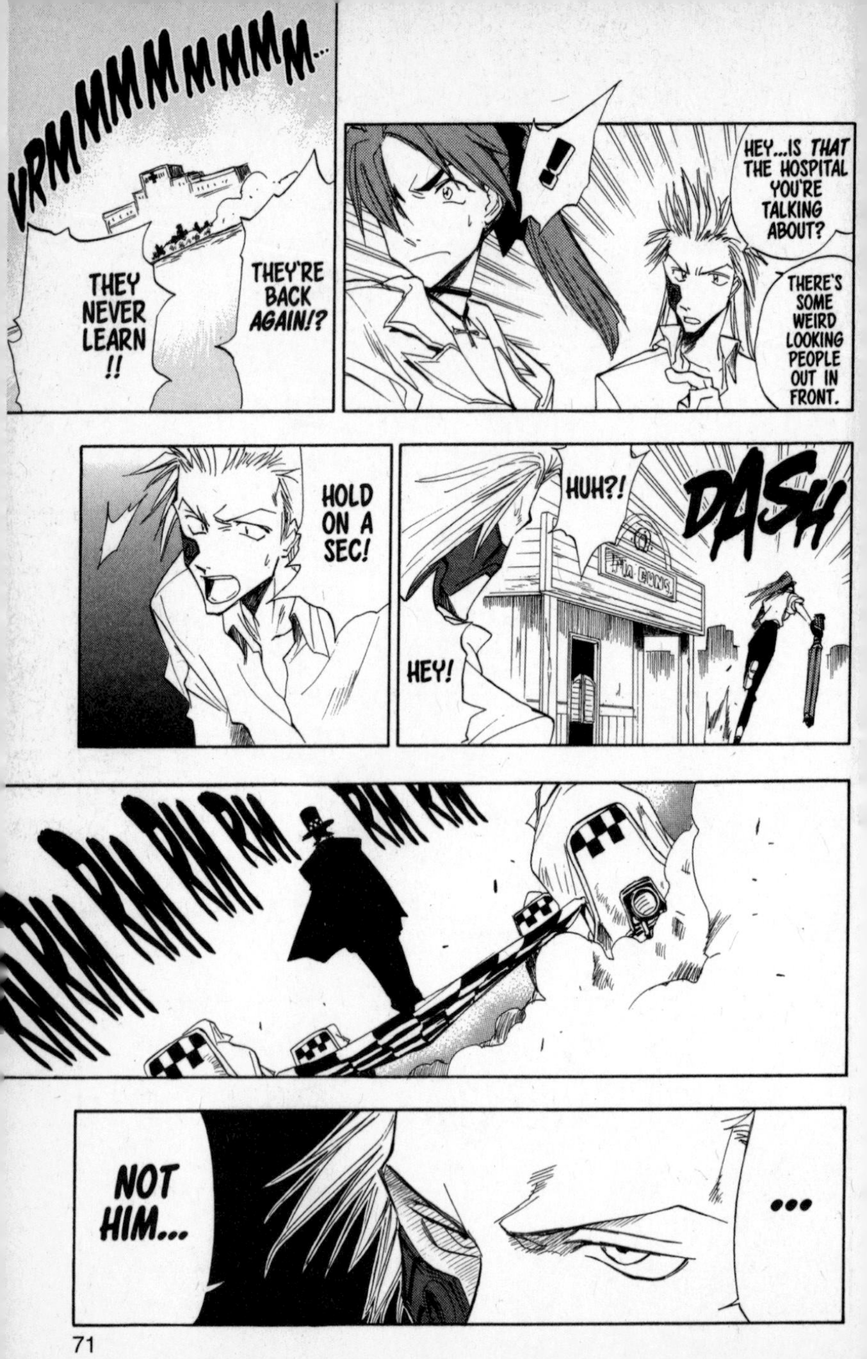
!
HEY...IS THAT THE HOSPITAL YOU'RE TALKING ABOUT?
THERE'S SOME WEIRD LOOKING PEOPLE OUT IN FRONT.
VRMMMMMMMMM...
THEY'RE BACK AGAIN!?
THEY NEVER LEARN!!
DASH
HUH?!
HEY!
HOLD ON A SEC!
RM RM RM RM RM RM RM RM RM RM
...
NOT HIM...

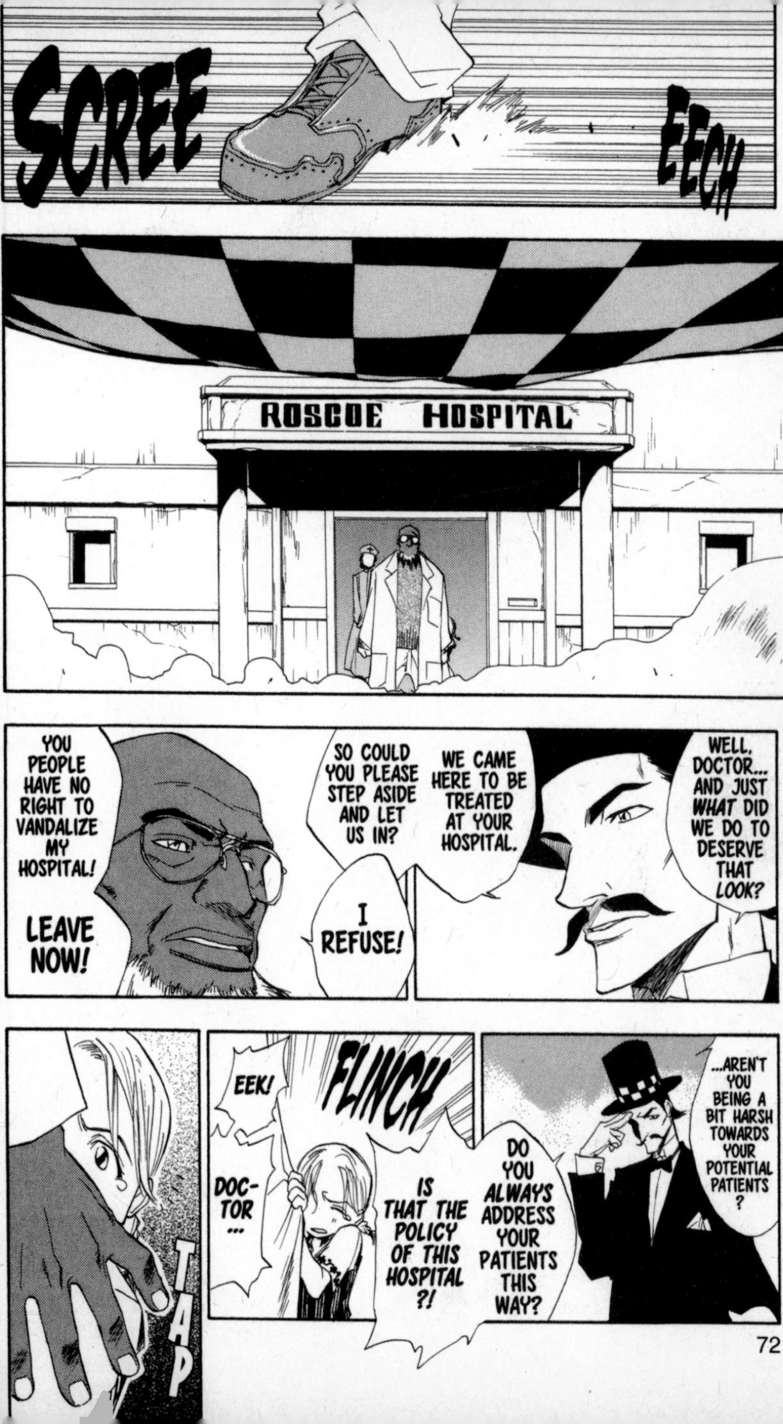
SCREE
EECH
ROSCOE HOSPITAL
WELL, DOCTOR... AND JUST WHAT DID WE DO TO DESERVE THAT LOOK?
WE CAME HERE TO BE TREATED AT YOUR HOSPITAL.
SO COULD YOU PLEASE STEP ASIDE AND LET US IN?
I REFUSE!
YOU PEOPLE HAVE NO RIGHT TO VANDALIZE MY HOSPITAL!
LEAVE NOW!
...AREN'T YOU BEING A BIT HARSH TOWARDS YOUR POTENTIAL PATIENTS?
DO YOU ALWAYS ADDRESS YOUR PATIENTS THIS WAY?
FLINCH
EEK!
IS THAT THE POLICY OF THIS HOSPITAL?!
DOC-TOR...
TAP

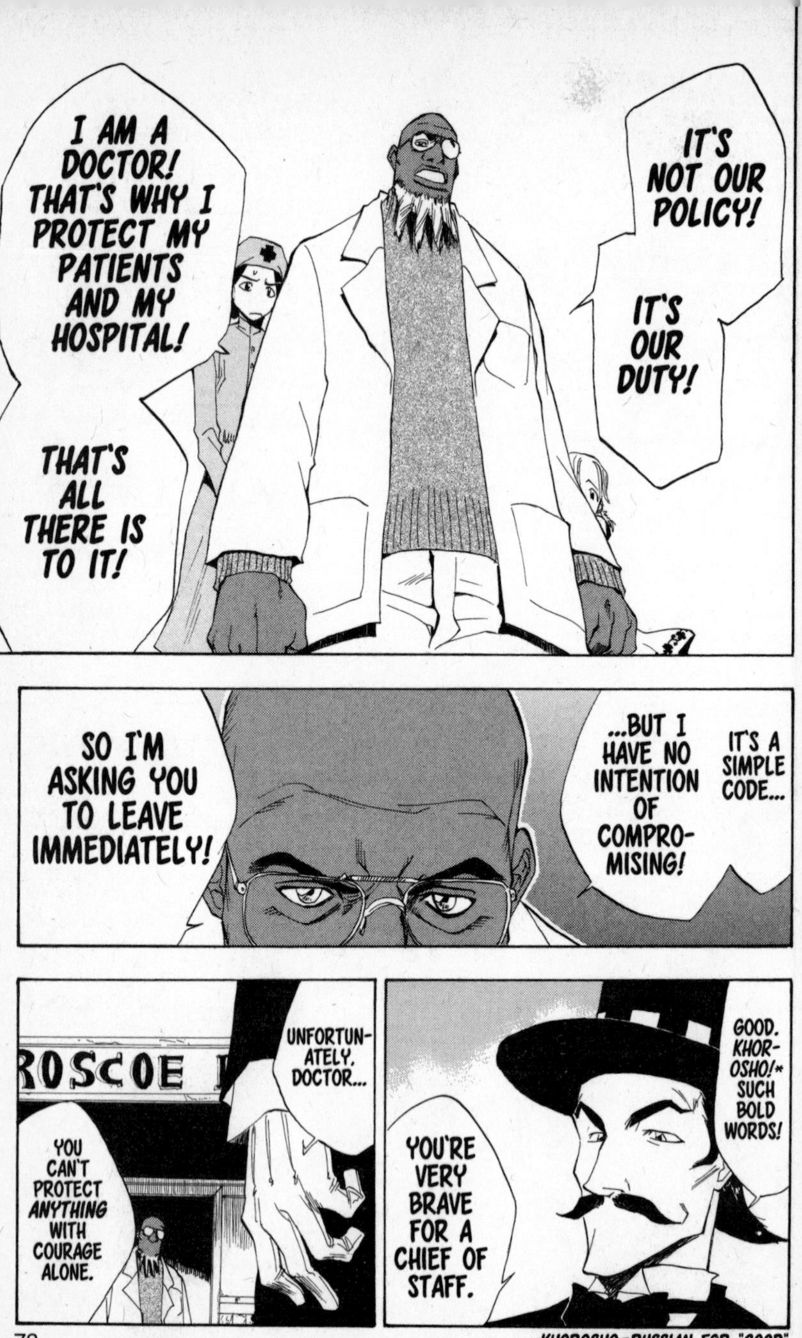
IT'S NOT OUR POLICY!
IT'S OUR DUTY!
I AM A DOCTOR! THAT'S WHY I PROTECT MY PATIENTS AND MY HOSPITAL!
THAT'S ALL THERE IS TO IT!
IT'S A SIMPLE CODE...
...BUT I HAVE NO INTENTION OF COMPRO-MISING!
SO I'M ASKING YOU TO LEAVE IMMEDIATELY!
GOOD. KHOR-OSHO!* SUCH BOLD WORDS!
YOU'RE VERY BRAVE FOR A CHIEF OF STAFF.
UNFORTUN-ATELY, DOCTOR...
ROSCOE
YOU CAN'T PROTECT ANYTHING WITH COURAGE ALONE.

*KHOROSHO=RUSSIAN FOR "GOOD"

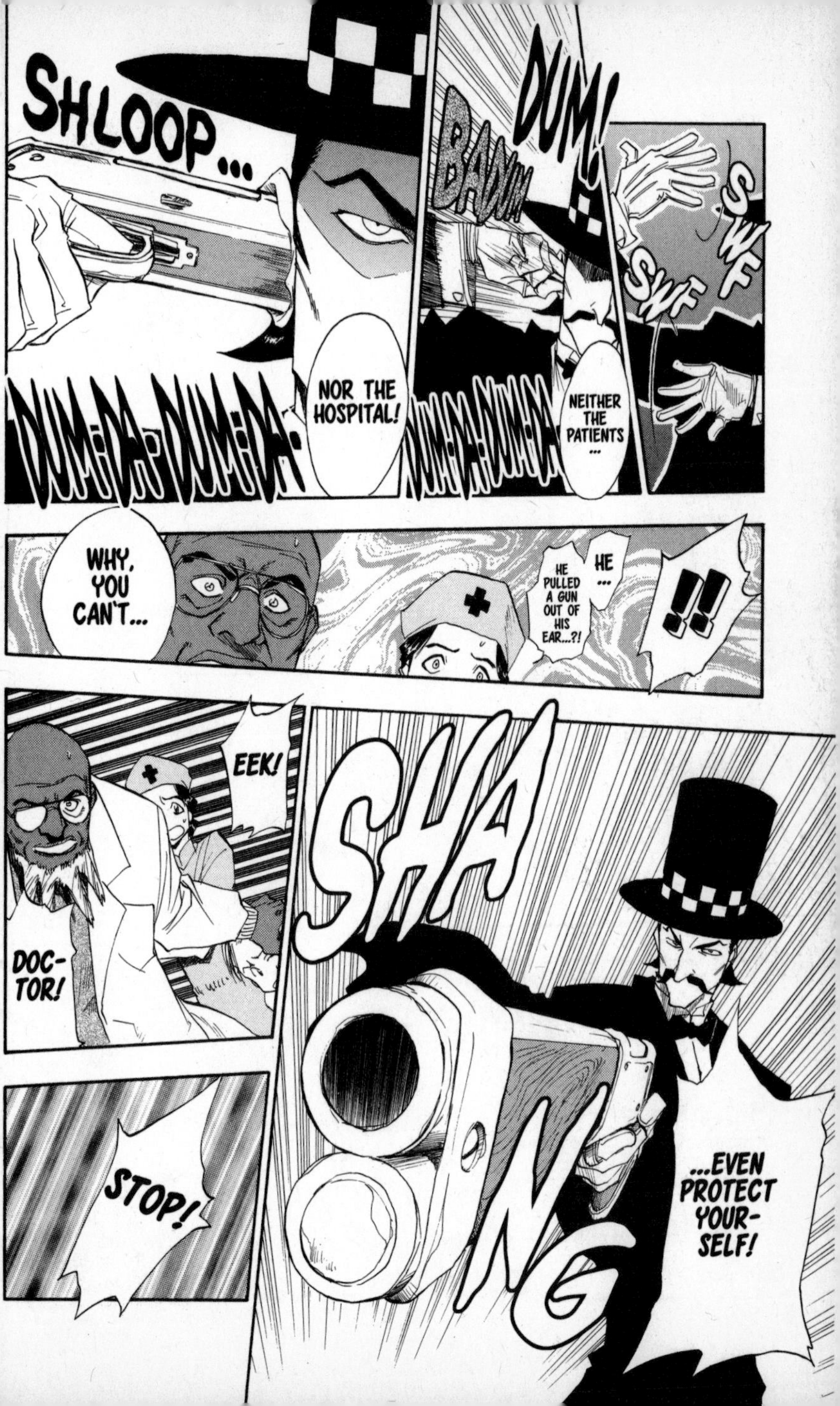
SWF
SWF
DUM!
BADUM!
NEITHER THE PATIENTS...
DUM-DA-DUM-DA
SHLOOP...
NOR THE HOSPITAL!
DUM-DA-DUM-DA-
!!
HE...
HE PULLED A GUN OUT OF HIS EAR...?!
WHY, YOU CAN'T...
SHANG
...EVEN PROTECT YOUR-SELF!
EEK!
DOC-TOR!
STOP!

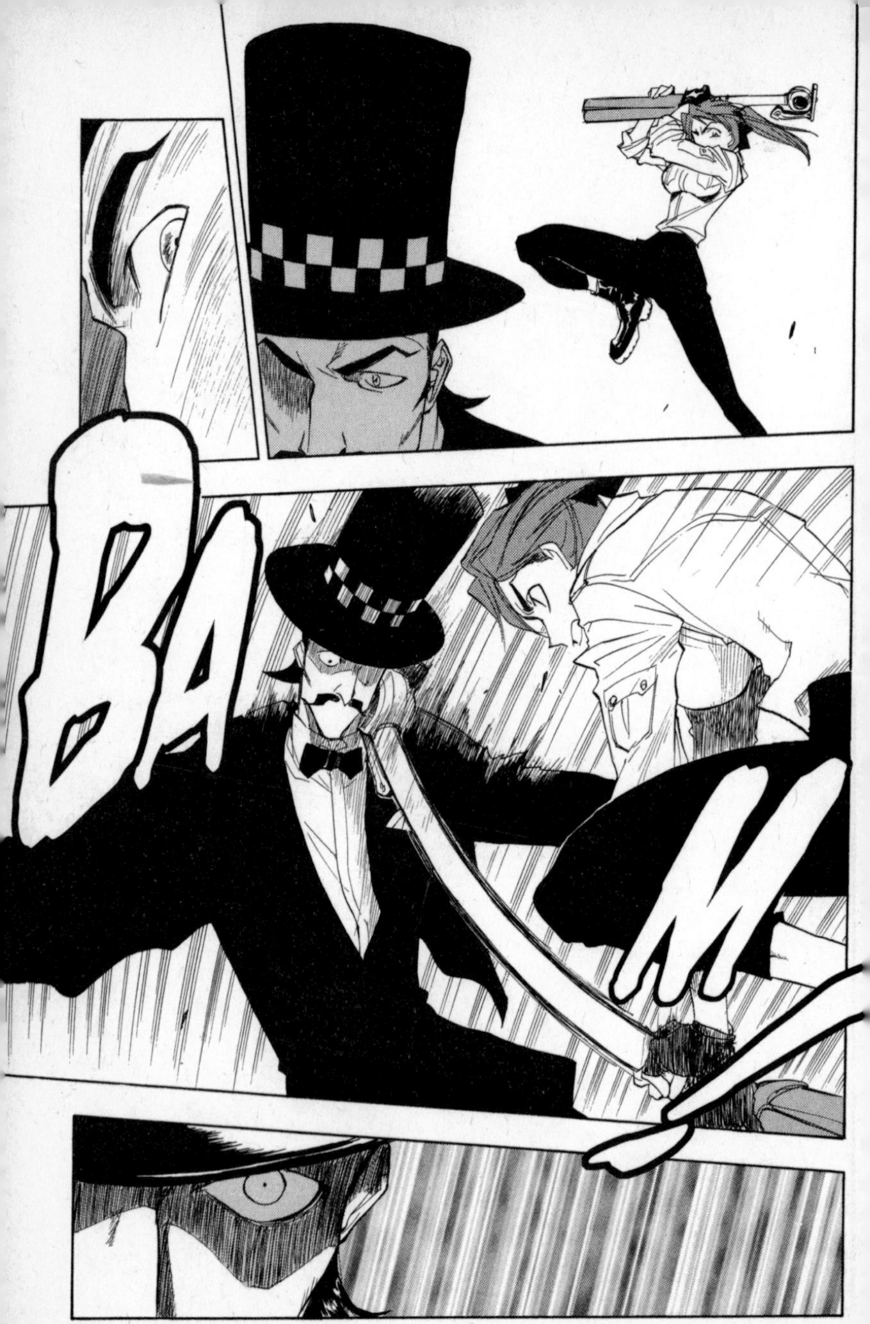
BAM

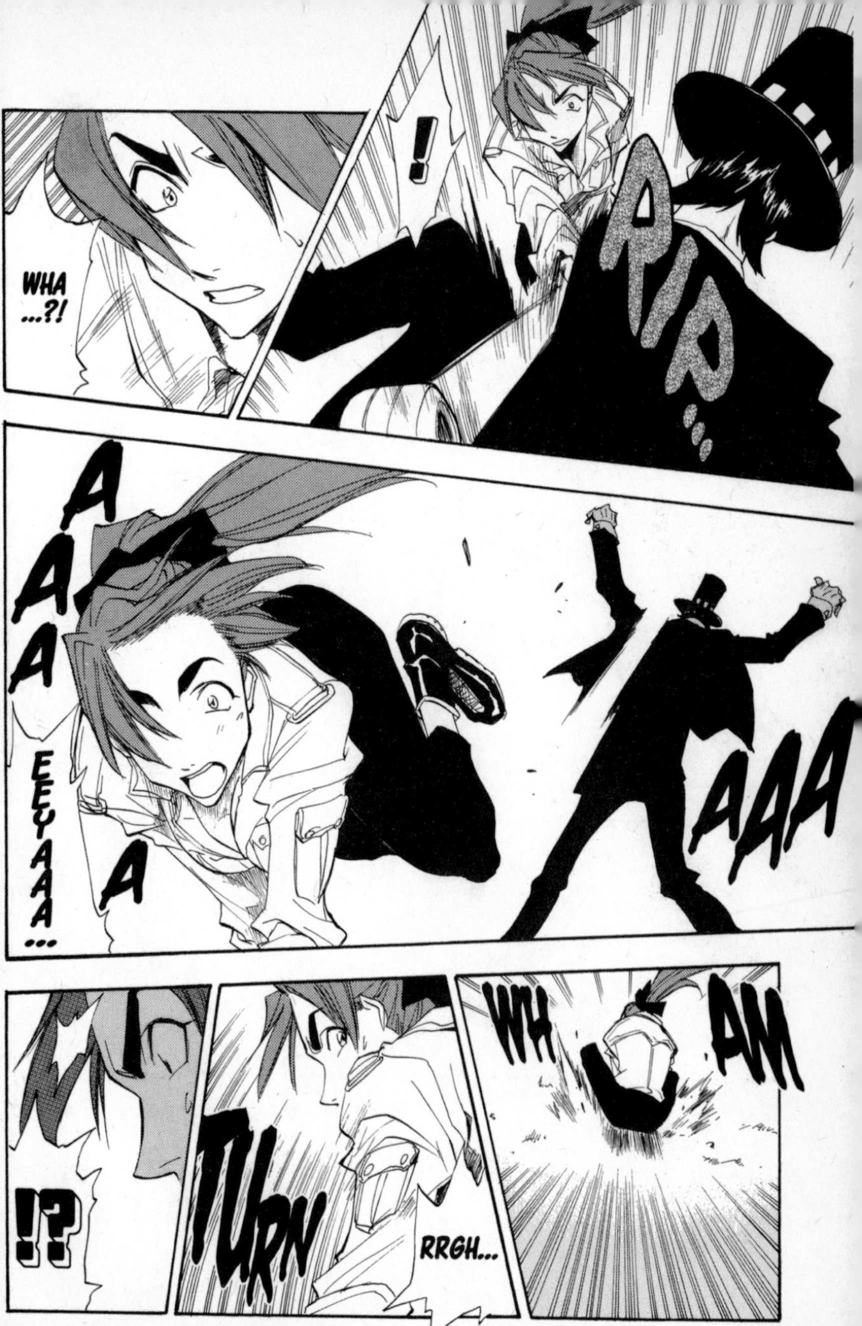
RIP...
!
WHA ...?!
AAA
AAAA
EEYAAA...
WHAM
TURN
RRGH...
!?

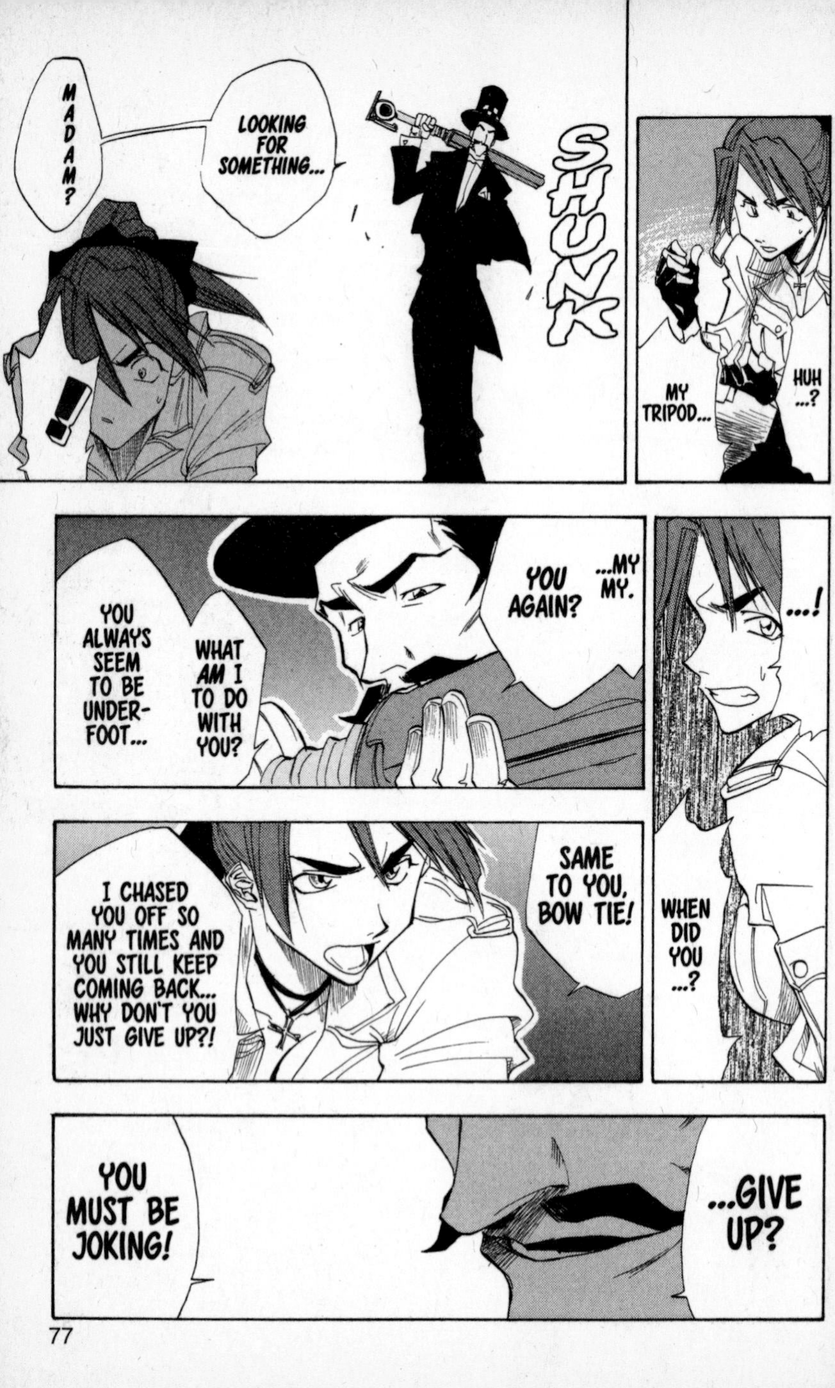
HUH ...?
MY TRIPOD...
SHUNK
LOOKING FOR SOMETHING...
MADAM?
!
...!
WHEN DID YOU ...?
...MY MY.
YOU AGAIN?
WHAT AM I TO DO WITH YOU?
YOU ALWAYS SEEM TO BE UNDER-FOOT...
SAME TO YOU, BOW TIE!
I CHASED YOU OFF SO MANY TIMES AND YOU STILL KEEP COMING BACK... WHY DON'T YOU JUST GIVE UP?!
...GIVE UP?
YOU MUST BE JOKING!

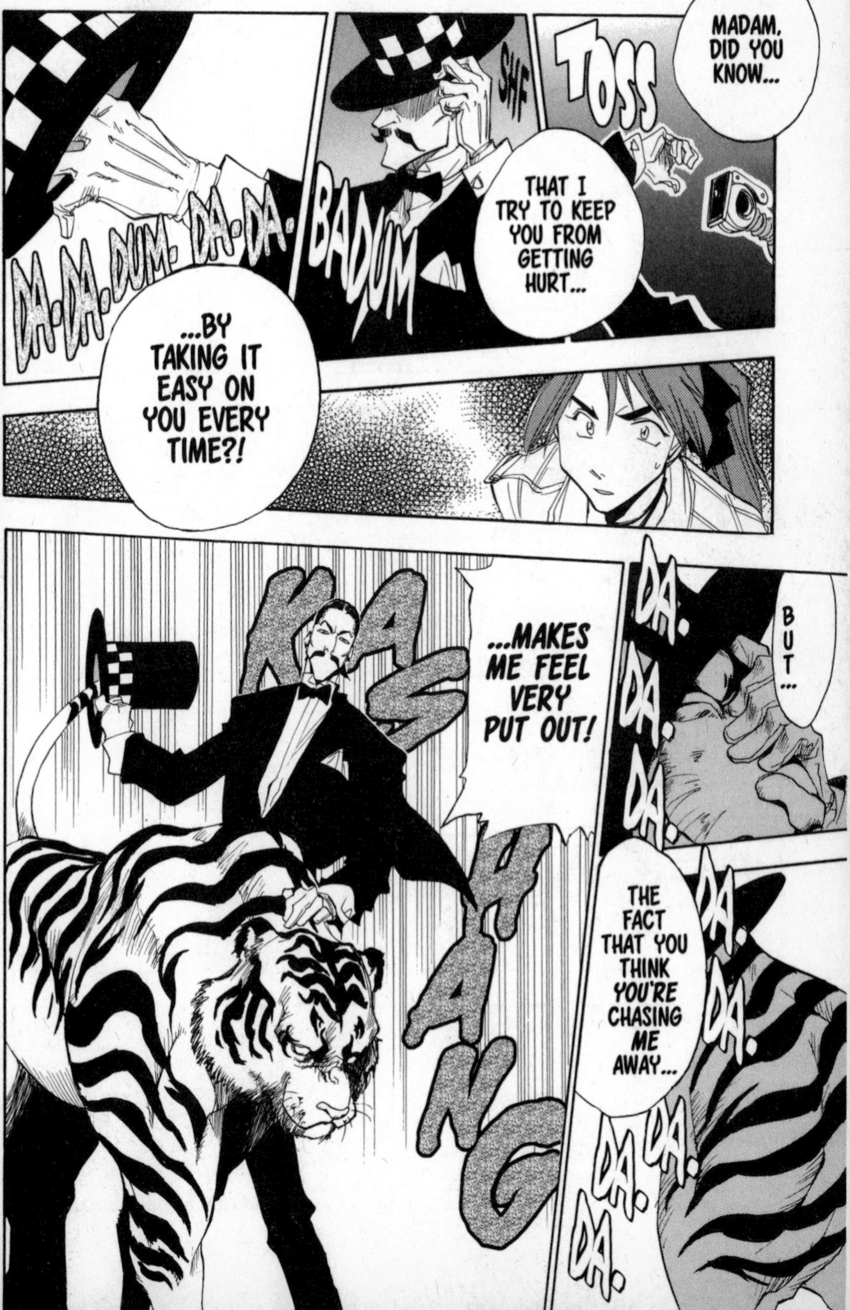
MADAM, DID YOU KNOW...
TOSS
SHF
THAT I TRY TO KEEP YOU FROM GETTING HURT...
BADUM
DA-DA-DUM. DA-DA-
...BY TAKING IT EASY ON YOU EVERY TIME?!
BUT...
DA. DA. DA. DA.
THE FACT THAT YOU THINK YOU'RE CHASING ME AWAY...
DA. DA. DA. DA. DA.
...MAKES ME FEEL VERY PUT OUT!
KASHANG

READ THIS WAY

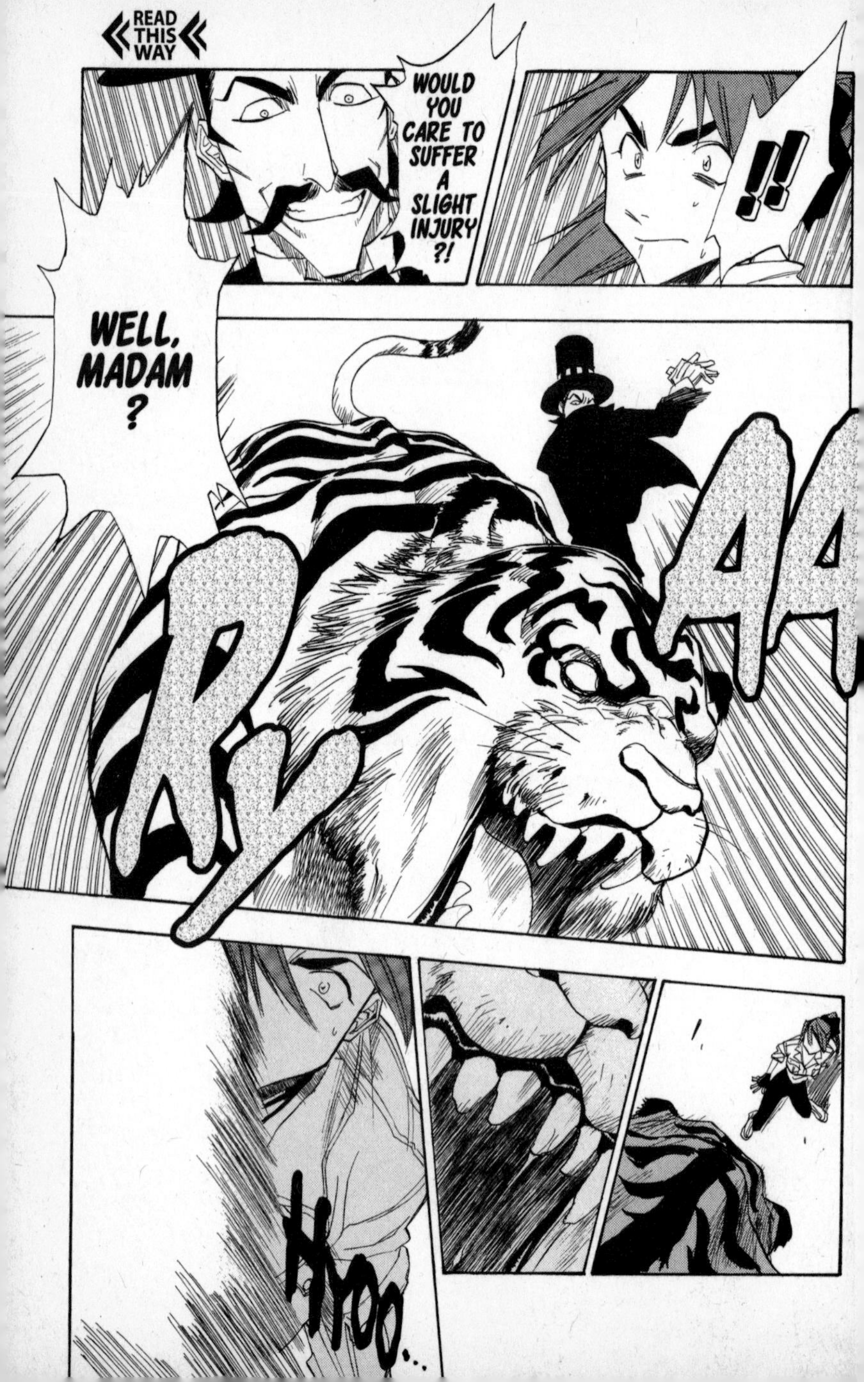
!!
WOULD YOU CARE TO SUFFER A SLIGHT INJURY?!
WELL, MADAM?
AA
R
!
HYOO...

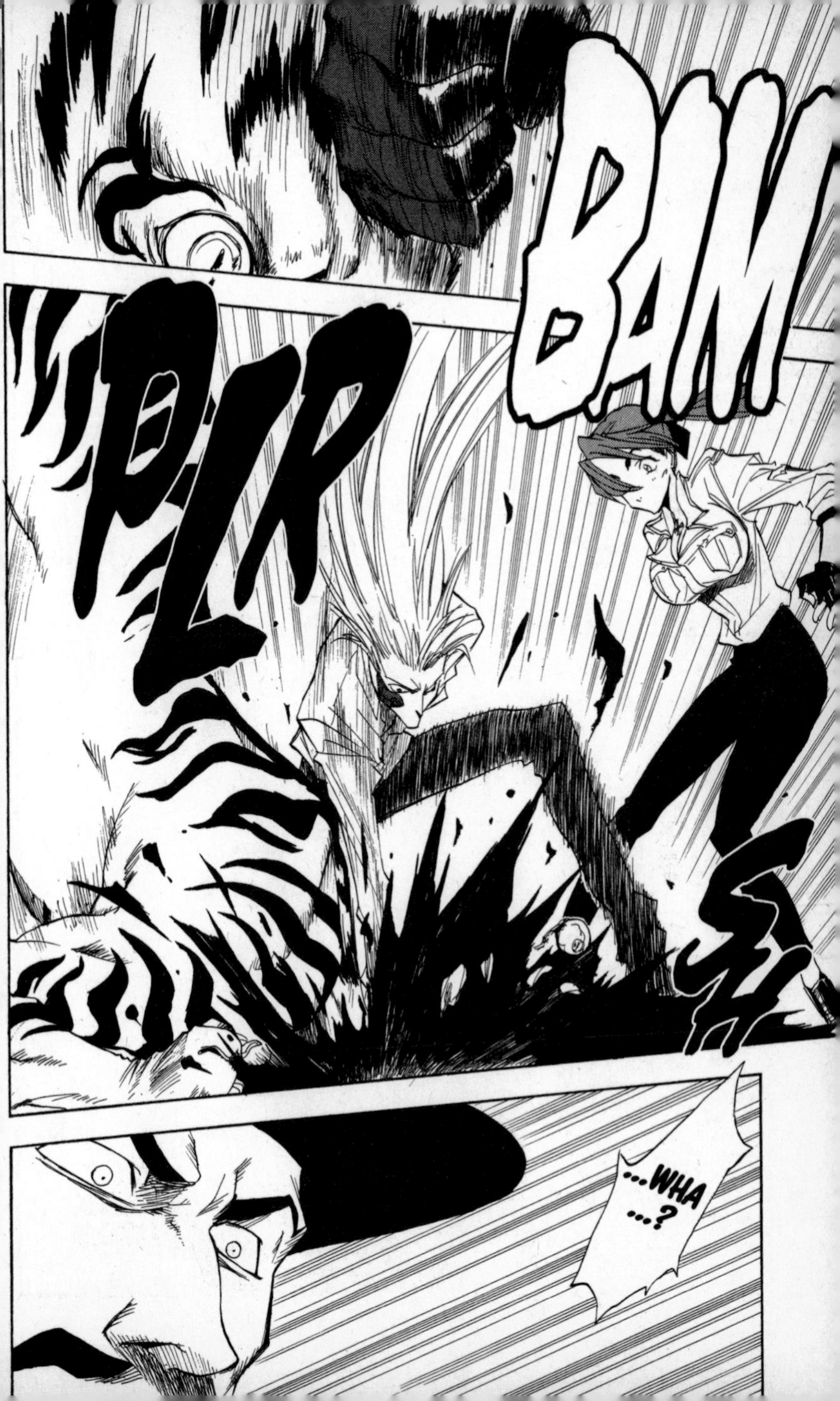
BAM
PLIP
SH
...WHA ...?

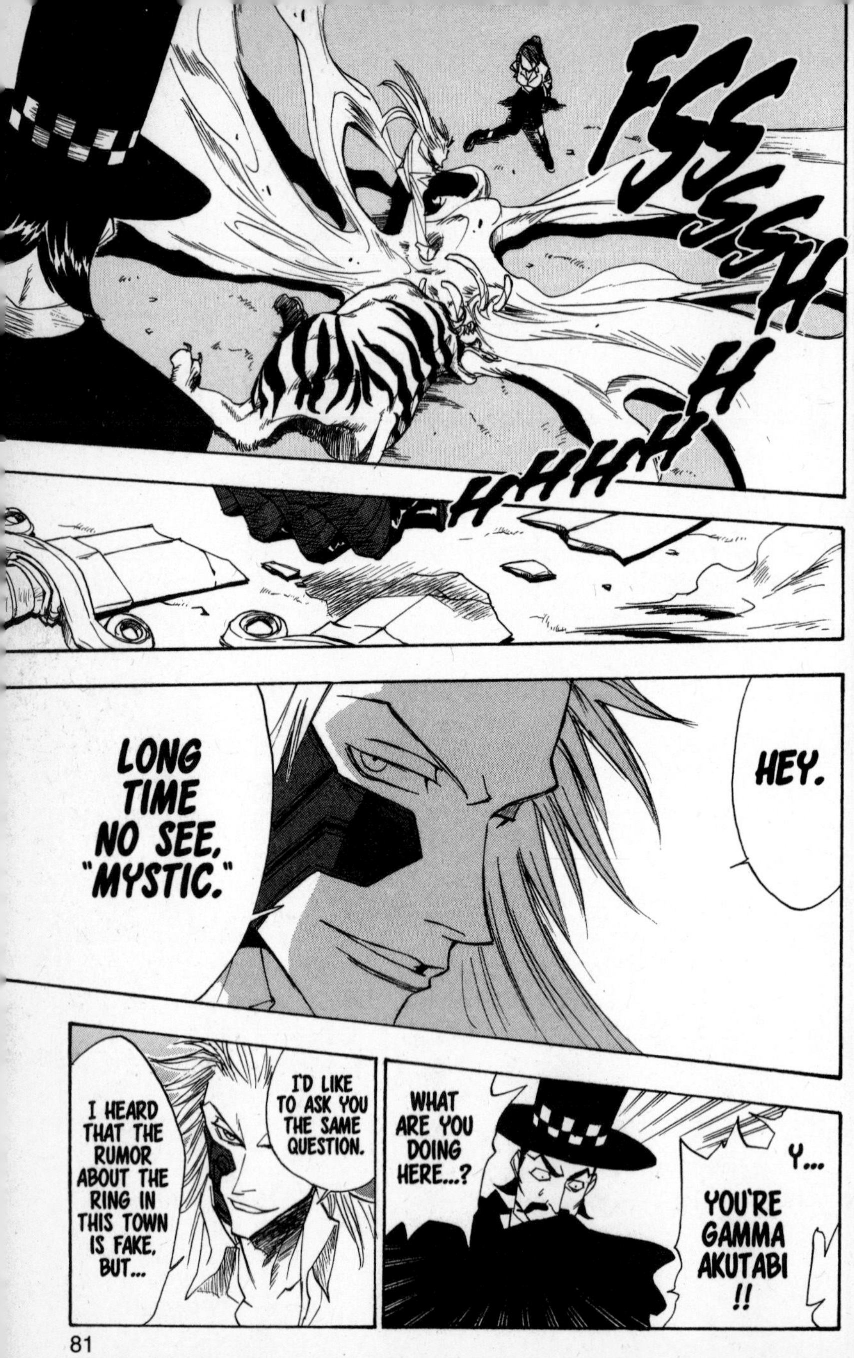
FSSSHHHHHHHH
HEY.
LONG TIME NO SEE, "MYSTIC."
Y...
YOU'RE GAMMA AKUTABI !!
WHAT ARE YOU DOING HERE...?
I'D LIKE TO ASK YOU THE SAME QUESTION.
I HEARD THAT THE RUMOR ABOUT THE RING IN THIS TOWN IS FAKE, BUT...

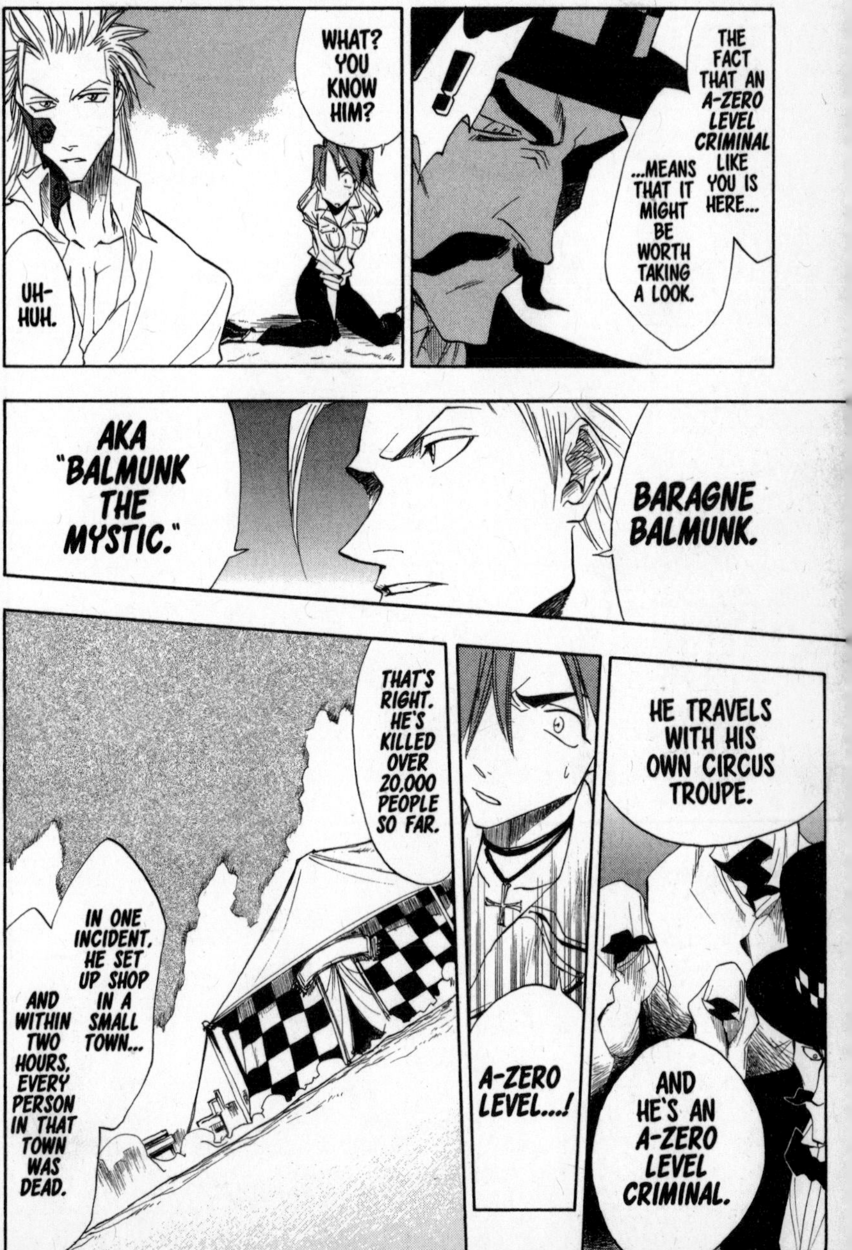
THE FACT THAT AN A-ZERO LEVEL CRIMINAL LIKE YOU IS HERE...
...MEANS THAT IT MIGHT BE WORTH TAKING A LOOK.
WHAT? YOU KNOW HIM?
UH-HUH.
BARAGNE BALMUNK.
AKA "BALMUNK THE MYSTIC."
HE TRAVELS WITH HIS OWN CIRCUS TROUPE.
AND HE'S AN A-ZERO LEVEL CRIMINAL.
A-ZERO LEVEL...!
THAT'S RIGHT. HE'S KILLED OVER 20,000 PEOPLE SO FAR.
IN ONE INCIDENT, HE SET UP SHOP IN A SMALL TOWN...
AND WITHIN TWO HOURS, EVERY PERSON IN THAT TOWN WAS DEAD.

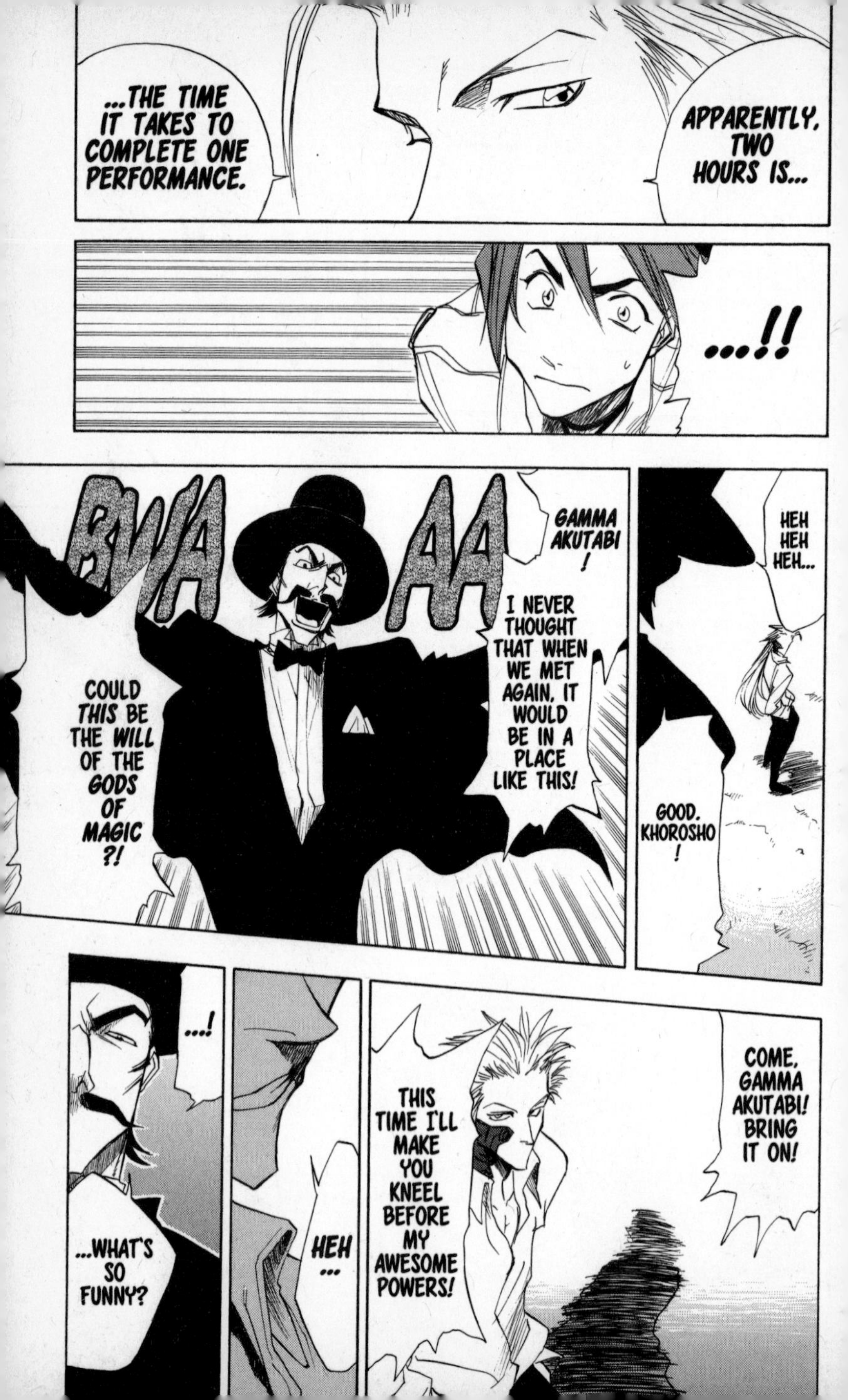
APPARENTLY, TWO HOURS IS...
...THE TIME IT TAKES TO COMPLETE ONE PERFORMANCE.
...!!
HEH HEH HEH...
GOOD. KHOROSHO!
BWAAA
GAMMA AKUTABI!
I NEVER THOUGHT THAT WHEN WE MET AGAIN, IT WOULD BE IN A PLACE LIKE THIS!
COULD THIS BE THE WILL OF THE GODS OF MAGIC?!
COME, GAMMA AKUTABI! BRING IT ON!
THIS TIME I'LL MAKE YOU KNEEL BEFORE MY AWESOME POWERS!
HEH...
...!
...WHAT'S SO FUNNY?

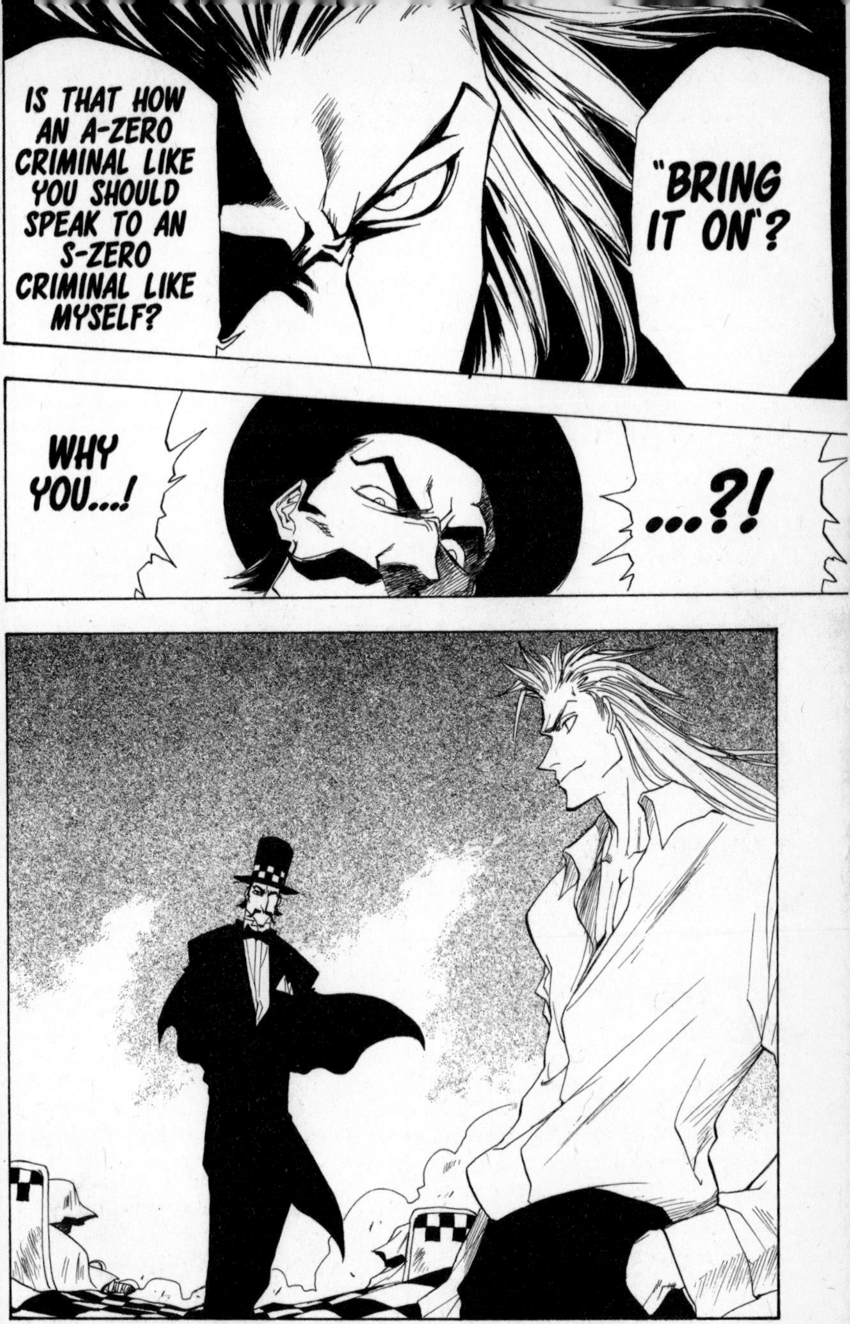
"BRING IT ON"?
IS THAT HOW AN A-ZERO CRIMINAL LIKE YOU SHOULD SPEAK TO AN S-ZERO CRIMINAL LIKE MYSELF?
...?!
WHY YOU...!

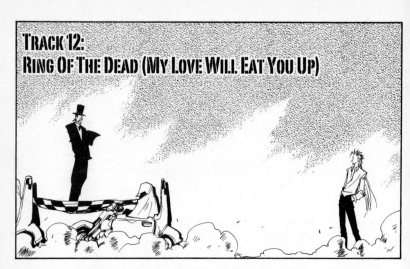

TRACK 12:
RING OF THE DEAD (MY LOVE WILL EAT YOU UP)
WHAT'S THE MATTER?
WEREN'T YOU GOING TO MAKE ME KNEEL?
WELL, BALMUNK?
NO, NO...
THIS WON'T DO AT ALL...
THE EXCITEMENT OF SEEING YOU AGAIN ALMOST MADE ME FORGET MY TRUE OBJECTIVE...

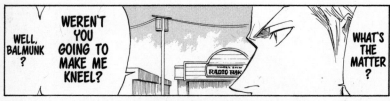

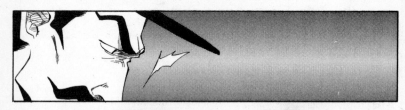

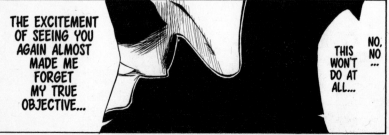

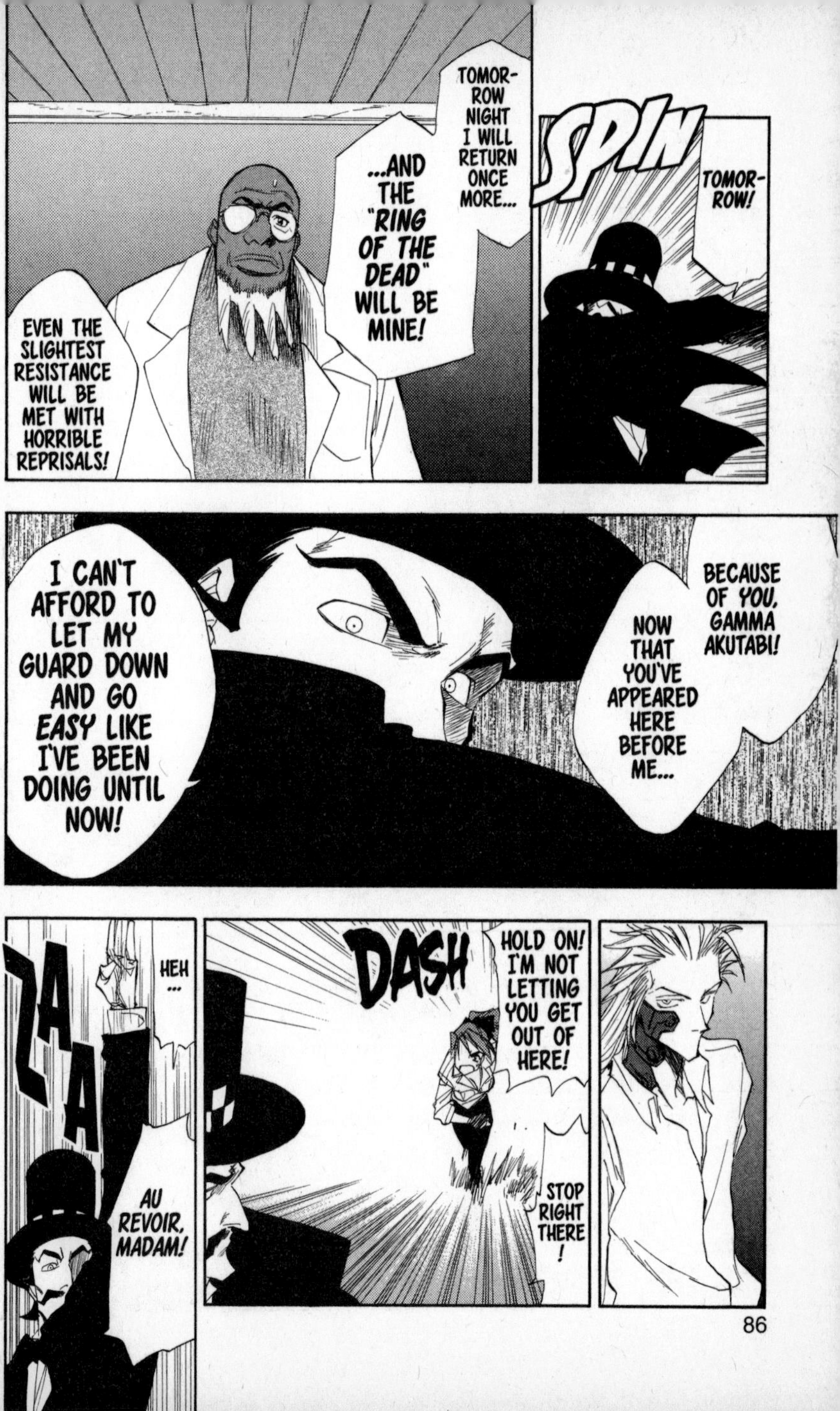
SPIN
TOMORROW!
TOMORROW NIGHT I WILL RETURN ONCE MORE...
...AND THE "RING OF THE DEAD" WILL BE MINE!
EVEN THE SLIGHTEST RESISTANCE WILL BE MET WITH HORRIBLE REPRISALS!
BECAUSE OF YOU, GAMMA AKUTABI!
NOW THAT YOU'VE APPEARED HERE BEFORE ME...
I CAN'T AFFORD TO LET MY GUARD DOWN AND GO *EASY* LIKE I'VE BEEN DOING UNTIL NOW!
HOLD ON! I'M NOT LETTING YOU GET OUT OF HERE!
DASH
STOP RIGHT THERE!
HEH...
ZAA
AU REVOIR, MADAM!

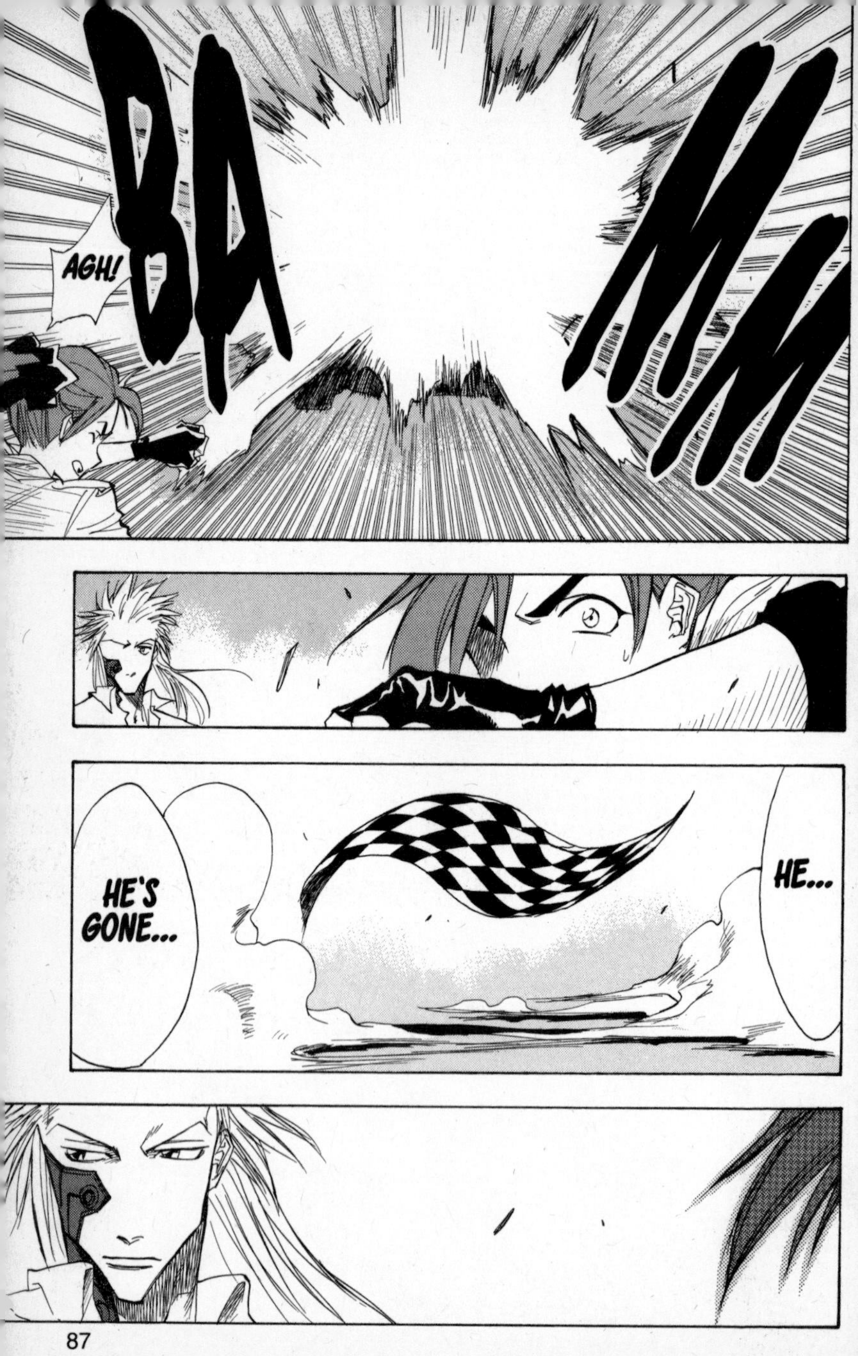
BAMM
AGH!
HE...
HE'S GONE...

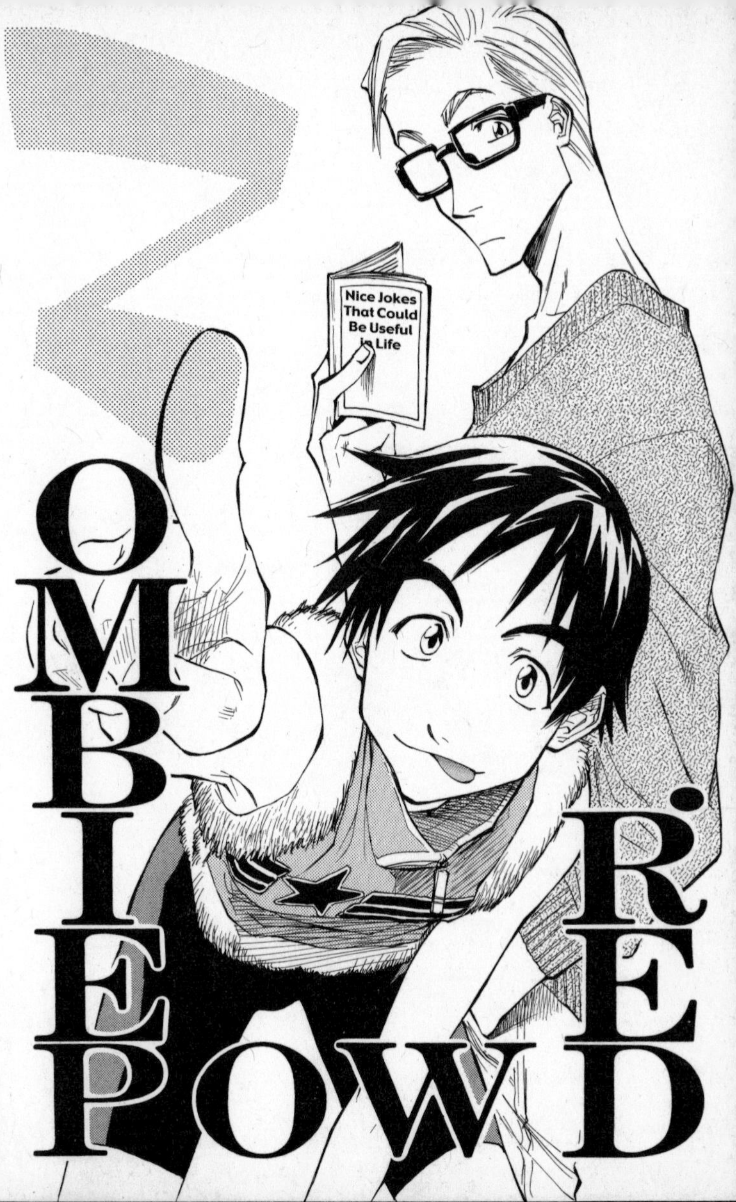
OMBIE
POWDER
Nice Jokes That Could Be Useful in Life

Track 12: Ring Of The Dead (My Love Will Eat You Up

READ THIS WAY

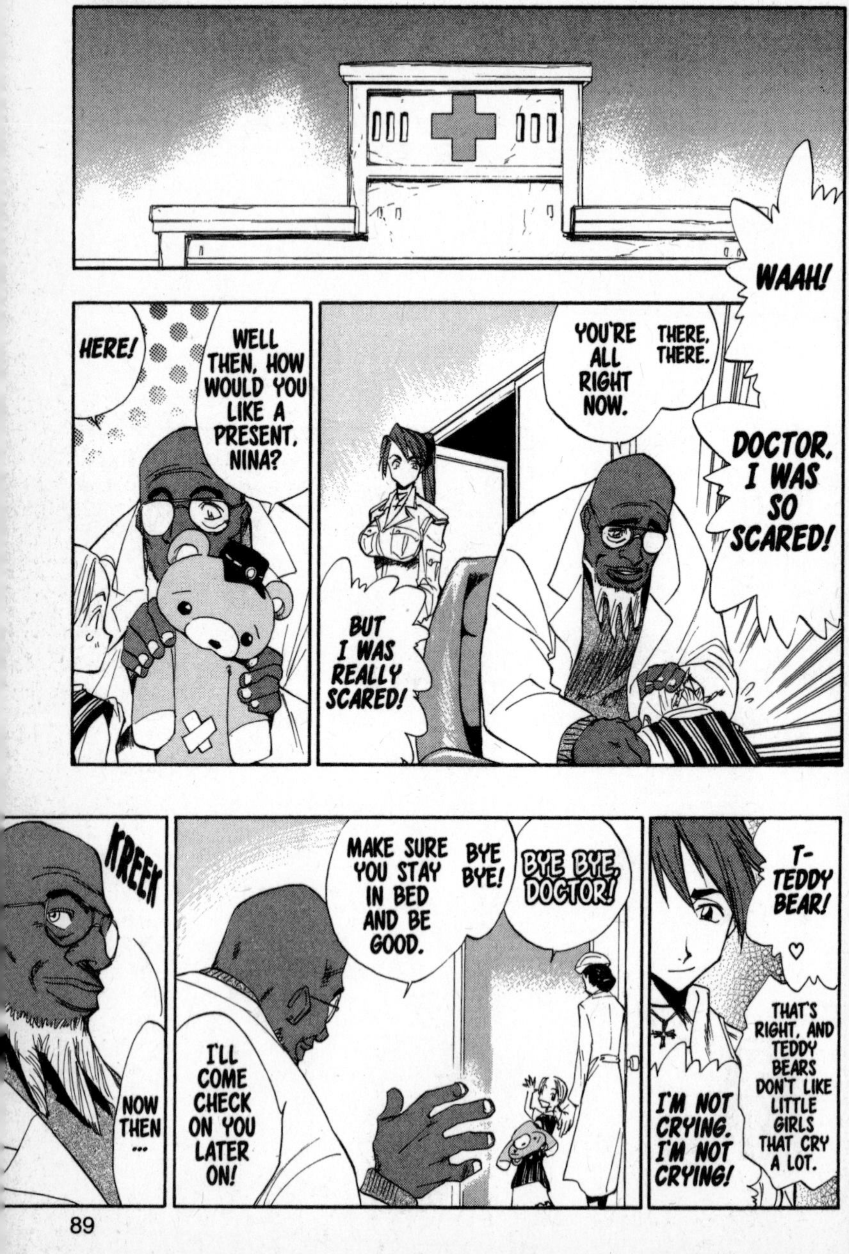

WAAH!
DOCTOR, I WAS SO SCARED!
THERE, THERE.
YOU'RE ALL RIGHT NOW.
BUT I WAS REALLY SCARED!
WELL THEN, HOW WOULD YOU LIKE A PRESENT, NINA?
HERE!
T-TEDDY BEAR! ♡
THAT'S RIGHT, AND TEDDY BEARS DON'T LIKE LITTLE GIRLS THAT CRY A LOT.
I'M NOT CRYING. I'M NOT CRYING!
BYE BYE, DOCTOR!
BYE BYE!
MAKE SURE YOU STAY IN BED AND BE GOOD.
I'LL COME CHECK ON YOU LATER ON!
KREEK
NOW THEN ...

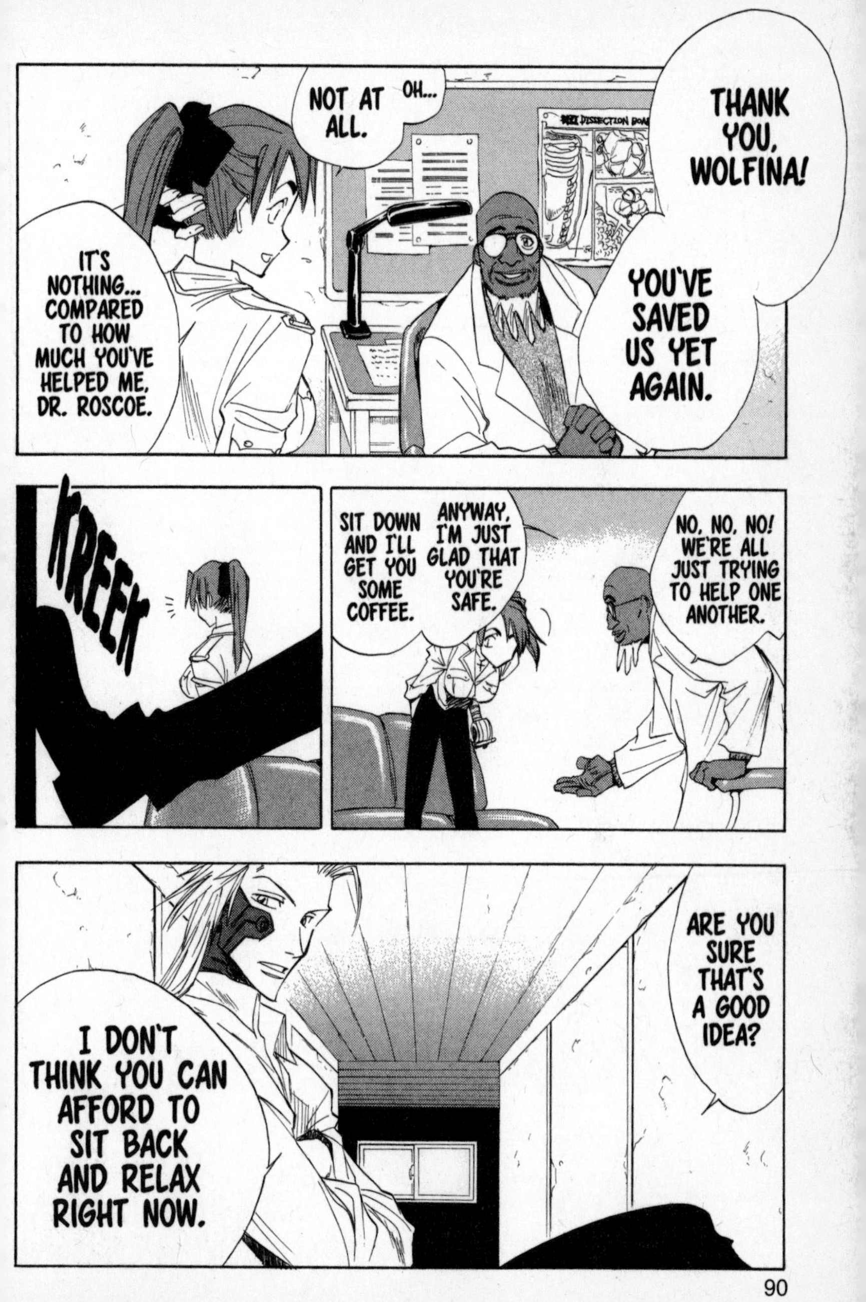
THANK YOU, WOLFINA!
YOU'VE SAVED US YET AGAIN.
OH...
NOT AT ALL.
IT'S NOTHING... COMPARED TO HOW MUCH YOU'VE HELPED ME, DR. ROSCOE.
NO, NO, NO! WE'RE ALL JUST TRYING TO HELP ONE ANOTHER.
ANYWAY, I'M JUST GLAD THAT YOU'RE SAFE.
SIT DOWN AND I'LL GET YOU SOME COFFEE.
KREEK
ARE YOU SURE THAT'S A GOOD IDEA?
I DON'T THINK YOU CAN AFFORD TO SIT BACK AND RELAX RIGHT NOW.

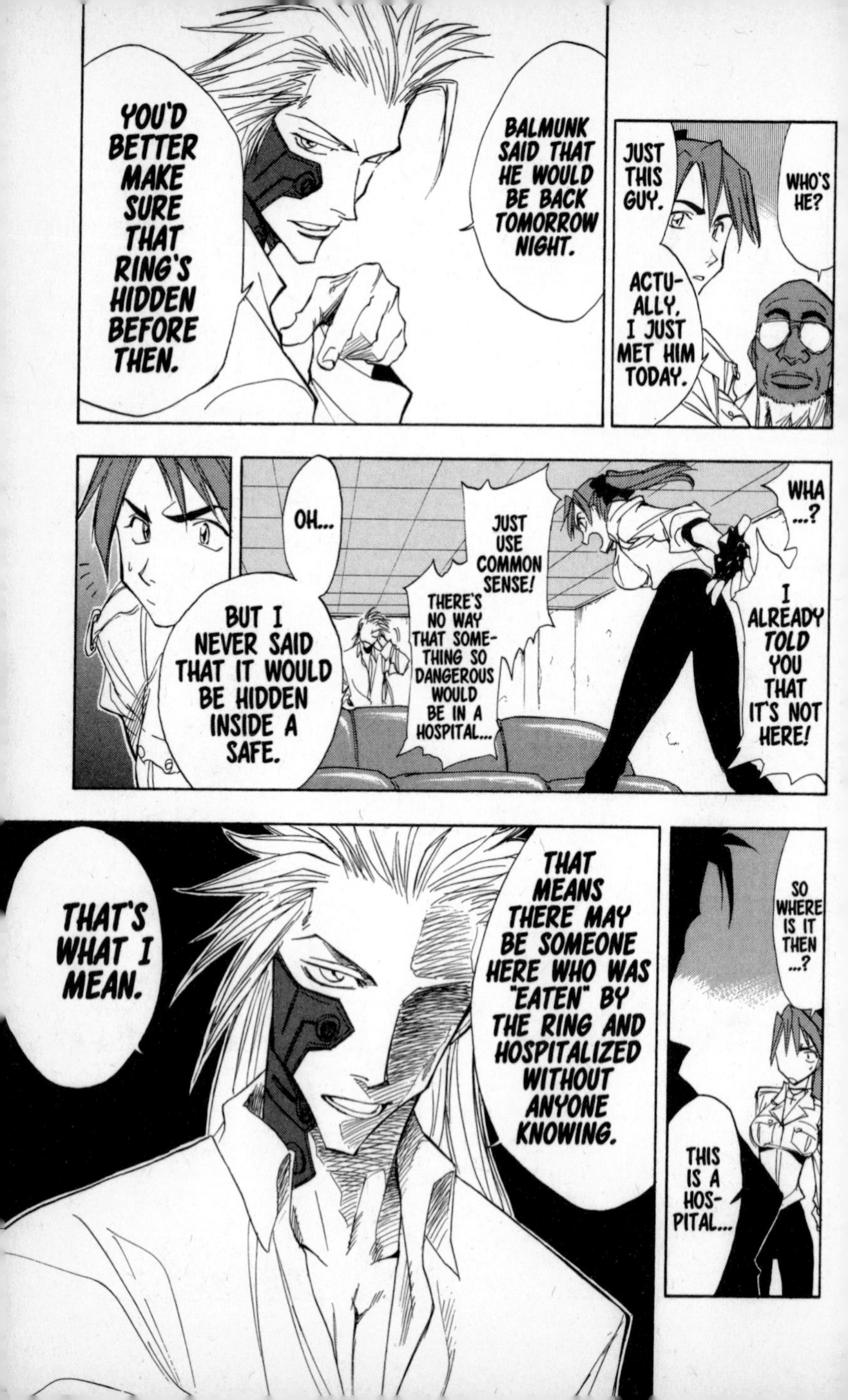
WHO'S HE?
JUST THIS GUY.
ACTU-ALLY, I JUST MET HIM TODAY.
BALMUNK SAID THAT HE WOULD BE BACK TOMORROW NIGHT.
YOU'D BETTER MAKE SURE THAT RING'S HIDDEN BEFORE THEN.
WHA ...?
I ALREADY TOLD YOU THAT IT'S NOT HERE!
JUST USE COMMON SENSE!
THERE'S NO WAY THAT SOME-THING SO DANGEROUS WOULD BE IN A HOSPITAL...
OH...
BUT I NEVER SAID THAT IT WOULD BE HIDDEN INSIDE A SAFE.
SO WHERE IS IT THEN ...?
THIS IS A HOS-PITAL...
THAT MEANS THERE MAY BE SOMEONE HERE WHO WAS "EATEN" BY THE RING AND HOSPITALIZED WITHOUT ANYONE KNOWING.
THAT'S WHAT I MEAN.

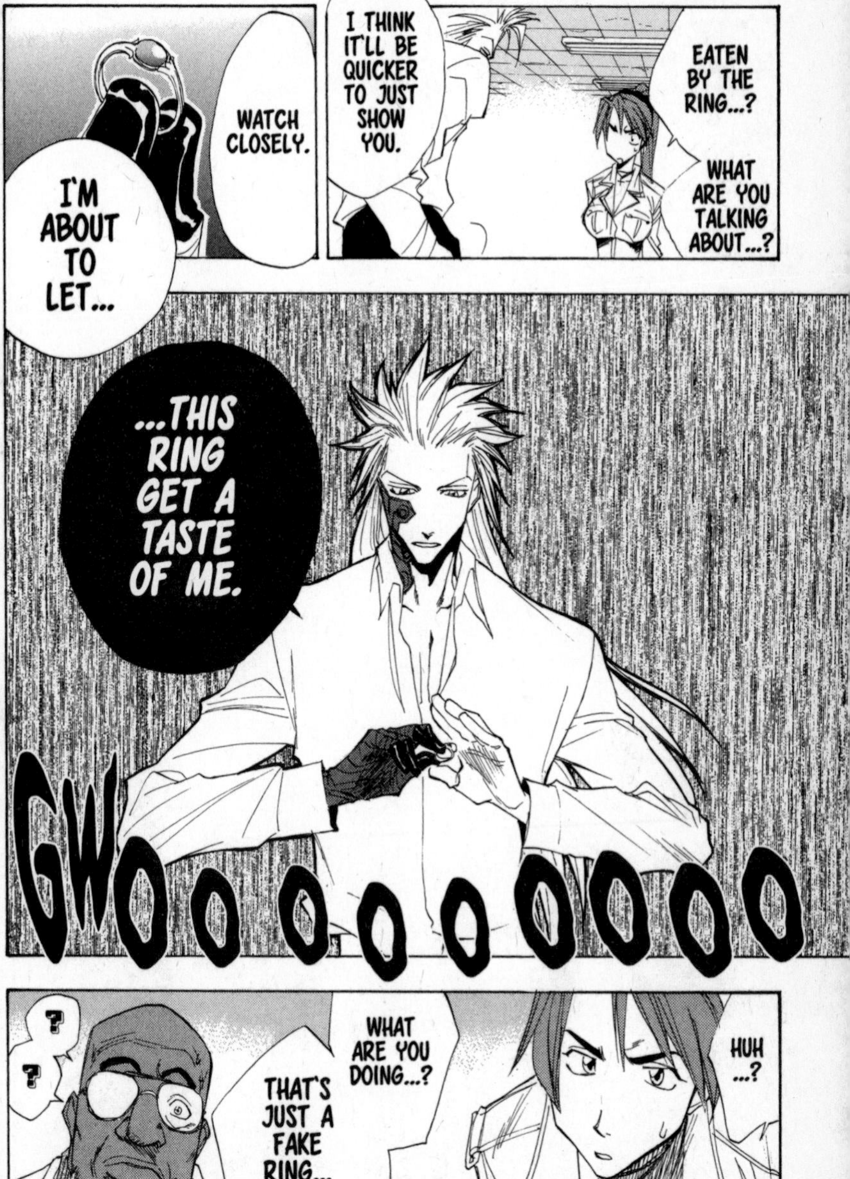
EATEN BY THE RING...?
WHAT ARE YOU TALKING ABOUT...?
I THINK IT'LL BE QUICKER TO JUST SHOW YOU.
WATCH CLOSELY.
I'M ABOUT TO LET...
...THIS RING GET A TASTE OF ME.
GWOOOOOOOOO
HUH...?
WHAT ARE YOU DOING...?
THAT'S JUST A FAKE RING...
?
?

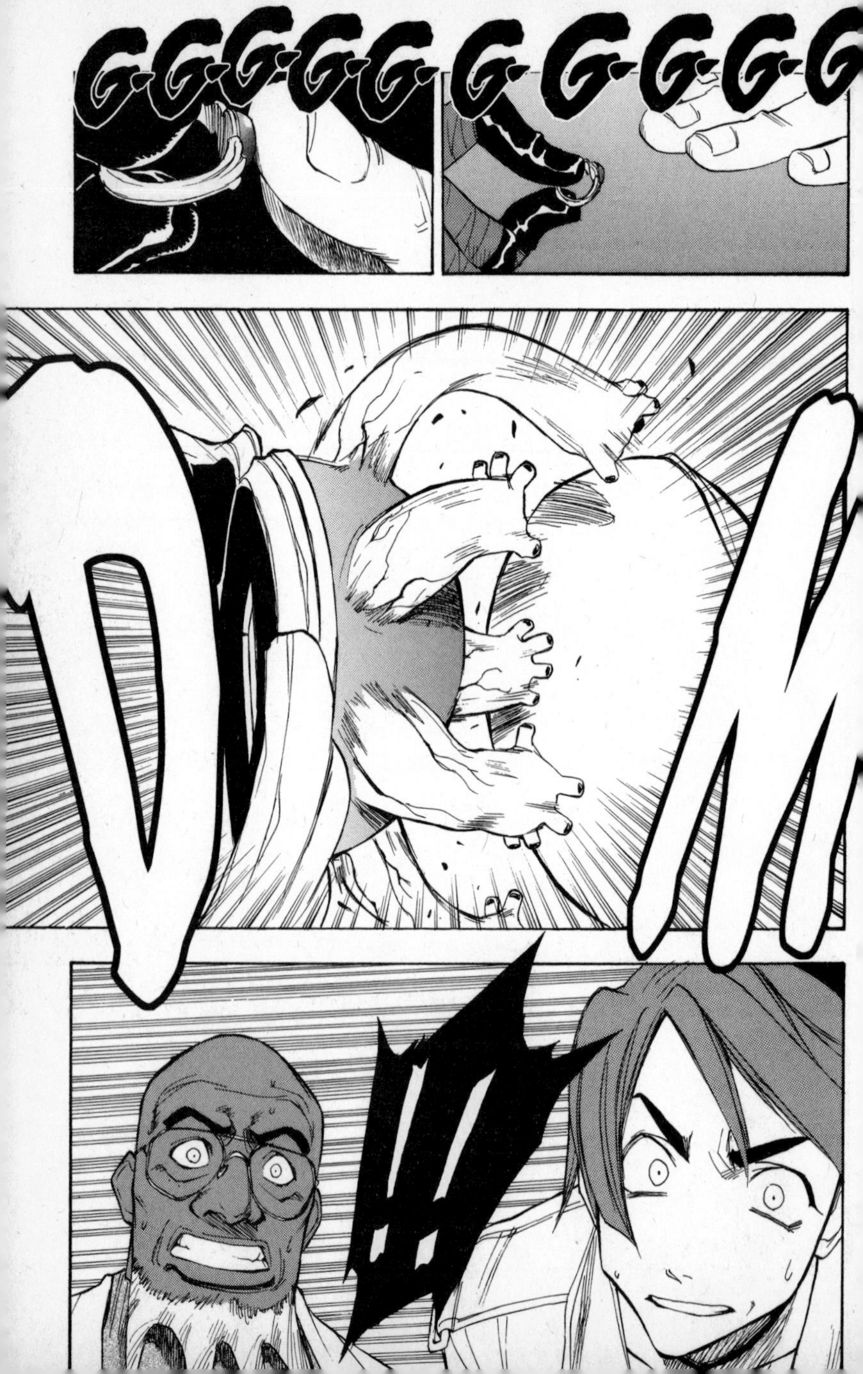

G-G-G-G-G-G-G-G-G-G
!!

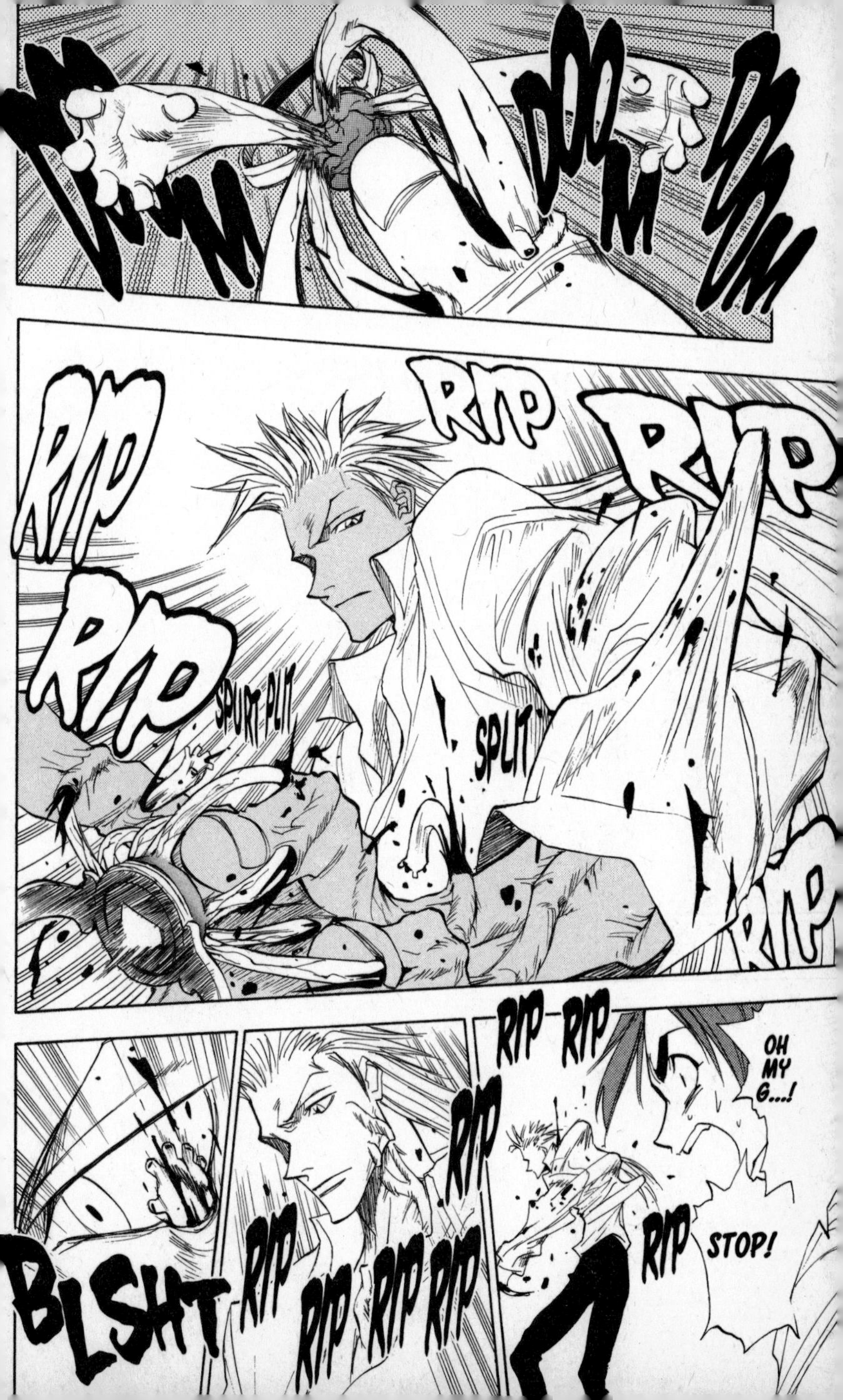
DOOM
DOOM
DOOM
RIP
RIP
RIP
RIP
SPLIT
SPURT PLIT
RIP
RIP RIP
OH MY G...!
RIP
STOP!
RIP
RIP
RIP RIP RIP
BLSHT

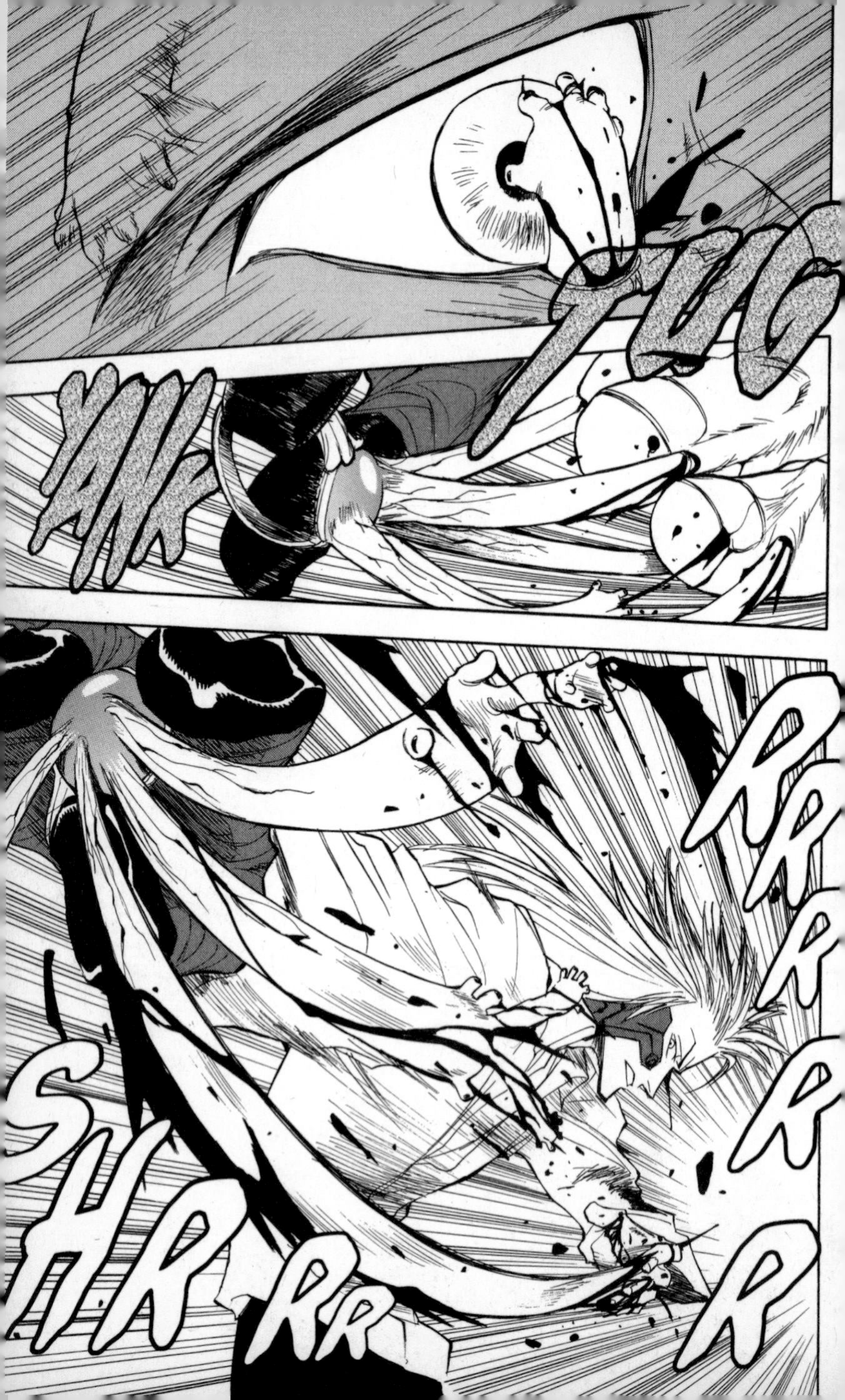
TUG
YANK
RRRRRR
SHRRR

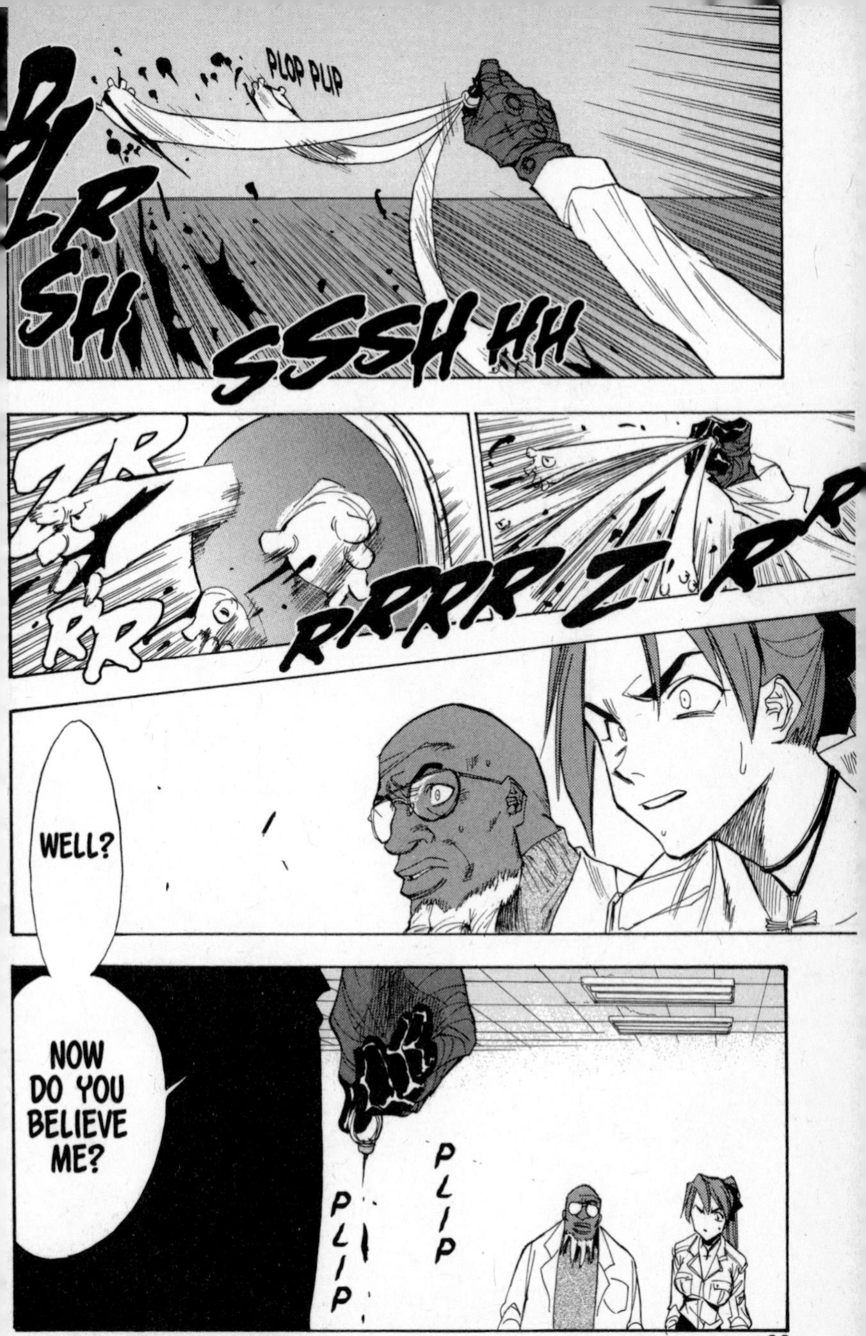
PLOP PLIP
BLRSH
SSSHHH
RRRRRZRR
ZRZRR
WELL?
NOW DO YOU BELIEVE ME?
PLIP
PLIP

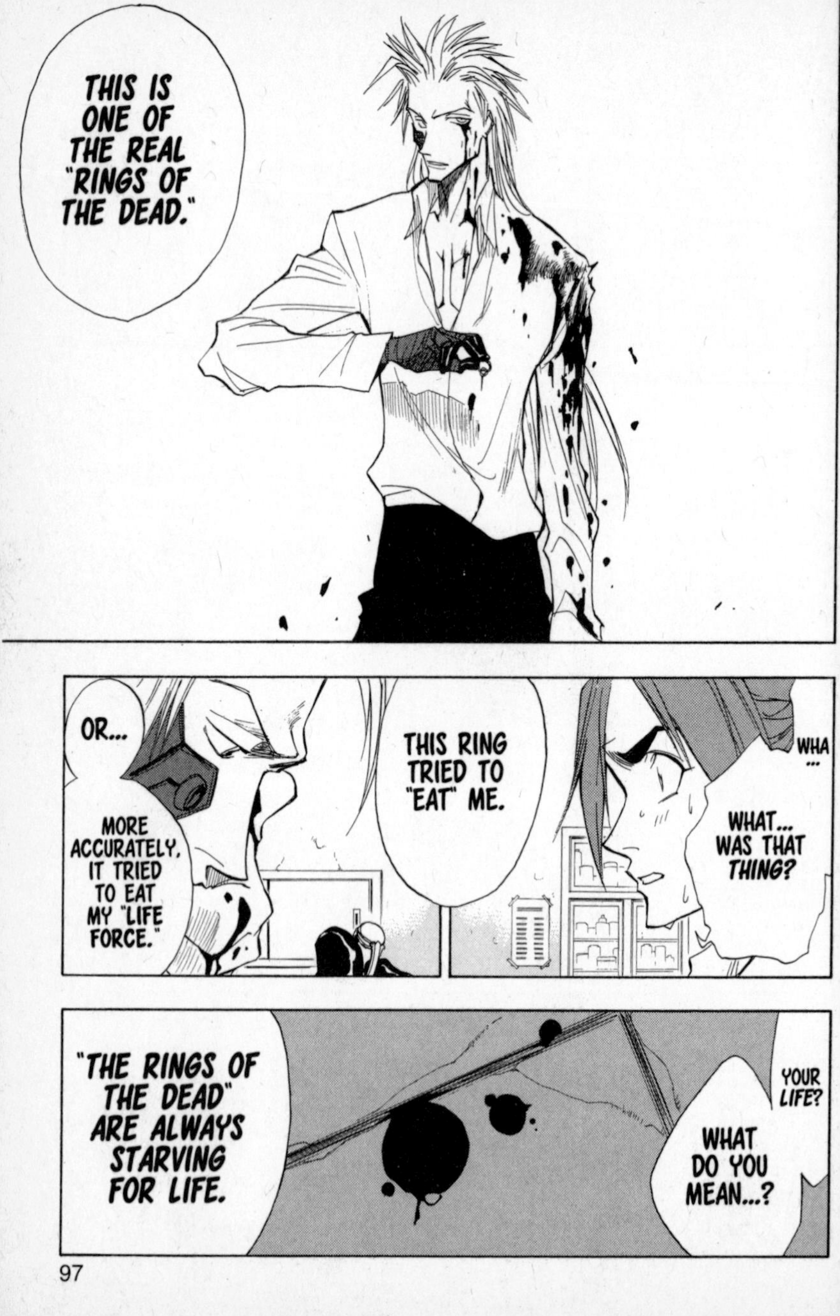
THIS IS ONE OF THE REAL "RINGS OF THE DEAD."
WHA...
WHAT... WAS THAT *THING*?
THIS RING TRIED TO "EAT" ME.
OR...
MORE ACCURATELY, IT TRIED TO EAT MY "LIFE FORCE."
YOUR LIFE?
WHAT DO YOU MEAN...?
"THE RINGS OF THE DEAD" ARE ALWAYS STARVING FOR LIFE.

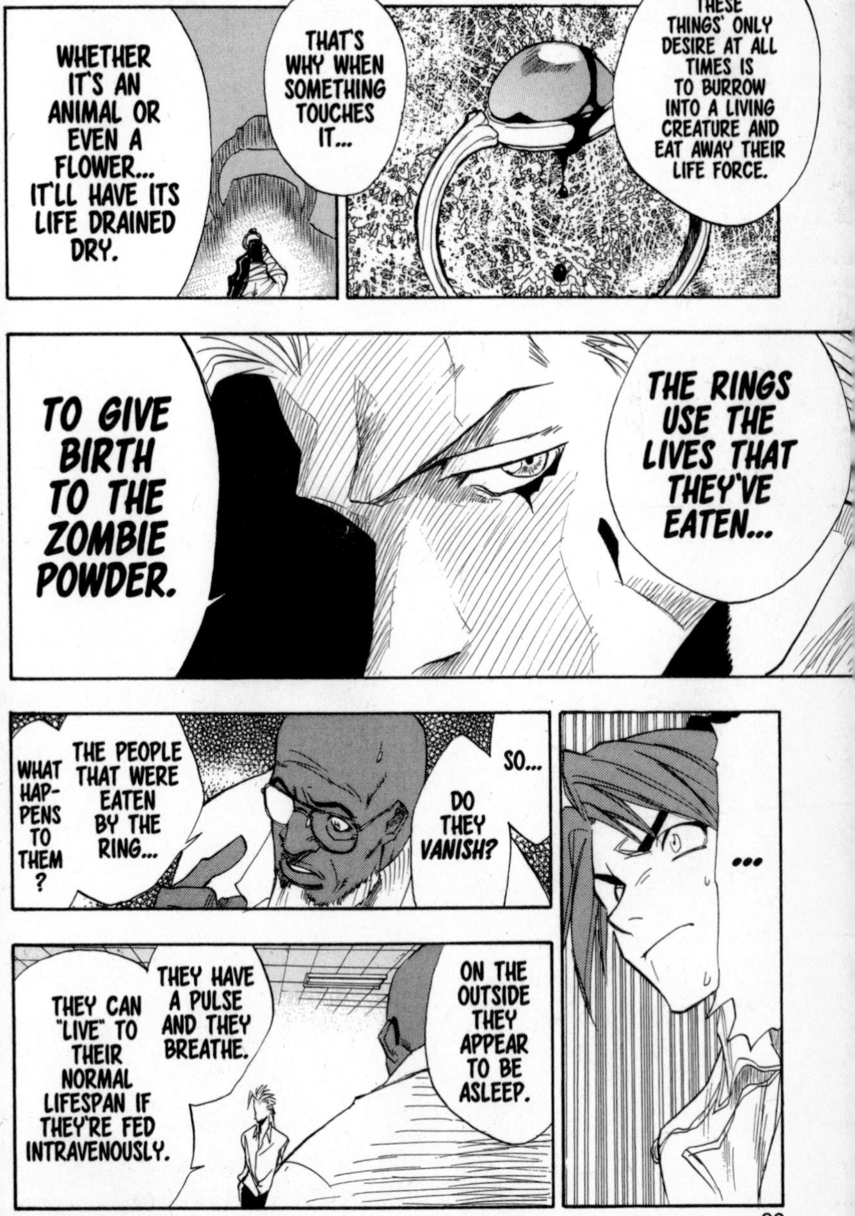
THESE THINGS' ONLY DESIRE AT ALL TIMES IS TO BURROW INTO A LIVING CREATURE AND EAT AWAY THEIR LIFE FORCE.
THAT'S WHY WHEN SOMETHING TOUCHES IT...
WHETHER IT'S AN ANIMAL OR EVEN A FLOWER... IT'LL HAVE ITS LIFE DRAINED DRY.
THE RINGS USE THE LIVES THAT THEY'VE EATEN...
TO GIVE BIRTH TO THE ZOMBIE POWDER.
...
SO...
DO THEY VANISH?
THE PEOPLE THAT WERE EATEN BY THE RING...
WHAT HAP-PENS TO THEM?
ON THE OUTSIDE THEY APPEAR TO BE ASLEEP.
THEY HAVE A PULSE AND THEY BREATHE.
THEY CAN "LIVE" TO THEIR NORMAL LIFESPAN IF THEY'RE FED INTRAVENOUSLY.

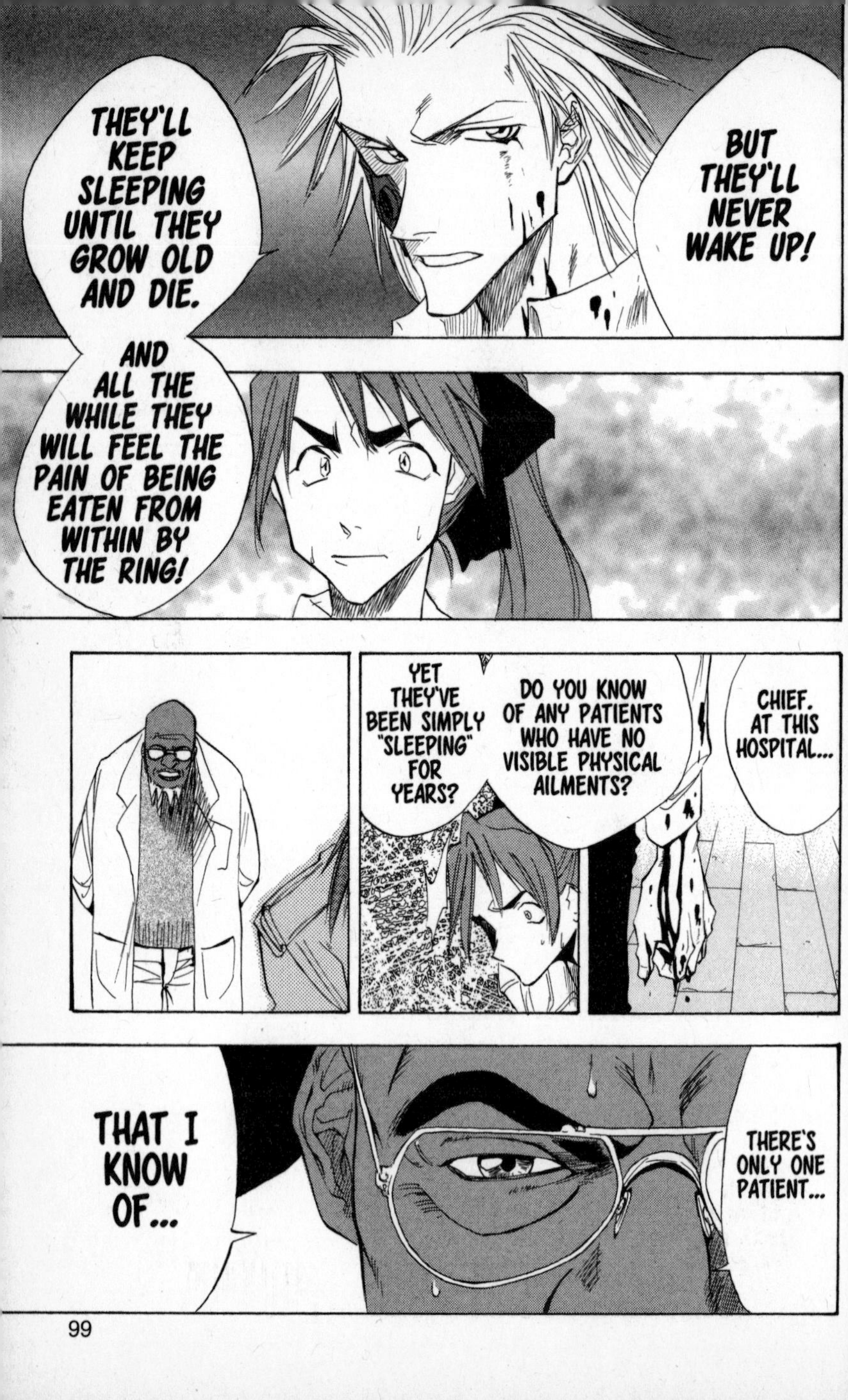
BUT THEY'LL NEVER WAKE UP!
THEY'LL KEEP SLEEPING UNTIL THEY GROW OLD AND DIE.
AND ALL THE WHILE THEY WILL FEEL THE PAIN OF BEING EATEN FROM WITHIN BY THE RING!
CHIEF. AT THIS HOSPITAL...
DO YOU KNOW OF ANY PATIENTS WHO HAVE NO VISIBLE PHYSICAL AILMENTS?
YET THEY'VE BEEN SIMPLY "SLEEPING" FOR YEARS?
THERE'S ONLY ONE PATIENT...
THAT I KNOW OF...

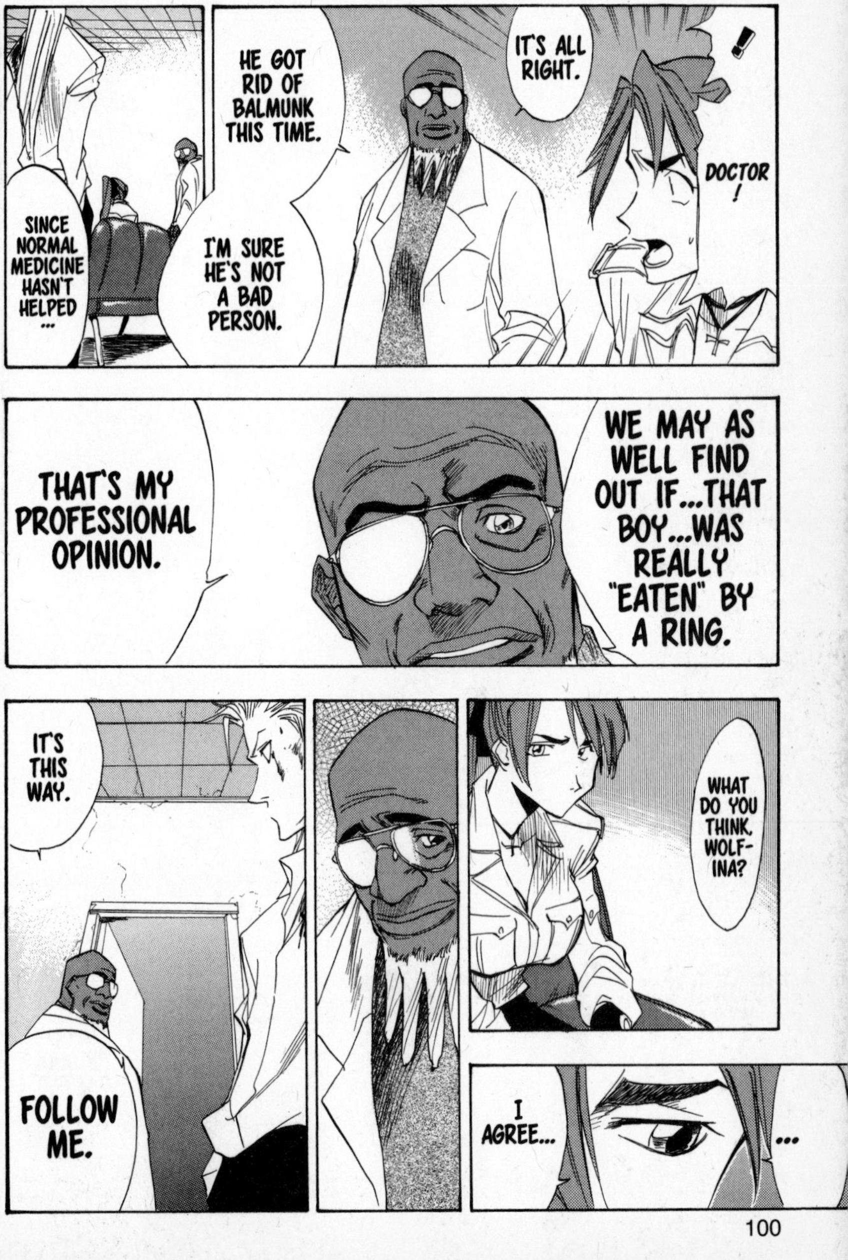
!
DOCTOR!
IT'S ALL RIGHT.
HE GOT RID OF BALMUNK THIS TIME.
I'M SURE HE'S NOT A BAD PERSON.
SINCE NORMAL MEDICINE HASN'T HELPED ...
WE MAY AS WELL FIND OUT IF...THAT BOY...WAS REALLY "EATEN" BY A RING.
THAT'S MY PROFESSIONAL OPINION.
WHAT DO YOU THINK, WOLF-INA?
...
I AGREE...
IT'S THIS WAY.
FOLLOW ME.

READ THIS WAY

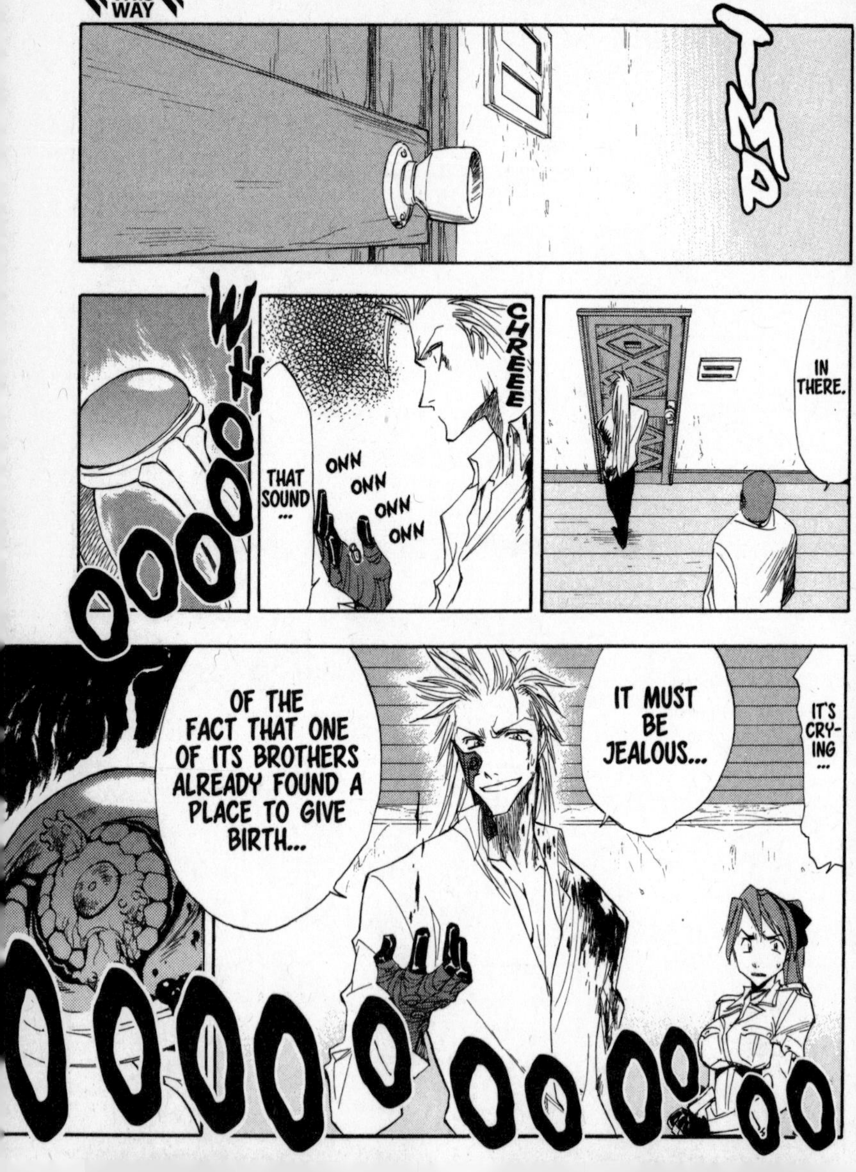
TMP
IN THERE.
CHREEE
ONN ONN ONN ONN
THAT SOUND...
WHOOOOOO
IT'S CRY-ING...
IT MUST BE JEALOUS...
OF THE FACT THAT ONE OF ITS BROTHERS ALREADY FOUND A PLACE TO GIVE BIRTH...
OOOOOOOOOOO

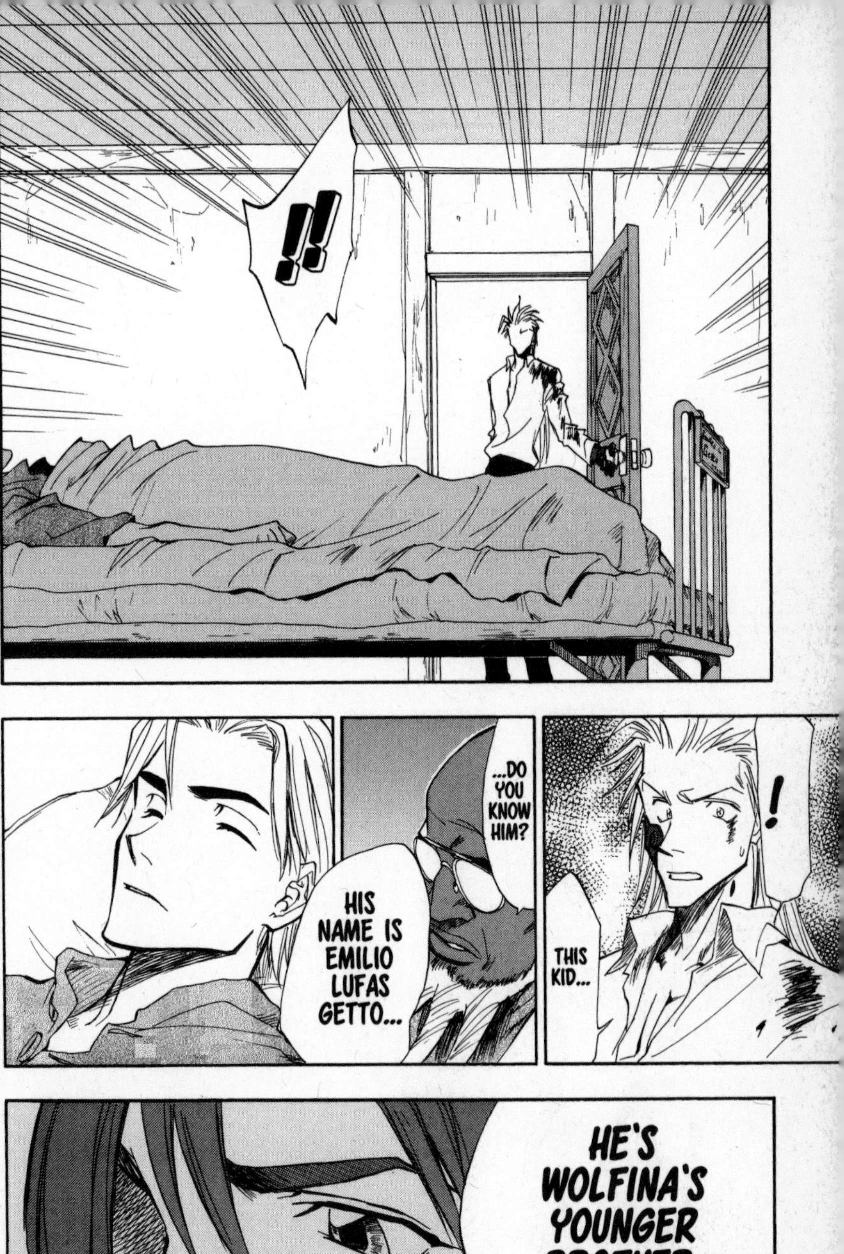
!!
!
THIS KID...
...DO YOU KNOW HIM?
HIS NAME IS EMILIO LUFAS GETTO...
HE'S WOLFINA'S YOUNGER BROTHER.

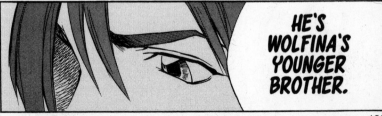

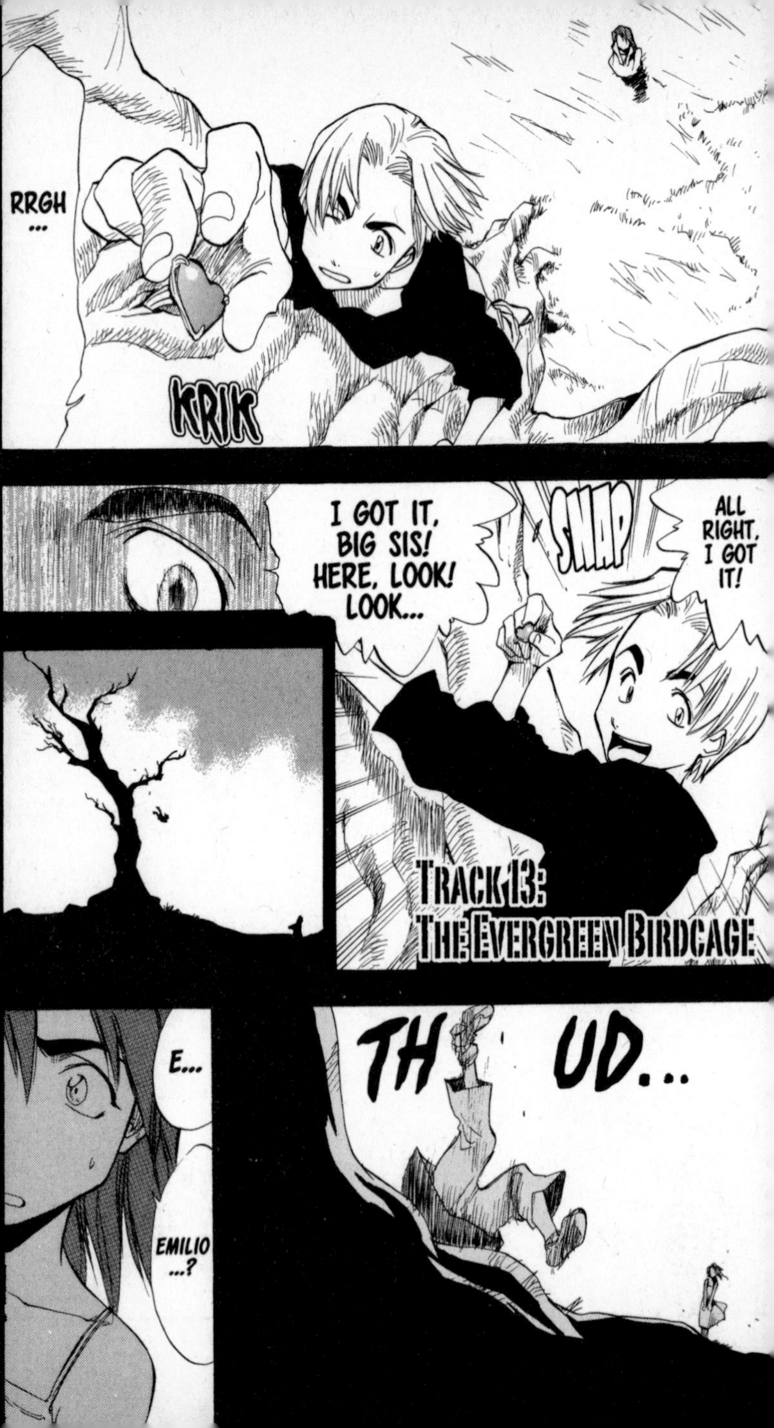
RRGH ...
KRIK
ALL RIGHT, I GOT IT!
SNAP
I GOT IT, BIG SIS! HERE, LOOK! LOOK...
TRACK 13: THE EVERGREEN BIRDCAGE
TH UD...
E...
EMILIO ...?

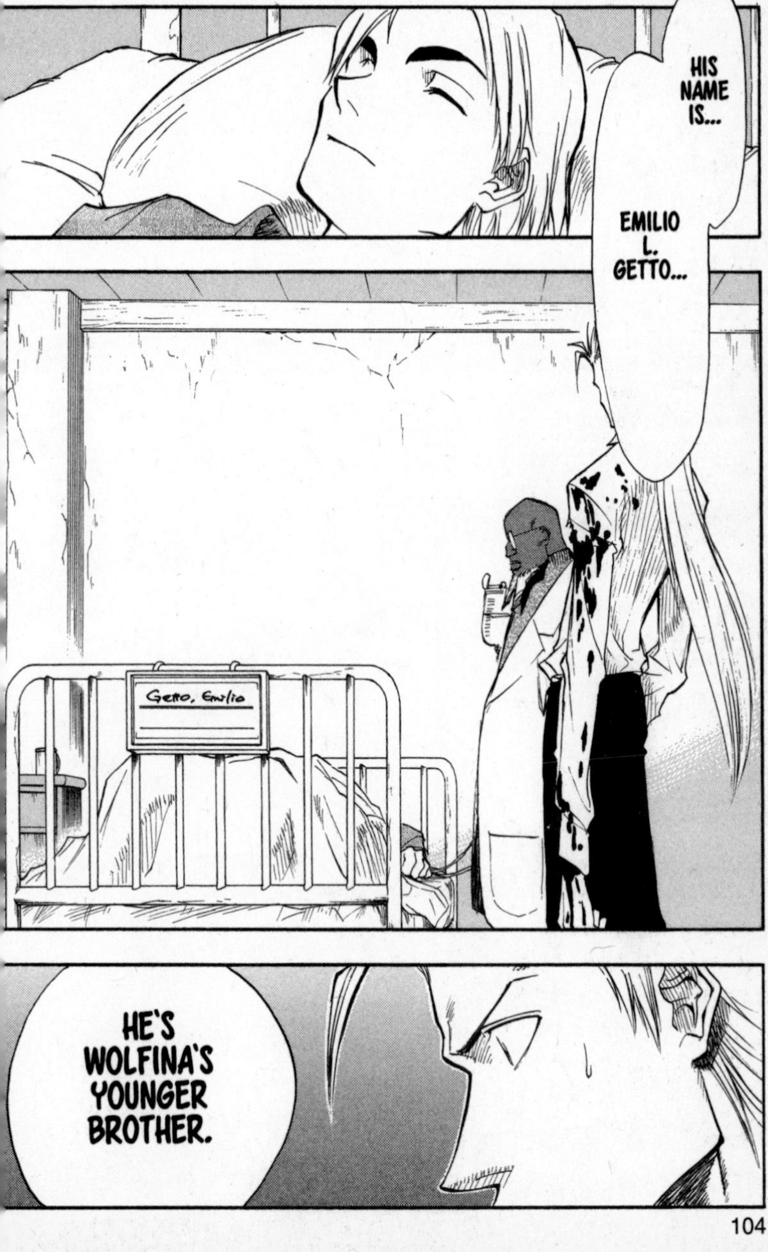
HIS NAME IS...
EMILIO L. GETTO...
Getto, Emilio
HE'S WOLFINA'S YOUNGER BROTHER.

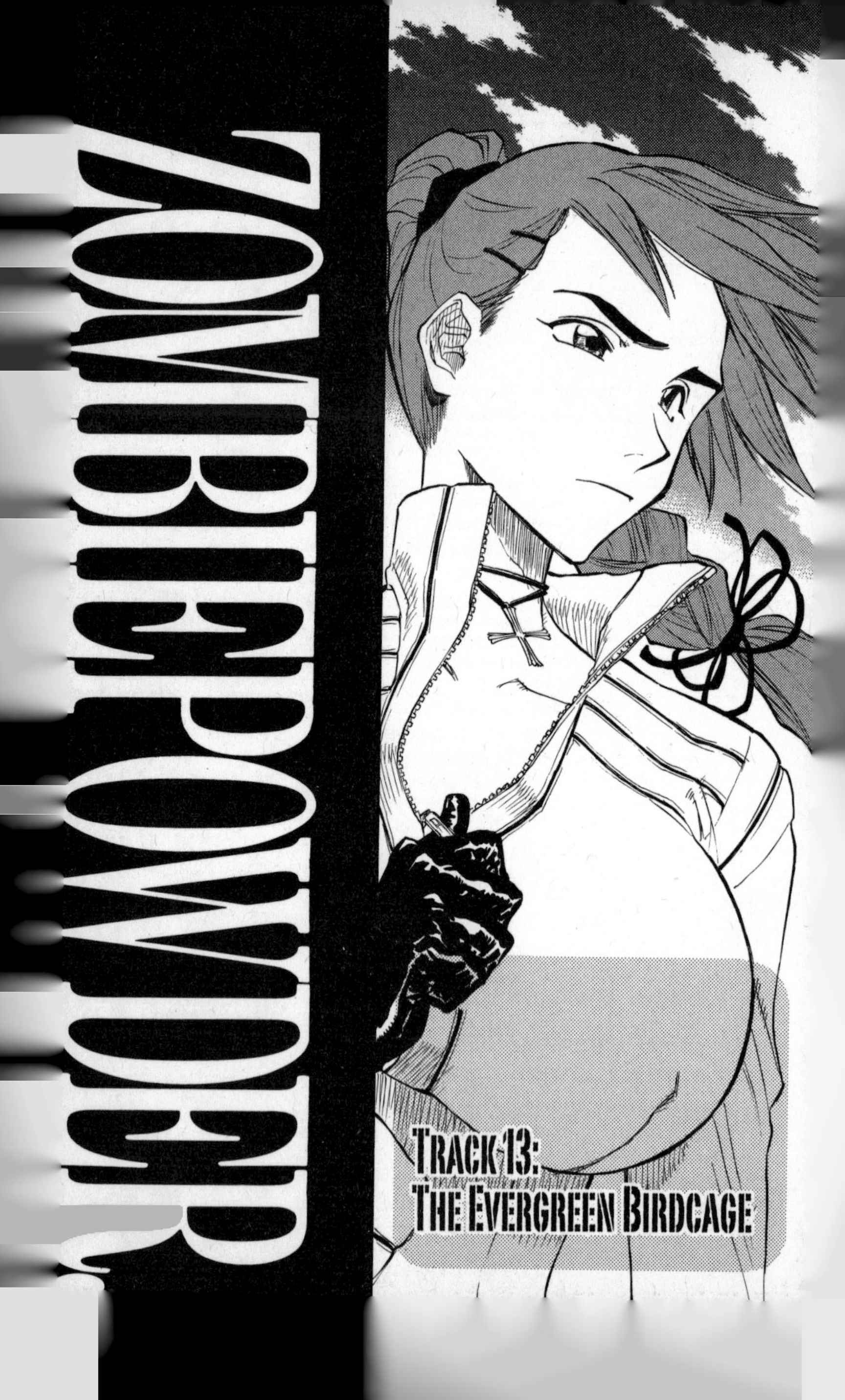
ZOMBIEPOWDER
TRACK 13:
THE EVERGREEN BIRDCAGE

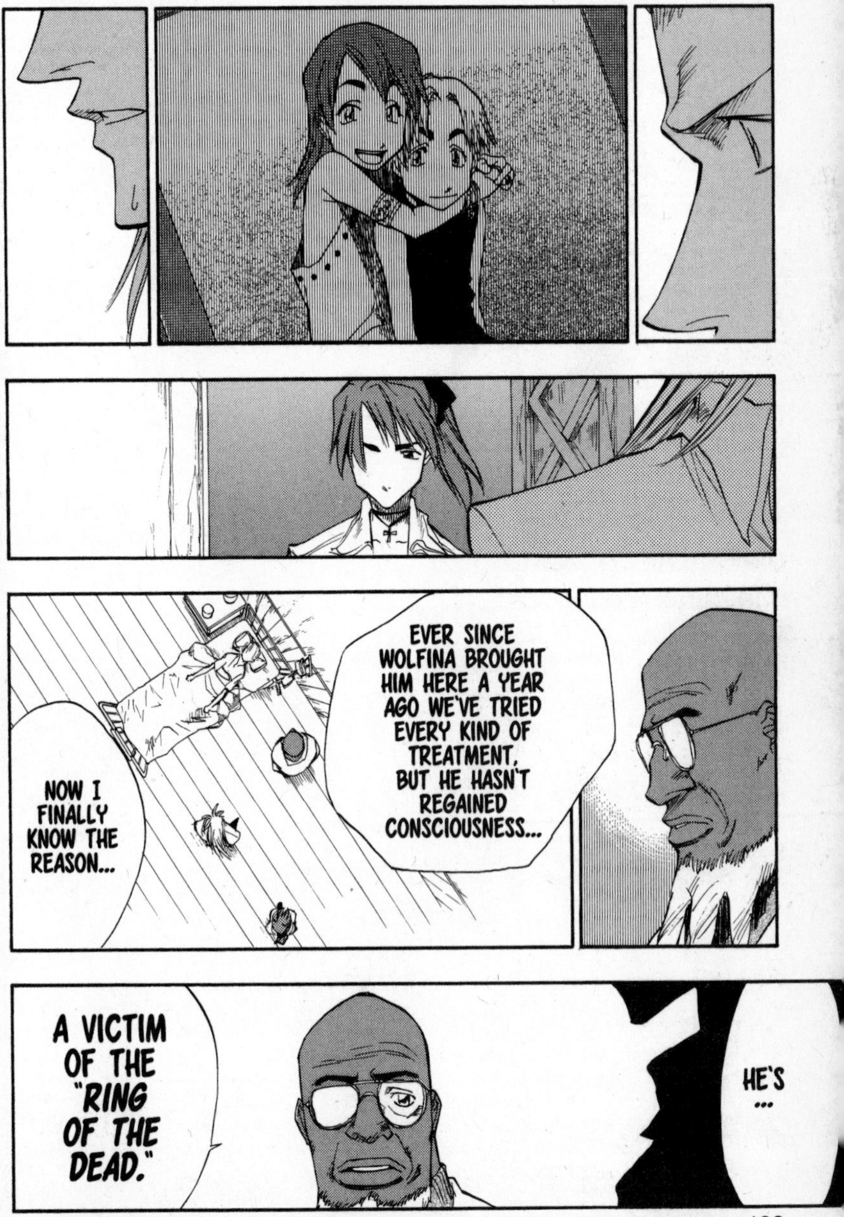
EVER SINCE WOLFINA BROUGHT HIM HERE A YEAR AGO WE'VE TRIED EVERY KIND OF TREATMENT, BUT HE HASN'T REGAINED CONSCIOUSNESS...
NOW I FINALLY KNOW THE REASON...
HE'S...
A VICTIM OF THE "RING OF THE DEAD."

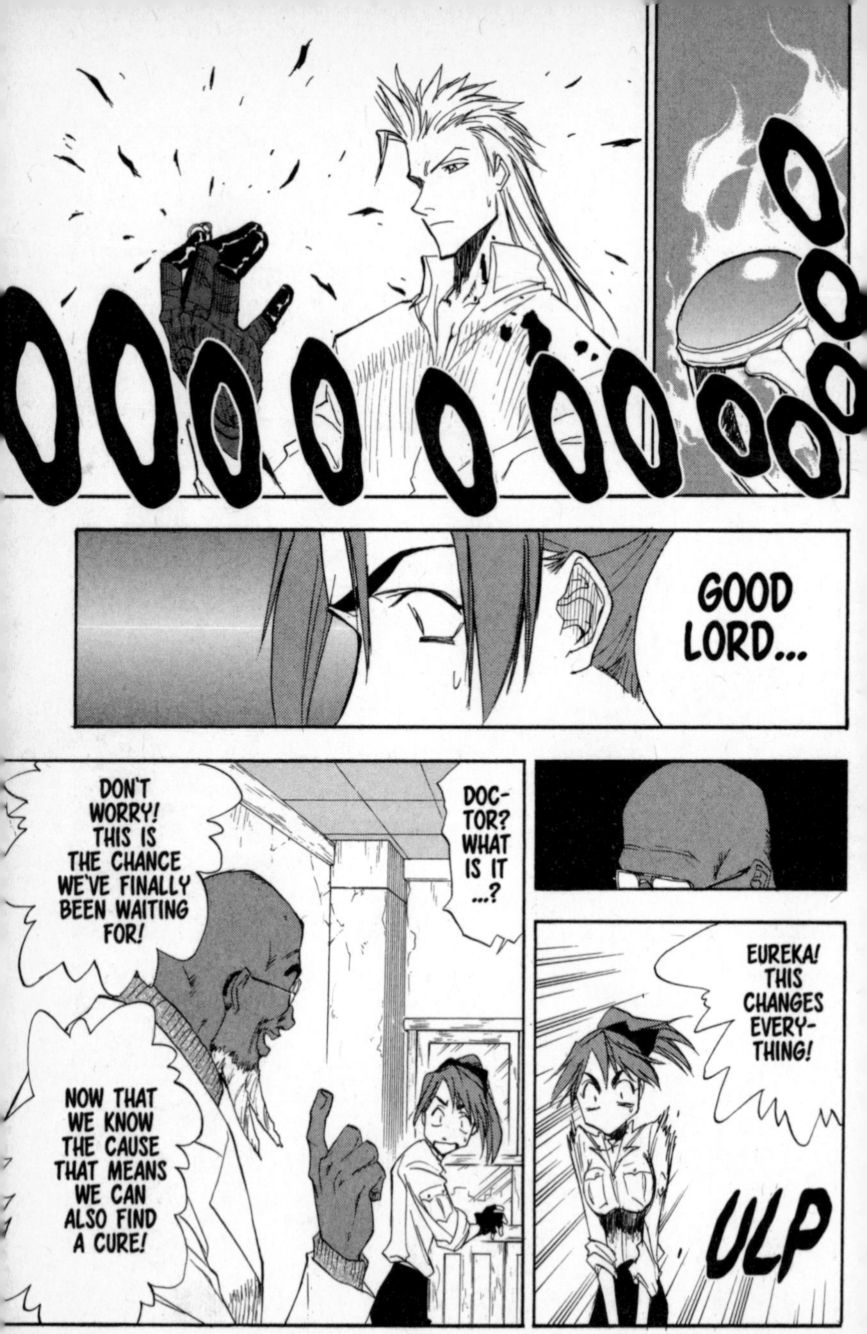
OOOOOOOOOOOOO
GOOD LORD...
EUREKA! THIS CHANGES EVERYTHING!
ULP
DOCTOR? WHAT IS IT ...?
DON'T WORRY! THIS IS THE CHANCE WE'VE FINALLY BEEN WAITING FOR!
NOW THAT WE KNOW THE CAUSE THAT MEANS WE CAN ALSO FIND A CURE!

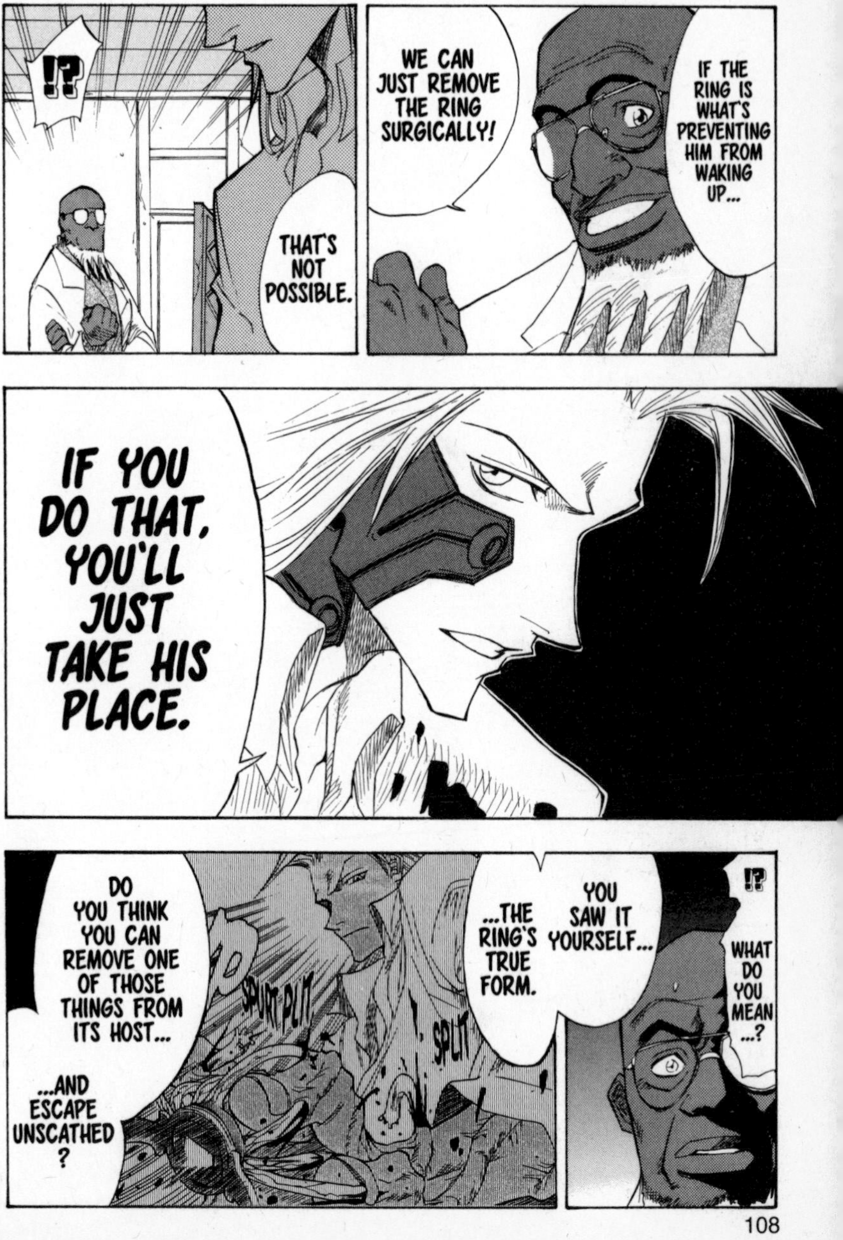
IF THE RING IS WHAT'S PREVENTING HIM FROM WAKING UP...
WE CAN JUST REMOVE THE RING SURGICALLY!
THAT'S NOT POSSIBLE.
!?
IF YOU DO THAT, YOU'LL JUST TAKE HIS PLACE.
!?
WHAT DO YOU MEAN ...?
YOU SAW IT YOURSELF...
...THE RING'S TRUE FORM.
SPLIT
SPURT PLIT
DO YOU THINK YOU CAN REMOVE ONE OF THOSE THINGS FROM ITS HOST...
...AND ESCAPE UNSCATHED ?

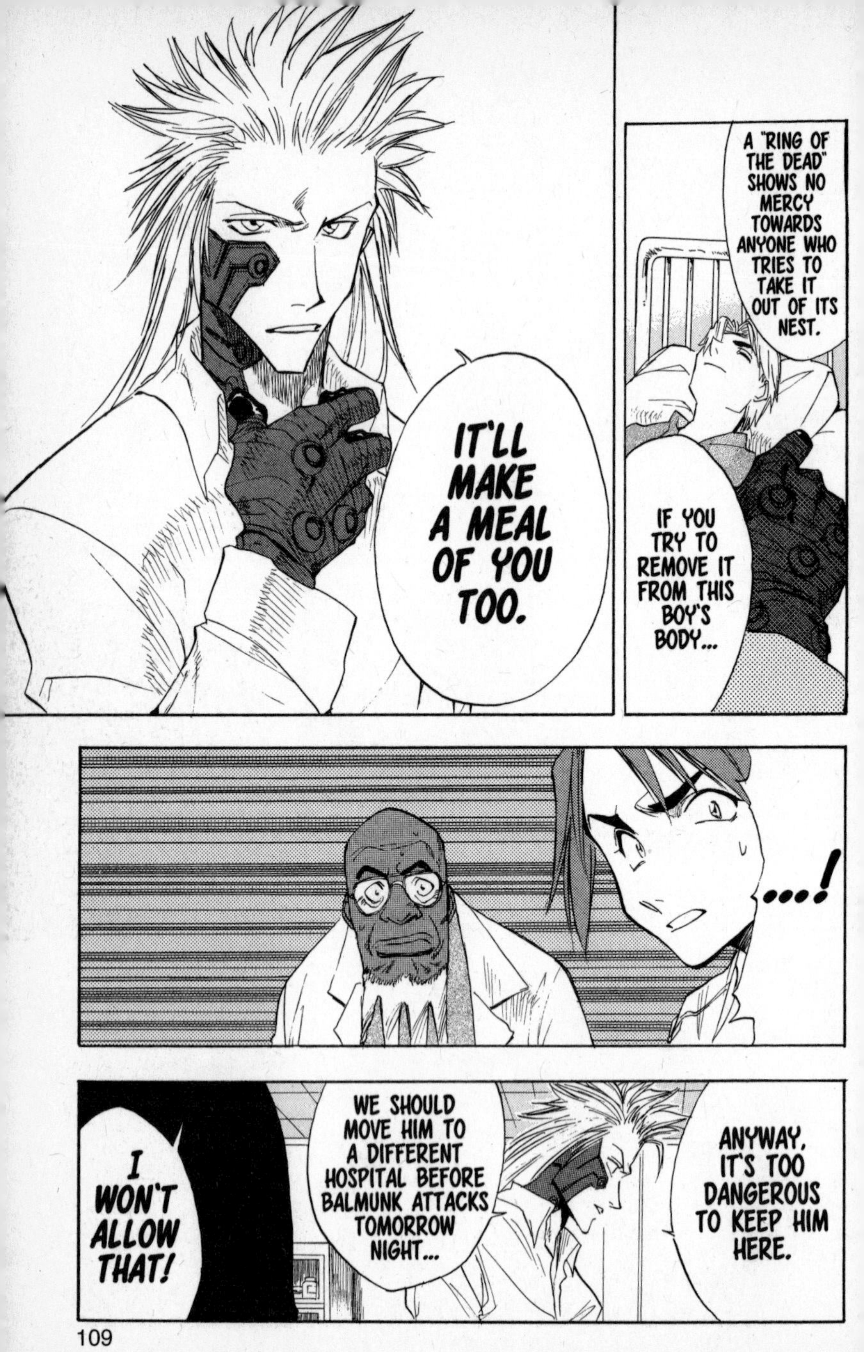
A "RING OF THE DEAD" SHOWS NO MERCY TOWARDS ANYONE WHO TRIES TO TAKE IT OUT OF ITS NEST.
IF YOU TRY TO REMOVE IT FROM THIS BOY'S BODY...
IT'LL MAKE A MEAL OF YOU TOO.
...!
ANYWAY, IT'S TOO DANGEROUS TO KEEP HIM HERE.
WE SHOULD MOVE HIM TO A DIFFERENT HOSPITAL BEFORE BALMUNK ATTACKS TOMORROW NIGHT...
I WON'T ALLOW THAT!

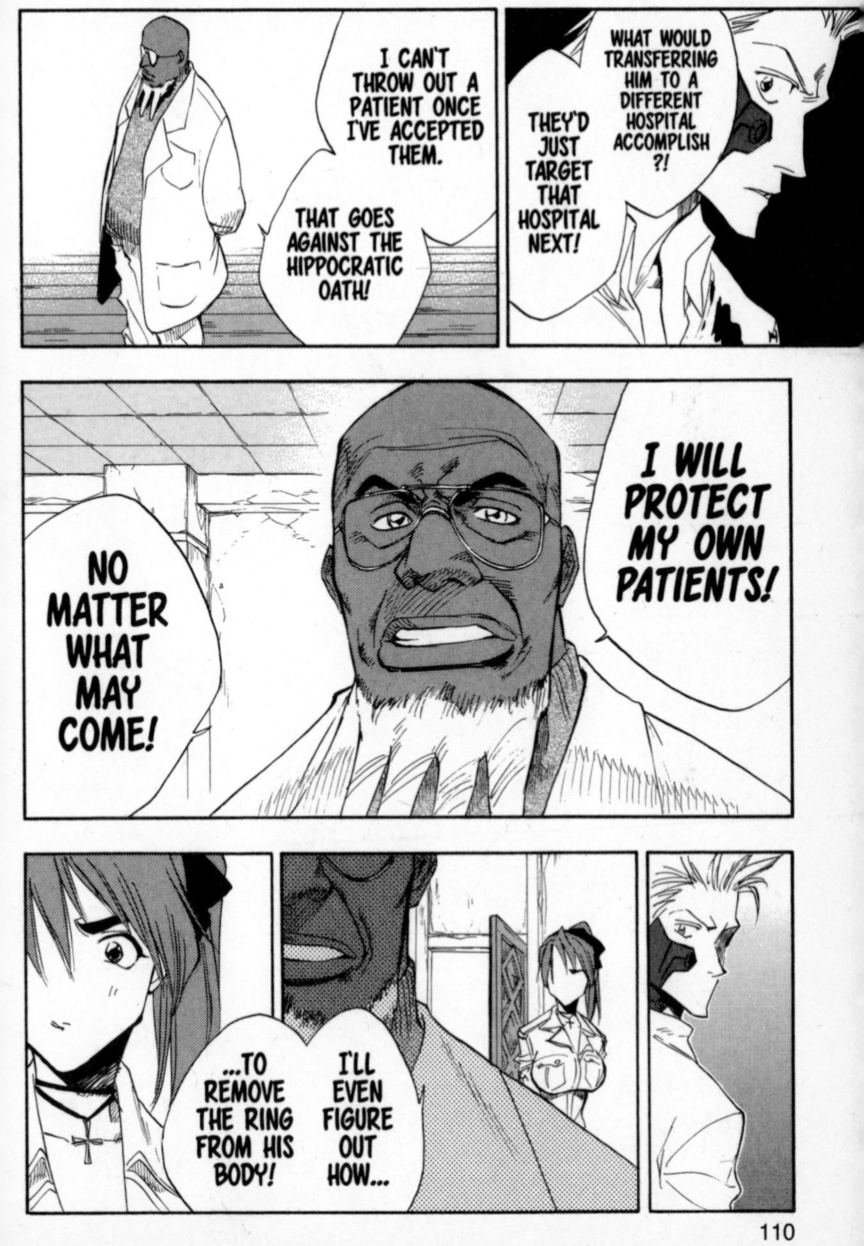
WHAT WOULD TRANSFERRING HIM TO A DIFFERENT HOSPITAL ACCOMPLISH ?!
THEY'D JUST TARGET THAT HOSPITAL NEXT!
I CAN'T THROW OUT A PATIENT ONCE I'VE ACCEPTED THEM.
THAT GOES AGAINST THE HIPPOCRATIC OATH!
I WILL PROTECT MY OWN PATIENTS!
NO MATTER WHAT MAY COME!
I'LL EVEN FIGURE OUT HOW...
...TO REMOVE THE RING FROM HIS BODY!

READ THIS WAY

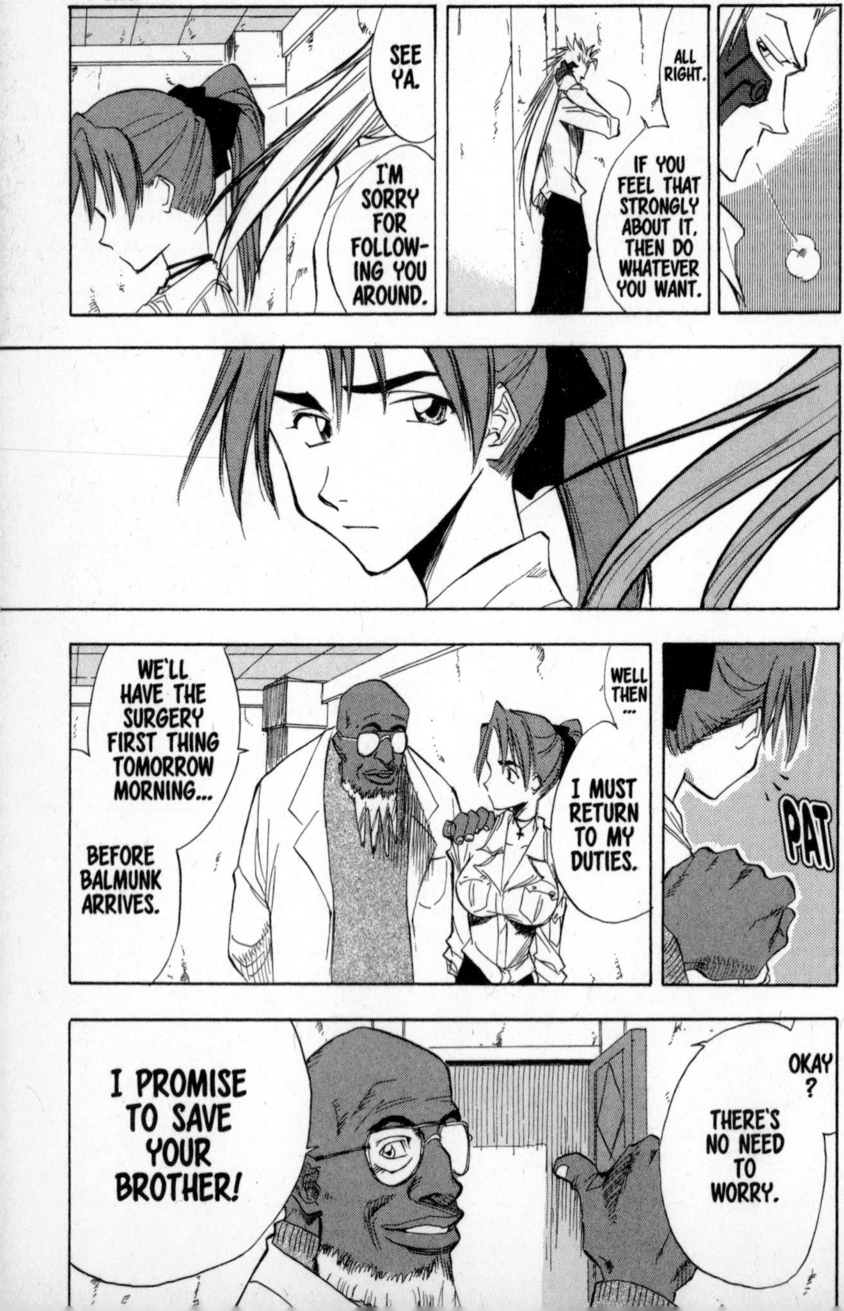
ALL RIGHT.
IF YOU FEEL THAT STRONGLY ABOUT IT, THEN DO WHATEVER YOU WANT.
SEE YA.
I'M SORRY FOR FOLLOWING YOU AROUND.
PAT
WELL THEN...
I MUST RETURN TO MY DUTIES.
WE'LL HAVE THE SURGERY FIRST THING TOMORROW MORNING...
BEFORE BALMUNK ARRIVES.
OKAY?
THERE'S NO NEED TO WORRY.
I PROMISE TO SAVE YOUR BROTHER!

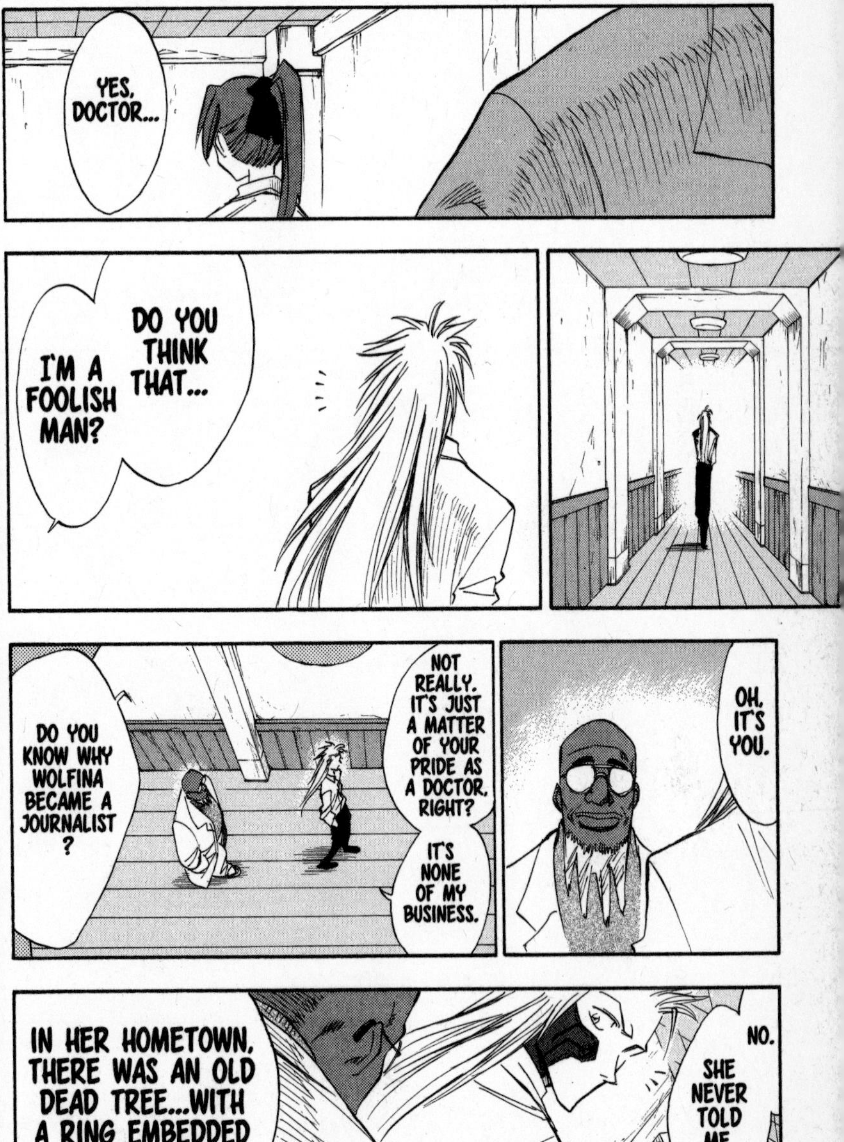
YES, DOCTOR...
DO YOU THINK THAT...
I'M A FOOLISH MAN?
OH, IT'S YOU.
NOT REALLY. IT'S JUST A MATTER OF YOUR PRIDE AS A DOCTOR, RIGHT?
IT'S NONE OF MY BUSINESS.
DO YOU KNOW WHY WOLFINA BECAME A JOURNALIST?
NO.
SHE NEVER TOLD ME.
IN HER HOMETOWN, THERE WAS AN OLD DEAD TREE...WITH A RING EMBEDDED AT THE TOP.

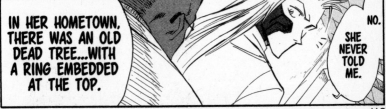

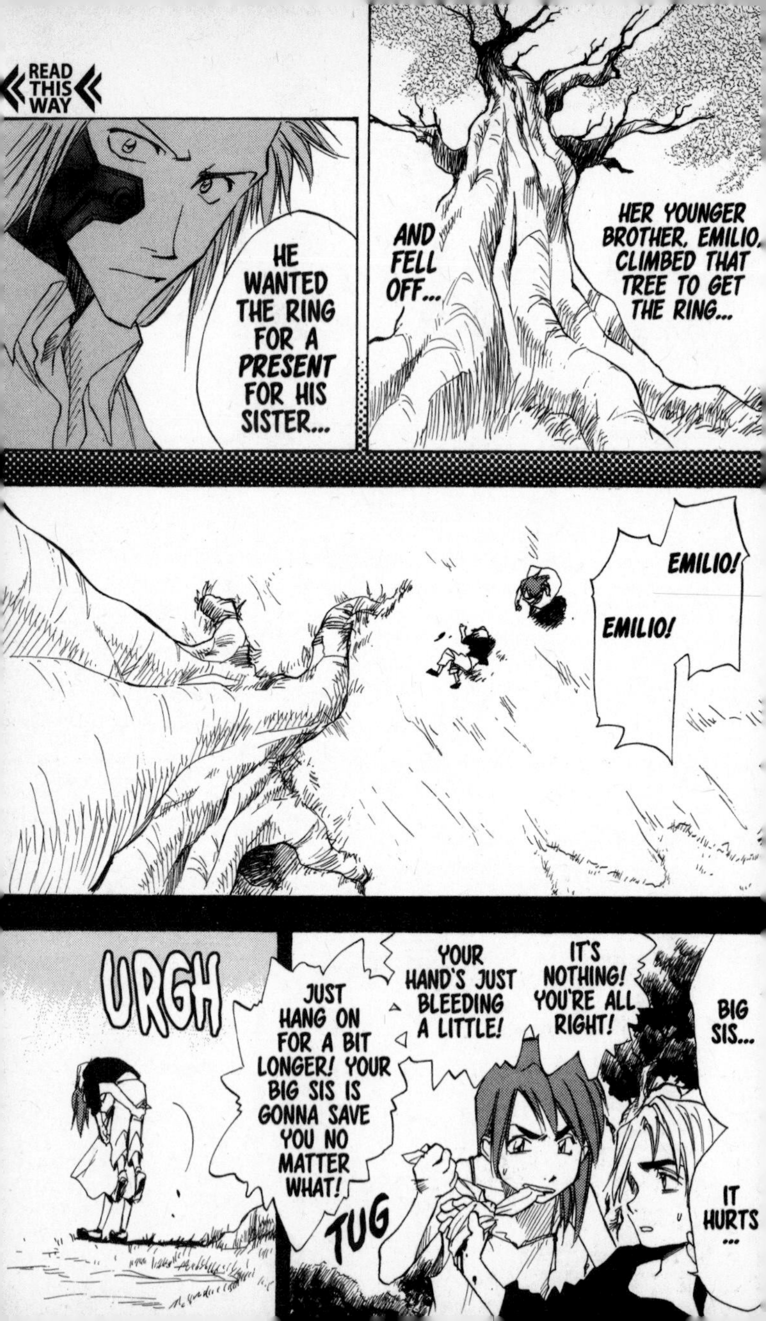
READ THIS WAY
HER YOUNGER BROTHER, EMILIO, CLIMBED THAT TREE TO GET THE RING...
AND FELL OFF...
HE WANTED THE RING FOR A PRESENT FOR HIS SISTER...
EMILIO!
EMILIO!
BIG SIS...
IT HURTS...
IT'S NOTHING! YOU'RE ALL RIGHT!
YOUR HAND'S JUST BLEEDING A LITTLE!
JUST HANG ON FOR A BIT LONGER! YOUR BIG SIS IS GONNA SAVE YOU NO MATTER WHAT!
TUG
URGH

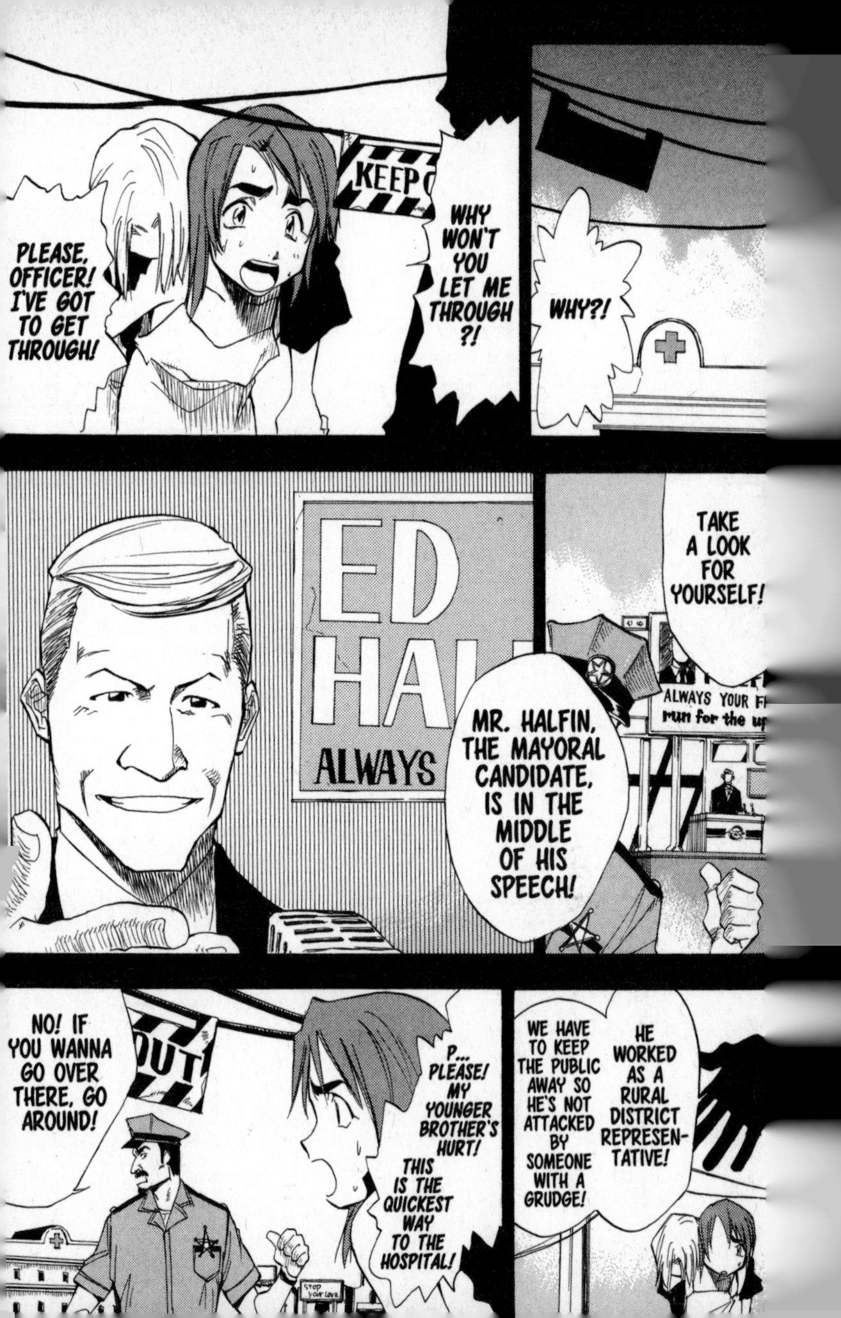
WHY?!
WHY WON'T YOU LET ME THROUGH?!
KEEP
PLEASE, OFFICER! I'VE GOT TO GET THROUGH!
TAKE A LOOK FOR YOURSELF!
ALWAYS YOUR F
run for the u
MR. HALFIN, THE MAYORAL CANDIDATE, IS IN THE MIDDLE OF HIS SPEECH!
ED HAL
ALWAYS
HE WORKED AS A RURAL DISTRICT REPRESENTATIVE!
WE HAVE TO KEEP THE PUBLIC AWAY SO HE'S NOT ATTACKED BY SOMEONE WITH A GRUDGE!
P... PLEASE! MY YOUNGER BROTHER'S HURT!
THIS IS THE QUICKEST WAY TO THE HOSPITAL!
OUT
NO! IF YOU WANNA GO OVER THERE, GO AROUND!

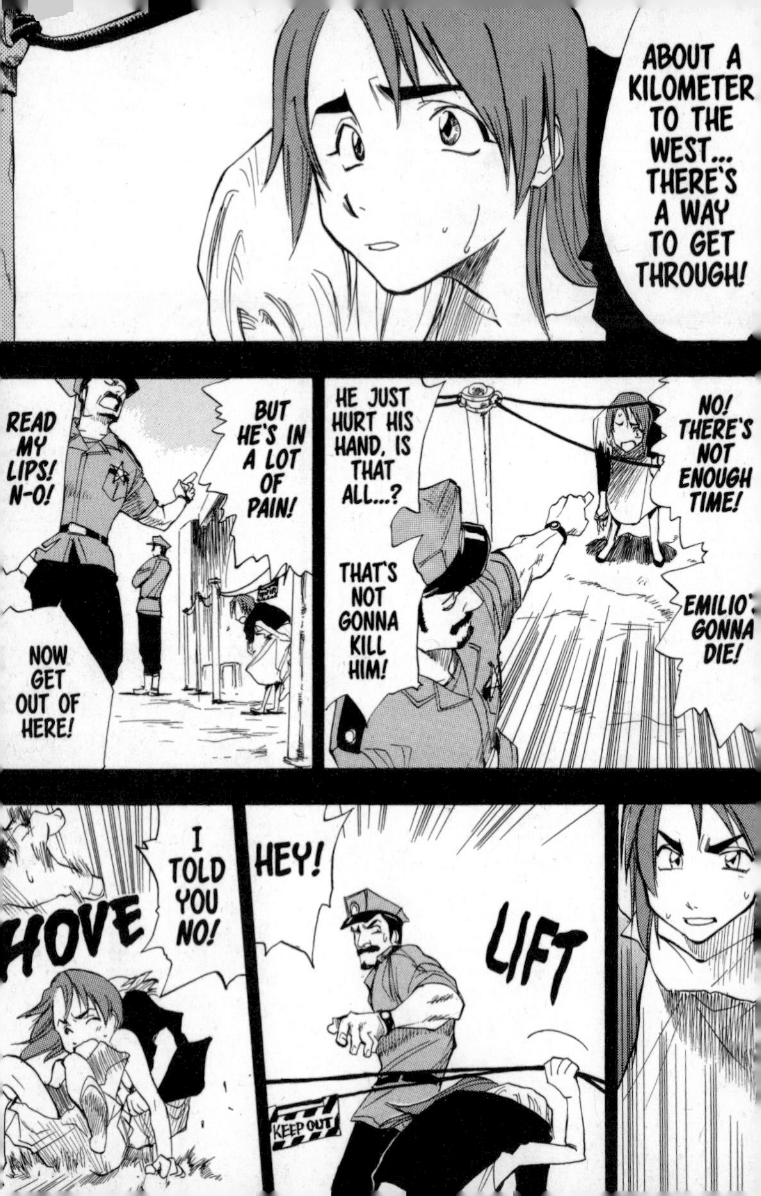
ABOUT A KILOMETER TO THE WEST... THERE'S A WAY TO GET THROUGH!
NO! THERE'S NOT ENOUGH TIME!
HE JUST HURT HIS HAND, IS THAT ALL...?
EMILIO'
GONNA DIE!
THAT'S NOT GONNA KILL HIM!
BUT HE'S IN A LOT OF PAIN!
READ MY LIPS! N-O!
NOW GET OUT OF HERE!
LIFT
HEY!
KEEP OUT
I TOLD YOU NO!
HOVE

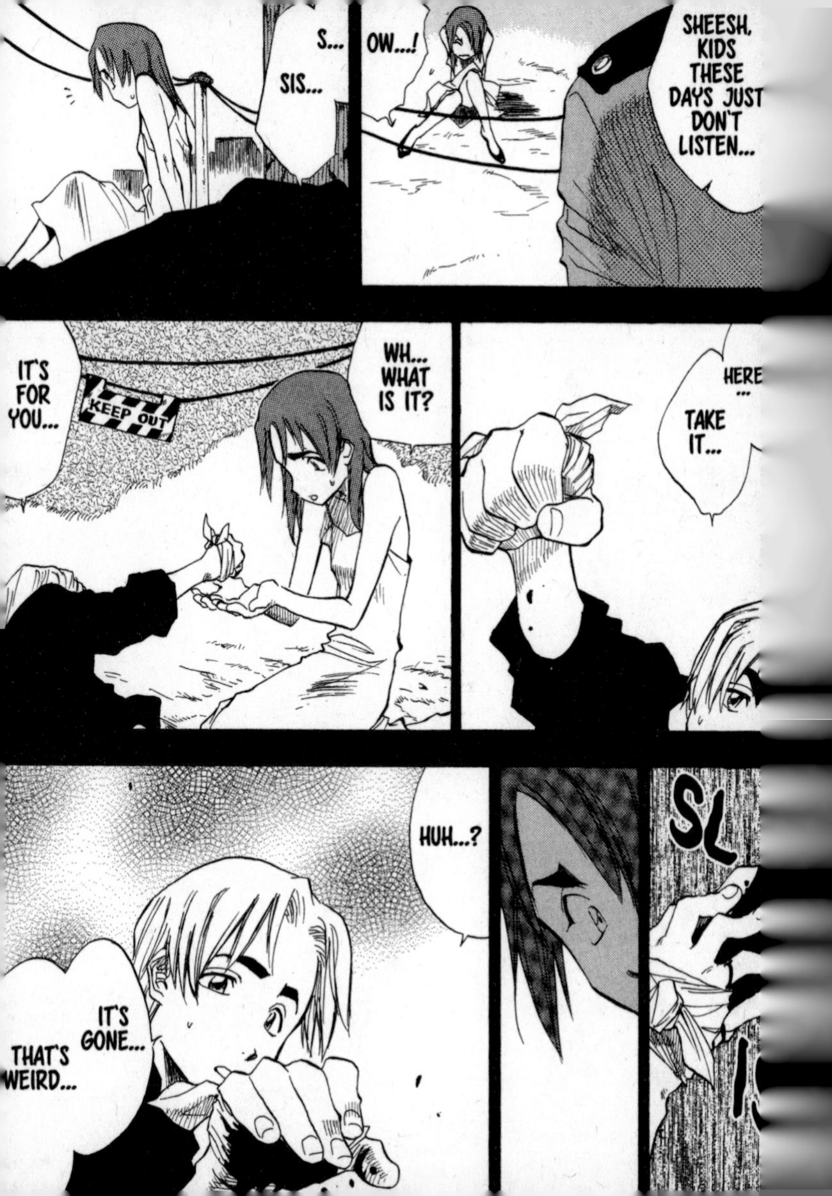
SHEESH, KIDS THESE DAYS JUST DON'T LISTEN...
OW...!
S...
SIS...
HERE... TAKE IT...
WH... WHAT IS IT?
IT'S FOR YOU...
SL
HUH...?
IT'S GONE...
THAT'S WEIRD...

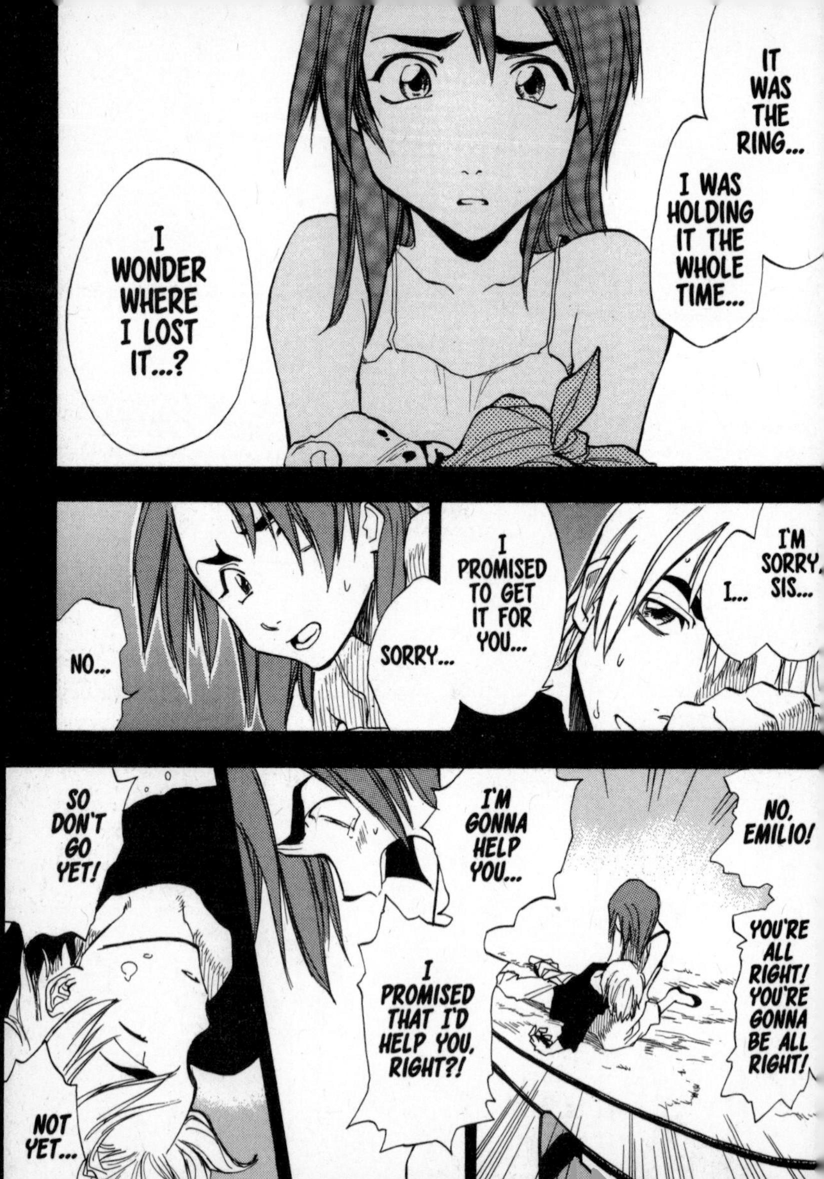
IT WAS THE RING...
I WAS HOLDING IT THE WHOLE TIME...
I WONDER WHERE I LOST IT...?
I'M SORRY, SIS...
I...
I PROMISED TO GET IT FOR YOU...
SORRY...
NO...
NO, EMILIO!
YOU'RE ALL RIGHT! YOU'RE GONNA BE ALL RIGHT!
I'M GONNA HELP YOU...
I PROMISED THAT I'D HELP YOU, RIGHT?!
SO DON'T GO YET!
NOT YET...

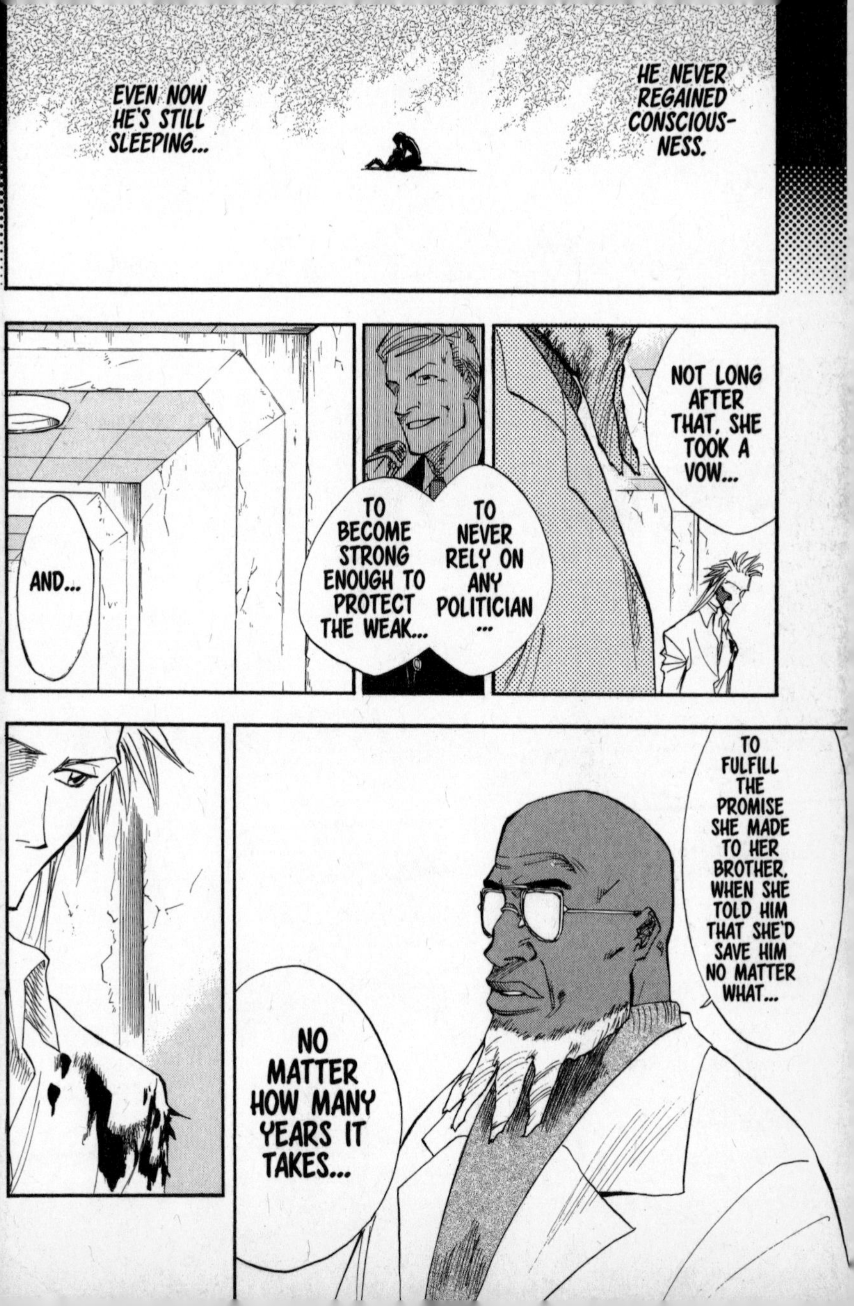
HE NEVER REGAINED CONSCIOUS-NESS.
EVEN NOW HE'S STILL SLEEPING...
NOT LONG AFTER THAT, SHE TOOK A VOW...
TO NEVER RELY ON ANY POLITICIAN...
TO BECOME STRONG ENOUGH TO PROTECT THE WEAK...
AND...
TO FULFILL THE PROMISE SHE MADE TO HER BROTHER, WHEN SHE TOLD HIM THAT SHE'D SAVE HIM NO MATTER WHAT...
NO MATTER HOW MANY YEARS IT TAKES...

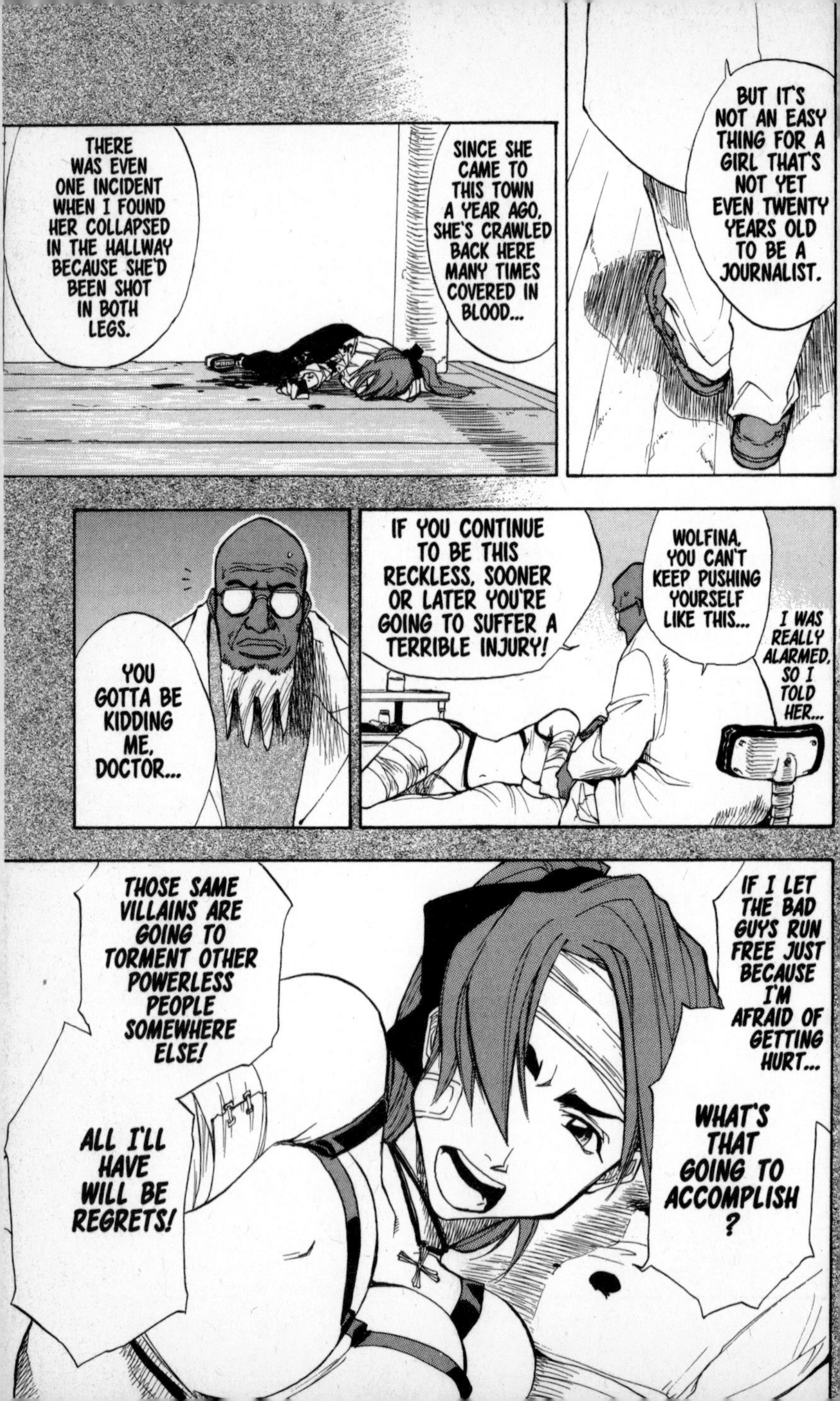
BUT IT'S NOT AN EASY THING FOR A GIRL THAT'S NOT YET EVEN TWENTY YEARS OLD TO BE A JOURNALIST.
SINCE SHE CAME TO THIS TOWN A YEAR AGO, SHE'S CRAWLED BACK HERE MANY TIMES COVERED IN BLOOD...
THERE WAS EVEN ONE INCIDENT WHEN I FOUND HER COLLAPSED IN THE HALLWAY BECAUSE SHE'D BEEN SHOT IN BOTH LEGS.
I WAS REALLY ALARMED, SO I TOLD HER...
WOLFINA, YOU CAN'T KEEP PUSHING YOURSELF LIKE THIS...
IF YOU CONTINUE TO BE THIS RECKLESS, SOONER OR LATER YOU'RE GOING TO SUFFER A TERRIBLE INJURY!
YOU GOTTA BE KIDDING ME, DOCTOR...
IF I LET THE BAD GUYS RUN FREE JUST BECAUSE I'M AFRAID OF GETTING HURT...
WHAT'S THAT GOING TO ACCOMPLISH?
THOSE SAME VILLAINS ARE GOING TO TORMENT OTHER POWERLESS PEOPLE SOMEWHERE ELSE!
ALL I'LL HAVE WILL BE REGRETS!

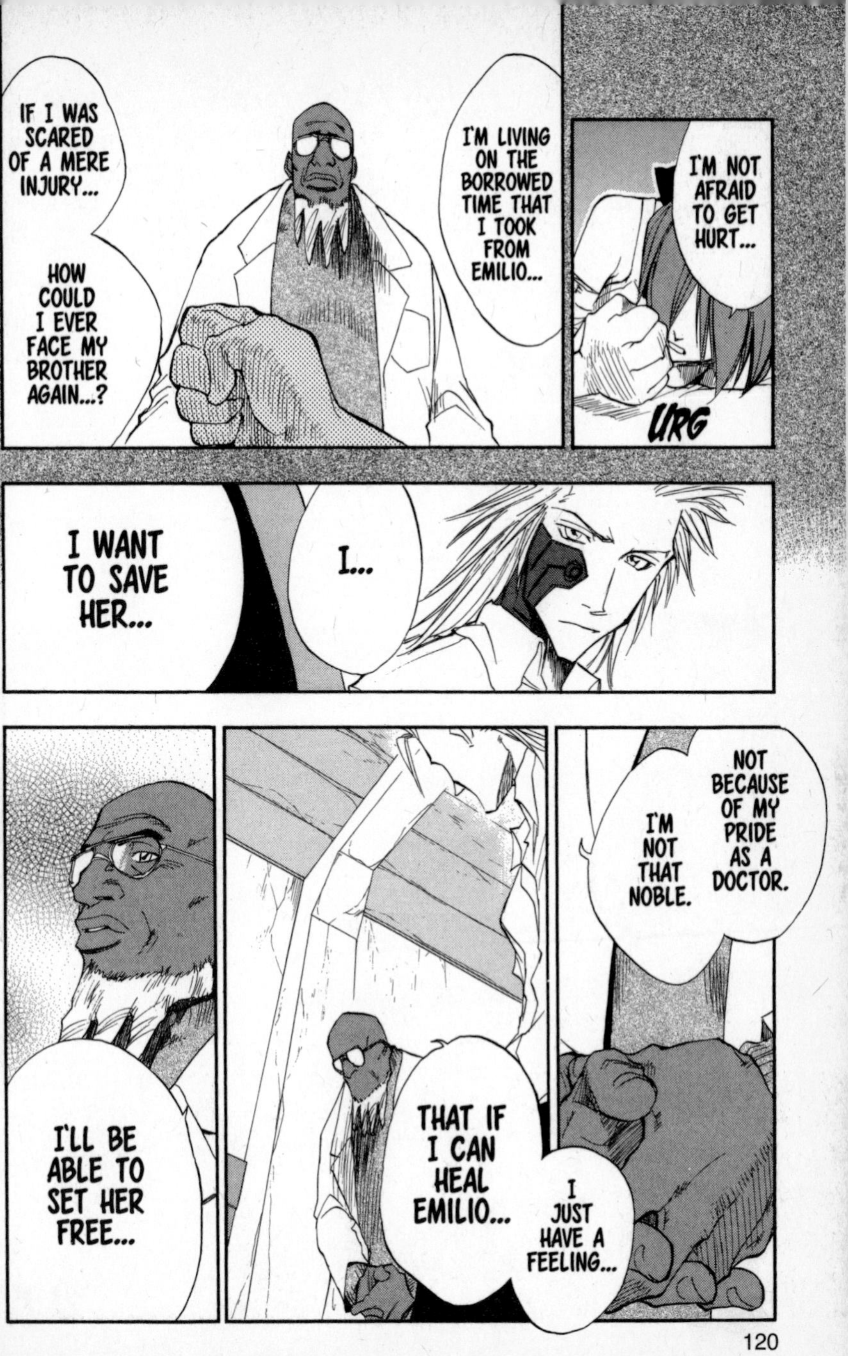
I'M NOT AFRAID TO GET HURT...
URG
I'M LIVING ON THE BORROWED TIME THAT I TOOK FROM EMILIO...
IF I WAS SCARED OF A MERE INJURY...
HOW COULD I EVER FACE MY BROTHER AGAIN...?
I...
I WANT TO SAVE HER...
NOT BECAUSE OF MY PRIDE AS A DOCTOR.
I'M NOT THAT NOBLE.
I JUST HAVE A FEELING...
THAT IF I CAN HEAL EMILIO...
I'LL BE ABLE TO SET HER FREE...

FROM THE PRISON OF LIVING ONLY FOR HER YOUNGER BROTHER'S SAKE...

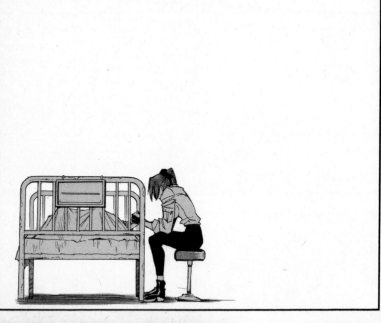

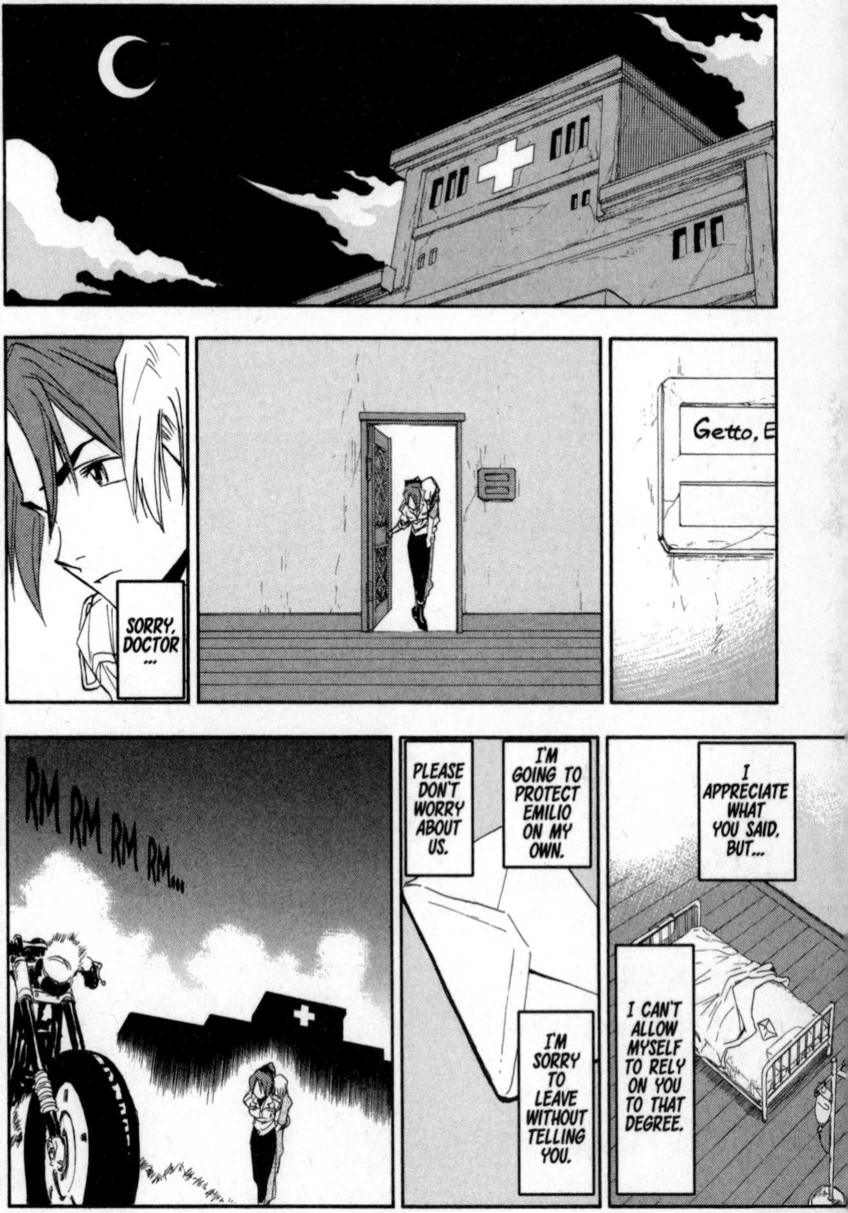
Getto, E
SORRY, DOCTOR ...
I APPRECIATE WHAT YOU SAID, BUT...
I CAN'T ALLOW MYSELF TO RELY ON YOU TO THAT DEGREE.
I'M GOING TO PROTECT EMILIO ON MY OWN.
PLEASE DON'T WORRY ABOUT US.
I'M SORRY TO LEAVE WITHOUT TELLING YOU.
RM RM RM RM...

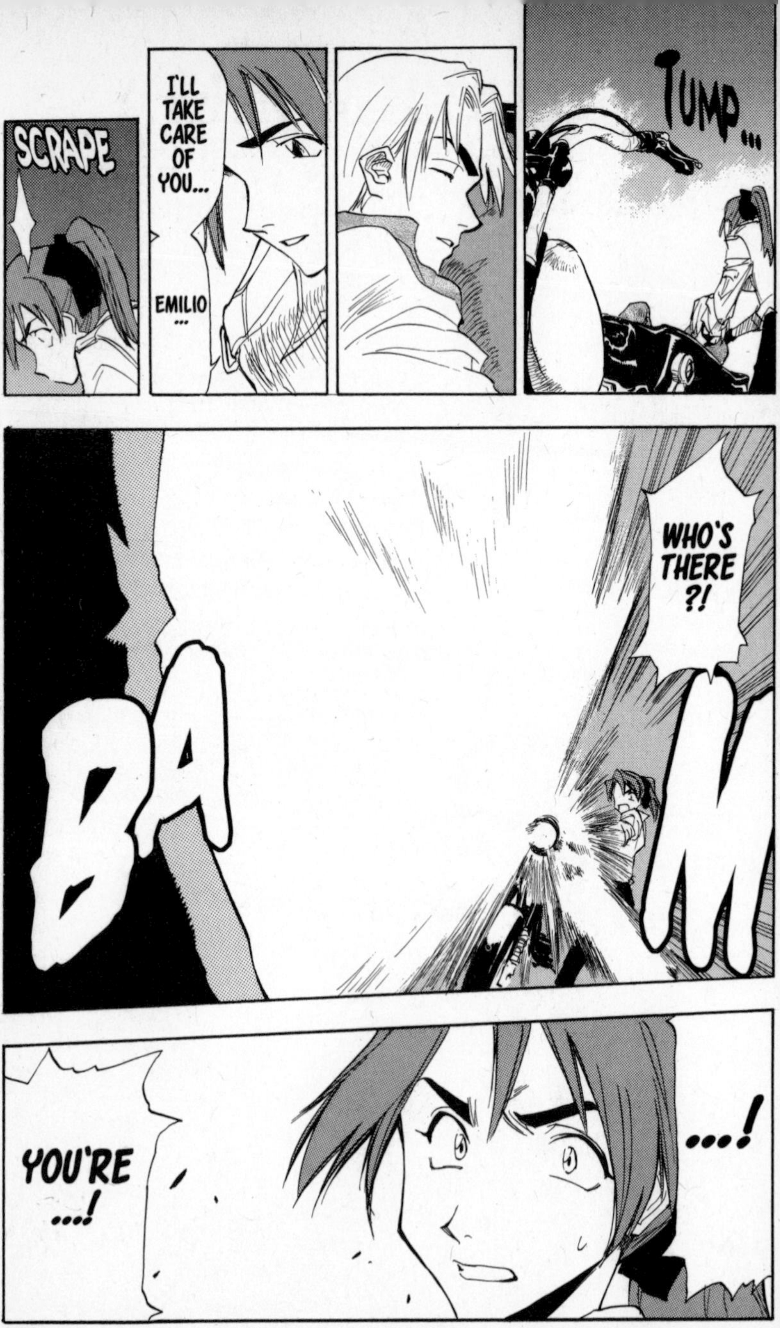
TUMP...
I'LL TAKE CARE OF YOU...
EMILIO...
SCRAPE
WHO'S THERE?!
BAM
...!
YOU'RE ...!

# B-side NAKED MONKEYS 8.

## Baragne Binoix Bartoreuil Balmunk
### バラーニュ・ビノワ・バルトルイユ・バルムンク

Height: 186 cm.
Weight: Unknown
Date of Birth: Unknown
Age: Unknown
Blood Type: Unknown
Hometown: Unknown

A psychopathic, mustachioed magician who goes by the title of "Mystic." Balmunk is a lover of leisure, who travels the world with a strange circus troupe. His favorite phrase is "Khorosho" (good), a Russian word, but for some reason everything else he says is in French. The spelling of his name is also reminiscent of French. Balmunk loves anything that's shocking. He hates anything that's not shocking. He loves to deal out punishment when the members of his troupe make a mistake. Although he subjects them to unimaginable torture, for some reason the troupe members seem to admire him. His hobby is collecting music boxes.

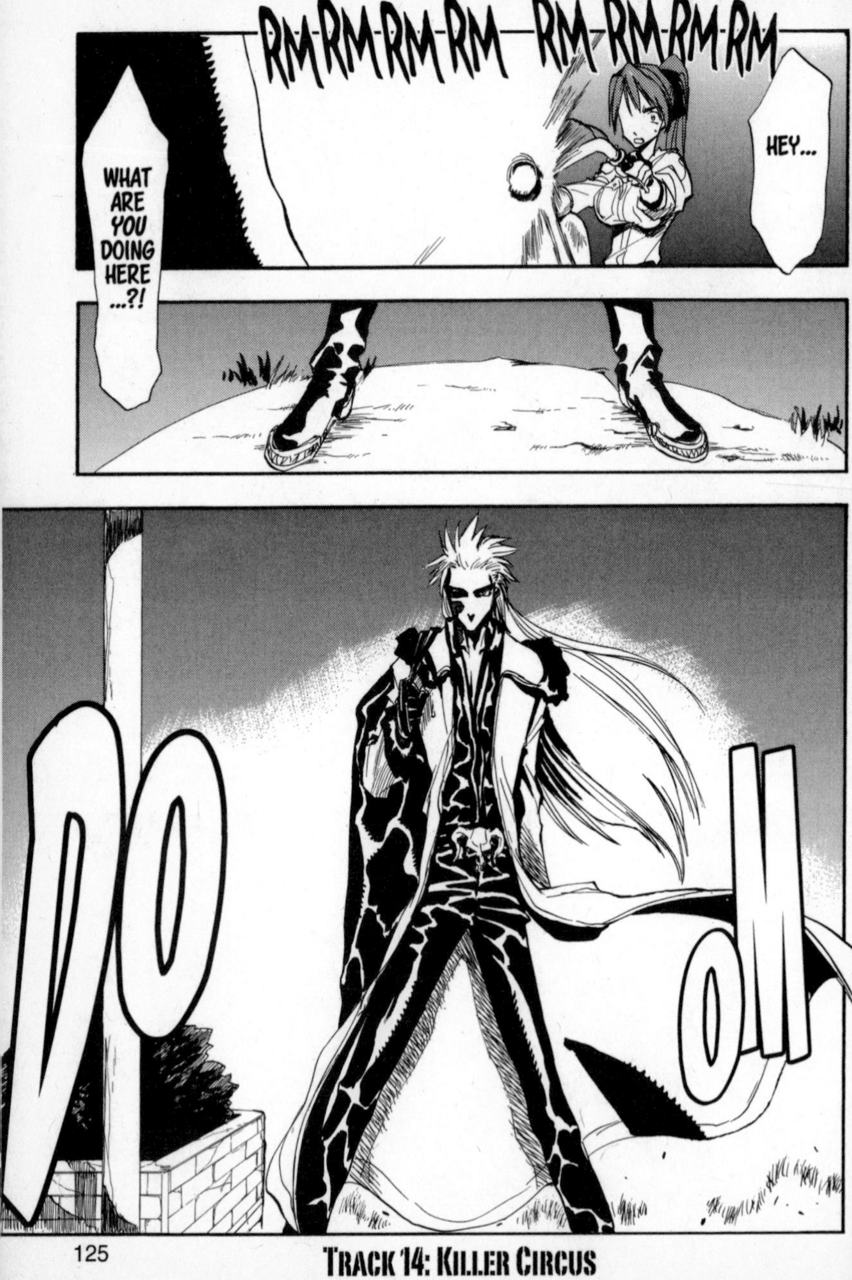
RM-RM-RM-RM RM-RM-RM-RM
HEY...
WHAT ARE YOU DOING HERE ...?!
DOOM



## Track 14: Killer Circus

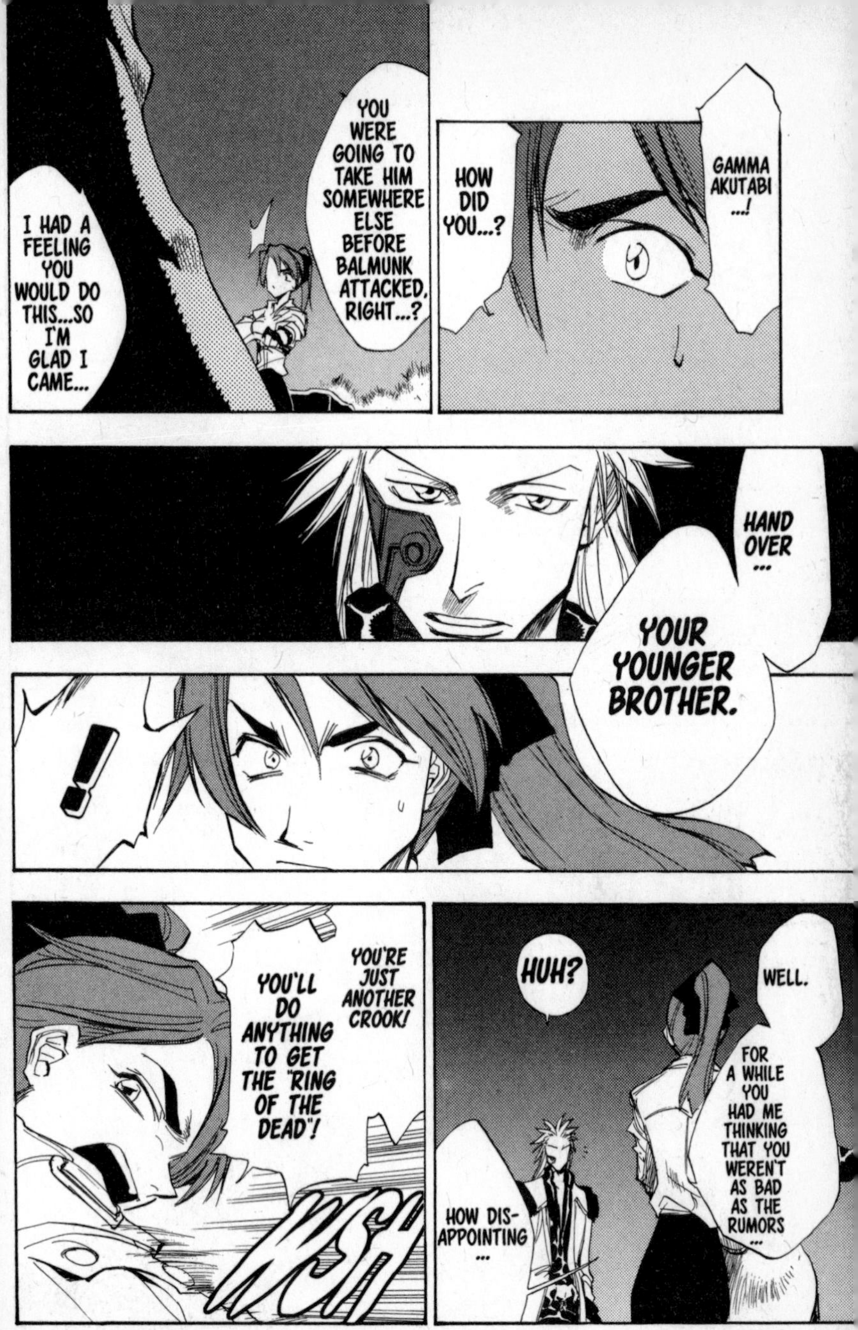
GAMMA AKUTABI ...!
HOW DID YOU...?
YOU WERE GOING TO TAKE HIM SOMEWHERE ELSE BEFORE BALMUNK ATTACKED, RIGHT...?
I HAD A FEELING YOU WOULD DO THIS...SO I'M GLAD I CAME...
HAND OVER ...
YOUR YOUNGER BROTHER.
!
WELL.
FOR A WHILE YOU HAD ME THINKING THAT YOU WEREN'T AS BAD AS THE RUMORS ...
HUH?
HOW DIS-APPOINTING ...
YOU'RE JUST ANOTHER CROOK!
YOU'LL DO ANYTHING TO GET THE "RING OF THE DEAD"!

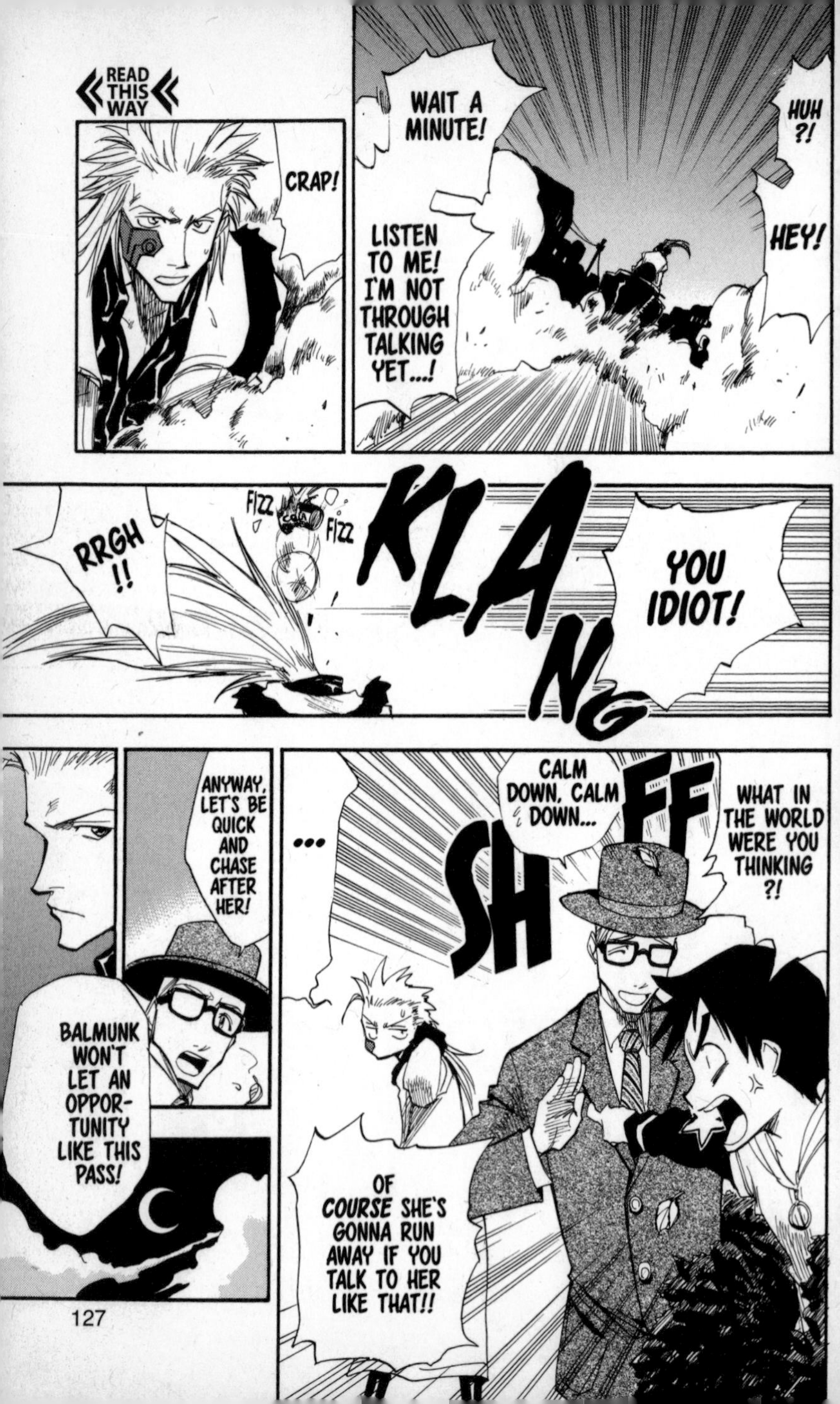
READ THIS WAY
HUH ?!
WAIT A MINUTE!
HEY!
LISTEN TO ME! I'M NOT THROUGH TALKING YET...!
CRAP!
YOU IDIOT!
KLANG
FIZZ
FIZZ
RRGH !!
WHAT IN THE WORLD WERE YOU THINKING ?!
CALM DOWN, CALM DOWN...
SHFF
...
OF COURSE SHE'S GONNA RUN AWAY IF YOU TALK TO HER LIKE THAT!!
ANYWAY, LET'S BE QUICK AND CHASE AFTER HER!
BALMUNK WON'T LET AN OPPOR-TUNITY LIKE THIS PASS!

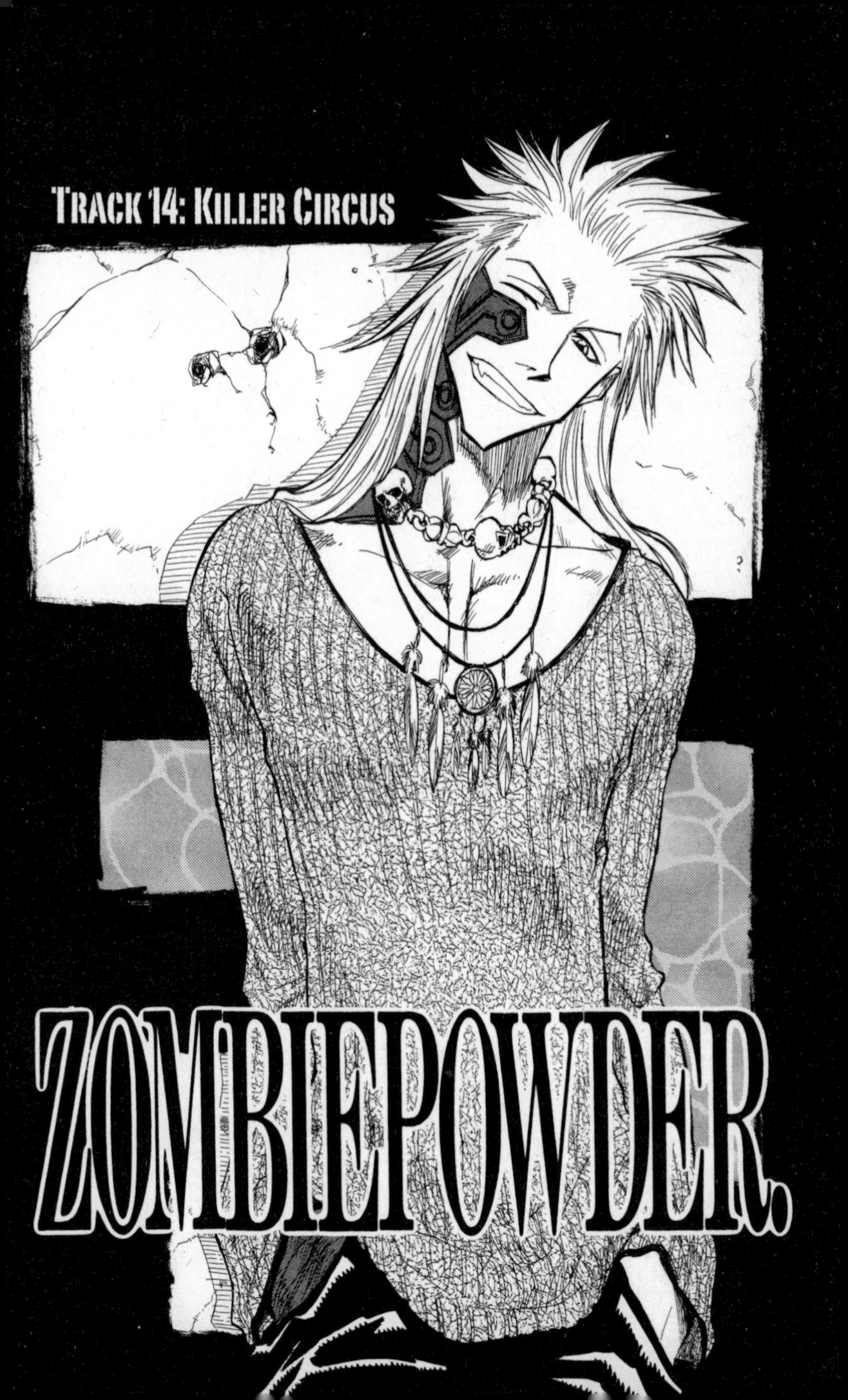
TRACK 14: KILLER CIRCUS
ZOMBIEPOWDER.

READ THIS WAY

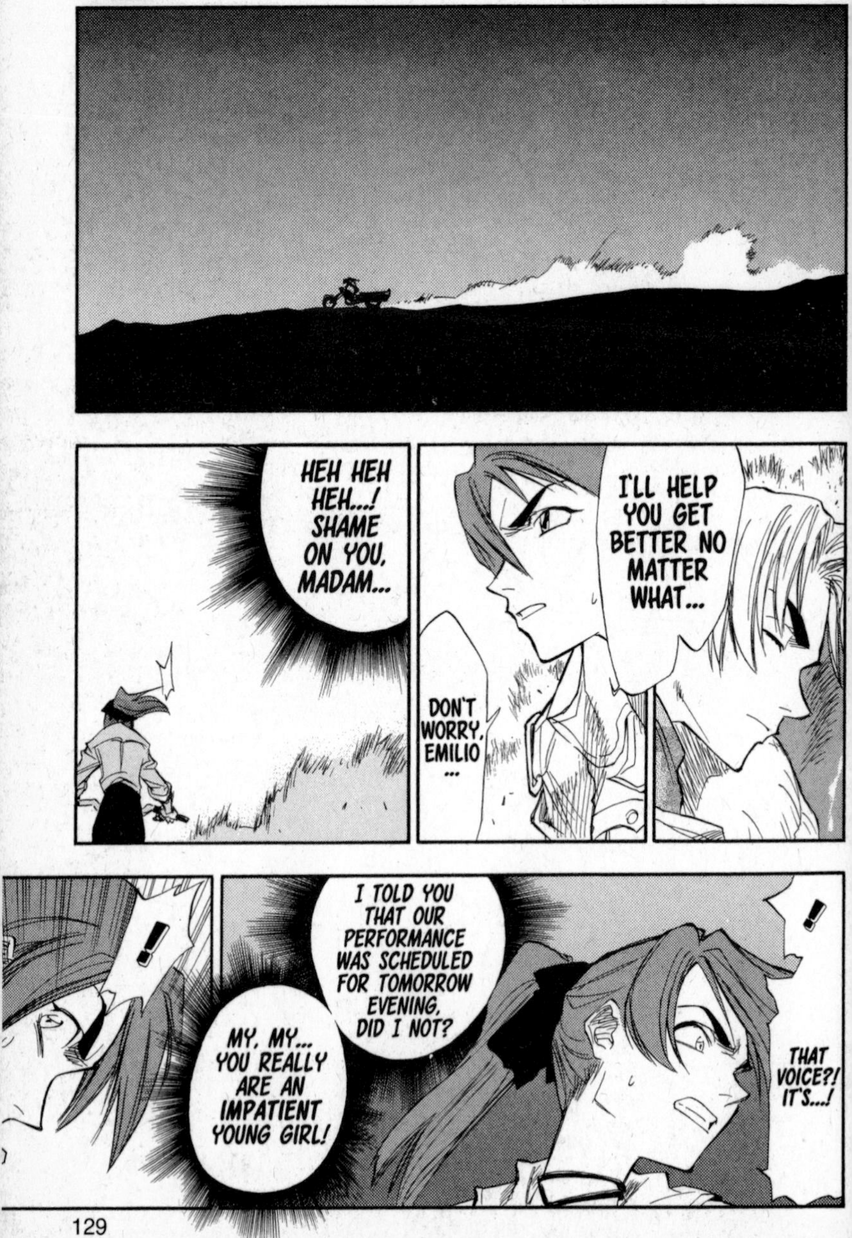

I'LL HELP YOU GET BETTER NO MATTER WHAT...
DON'T WORRY, EMILIO ...
HEH HEH HEH...! SHAME ON YOU, MADAM...
!
THAT VOICE?! IT'S...!
I TOLD YOU THAT OUR PERFORMANCE WAS SCHEDULED FOR TOMORROW EVENING, DID I NOT?
MY, MY... YOU REALLY ARE AN IMPATIENT YOUNG GIRL!
!

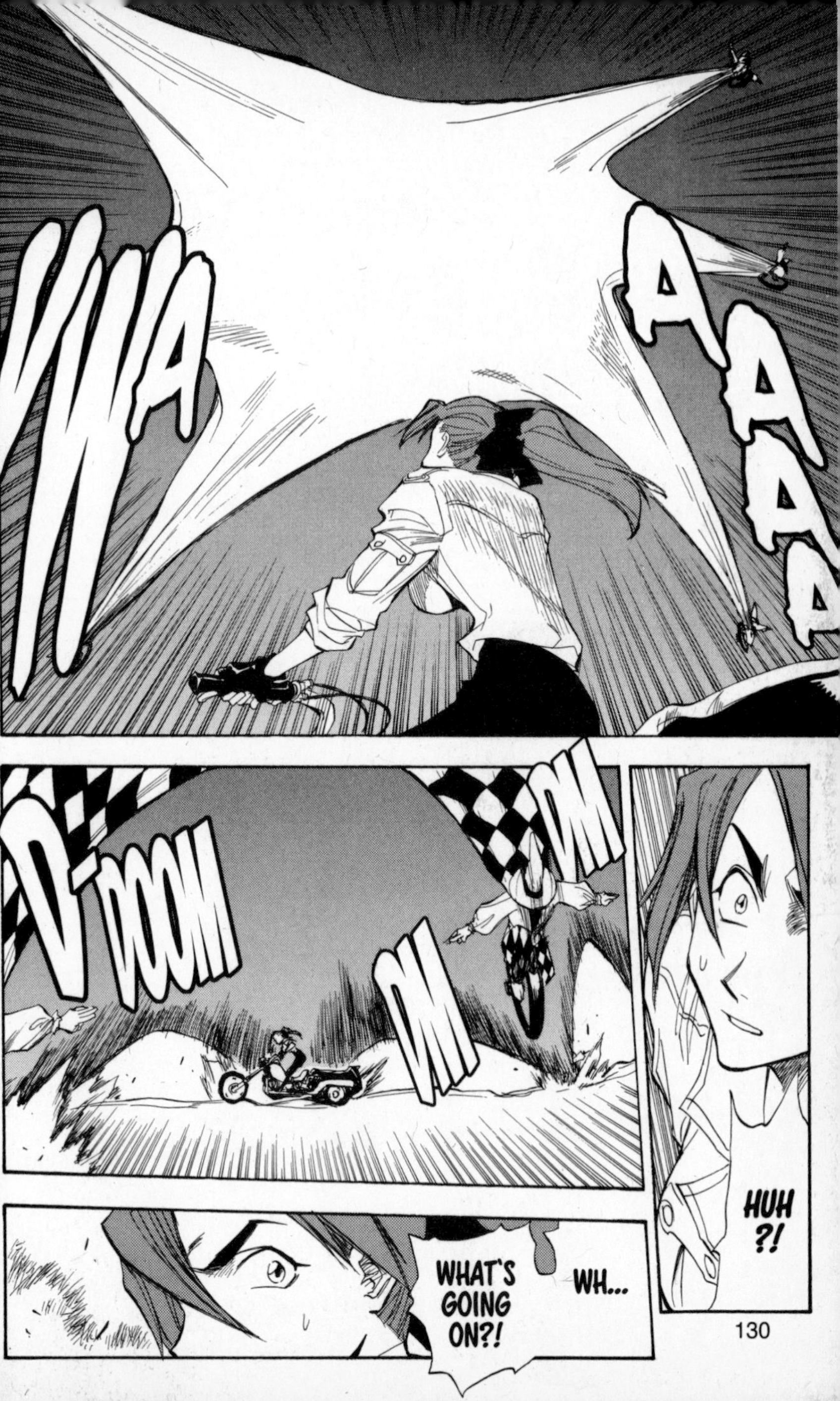
WHAAAAA
HUH ?!
D-DOOM
OM
OM
WH...
WHAT'S GOING ON?!

READ THIS WAY

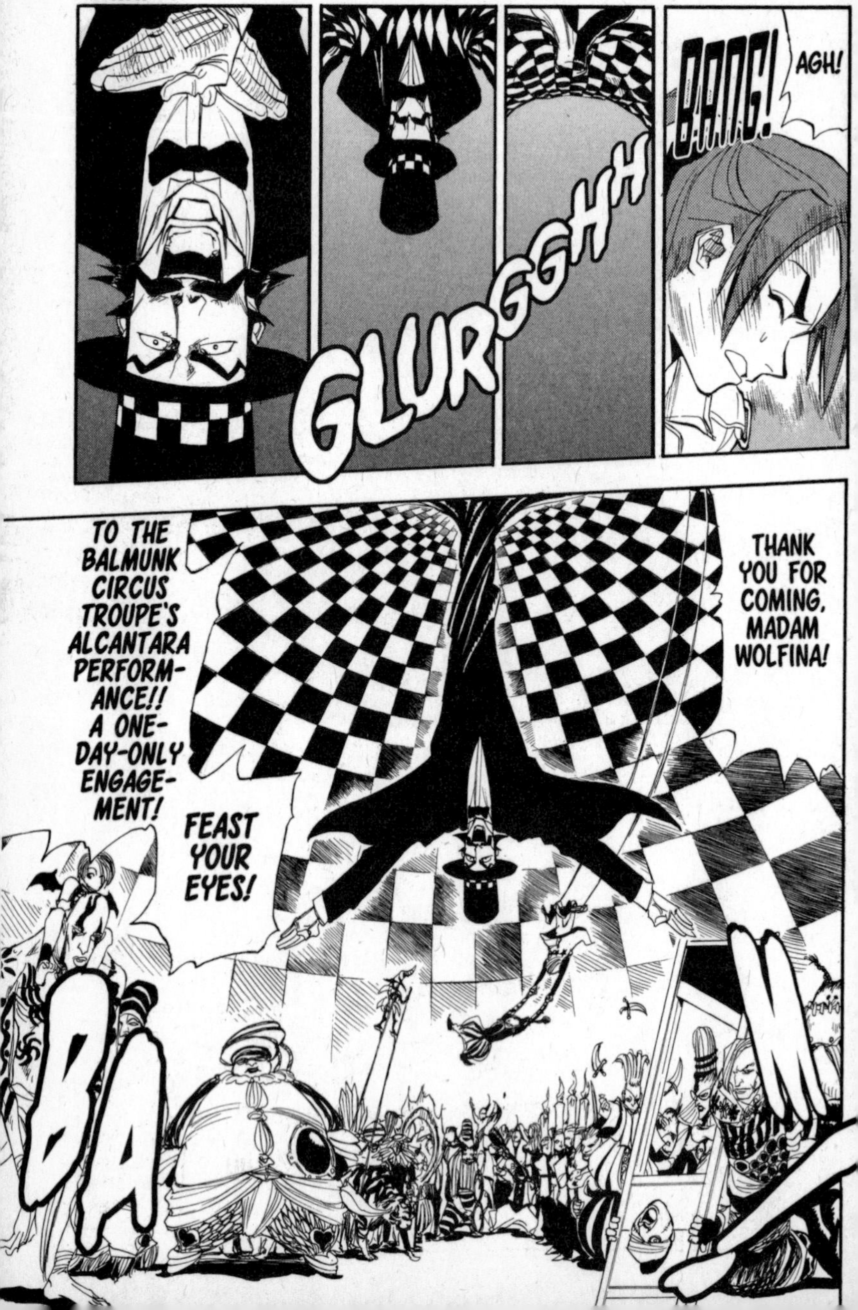
AGH!
BANG!
GLURGGHH
THANK YOU FOR COMING, MADAM WOLFINA!
TO THE BALMUNK CIRCUS TROUPE'S ALCANTARA PERFORMANCE!! A ONE-DAY-ONLY ENGAGEMENT!
FEAST YOUR EYES!
BAM

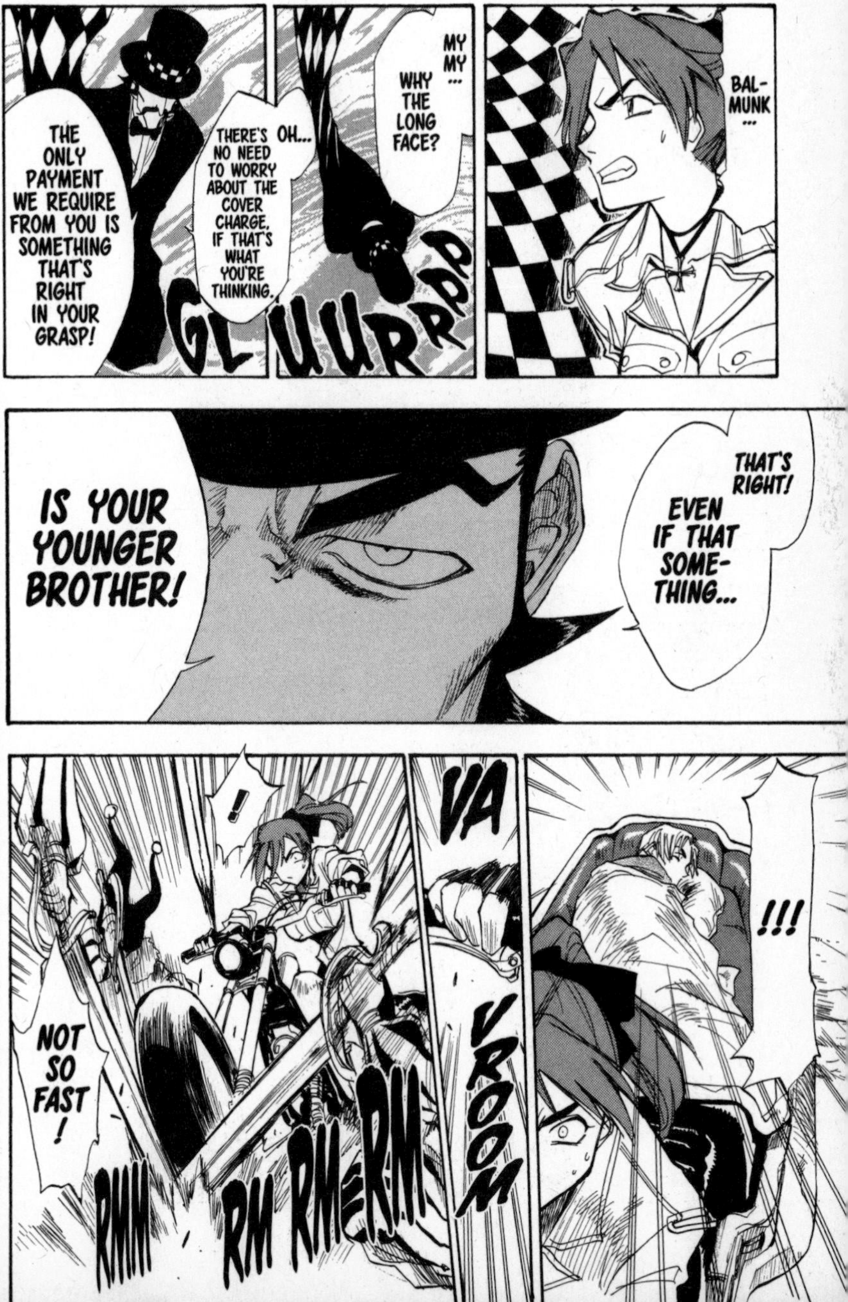
BAL-MUNK...
MY MY... WHY THE LONG FACE?
OH...
THERE'S NO NEED TO WORRY ABOUT THE COVER CHARGE, IF THAT'S WHAT YOU'RE THINKING.
GLUURRPP
THE ONLY PAYMENT WE REQUIRE FROM YOU IS SOMETHING THAT'S RIGHT IN YOUR GRASP!
THAT'S RIGHT!
EVEN IF THAT SOME-THING...
IS YOUR YOUNGER BROTHER!
!!!
VA
VROOM
!
NOT SO FAST!
RMM RM RM RM

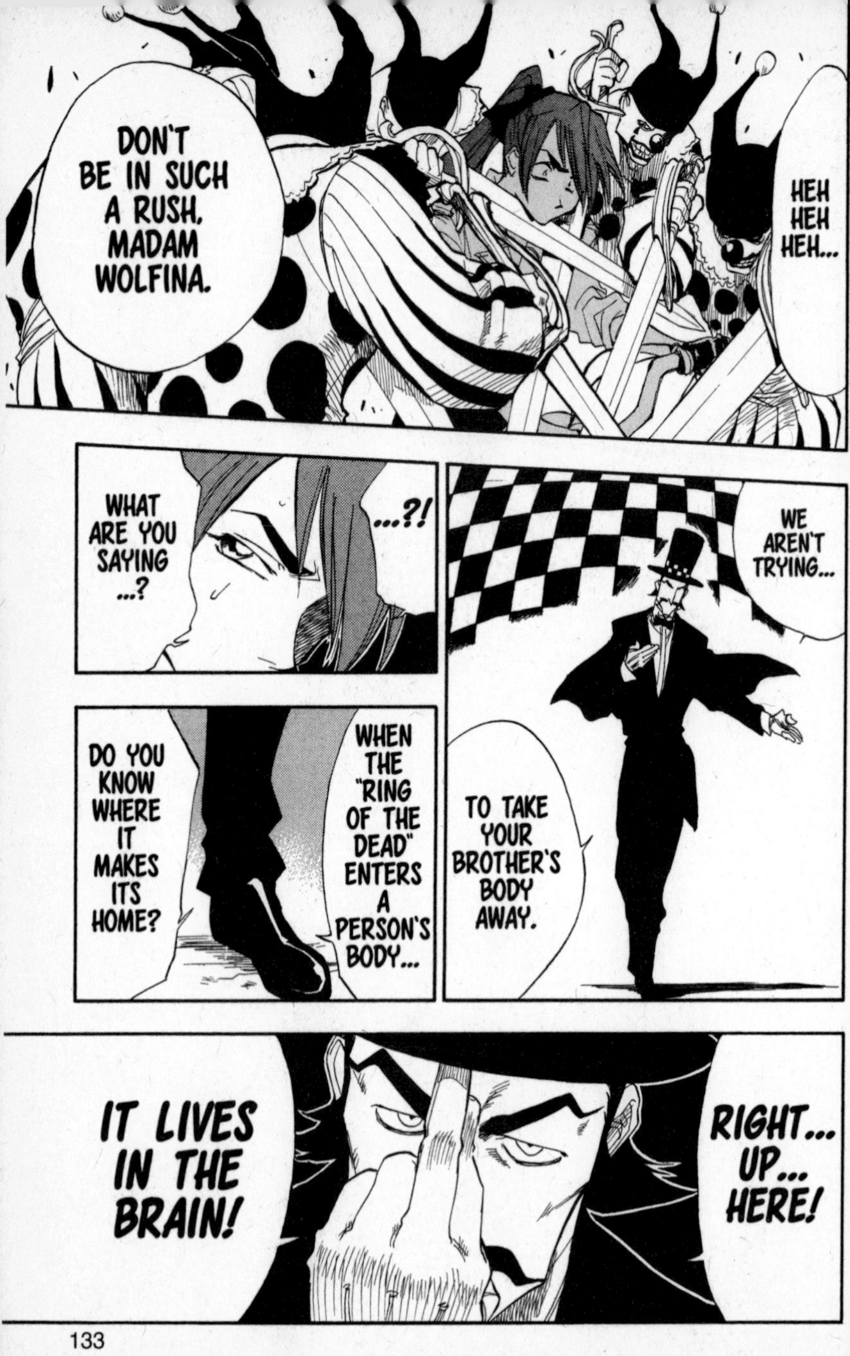
HEH HEH HEH...
DON'T BE IN SUCH A RUSH, MADAM WOLFINA.
WE AREN'T TRYING...
TO TAKE YOUR BROTHER'S BODY AWAY.
...?!
WHAT ARE YOU SAYING ...?
WHEN THE "RING OF THE DEAD" ENTERS A PERSON'S BODY...
DO YOU KNOW WHERE IT MAKES ITS HOME?
RIGHT... UP... HERE!
IT LIVES IN THE BRAIN!

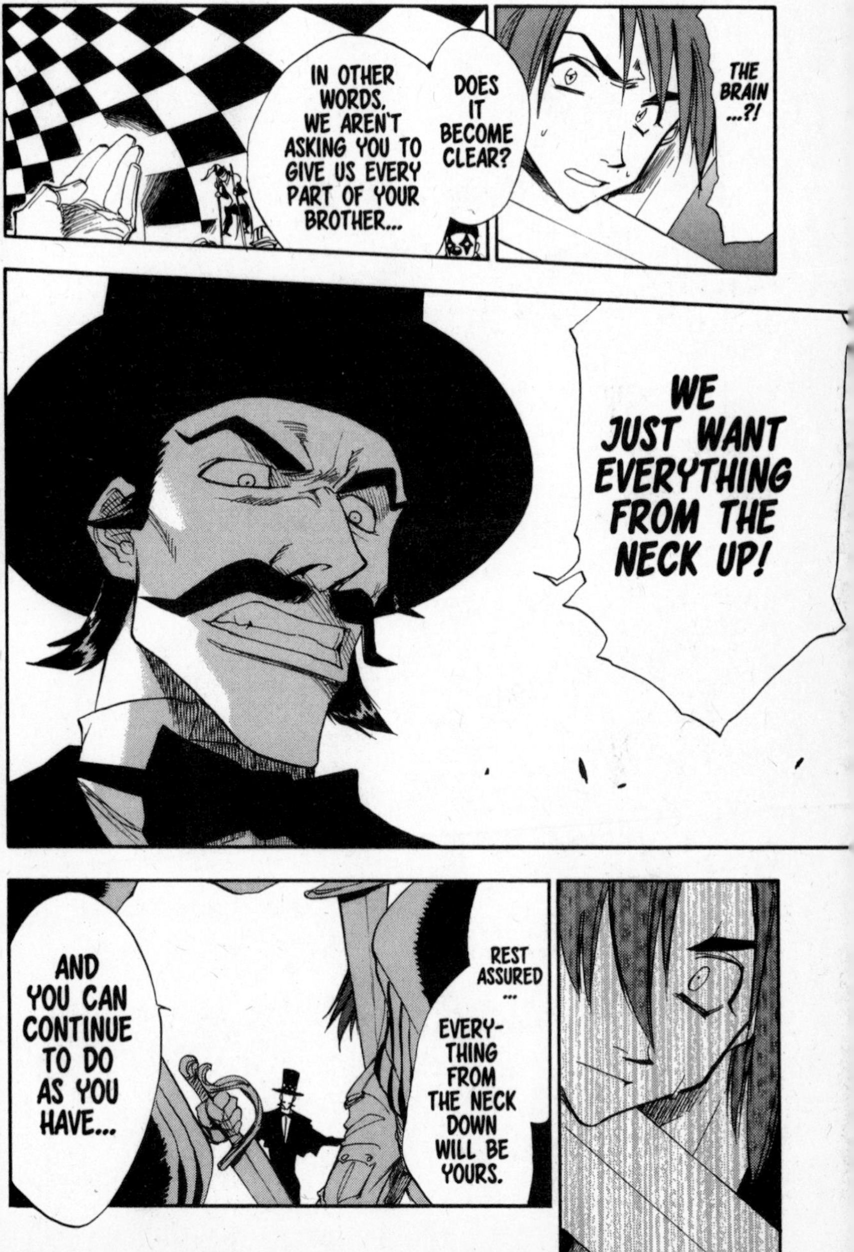
THE BRAIN ...?!
DOES IT BECOME CLEAR?
IN OTHER WORDS, WE AREN'T ASKING YOU TO GIVE US EVERY PART OF YOUR BROTHER...
WE JUST WANT EVERYTHING FROM THE NECK UP!
REST ASSURED ...
EVERY-THING FROM THE NECK DOWN WILL BE YOURS.
AND YOU CAN CONTINUE TO DO AS YOU HAVE...

READ THIS WAY

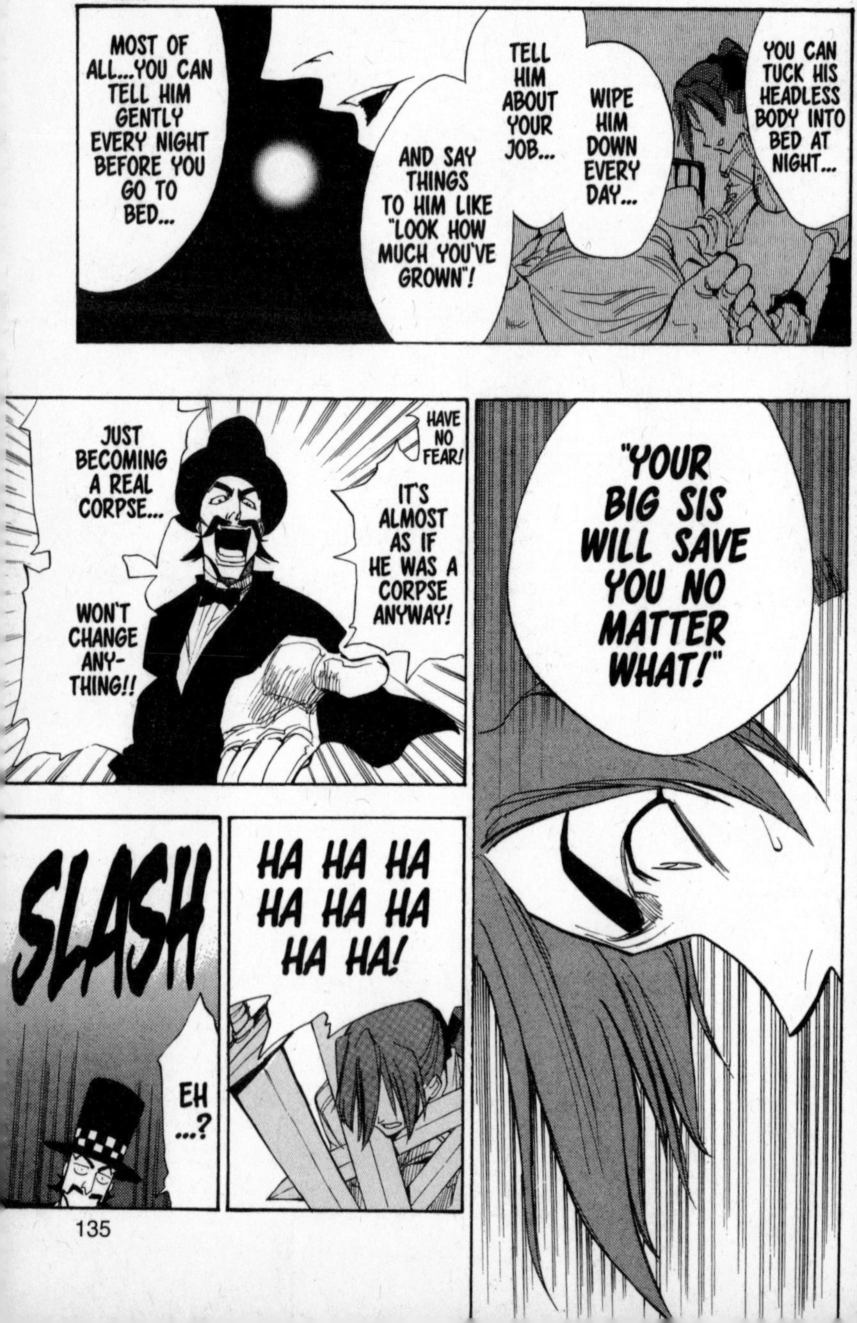

YOU CAN TUCK HIS HEADLESS BODY INTO BED AT NIGHT...
WIPE HIM DOWN EVERY DAY...
TELL HIM ABOUT YOUR JOB...
AND SAY THINGS TO HIM LIKE "LOOK HOW MUCH YOU'VE GROWN"!
MOST OF ALL...YOU CAN TELL HIM GENTLY EVERY NIGHT BEFORE YOU GO TO BED...
"YOUR BIG SIS WILL SAVE YOU NO MATTER WHAT!"
HAVE NO FEAR!
IT'S ALMOST AS IF HE WAS A CORPSE ANYWAY!
JUST BECOMING A REAL CORPSE...
WON'T CHANGE ANY-THING!!
HA HA HA HA HA HA HA HA!
SLASH
EH ...?

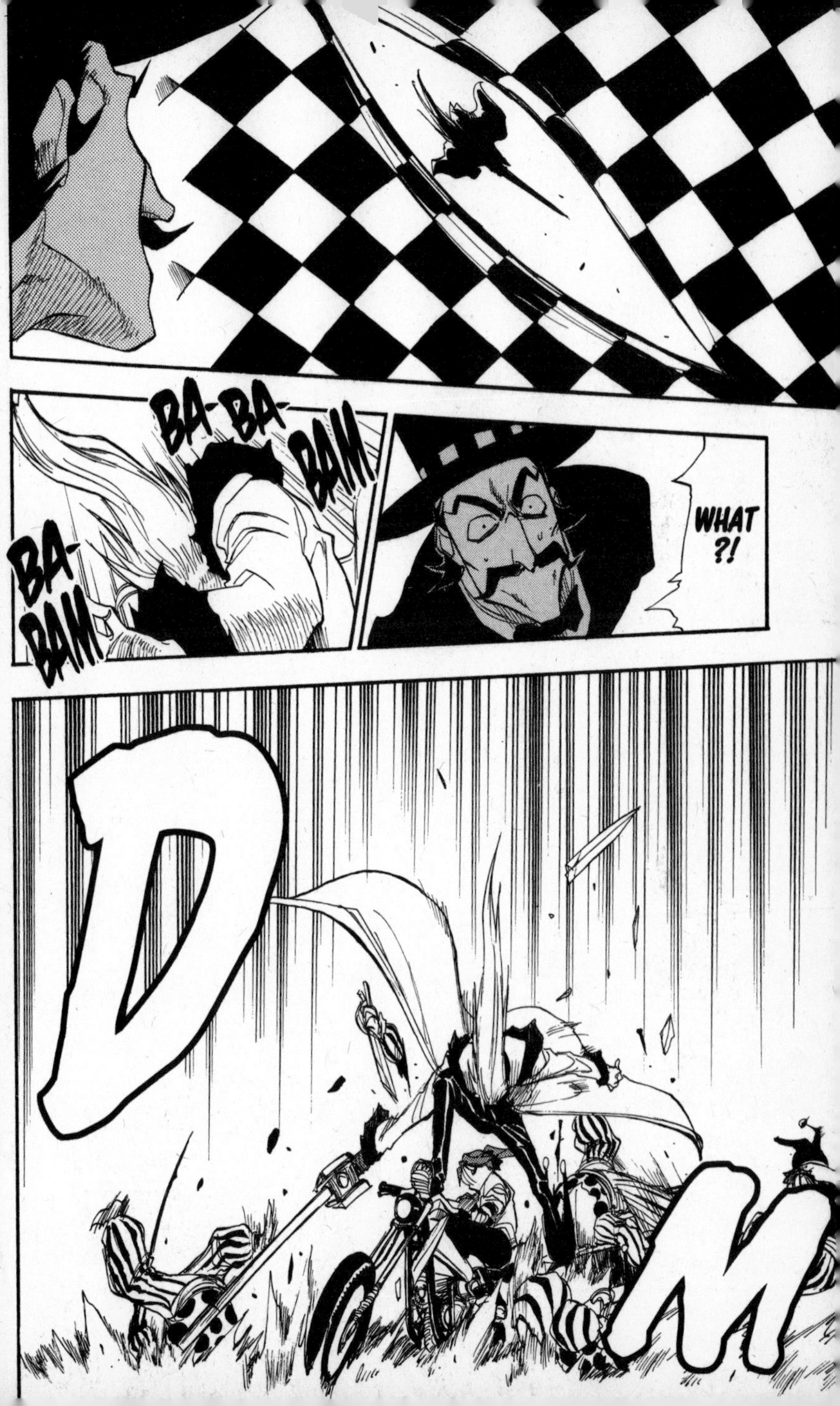
WHAT ?!
BA-BA-BAM
BA-BAM
D M

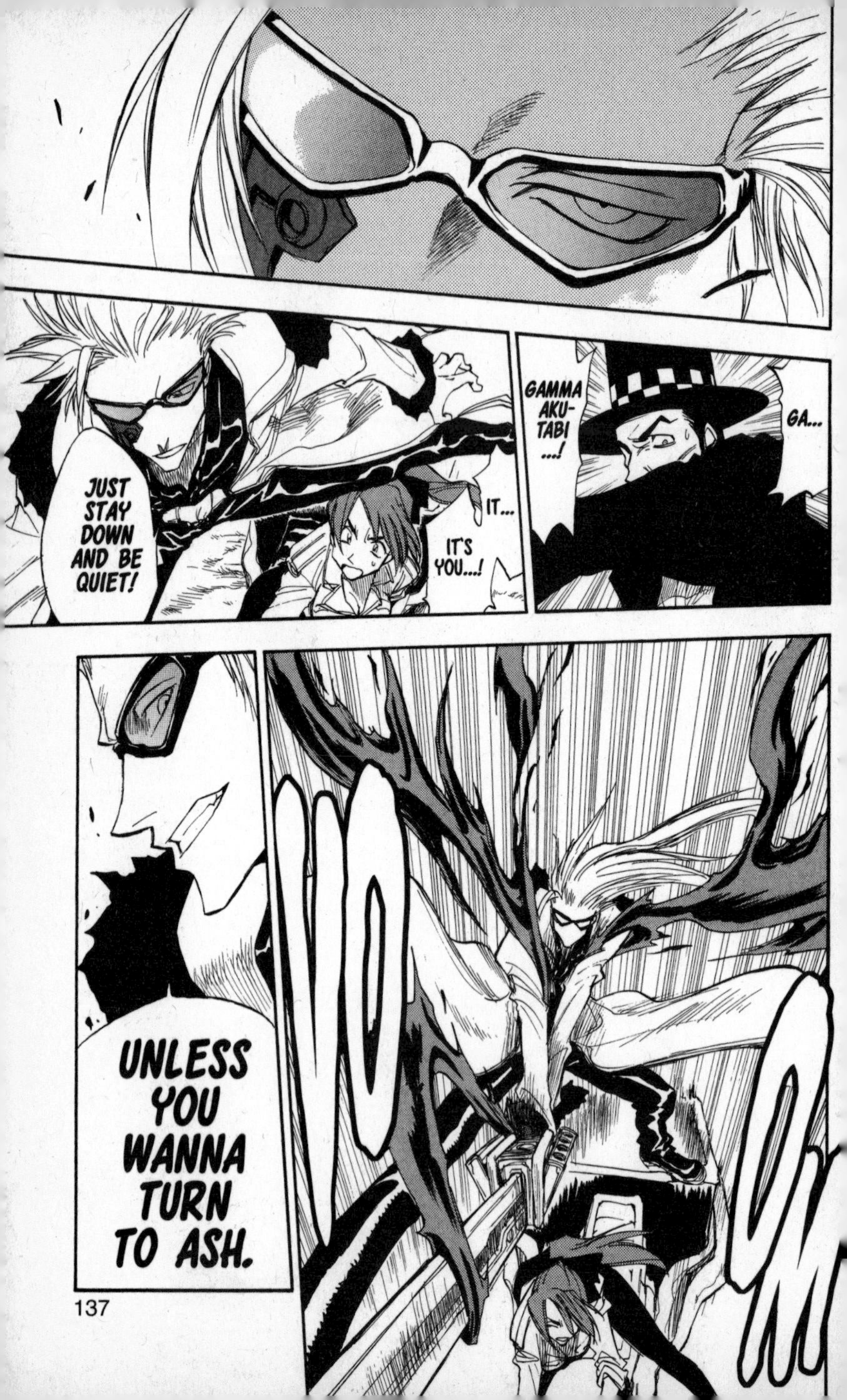
GA...
GAMMA AKUTABI ...!
IT...
IT'S YOU...!
JUST STAY DOWN AND BE QUIET!
UNLESS YOU WANNA TURN TO ASH.

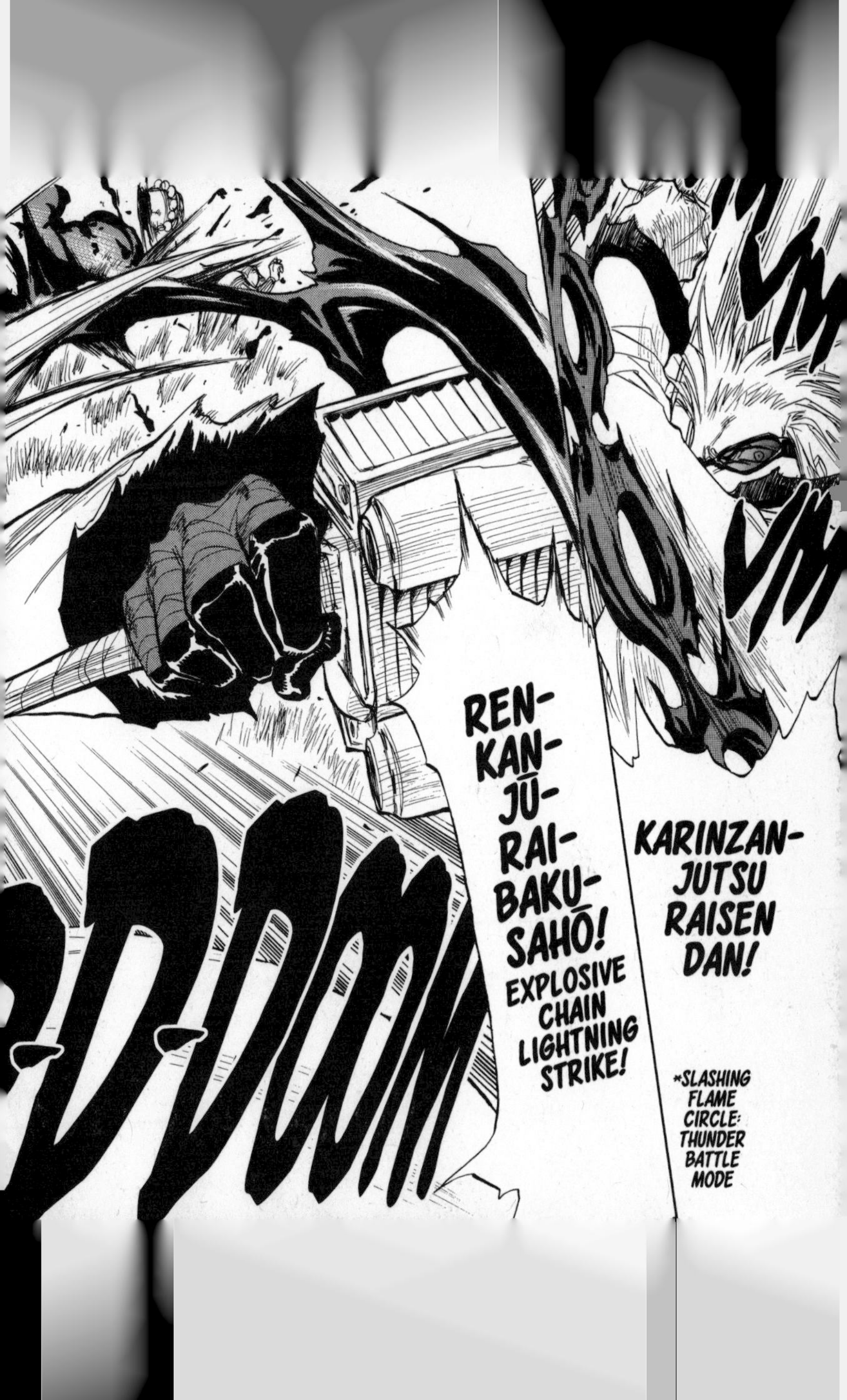
KARINZAN-JUTSU RAISEN DAN!
*SLASHING FLAME CIRCLE: THUNDER BATTLE MODE
REN-KAN-JŪ-RAI-BAKU-SAHŌ!
EXPLOSIVE CHAIN LIGHTNING STRIKE!

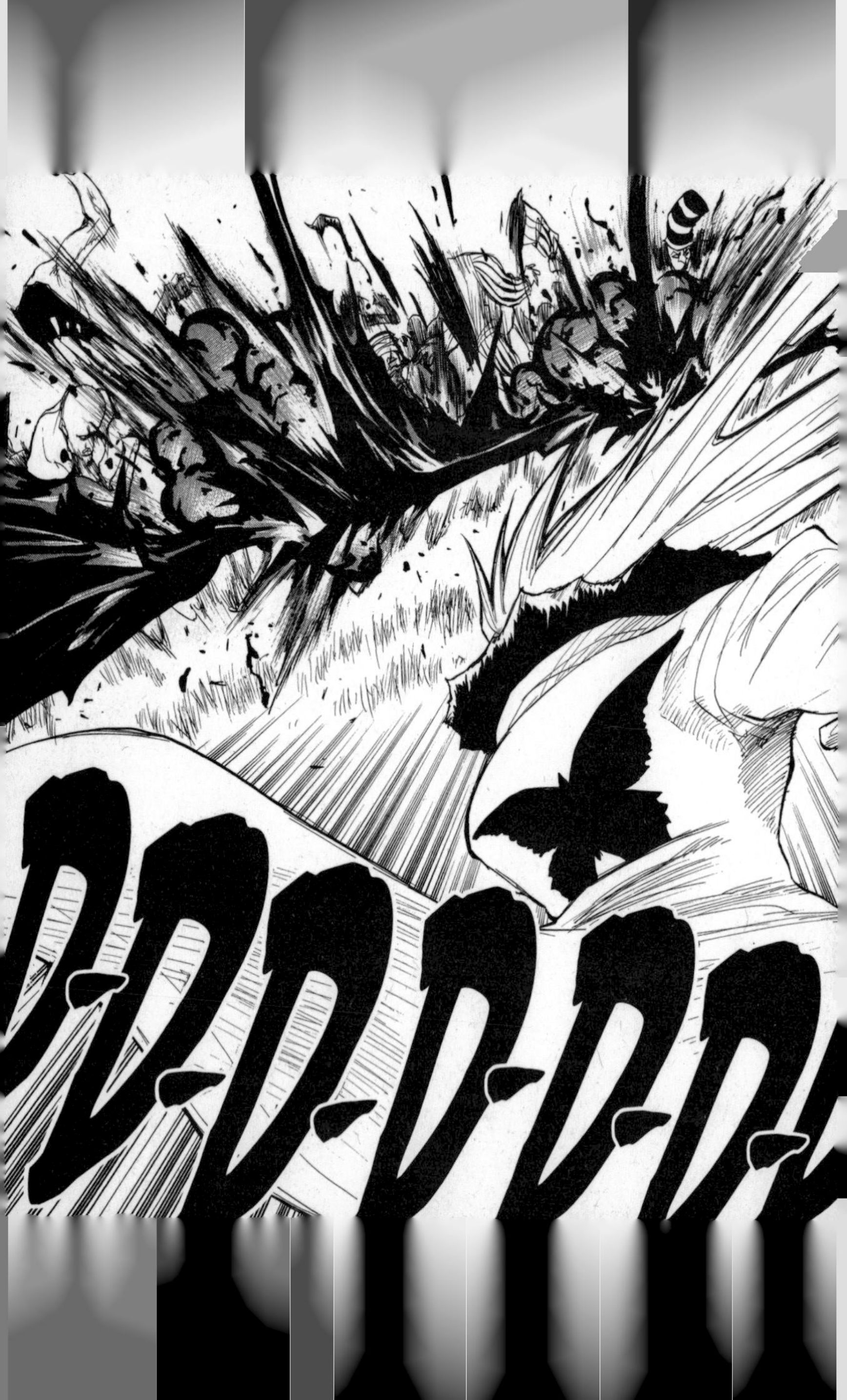

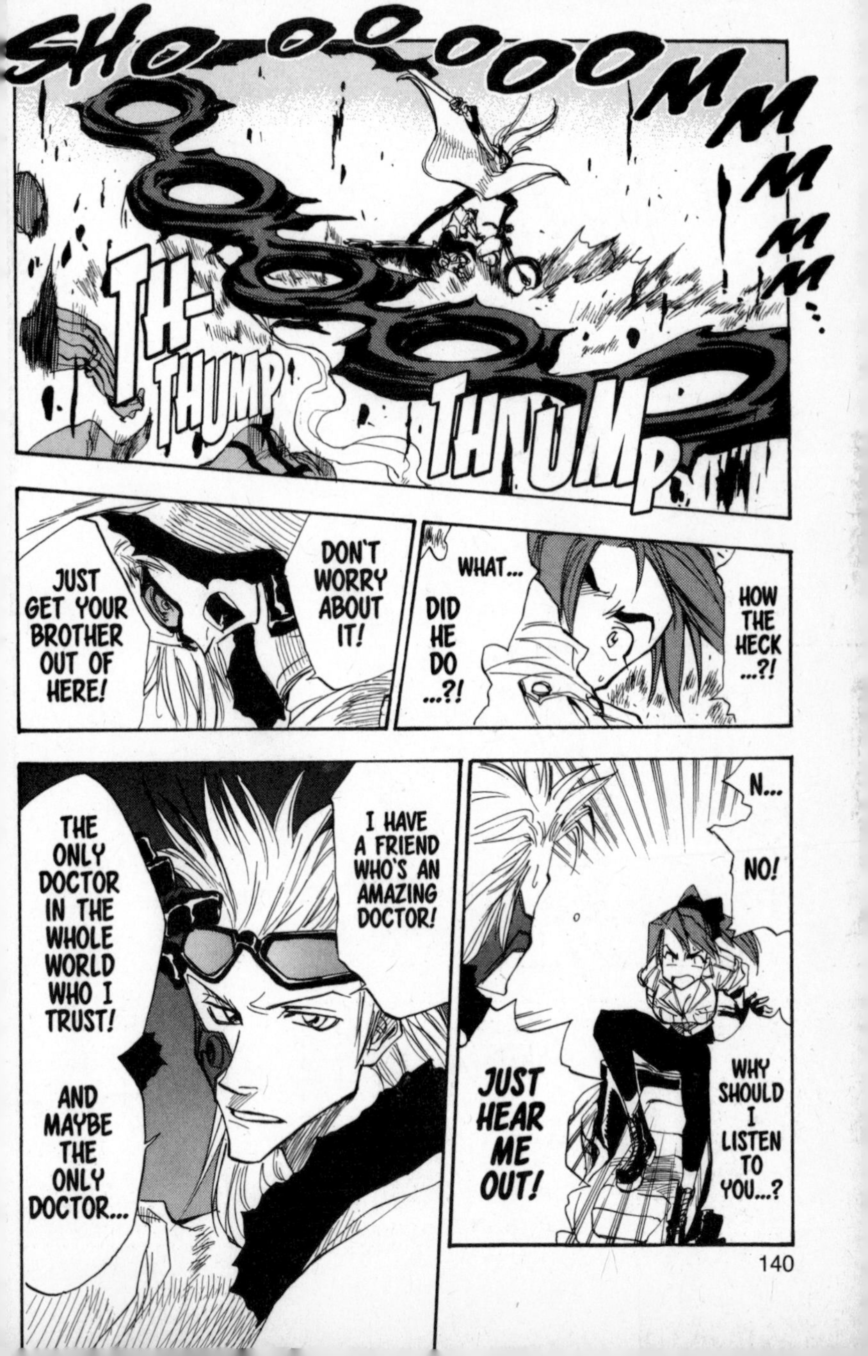
SHO-O-O-OOOOMMMMMMM
THUMP
TH-THUMP
HOW THE HECK ...?!
WHAT...
DID HE DO ...?!
DON'T WORRY ABOUT IT!
JUST GET YOUR BROTHER OUT OF HERE!
N...
NO!
WHY SHOULD I LISTEN TO YOU...?
JUST HEAR ME OUT!
I HAVE A FRIEND WHO'S AN AMAZING DOCTOR!
THE ONLY DOCTOR IN THE WHOLE WORLD WHO I TRUST!
AND MAYBE THE ONLY DOCTOR...

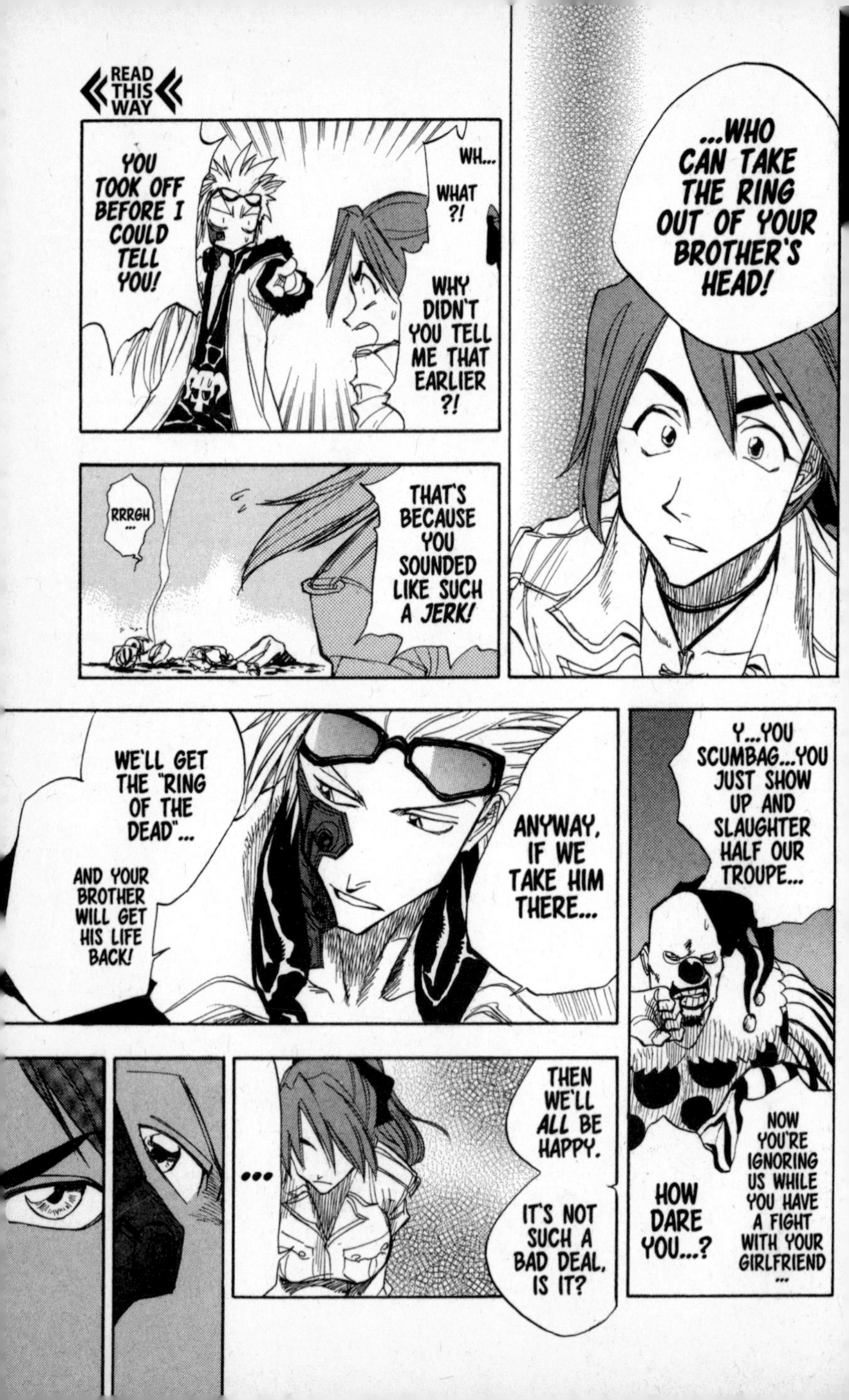
READ THIS WAY
...WHO CAN TAKE THE RING OUT OF YOUR BROTHER'S HEAD!
WH...
WHAT ?!
WHY DIDN'T YOU TELL ME THAT EARLIER ?!
YOU TOOK OFF BEFORE I COULD TELL YOU!
THAT'S BECAUSE YOU SOUNDED LIKE SUCH A *JERK!*
RRRGH ...
Y...YOU SCUMBAG...YOU JUST SHOW UP AND SLAUGHTER HALF OUR TROUPE...
NOW YOU'RE IGNORING US WHILE YOU HAVE A FIGHT WITH YOUR GIRLFRIEND ...
HOW DARE YOU...?
ANYWAY, IF WE TAKE HIM THERE...
WE'LL GET THE "RING OF THE DEAD"...
AND YOUR BROTHER WILL GET HIS LIFE BACK!
THEN WE'LL *ALL* BE HAPPY.
IT'S NOT SUCH A BAD DEAL, IS IT?
...

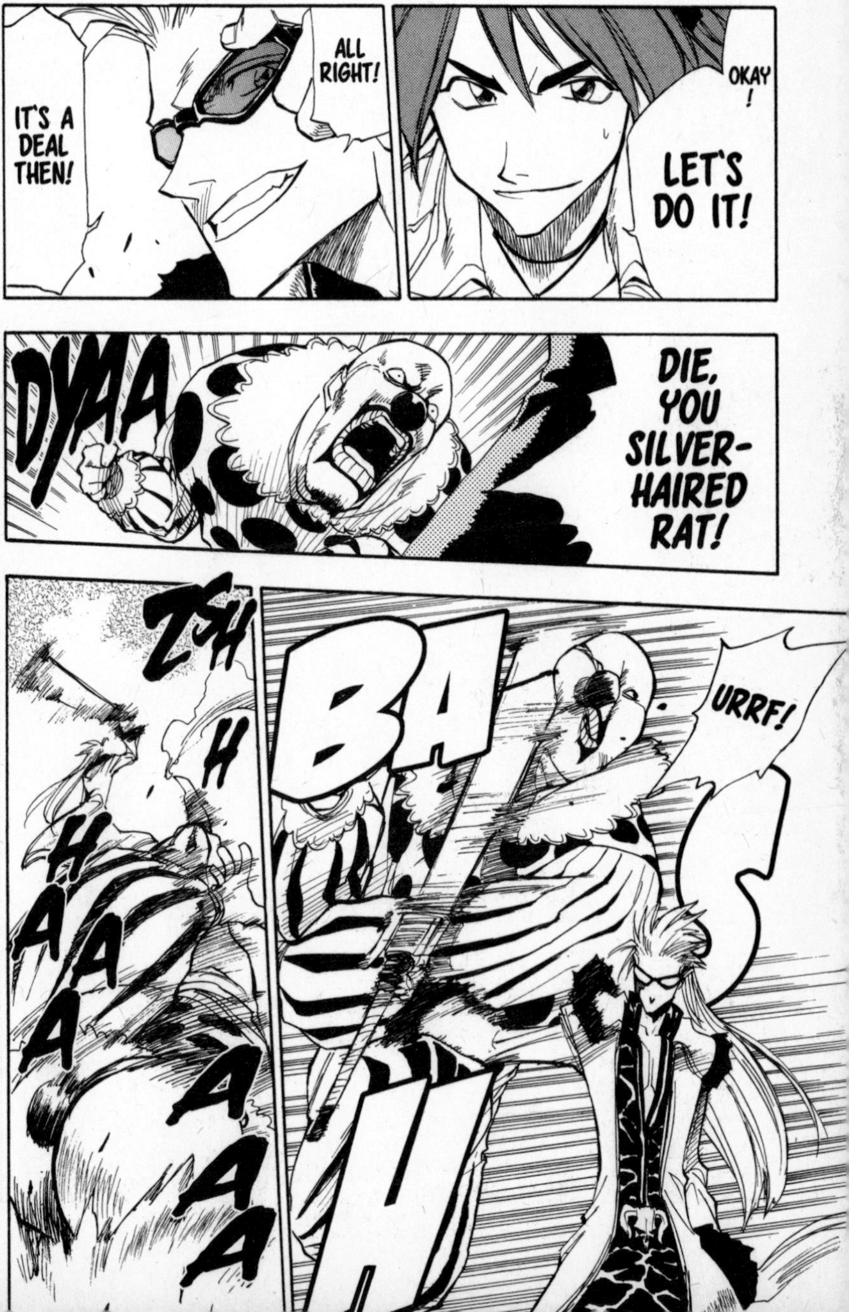
OKAY!
LET'S DO IT!
ALL RIGHT!
IT'S A DEAL THEN!
DIE, YOU SILVER-HAIRED RAT!
DYAA
URRF!
BASH
ZSHHH
HAAAAAAAAA

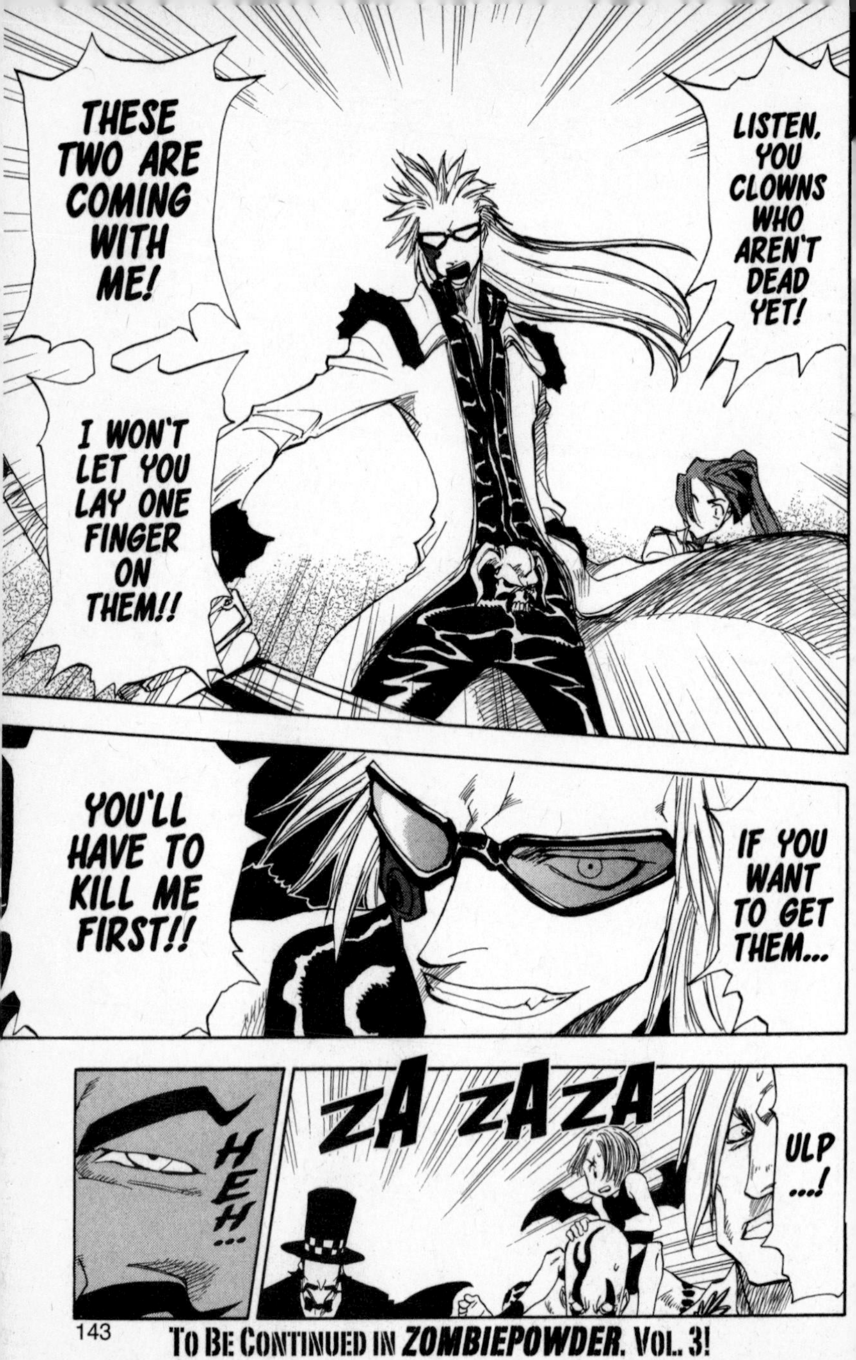
LISTEN, YOU CLOWNS WHO AREN'T DEAD YET!
THESE TWO ARE COMING WITH ME!
I WON'T LET YOU LAY ONE FINGER ON THEM!!
IF YOU WANT TO GET THEM...
YOU'LL HAVE TO KILL ME FIRST!!
ULP ...!
ZA ZAZA
HEH...



To Be Continued in *ZOMBIEPOWDER*. Vol. 3!

# Bonus Track. **1.**

# Ultra Unholy Hearted Machine.

→ Because the readers demanded it, next we have a special bonus: my very first short manga story!

→ This is my debut work, "Ultra Unholy Hearted Machine." I drew it when I was 18 years old and I just drew what I felt like drawing. It has the same cynical dialogue as my current work, however.

→ Well...I tried to write some legitimate-sounding commentary, but actually, I just wanted to say one thing: I like Tinatina. That's all.

**Tinatina**
  (Predea Corp. NHM-72B
TEST TYPE "Q2")
Height: 151 cm
Weight: 167 kg
Blood Type:
FFF-105. ver.6
Body Data
Transmission Liquid

**Bäinhardt Rosner**

Height: 182 cm
Weight: 71 kg
Blood Type: BO (+)

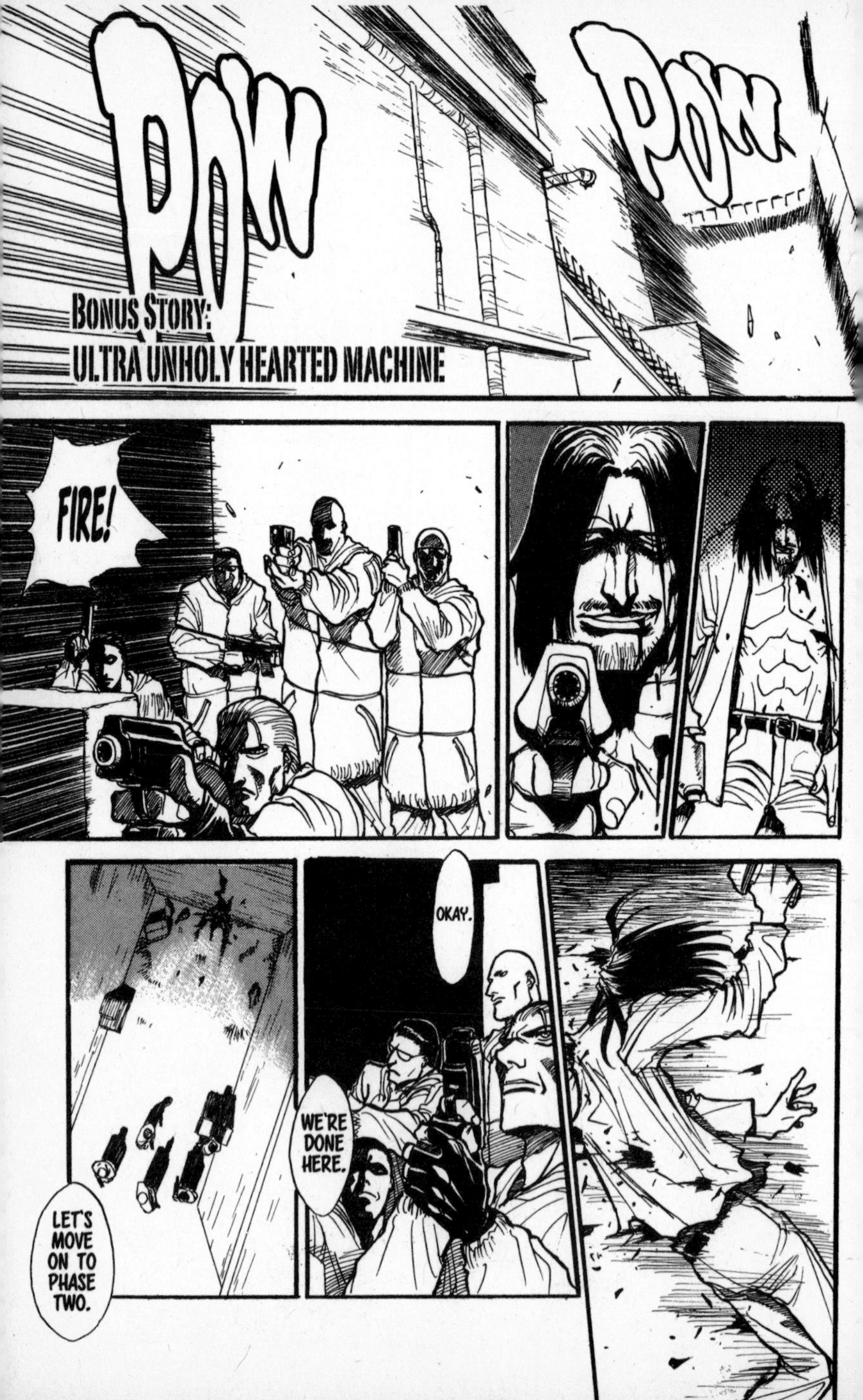
POW
POW
BONUS STORY:
ULTRA UNHOLY HEARTED MACHINE
FIRE!
OKAY.
WE'RE DONE HERE.
LET'S MOVE ON TO PHASE TWO.

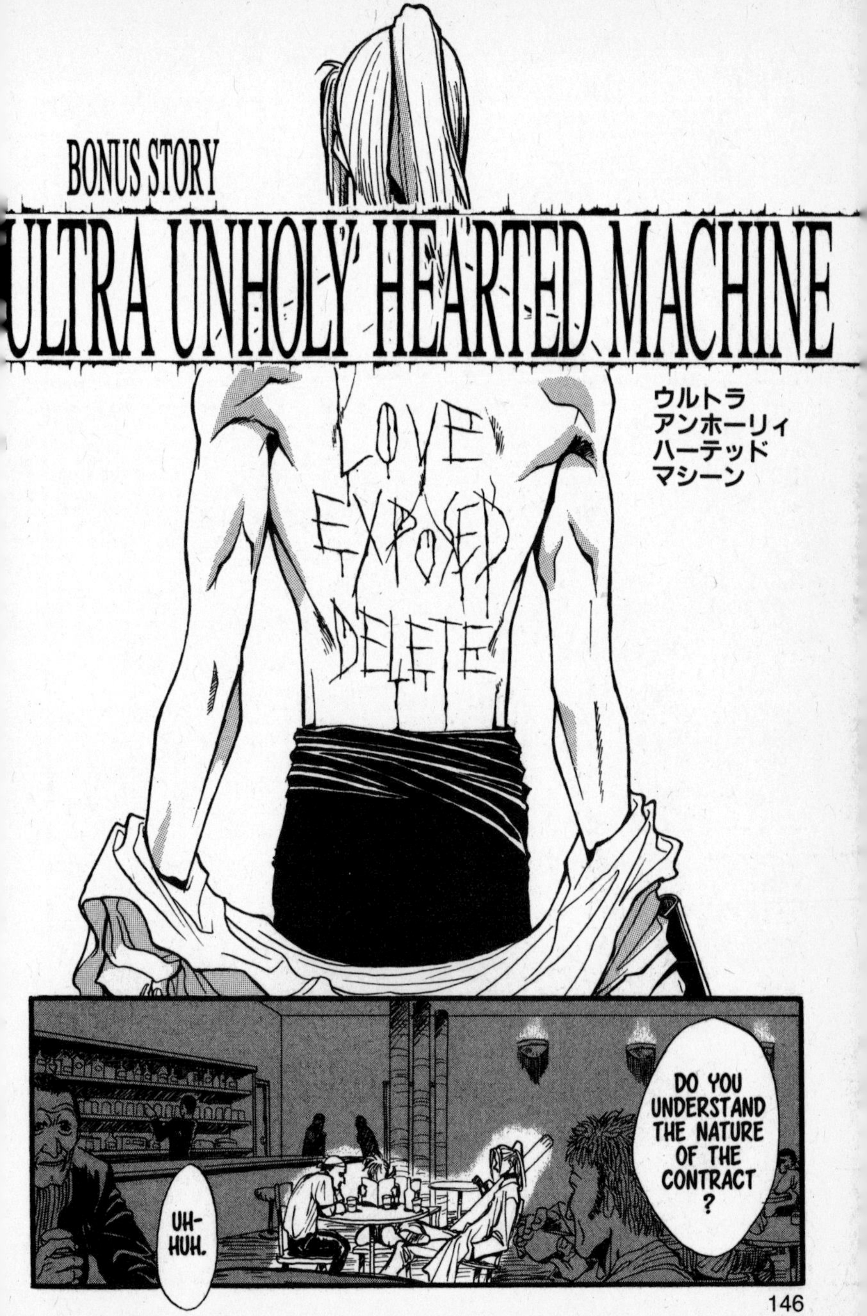
BONUS STORY
ULTRA UNHOLY HEARTED MACHINE
ウルトラ
アンホーリィ
ハーテッド
マシーン
LOVE
EXPOSED
DELETE
DO YOU UNDERSTAND THE NATURE OF THE CONTRACT ?
UH-HUH.

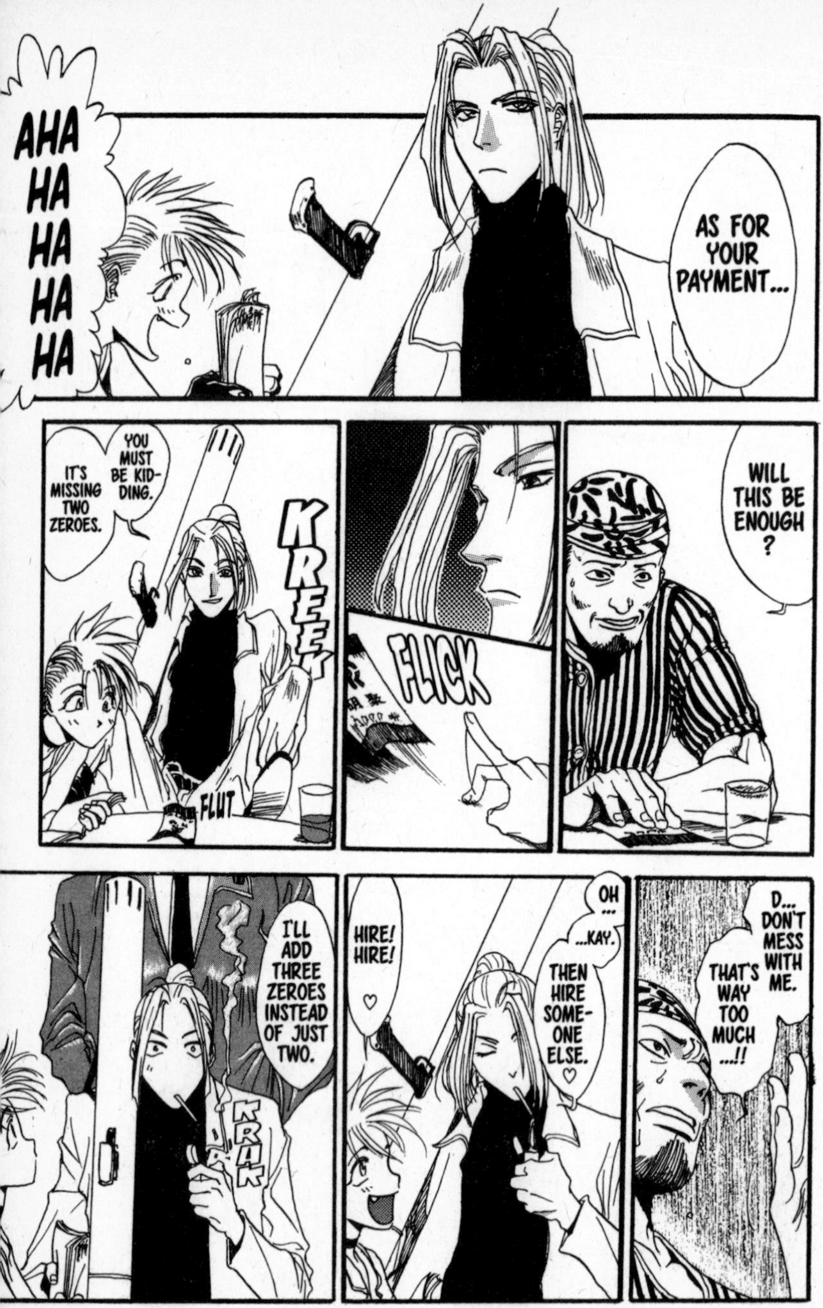
AS FOR YOUR PAYMENT...
AHA HA HA HA HA
WILL THIS BE ENOUGH?
FLICK
YOU MUST BE KID-DING.
IT'S MISSING TWO ZEROES.
KREEK
FLUT
D... DON'T MESS WITH ME.
THAT'S WAY TOO MUCH...!!
OH... ...KAY.
THEN HIRE SOME-ONE ELSE. ♡
HIRE! HIRE! ♡
I'LL ADD THREE ZEROES INSTEAD OF JUST TWO.
KRAK

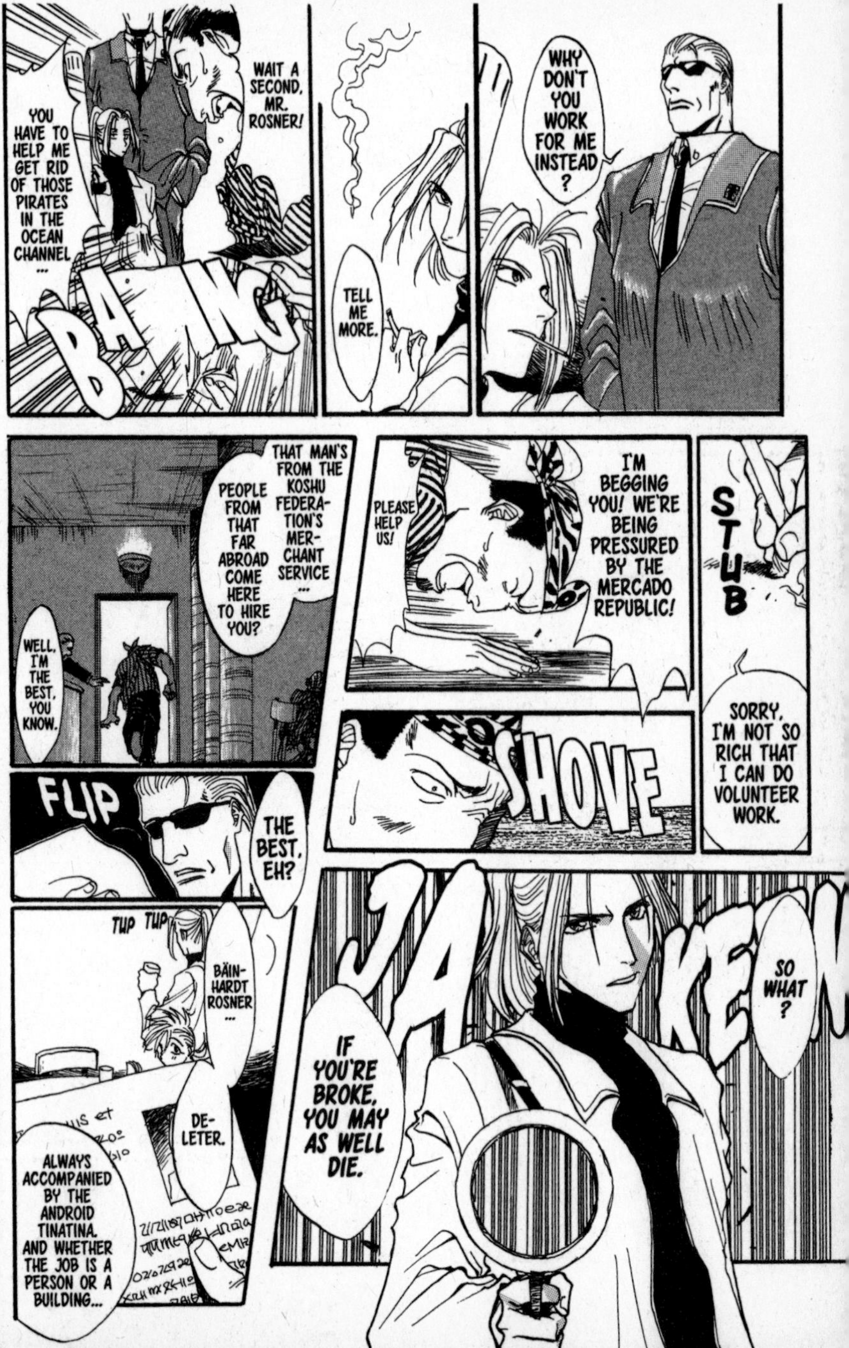
WHY DON'T YOU WORK FOR ME INSTEAD?
TELL ME MORE.
WAIT A SECOND, MR. ROSNER!
YOU HAVE TO HELP ME GET RID OF THOSE PIRATES IN THE OCEAN CHANNEL...
STUB
SORRY, I'M NOT SO RICH THAT I CAN DO VOLUNTEER WORK.
I'M BEGGING YOU! WE'RE BEING PRESSURED BY THE MERCADO REPUBLIC!
PLEASE HELP US!
SHOVE
THAT MAN'S FROM THE KOSHU FEDERATION'S MERCHANT SERVICE...
PEOPLE FROM THAT FAR ABROAD COME HERE TO HIRE YOU?
WELL, I'M THE BEST, YOU KNOW.
THE BEST, EH?
FLIP
SO WHAT?
IF YOU'RE BROKE, YOU MAY AS WELL DIE.
TUP TUP
BÄINHARDT ROSNER...
DELETER.
ALWAYS ACCOMPANIED BY THE ANDROID TINATINA. AND WHETHER THE JOB IS A PERSON OR A BUILDING...

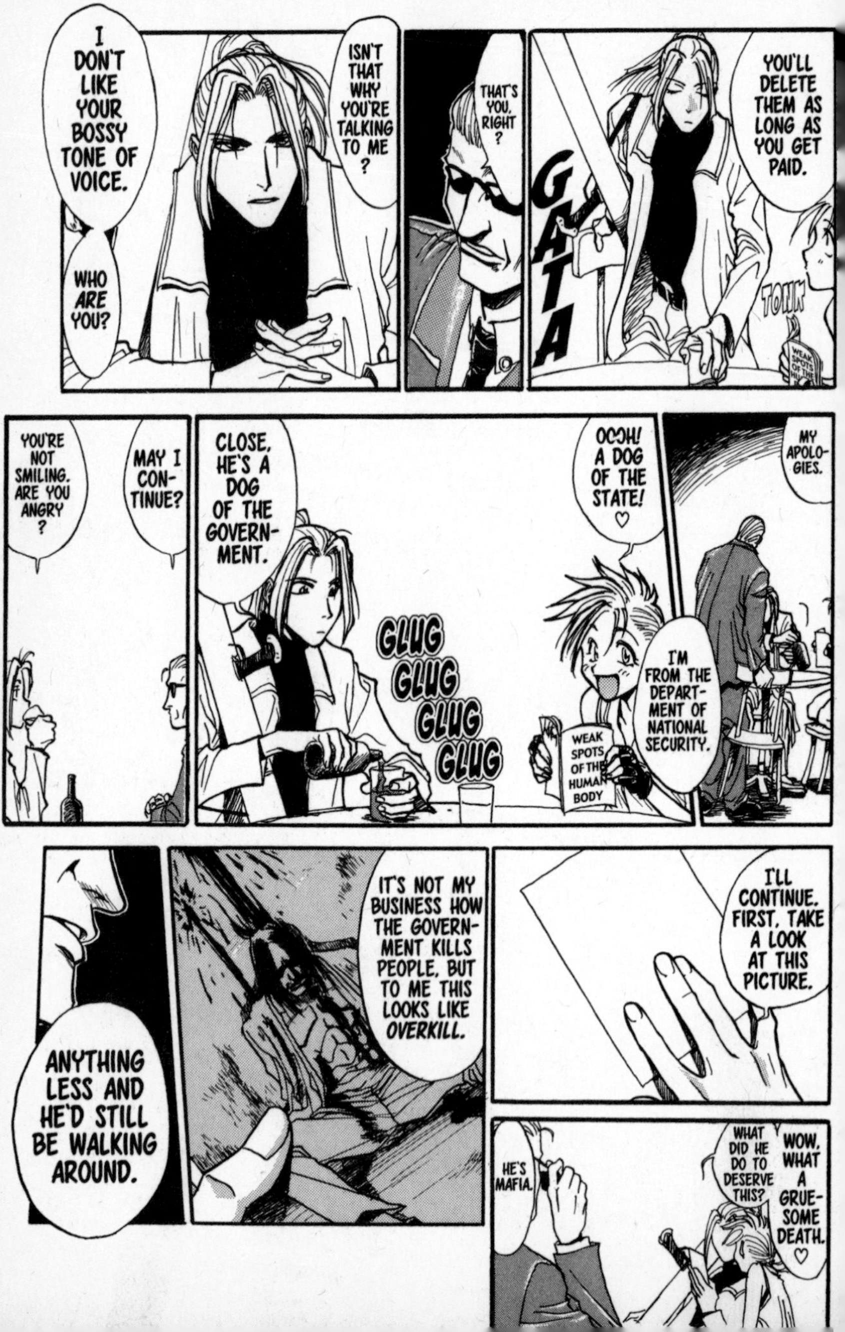
YOU'LL DELETE THEM AS LONG AS YOU GET PAID.
GATA
TONK
THAT'S YOU, RIGHT?
ISN'T THAT WHY YOU'RE TALKING TO ME?
I DON'T LIKE YOUR BOSSY TONE OF VOICE.
WHO ARE YOU?
MY APOLOGIES.
OOOH! A DOG OF THE STATE! ♡
I'M FROM THE DEPARTMENT OF NATIONAL SECURITY.
CLOSE, HE'S A DOG OF THE GOVERNMENT.
GLUG GLUG GLUG GLUG
WEAK SPOTS OF THE HUMAN BODY
MAY I CONTINUE?
YOU'RE NOT SMILING. ARE YOU ANGRY?
I'LL CONTINUE. FIRST, TAKE A LOOK AT THIS PICTURE.
WOW, WHAT A GRUESOME DEATH. ♡
WHAT DID HE DO TO DESERVE THIS?
HE'S MAFIA.
IT'S NOT MY BUSINESS HOW THE GOVERNMENT KILLS PEOPLE, BUT TO ME THIS LOOKS LIKE OVERKILL.
ANYTHING LESS AND HE'D STILL BE WALKING AROUND.

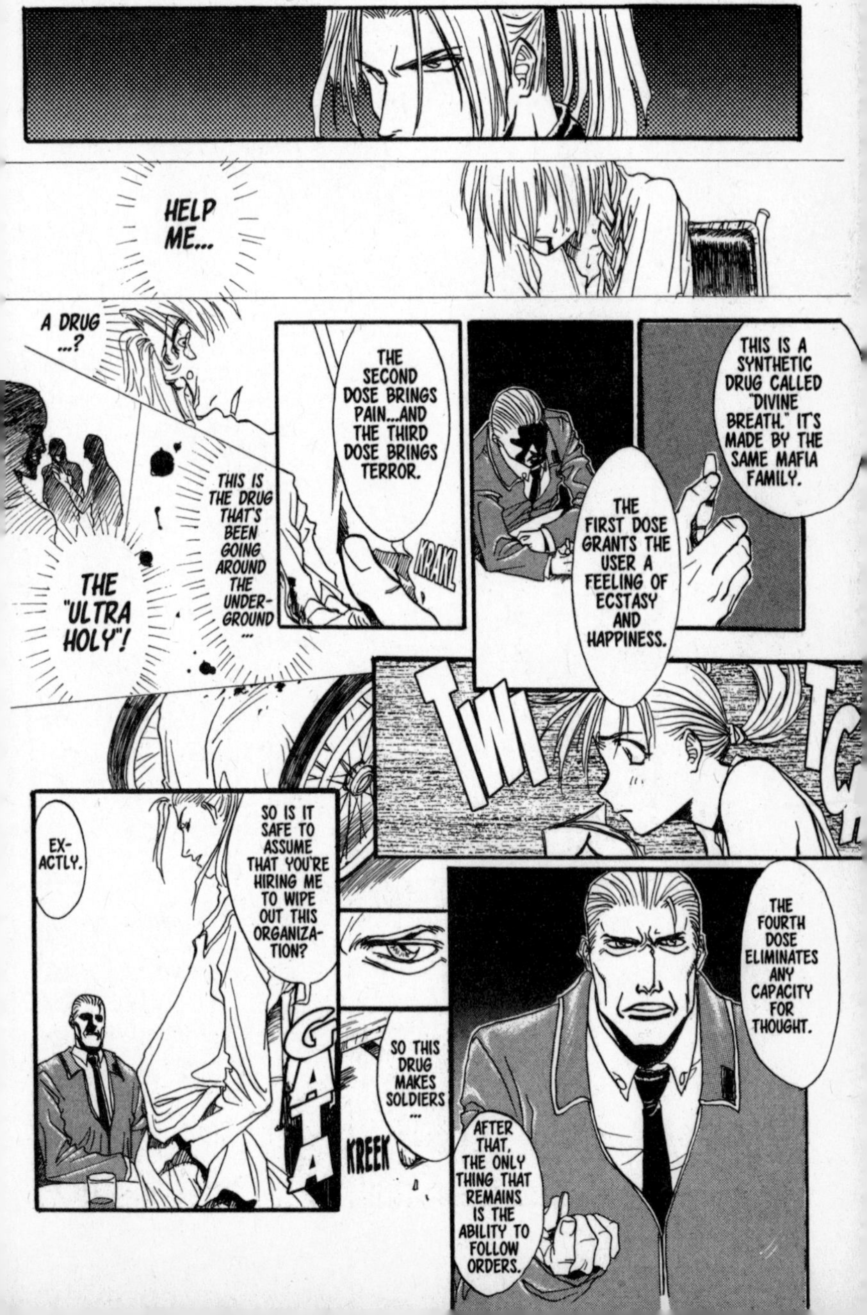
HELP ME...
THIS IS A SYNTHETIC DRUG CALLED "DIVINE BREATH." IT'S MADE BY THE SAME MAFIA FAMILY.
THE FIRST DOSE GRANTS THE USER A FEELING OF ECSTASY AND HAPPINESS.
THE SECOND DOSE BRINGS PAIN...AND THE THIRD DOSE BRINGS TERROR.
KRAKL
A DRUG ...?
THIS IS THE DRUG THAT'S BEEN GOING AROUND THE UNDER-GROUND ...
THE "ULTRA HOLY"!
THE FOURTH DOSE ELIMINATES ANY CAPACITY FOR THOUGHT.
AFTER THAT, THE ONLY THING THAT REMAINS IS THE ABILITY TO FOLLOW ORDERS.
SO THIS DRUG MAKES SOLDIERS ...
GATA
KREEK
SO IS IT SAFE TO ASSUME THAT YOU'RE HIRING ME TO WIPE OUT THIS ORGANIZA-TION?
EX-ACTLY.

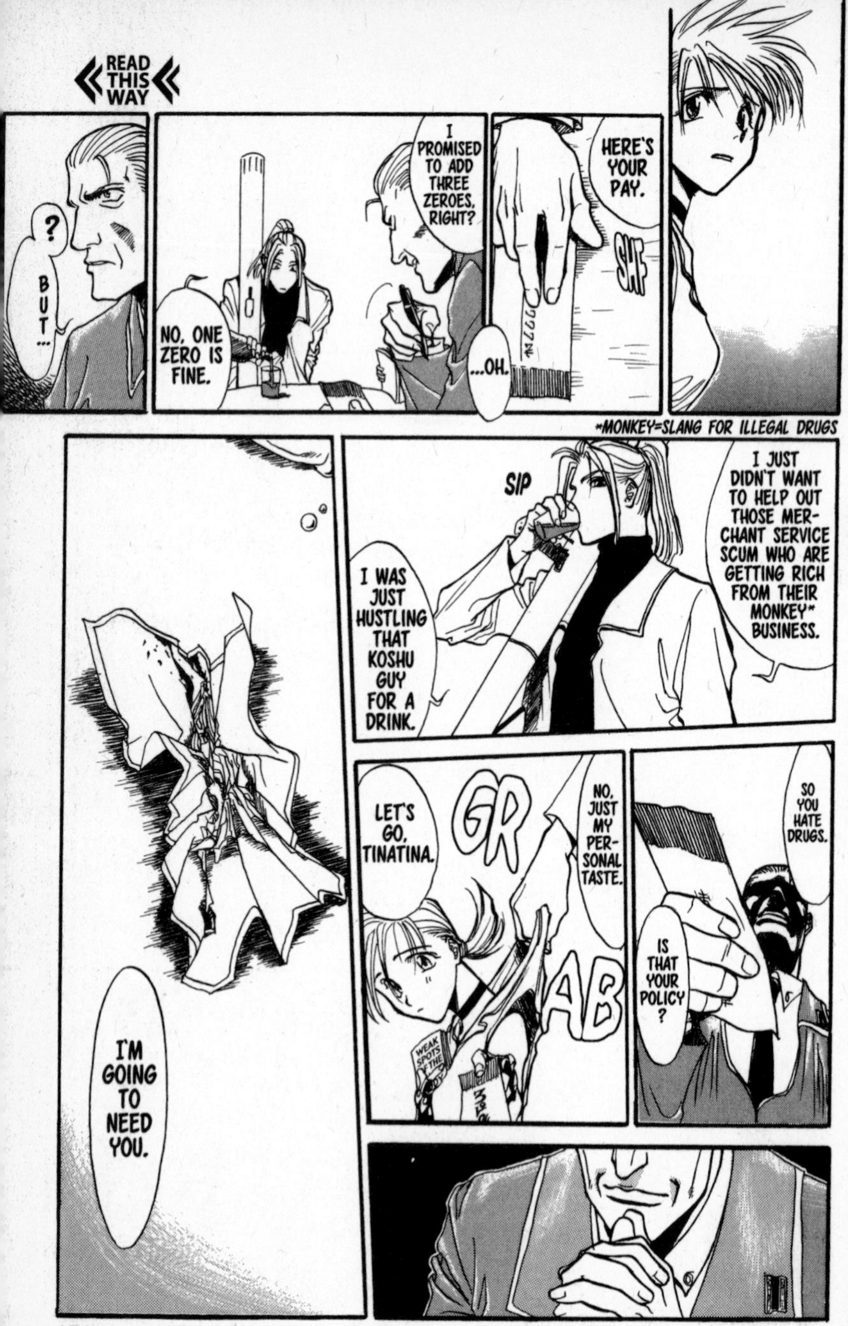
READ THIS WAY
HERE'S YOUR PAY.
SHF
...OH.
I PROMISED TO ADD THREE ZEROES, RIGHT?
NO, ONE ZERO IS FINE.
?
BUT...
*MONKEY=SLANG FOR ILLEGAL DRUGS
SIP
I JUST DIDN'T WANT TO HELP OUT THOSE MER-CHANT SERVICE SCUM WHO ARE GETTING RICH FROM THEIR MONKEY* BUSINESS.
I WAS JUST HUSTLING THAT KOSHU GUY FOR A DRINK.
SO YOU HATE DRUGS.
IS THAT YOUR POLICY?
NO, JUST MY PER-SONAL TASTE.
GRAB
LET'S GO, TINATINA.
WEAK SPOTS OF THE BODY
I'M GOING TO NEED YOU.

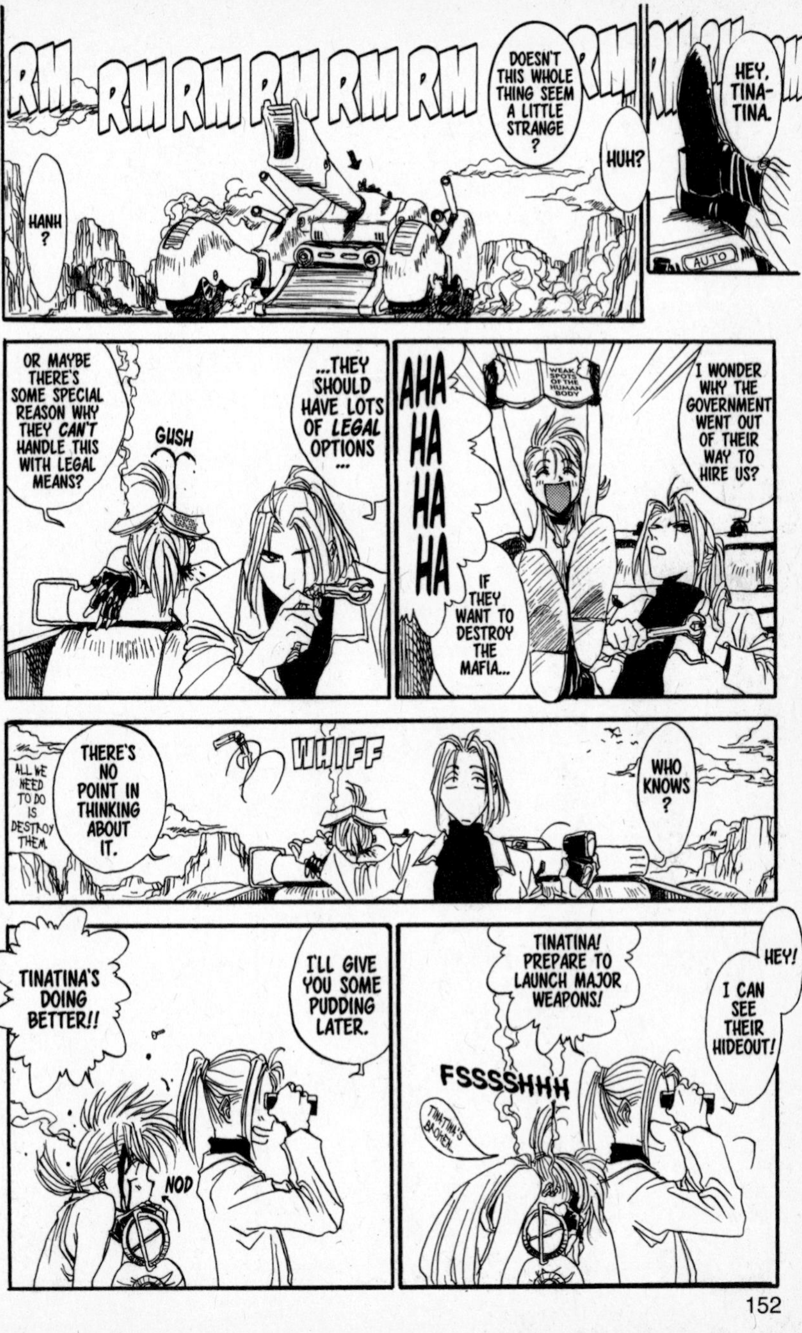
RM RM RM RM RM RM RM RM RM RM
AUTO
HEY, TINA-TINA.
HUH?
DOESN'T THIS WHOLE THING SEEM A LITTLE STRANGE?
HANH?
I WONDER WHY THE GOVERNMENT WENT OUT OF THEIR WAY TO HIRE US?
WEAK SPOTS OF THE HUMAN BODY
AHA HA HA HA HA
IF THEY WANT TO DESTROY THE MAFIA...
...THEY SHOULD HAVE LOTS OF *LEGAL* OPTIONS...
GUSH
OR MAYBE THERE'S SOME SPECIAL REASON WHY THEY *CAN'T* HANDLE THIS WITH LEGAL MEANS?
WHO KNOWS?
WHIFF
THERE'S NO POINT IN THINKING ABOUT IT.
ALL WE NEED TO DO IS DESTROY THEM.
HEY!
I CAN SEE THEIR HIDEOUT!
TINATINA! PREPARE TO LAUNCH MAJOR WEAPONS!
FSSSSHHH
TINATINA'S BROKEN.
I'LL GIVE YOU SOME PUDDING LATER.
TINATINA'S DOING BETTER!!
NOD

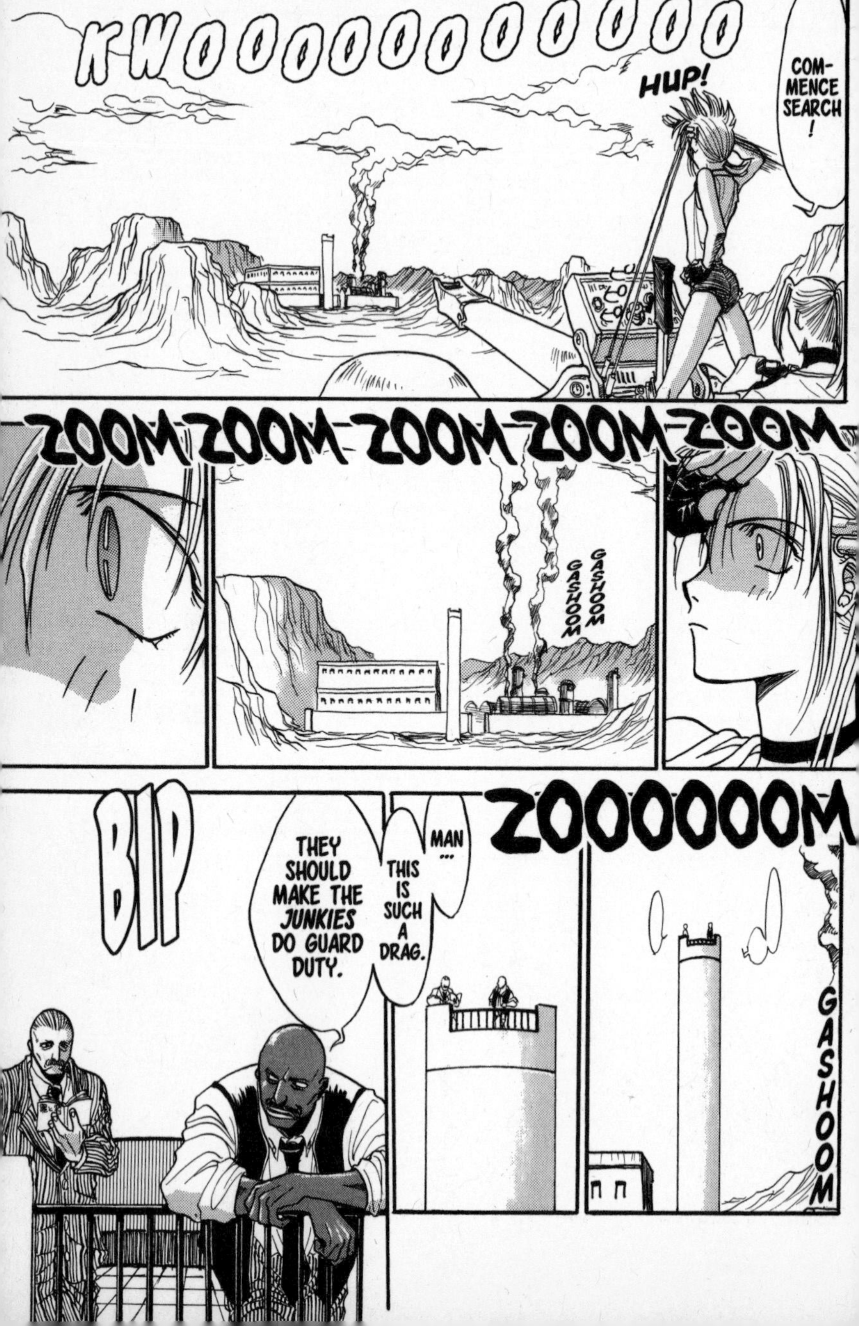
COM-
MENCE
SEARCH
!
HUP!
KWOOOOOOOOOOOO
ZOOM ZOOM ZOOM ZOOM ZOOM
GASHOOM
GASHOOM
ZOOOOOOM
GASHOOM
MAN
...
THIS IS SUCH A DRAG.
THEY SHOULD MAKE THE JUNKIES DO GUARD DUTY.
BIP

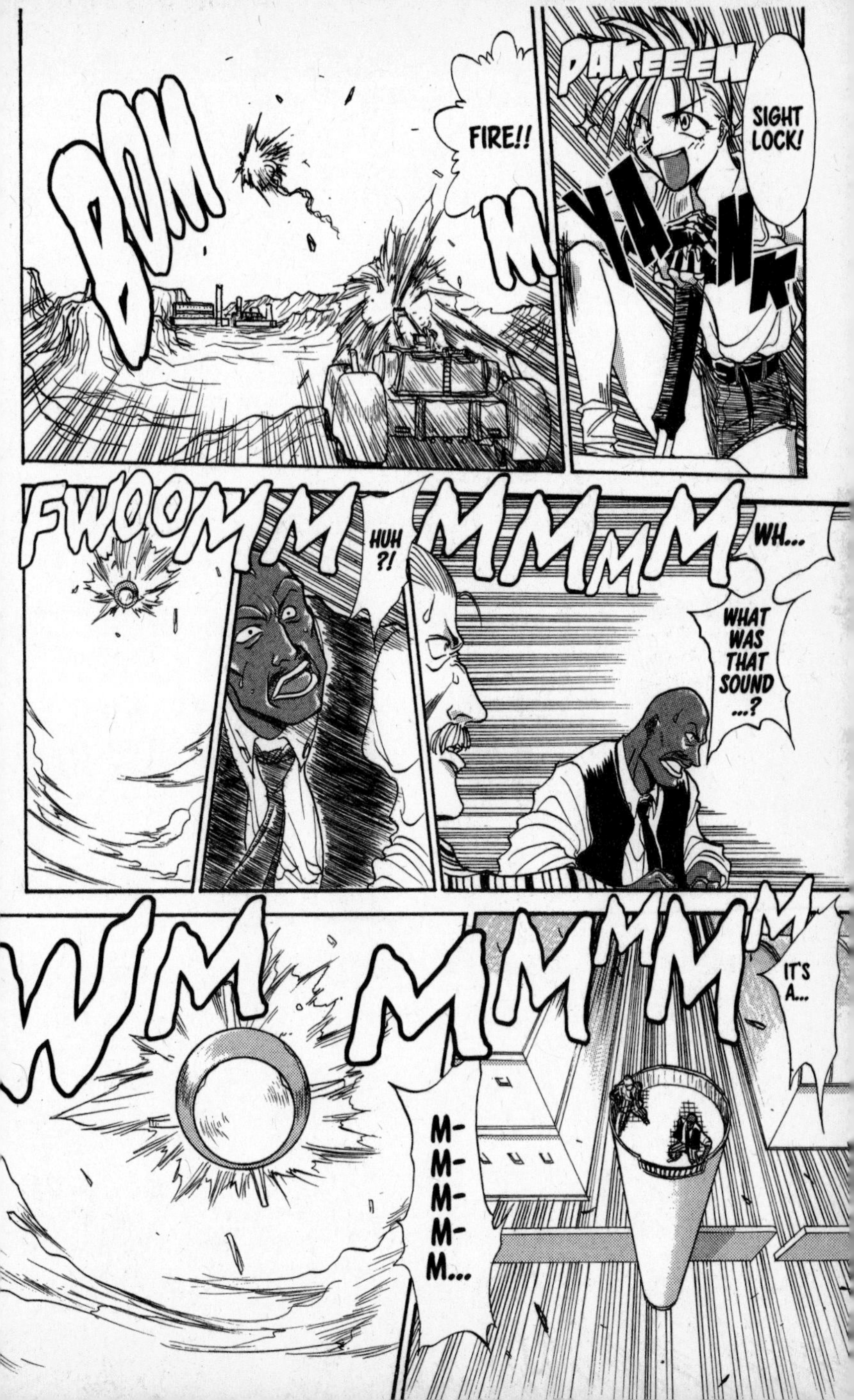

PAREEEEN
SIGHT LOCK!
YANK
FIRE!!
M
BOM
MMMMM
WH...
WHAT WAS THAT SOUND ...?
HUH ?!
FWOOMM
MMMMM
WM
IT'S A...
M-M-MMM-MMM-M...

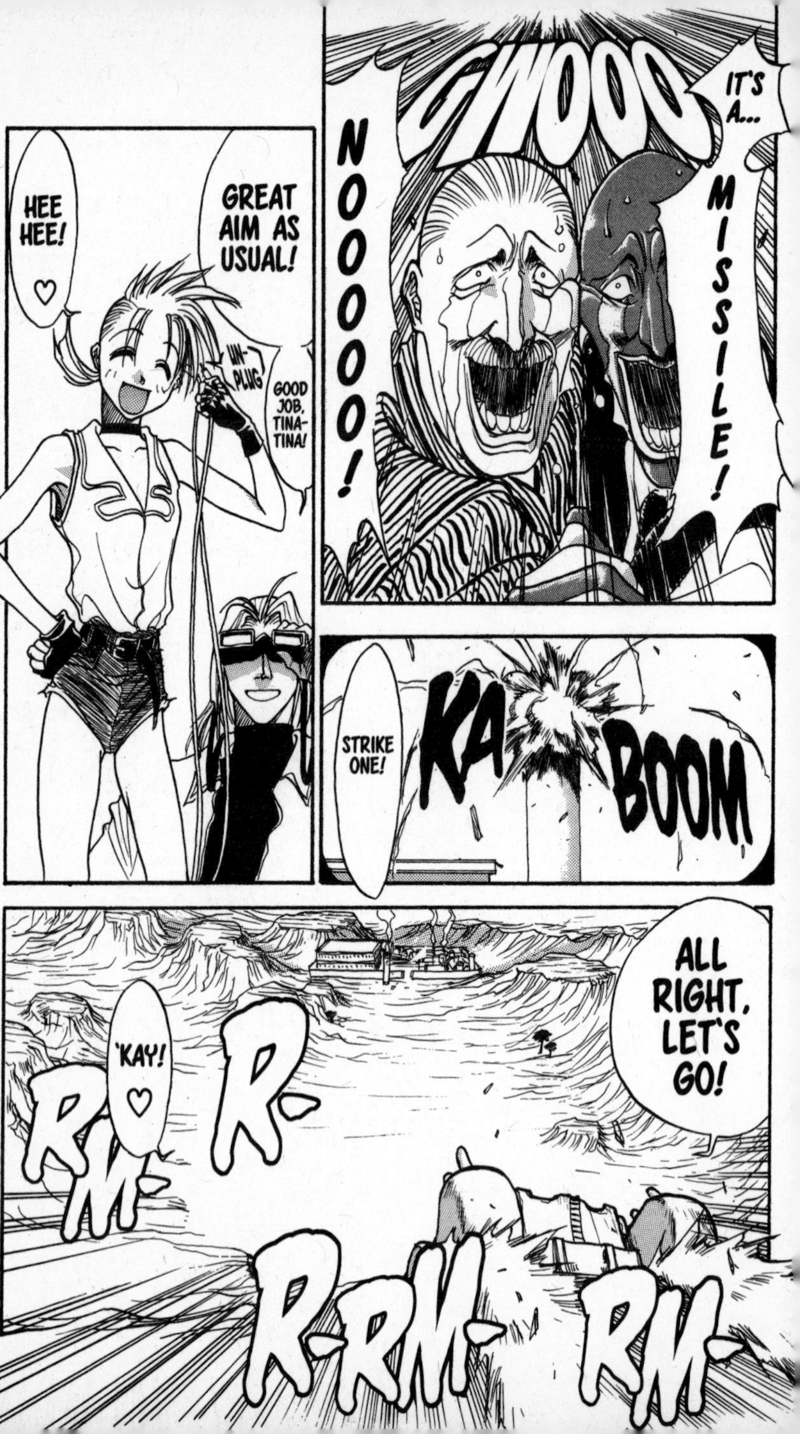

IT'S A...
GWOOO
MISSILE!
NOOOOOOO!
KA BOOM
STRIKE ONE!
GREAT AIM AS USUAL!
HEE HEE! ♡
GOOD JOB, TINA-TINA!
UN-PLUG
ALL RIGHT, LET'S GO!
R R
'KAY! ♡
RM
R-RM RM

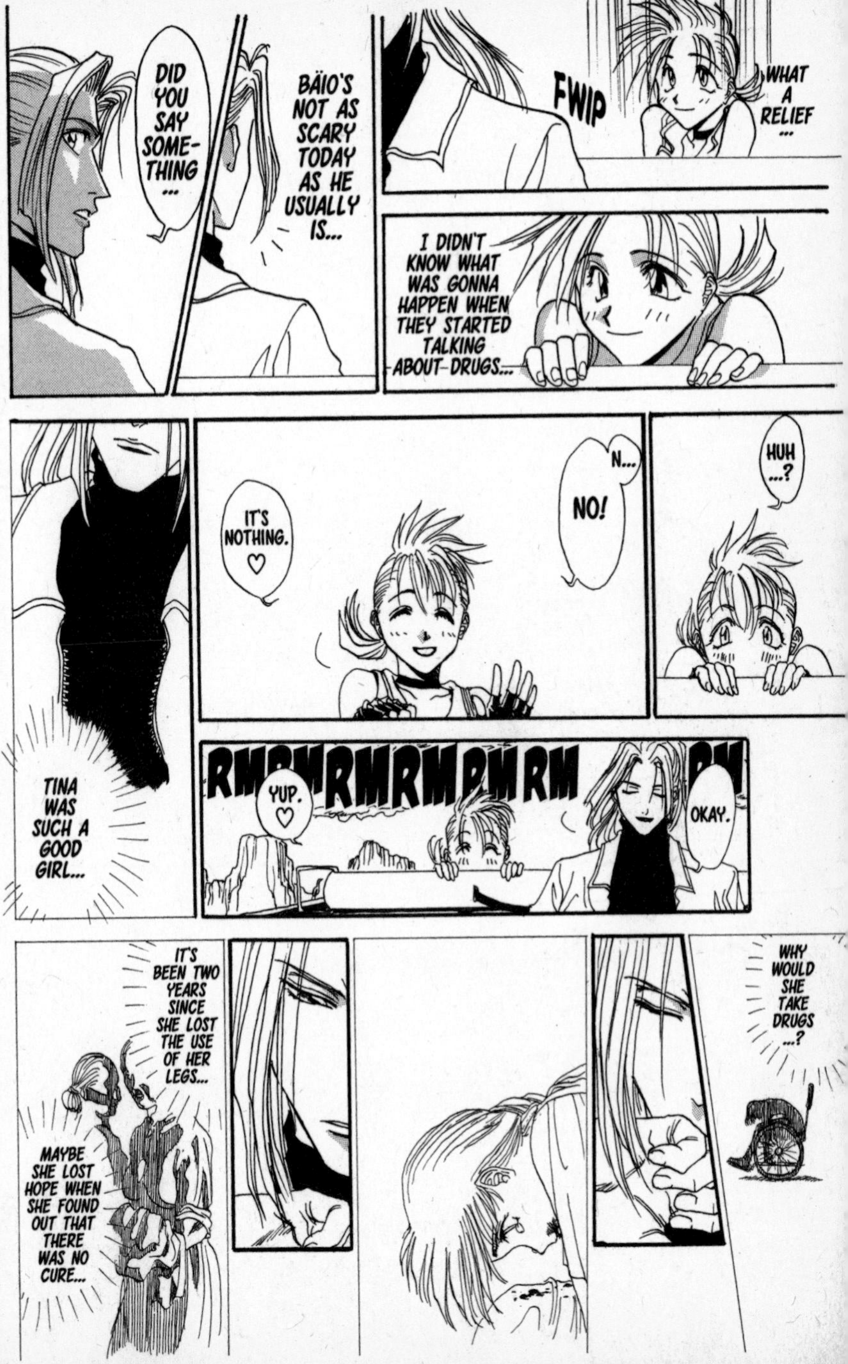
FWIP
WHAT A RELIEF...
I DIDN'T KNOW WHAT WAS GONNA HAPPEN WHEN THEY STARTED TALKING ABOUT DRUGS...
BÄIO'S NOT AS SCARY TODAY AS HE USUALLY IS...
DID YOU SAY SOMETHING...
HUH...?
N... NO!
IT'S NOTHING. ♡
OKAY.
YUP. ♡
RMRMRMRMRMRMRM
TINA WAS SUCH A GOOD GIRL...
WHY WOULD SHE TAKE DRUGS...?
IT'S BEEN TWO YEARS SINCE SHE LOST THE USE OF HER LEGS...
MAYBE SHE LOST HOPE WHEN SHE FOUND OUT THAT THERE WAS NO CURE...

READ THIS WAY

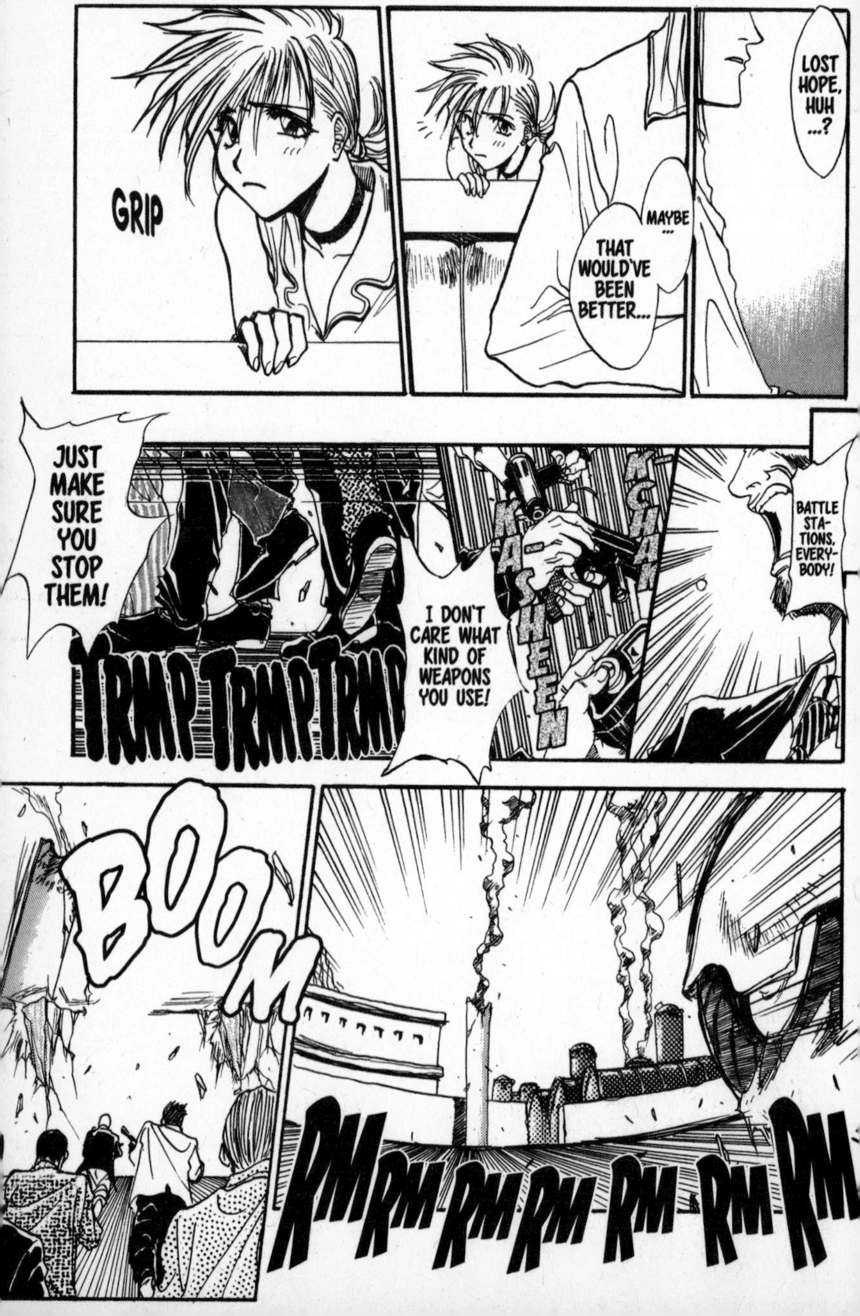
LOST HOPE, HUH ...?
MAYBE ...
THAT WOULD'VE BEEN BETTER...
GRIP
BATTLE STA-TIONS, EVERY-BODY!
K-CHAK
KA-SHEEN
I DON'T CARE WHAT KIND OF WEAPONS YOU USE!
JUST MAKE SURE YOU STOP THEM!
TRMP TRMP TRMP
RM RM RM RM RM RM RM RM
BOOM

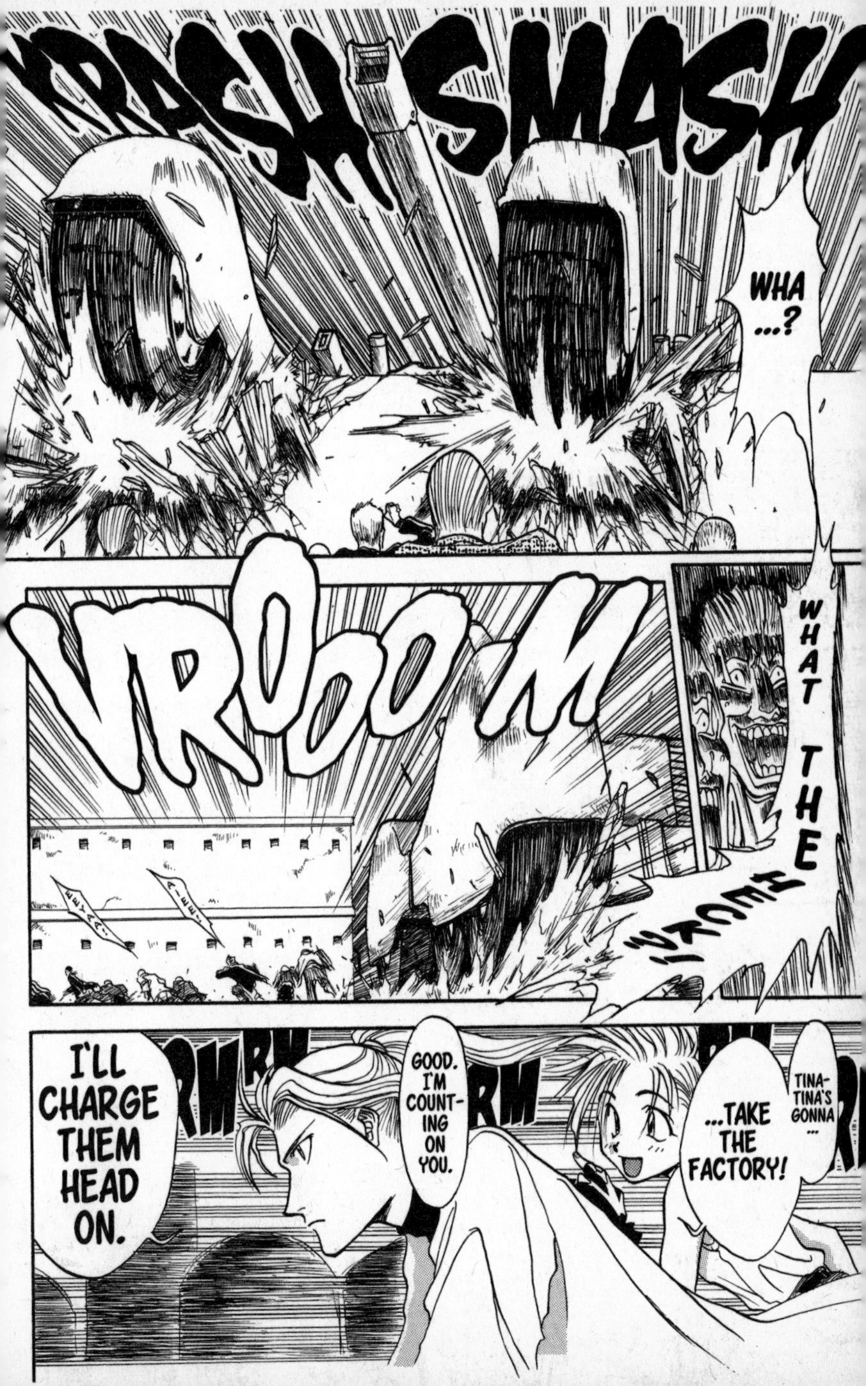

KRASH
SMASH
WHA ...?
WHAT THE HECK!?
VROOOM
TINA-TINA'S GONNA ...
...TAKE THE FACTORY!
RM RM
GOOD. I'M COUNTING ON YOU.
I'LL CHARGE THEM HEAD ON.

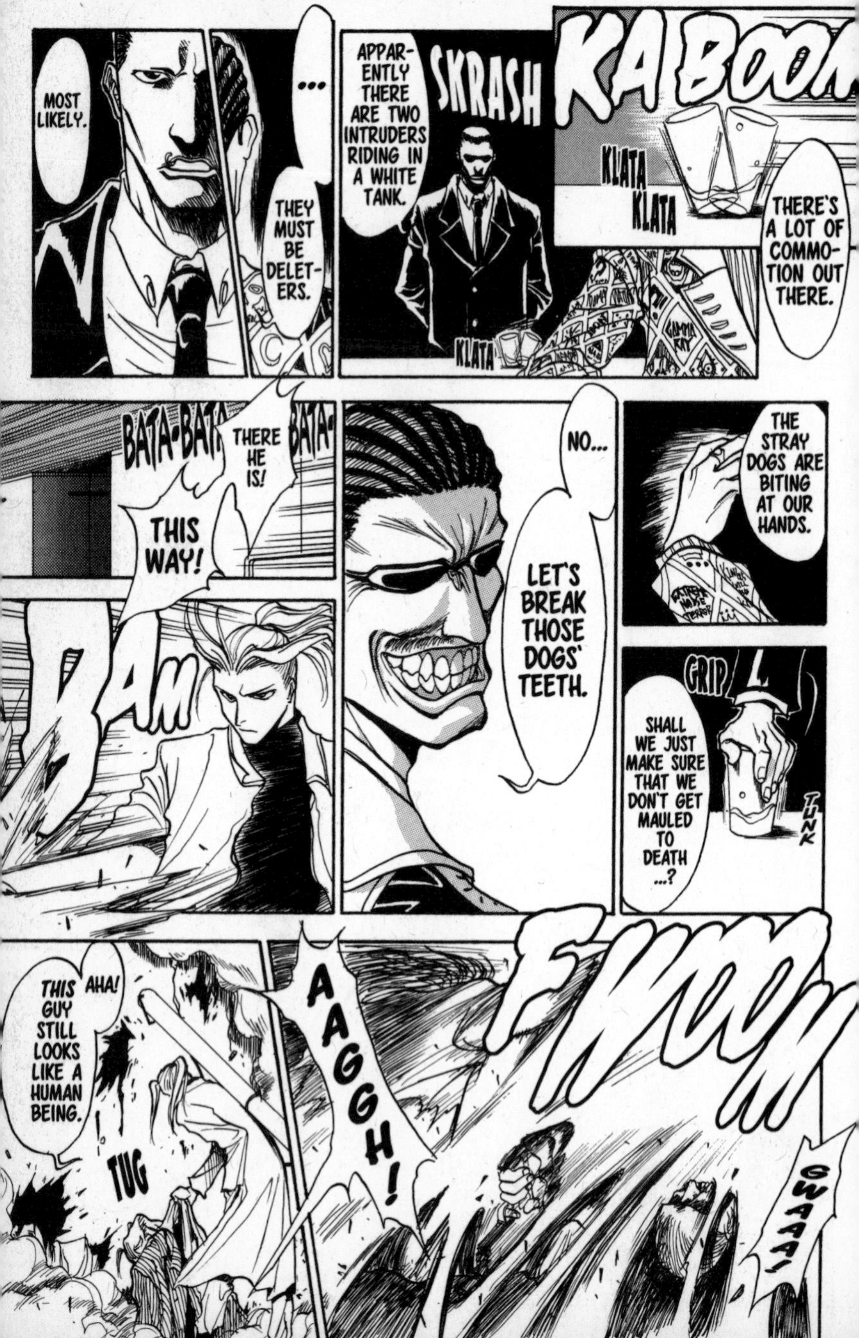
KA BOOM
KLATA KLATA
THERE'S A LOT OF COMMOTION OUT THERE.
KLATA
SKRASH
APPARENTLY THERE ARE TWO INTRUDERS RIDING IN A WHITE TANK.
...
THEY MUST BE DELETERS.
MOST LIKELY.
THE STRAY DOGS ARE BITING AT OUR HANDS.
GRIP
SHALL WE JUST MAKE SURE THAT WE DON'T GET MAULED TO DEATH ...?
TUNK
NO...
LET'S BREAK THOSE DOGS' TEETH.
BATA-BATA-BATA-
THERE HE IS!
THIS WAY!
BAM
GWAAA!
AAGGH!
AHA!
THIS GUY STILL LOOKS LIKE A HUMAN BEING.
TUG

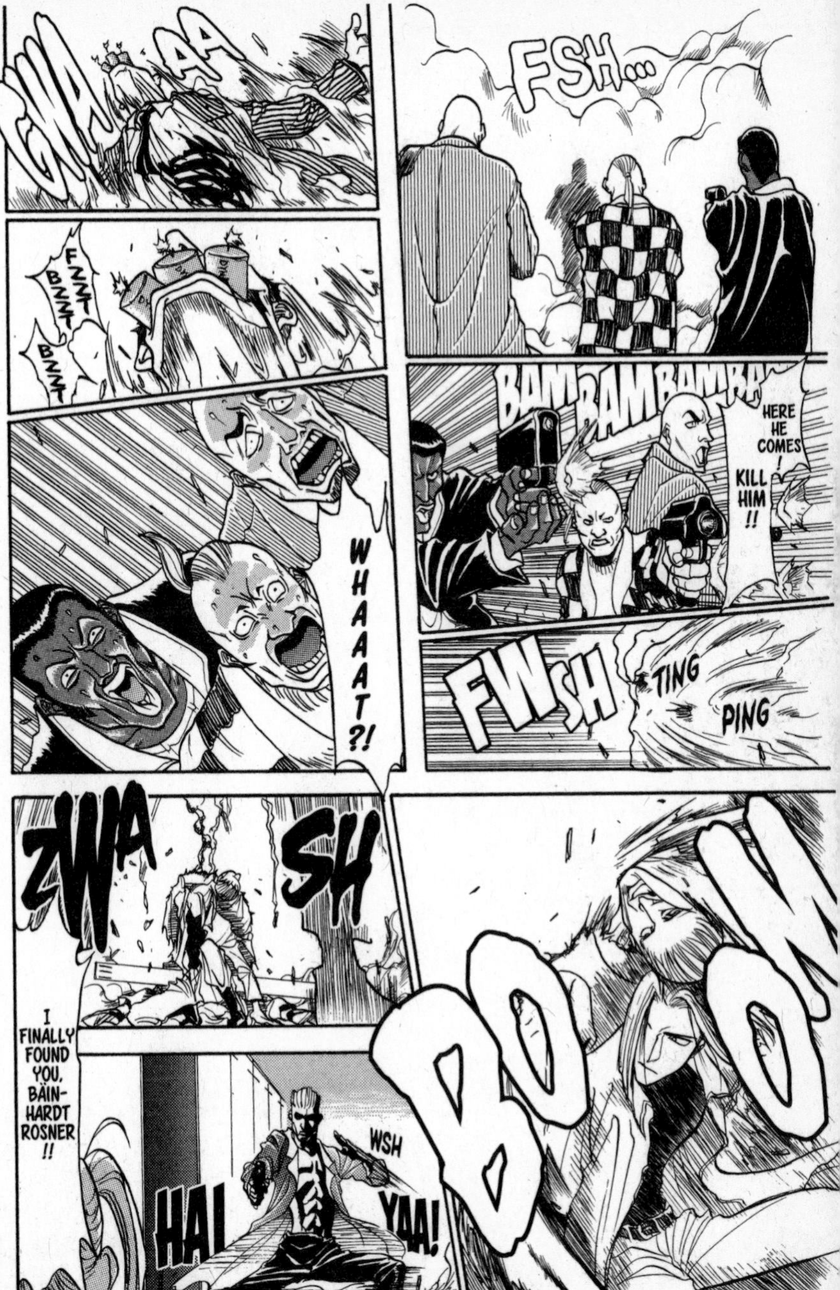
FSH...
GWA
AA
FZZZT
BZZZT
BZZZT
BZZZT
BAM BAM BAM BAM
HERE HE COMES! KILL HIM!!
FWSH
TING
PING
WHAAAAT?!
BOOM
ZWASH
I FINALLY FOUND YOU, BÄIN-HARDT ROSNER!!
WSH
HAI
YAA!

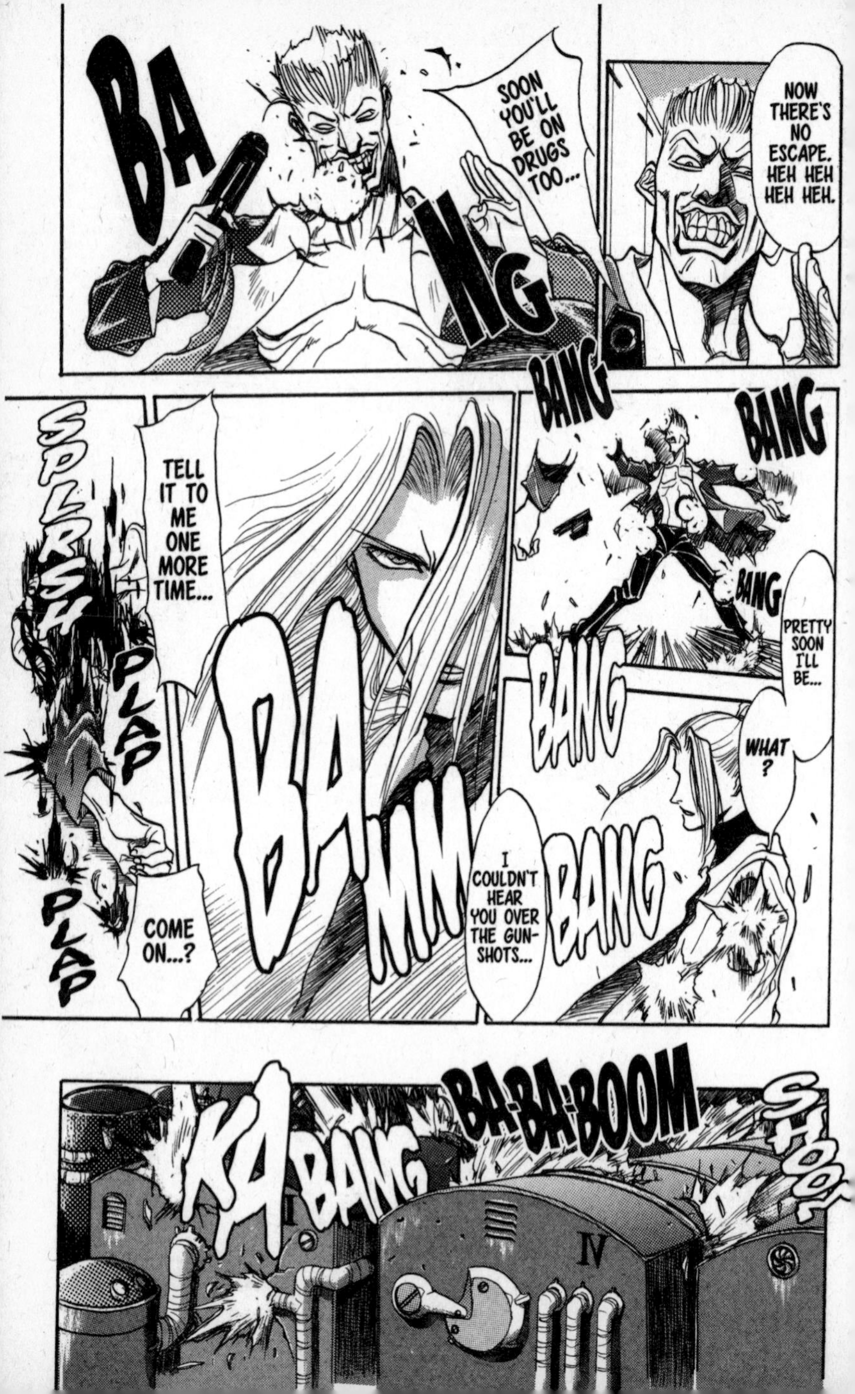
NOW THERE'S NO ESCAPE. HEH HEH HEH HEH.
BANG
SOON YOU'LL BE ON DRUGS TOO...
BANG
BANG
BANG
BANG
PRETTY SOON I'LL BE...
BANG
WHAT?
BANG
I COULDN'T HEAR YOU OVER THE GUN-SHOTS...
TELL IT TO ME ONE MORE TIME...
BAMM
SPLASH
PLAP
PLAP
COME ON...?
BA-BA-BOOM
KA BANG
IV
I

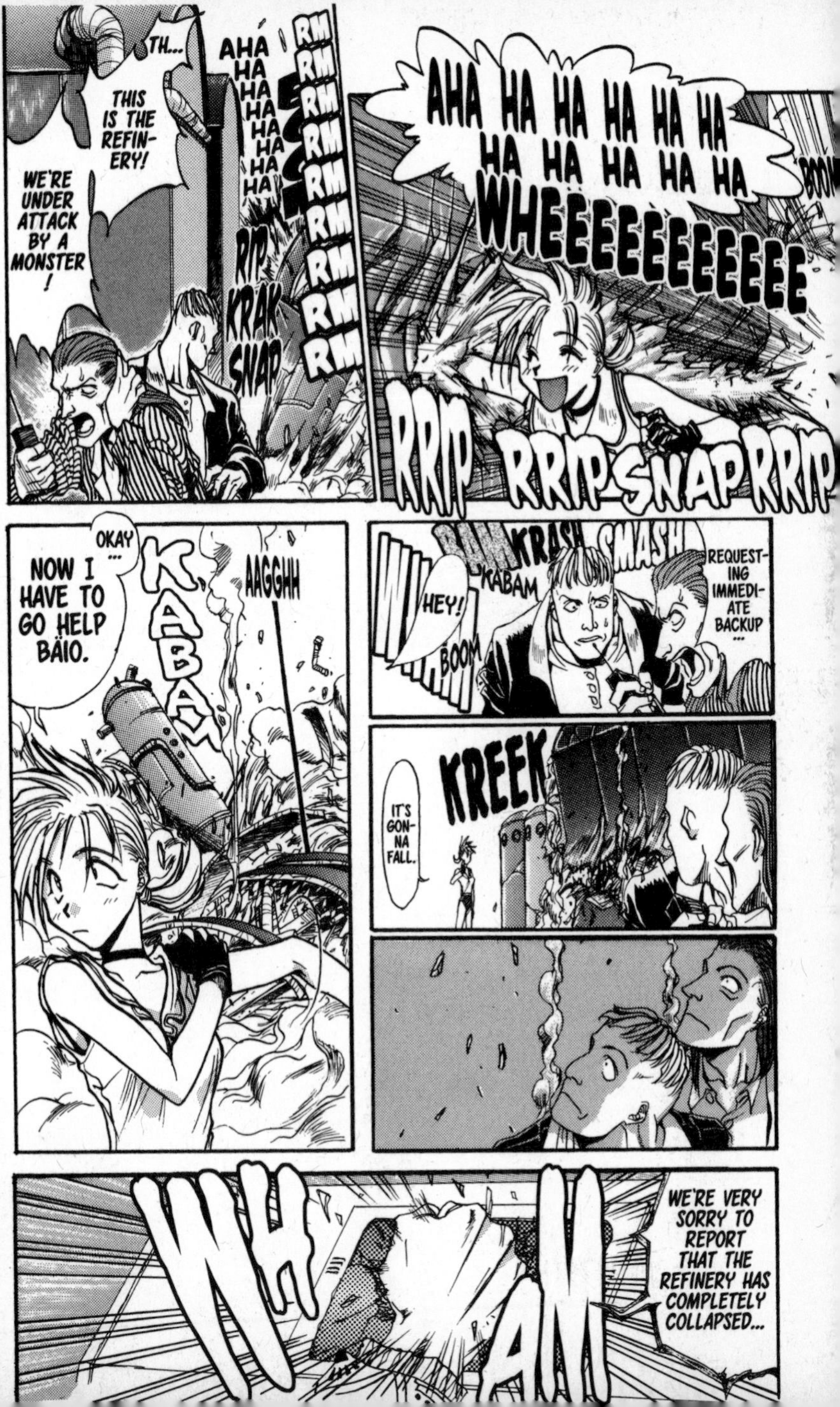
AHA HA HA HA HA HA
HA HA HA HA HA
WHEEEEEEEEEEE
BOOM
RRIP RRIP SNAP RRRIP
TH...
THIS IS THE REFIN-ERY!
WE'RE UNDER ATTACK BY A MONSTER!
AHA HA HA HA HA HA HA HA HA
RM RM RM RM RM RM RM RM RM RM
RIP KRAK SNAP
KRASH SMASH
KABAM
HEY!
BOOM
REQUEST-ING IMMEDI-ATE BACKUP...
KREEK
IT'S GON-NA FALL.
OKAY...
NOW I HAVE TO GO HELP BÄIO.
KABAM
AAGGHH
WHAM
WE'RE VERY SORRY TO REPORT THAT THE REFINERY HAS COMPLETELY COLLAPSED...

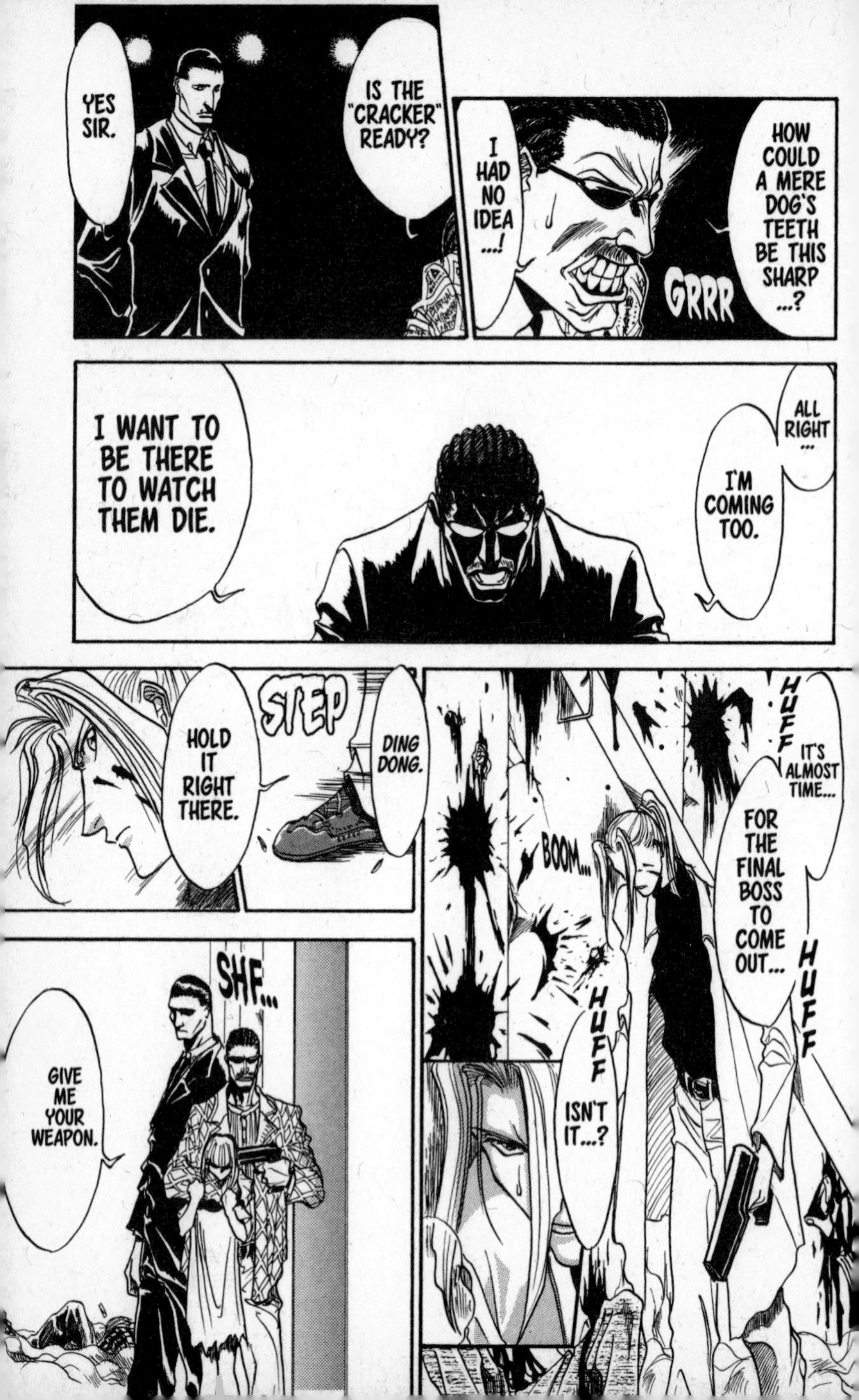
HOW COULD A MERE DOG'S TEETH BE THIS SHARP...?
GRRR
I HAD NO IDEA...!
IS THE "CRACKER" READY?
YES SIR.
ALL RIGHT...
I'M COMING TOO.
I WANT TO BE THERE TO WATCH THEM DIE.
HUFF
IT'S ALMOST TIME...
FOR THE FINAL BOSS TO COME OUT...
HUFF
BOOM...
HUFF
ISN'T IT...?
DING DONG.
STEP
HOLD IT RIGHT THERE.
SHF...
GIVE ME YOUR WEAPON.

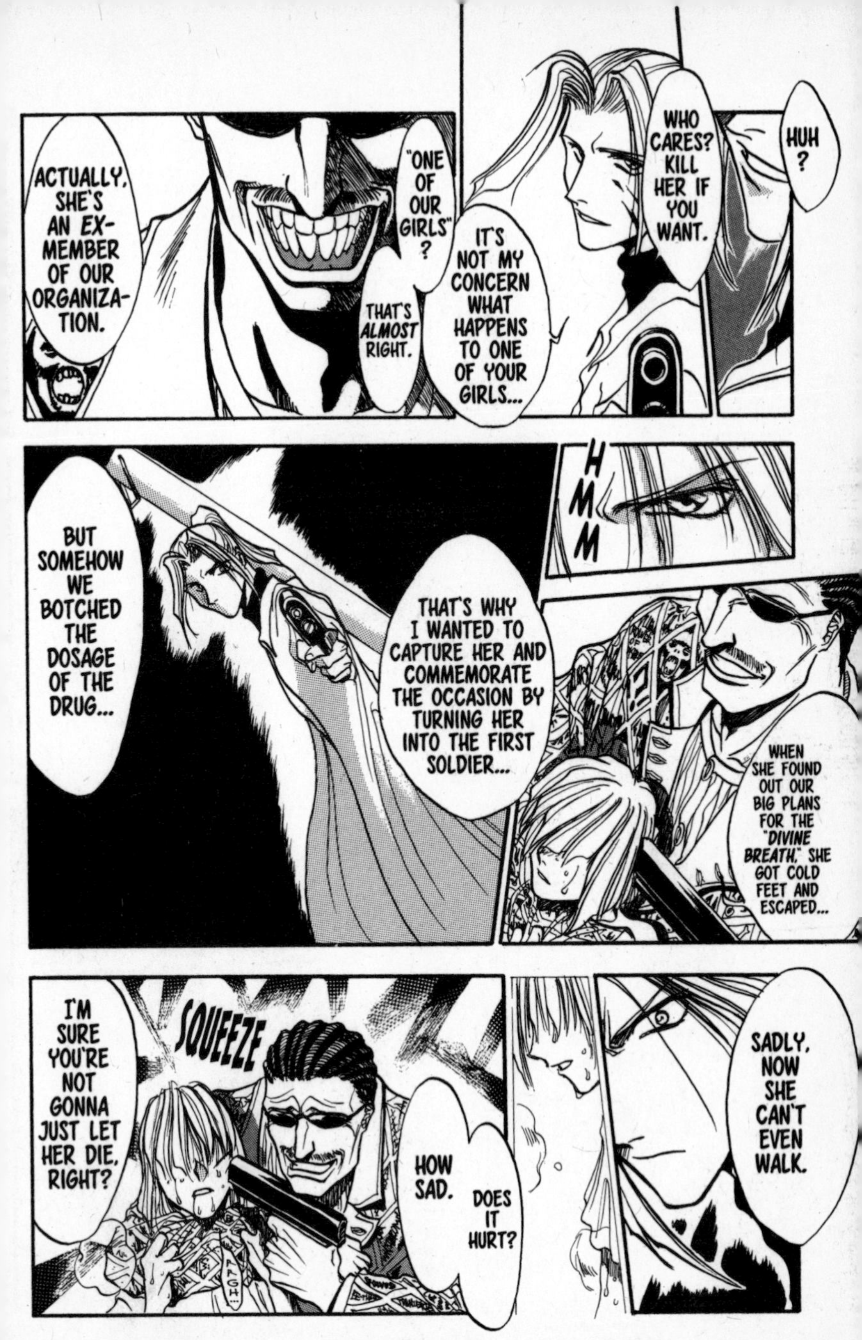
HUH?
WHO CARES? KILL HER IF YOU WANT.
IT'S NOT MY CONCERN WHAT HAPPENS TO ONE OF YOUR GIRLS...
"ONE OF OUR GIRLS"?
THAT'S ALMOST RIGHT.
ACTUALLY, SHE'S AN EX-MEMBER OF OUR ORGANIZATION.
HMMM
WHEN SHE FOUND OUT OUR BIG PLANS FOR THE "DIVINE BREATH," SHE GOT COLD FEET AND ESCAPED...
THAT'S WHY I WANTED TO CAPTURE HER AND COMMEMORATE THE OCCASION BY TURNING HER INTO THE FIRST SOLDIER...
BUT SOMEHOW WE BOTCHED THE DOSAGE OF THE DRUG...
SADLY, NOW SHE CAN'T EVEN WALK.
DOES IT HURT?
HOW SAD.
SQUEEZE
I'M SURE YOU'RE NOT GONNA JUST LET HER DIE, RIGHT?
ARGH...

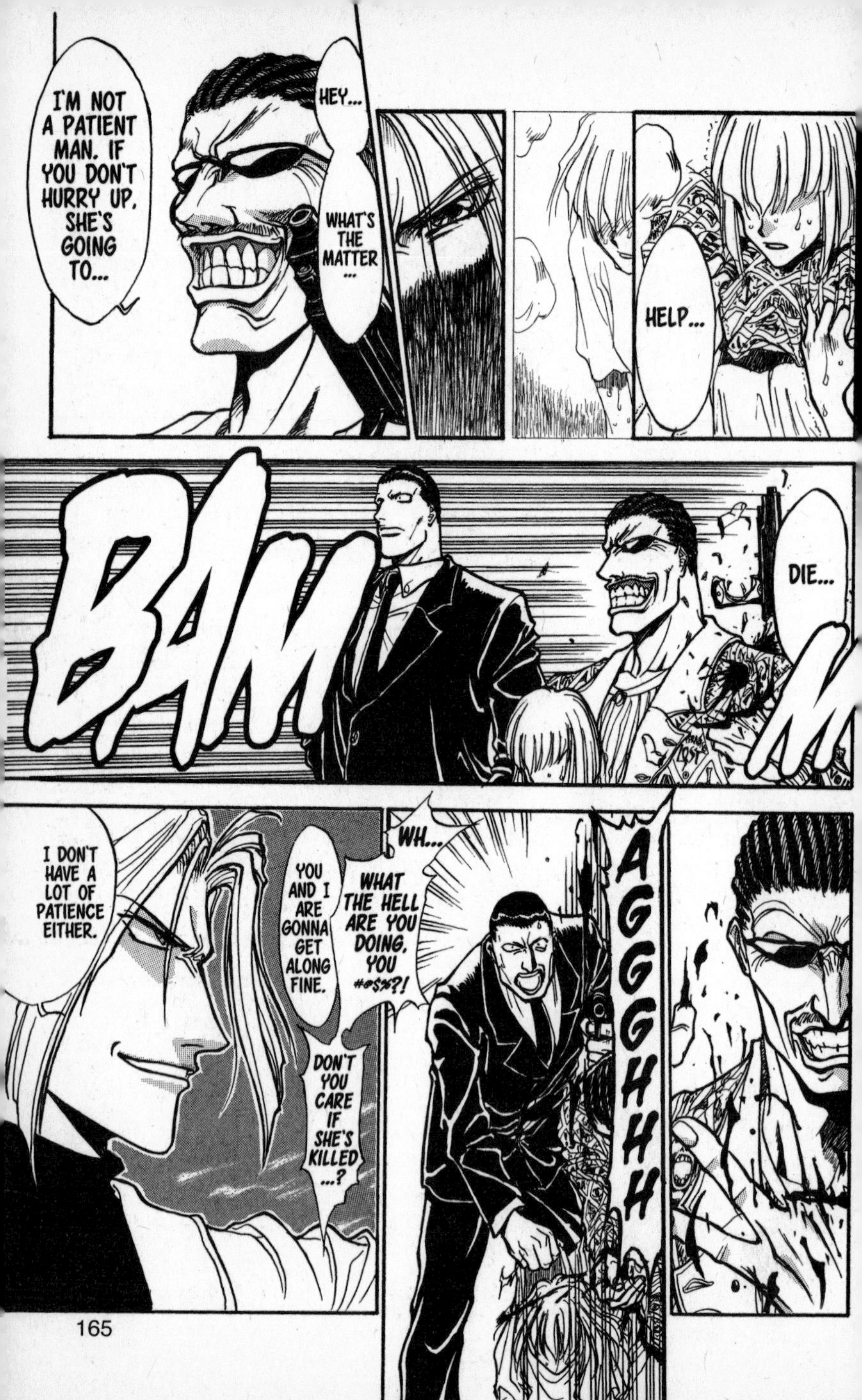

HELP...
HEY...
WHAT'S THE MATTER...
I'M NOT A PATIENT MAN. IF YOU DON'T HURRY UP, SHE'S GOING TO...
DIE...
BAMM
AGGGHHHH
WH...
WHAT THE HELL ARE YOU DOING, YOU #@$%?!
DON'T YOU CARE IF SHE'S KILLED...?
I DON'T HAVE A LOT OF PATIENCE EITHER.
YOU AND I ARE GONNA GET ALONG FINE.

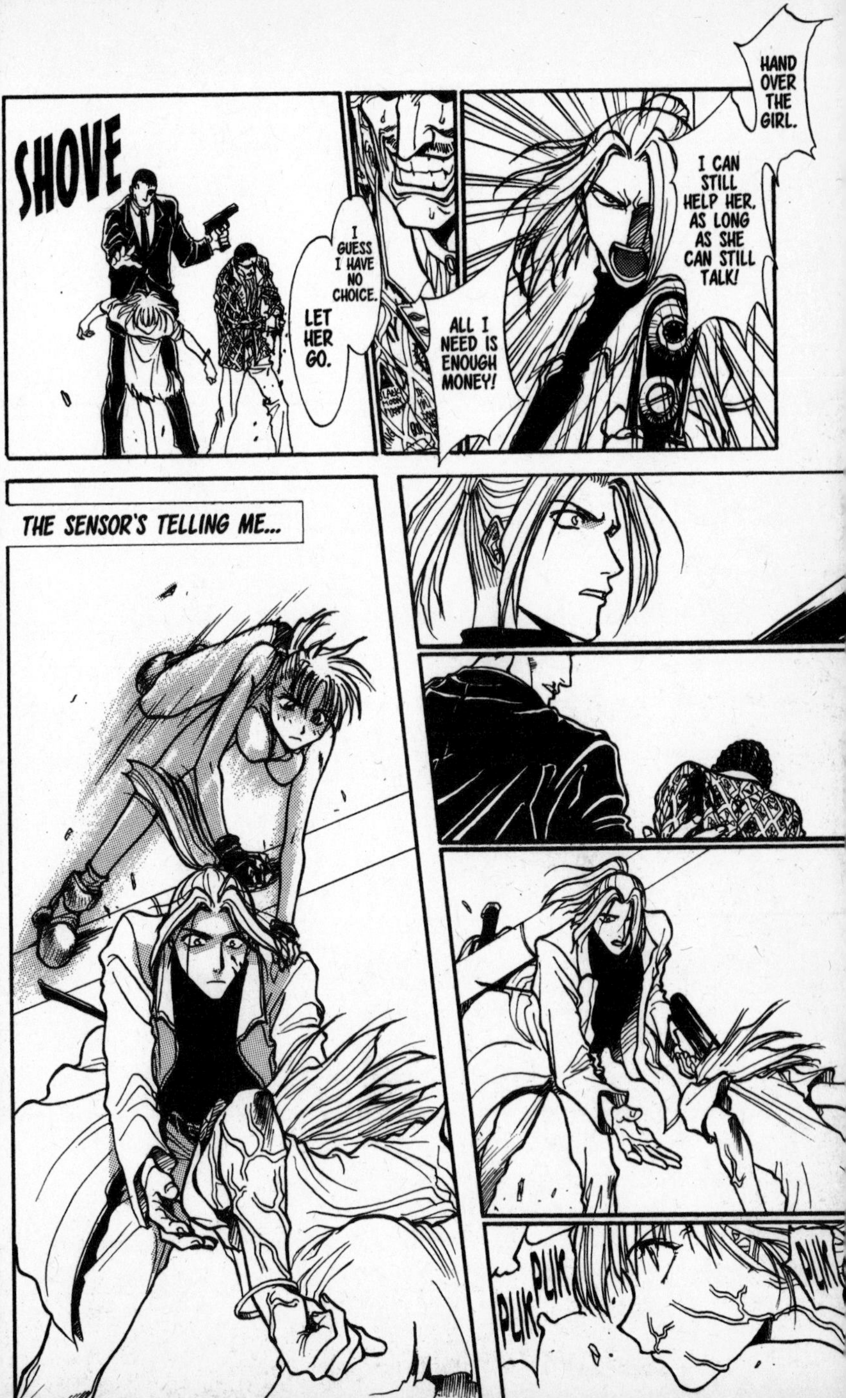
HAND OVER THE GIRL.
I CAN STILL HELP HER. AS LONG AS SHE CAN STILL TALK!
ALL I NEED IS ENOUGH MONEY!
I GUESS I HAVE NO CHOICE.
LET HER GO.
SHOVE
PUK
PUK
PUK
PUK
THE SENSOR'S TELLING ME...

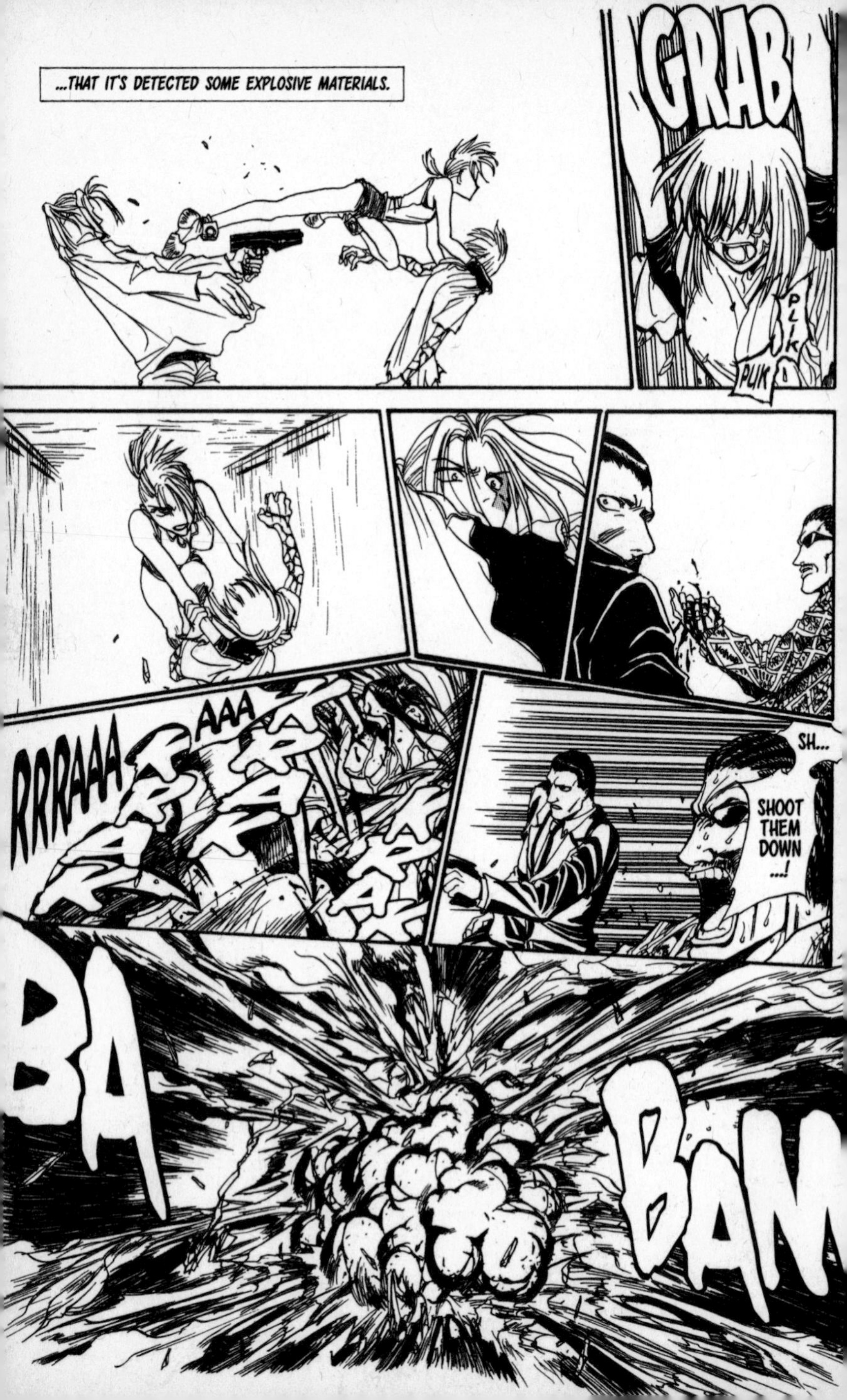
GRAB
PLIK
PUK
...THAT IT'S DETECTED SOME EXPLOSIVE MATERIALS.
SH...
SHOOT THEM DOWN ...!
AAA
RRRAAA
BA
BAM

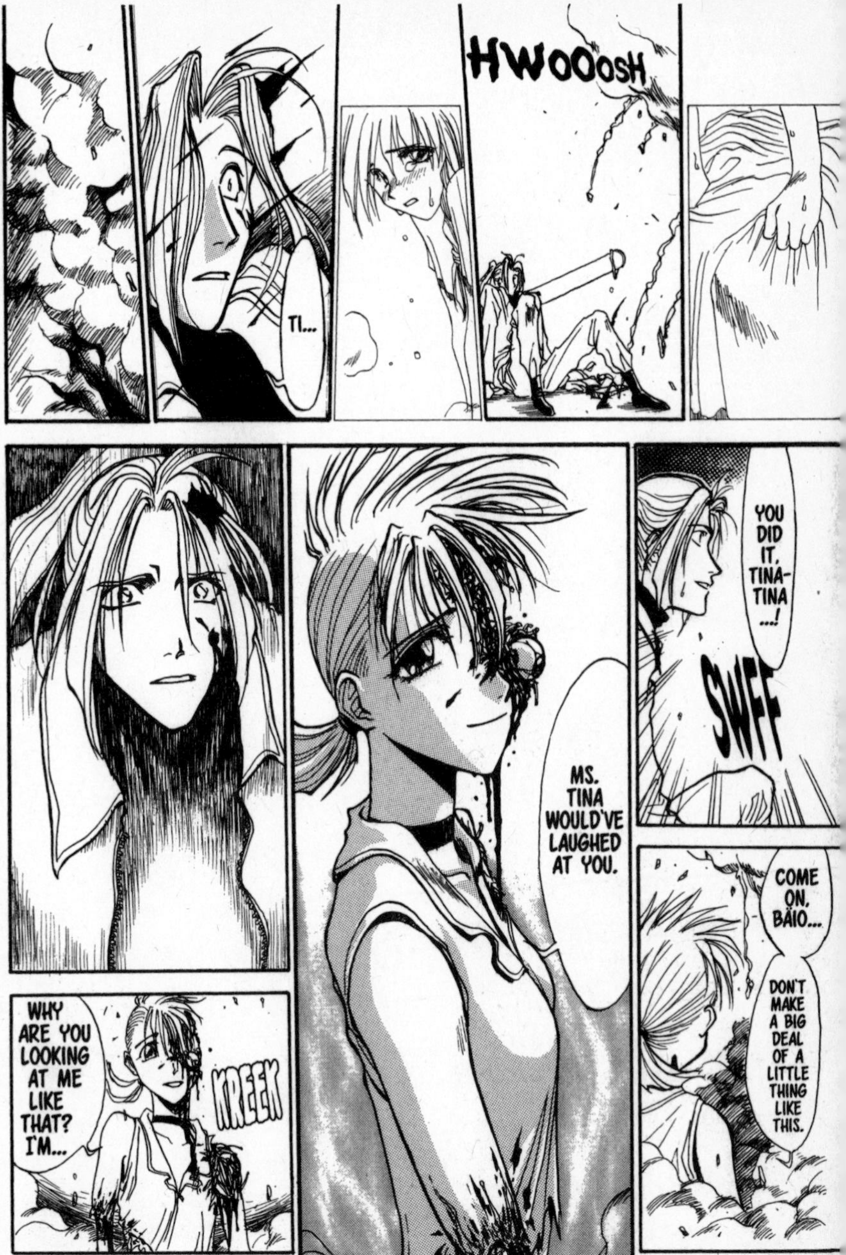
HWOOOSH
TI...
YOU DID IT, TINA-TINA...!
SWFF
COME ON, BÄIO...
DON'T MAKE A BIG DEAL OF A LITTLE THING LIKE THIS.
MS. TINA WOULD'VE LAUGHED AT YOU.
WHY ARE YOU LOOKING AT ME LIKE THAT? I'M...
KREEK

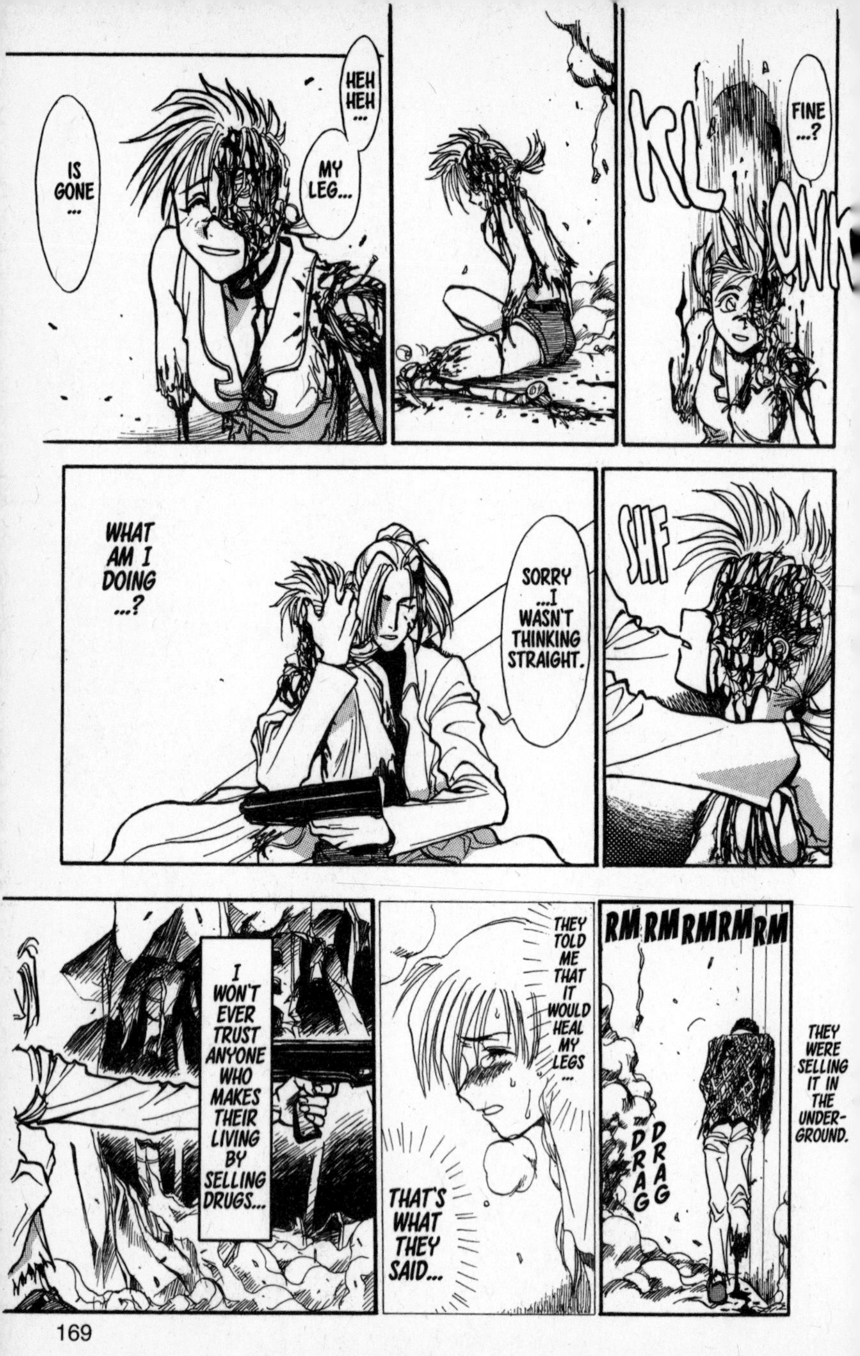
KLONK
FINE ...?
HEH HEH ...
MY LEG...
IS GONE ...
SHF
SORRY ...I WASN'T THINKING STRAIGHT.
WHAT AM I DOING ...?
RM RM RM RM RM
THEY WERE SELLING IT IN THE UNDER-GROUND.
DRAG DRAG
THEY TOLD ME THAT IT WOULD HEAL MY LEGS ...
THAT'S WHAT THEY SAID...
I WON'T EVER TRUST ANYONE WHO MAKES THEIR LIVING BY SELLING DRUGS...

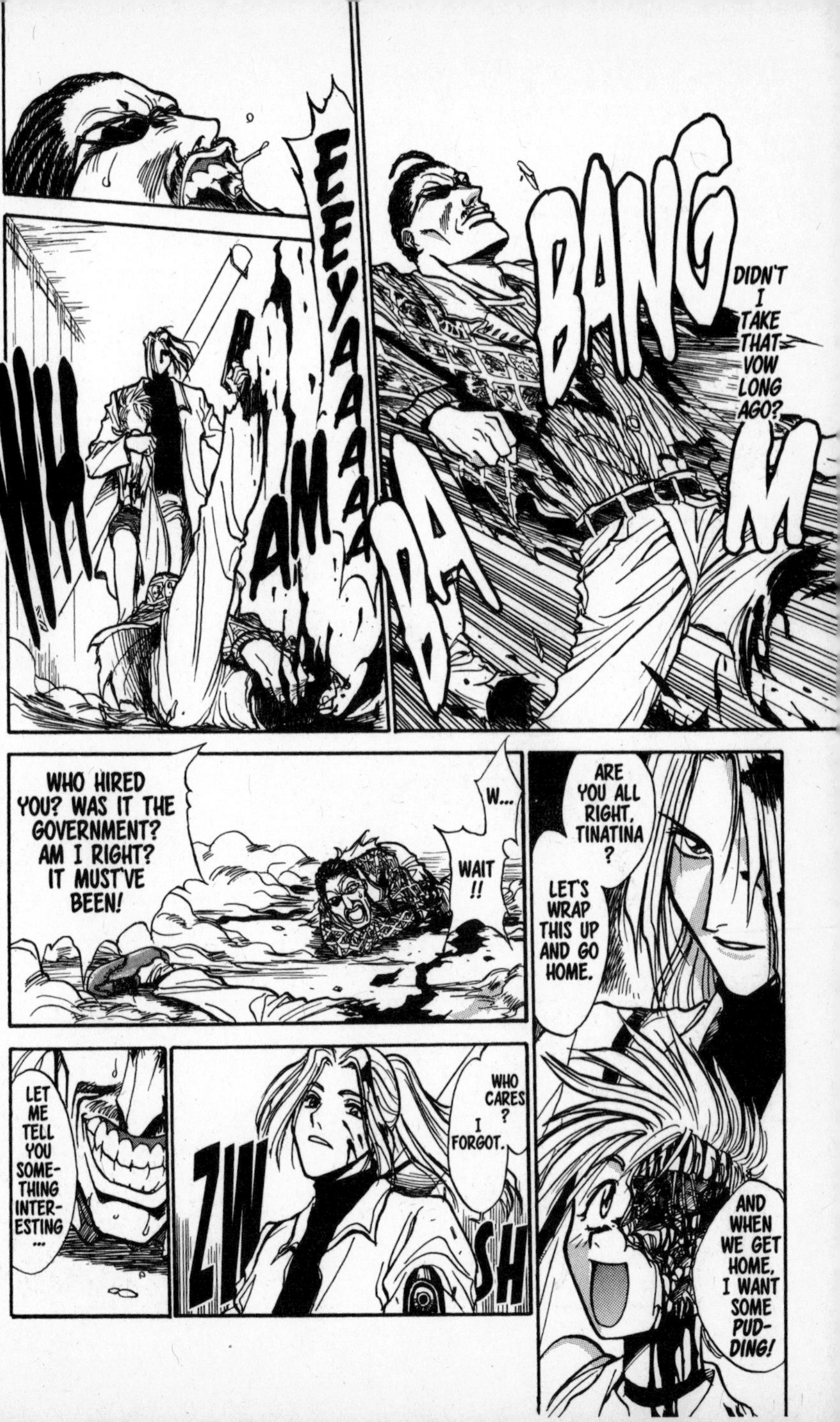
BANG
DIDN'T I TAKE THAT VOW LONG AGO?
BAM
EEYAAAAAA
WHAM
ARE YOU ALL RIGHT, TINATINA?
LET'S WRAP THIS UP AND GO HOME.
AND WHEN WE GET HOME, I WANT SOME PUD-DING!
W...
WAIT!!
WHO HIRED YOU? WAS IT THE GOVERNMENT? AM I RIGHT? IT MUST'VE BEEN!
WHO CARES? I FORGOT.
ZWISH
LET ME TELL YOU SOME-THING INTER-ESTING...

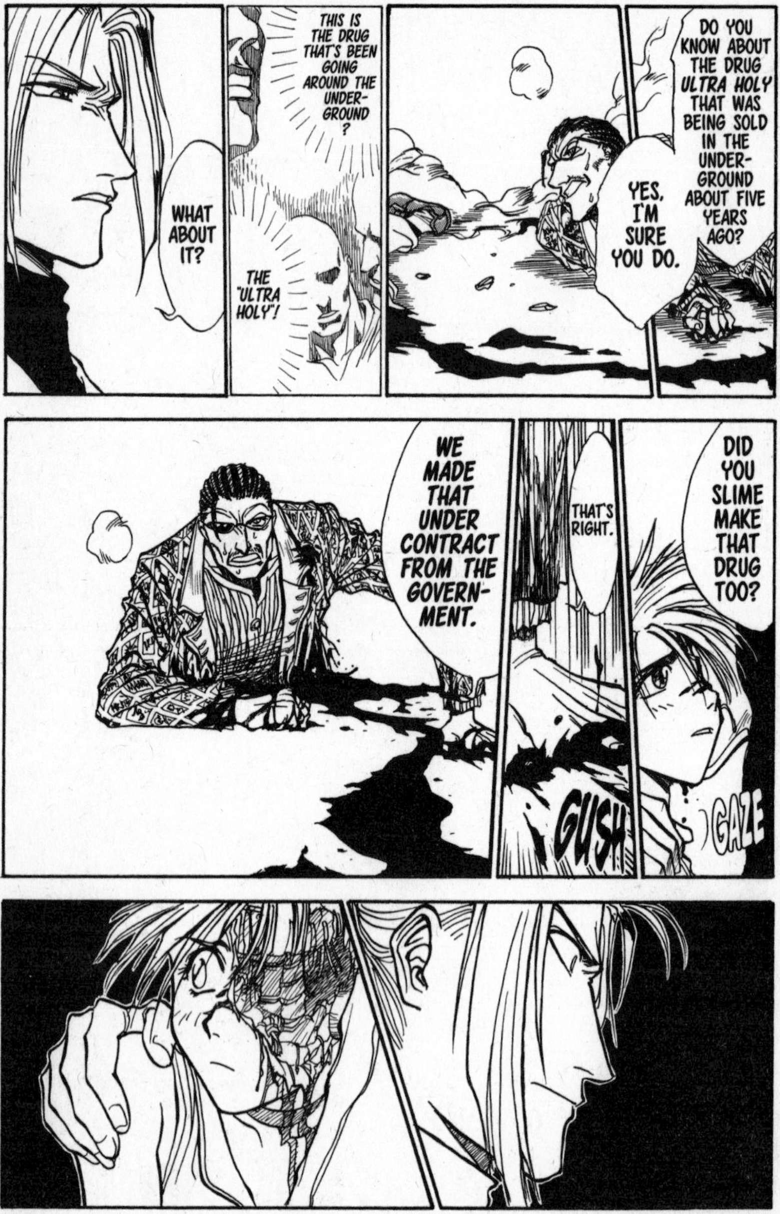
DO YOU KNOW ABOUT THE DRUG *ULTRA HOLY* THAT WAS BEING SOLD IN THE UNDERGROUND ABOUT FIVE YEARS AGO?
YES, I'M SURE YOU DO.
THIS IS THE DRUG THAT'S BEEN GOING AROUND THE UNDERGROUND?
THE "ULTRA HOLY"!
WHAT ABOUT IT?
DID YOU SLIME MAKE THAT DRUG TOO?
GAZE
THAT'S RIGHT.
GUSH
WE MADE THAT UNDER CONTRACT FROM THE GOVERNMENT.

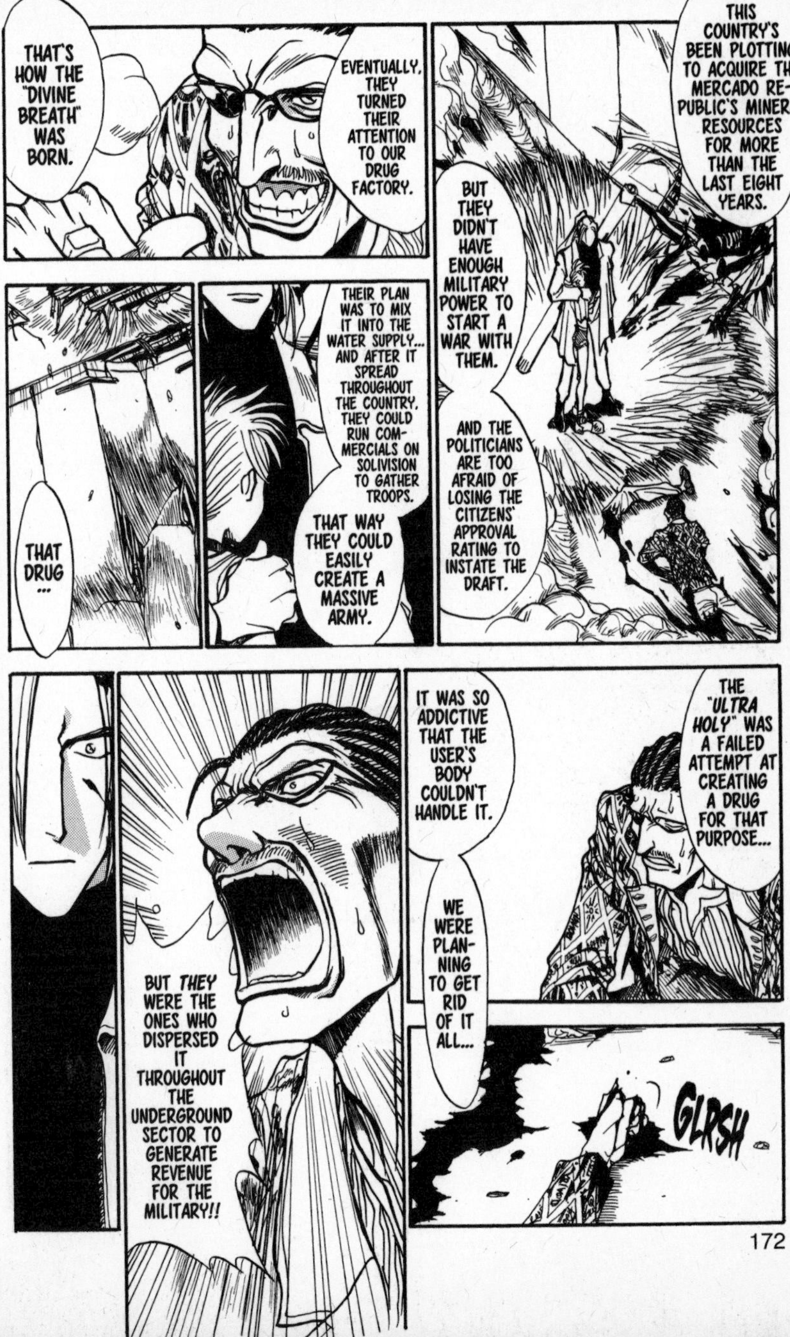
THIS COUNTRY'S BEEN PLOTTING TO ACQUIRE THE MERCADO REPUBLIC'S MINERAL RESOURCES FOR MORE THAN THE LAST EIGHT YEARS.
BUT THEY DIDN'T HAVE ENOUGH MILITARY POWER TO START A WAR WITH THEM.
AND THE POLITICIANS ARE TOO AFRAID OF LOSING THE CITIZENS' APPROVAL RATING TO INSTATE THE DRAFT.
EVENTUALLY, THEY TURNED THEIR ATTENTION TO OUR DRUG FACTORY.
THAT'S HOW THE "DIVINE BREATH" WAS BORN.
THEIR PLAN WAS TO MIX IT INTO THE WATER SUPPLY... AND AFTER IT SPREAD THROUGHOUT THE COUNTRY, THEY COULD RUN COMMERCIALS ON SOLIVISION TO GATHER TROOPS.
THAT WAY THEY COULD EASILY CREATE A MASSIVE ARMY.
THAT DRUG...
THE "*ULTRA HOLY*" WAS A FAILED ATTEMPT AT CREATING A DRUG FOR THAT PURPOSE...
IT WAS SO ADDICTIVE THAT THE USER'S BODY COULDN'T HANDLE IT.
WE WERE PLANNING TO GET RID OF IT ALL...
GLRSH
BUT *THEY* WERE THE ONES WHO DISPERSED IT THROUGHOUT THE UNDERGROUND SECTOR TO GENERATE REVENUE FOR THE MILITARY!!

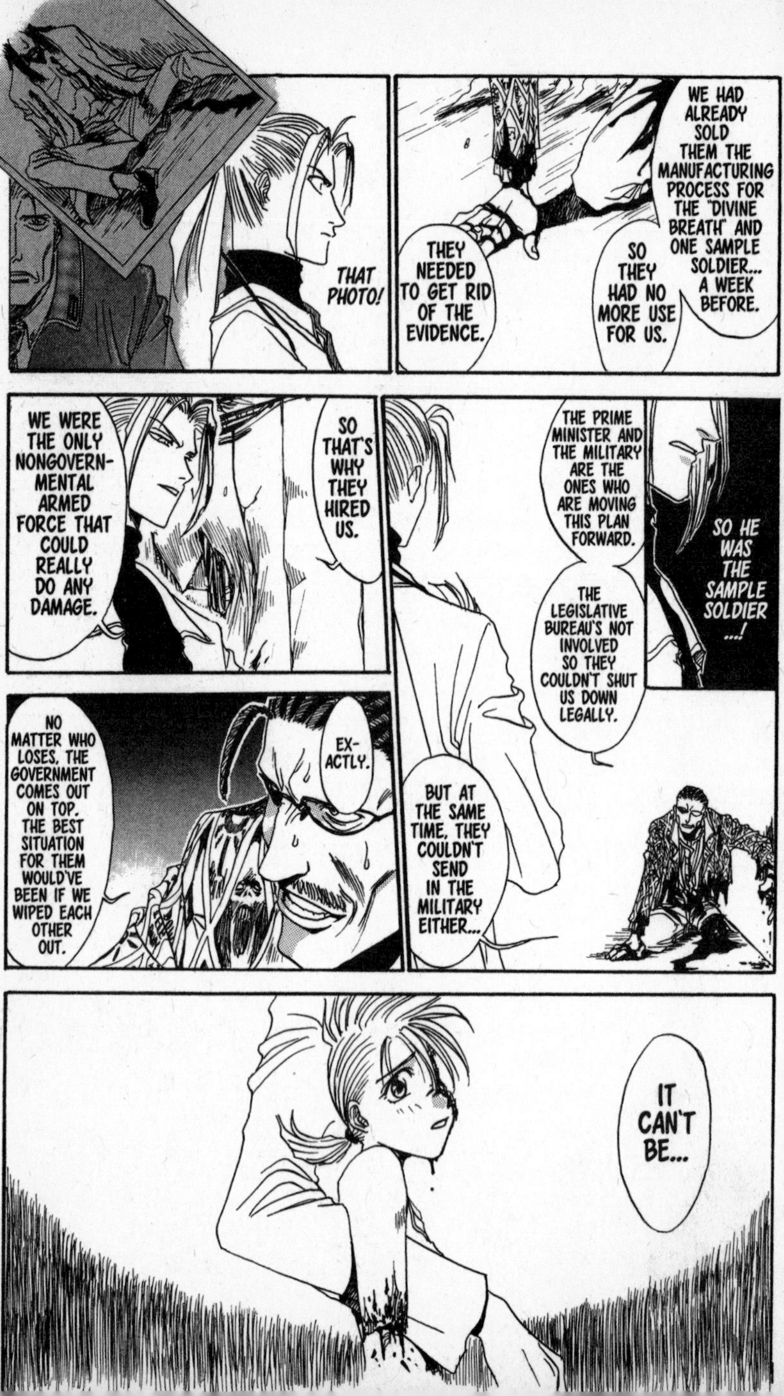
WE HAD ALREADY SOLD THEM THE MANUFACTURING PROCESS FOR THE "DIVINE BREATH" AND ONE SAMPLE SOLDIER... A WEEK BEFORE.
SO THEY HAD NO MORE USE FOR US.
THEY NEEDED TO GET RID OF THE EVIDENCE.
THAT PHOTO!
SO HE WAS THE SAMPLE SOLDIER...!
THE PRIME MINISTER AND THE MILITARY ARE THE ONES WHO ARE MOVING THIS PLAN FORWARD.
THE LEGISLATIVE BUREAU'S NOT INVOLVED SO THEY COULDN'T SHUT US DOWN LEGALLY.
BUT AT THE SAME TIME, THEY COULDN'T SEND IN THE MILITARY EITHER...
SO THAT'S WHY THEY HIRED US.
WE WERE THE ONLY NONGOVERNMENTAL ARMED FORCE THAT COULD REALLY DO ANY DAMAGE.
EXACTLY.
NO MATTER WHO LOSES, THE GOVERNMENT COMES OUT ON TOP. THE BEST SITUATION FOR THEM WOULD'VE BEEN IF WE WIPED EACH OTHER OUT.
IT CAN'T BE...

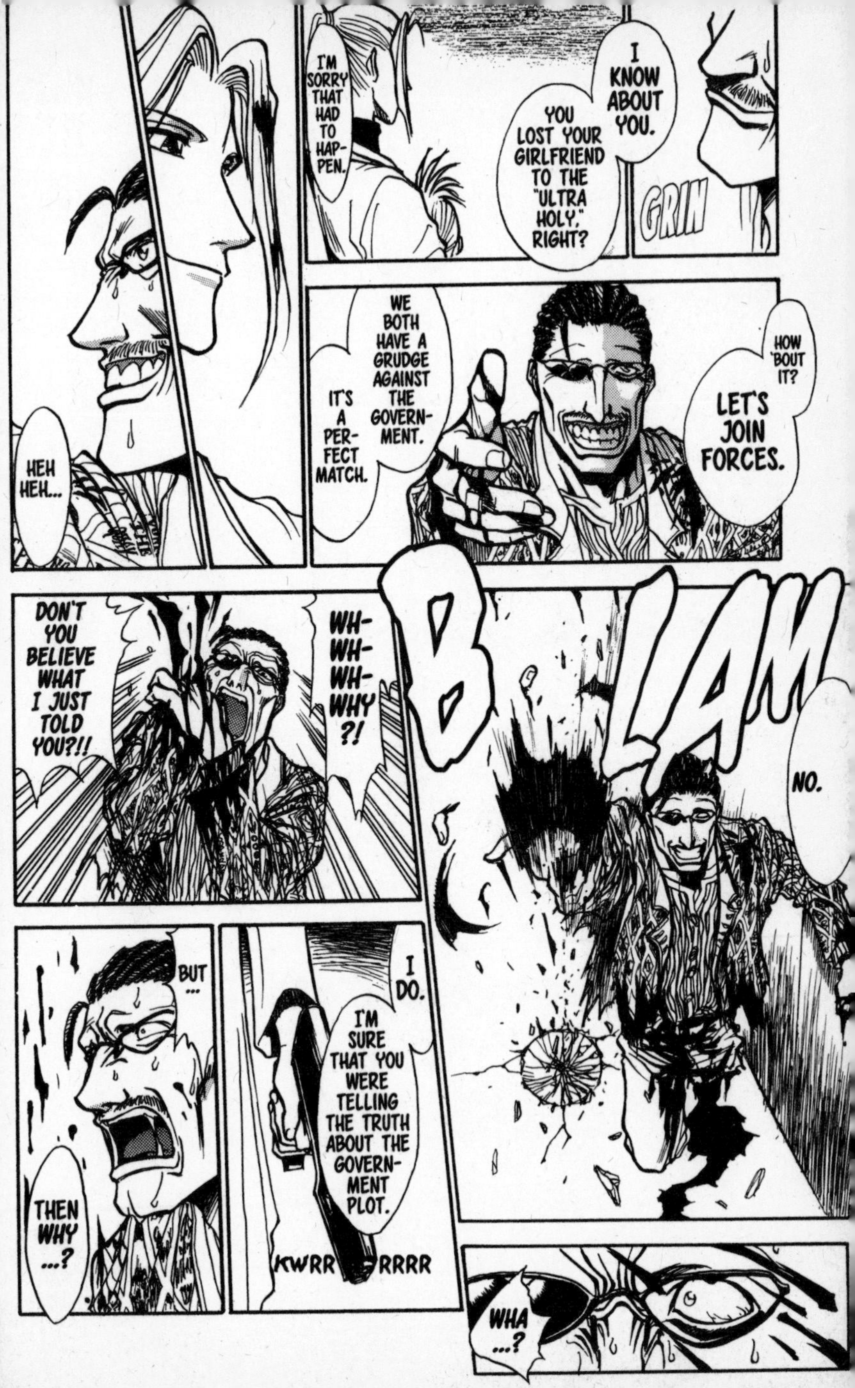
I KNOW ABOUT YOU.
YOU LOST YOUR GIRLFRIEND TO THE "ULTRA HOLY," RIGHT?
GRIN
I'M SORRY THAT HAD TO HAP-PEN.
HOW 'BOUT IT?
LET'S JOIN FORCES.
WE BOTH HAVE A GRUDGE AGAINST THE GOVERN-MENT.
IT'S A PER-FECT MATCH.
HEH HEH...
BLAM
NO.
WH-WH-WH-WHY?!
DON'T YOU BELIEVE WHAT I JUST TOLD YOU?!!
I DO.
I'M SURE THAT YOU WERE TELLING THE TRUTH ABOUT THE GOVERN-MENT PLOT.
KWRR RRRR
BUT...
THEN WHY...?
WHA...?

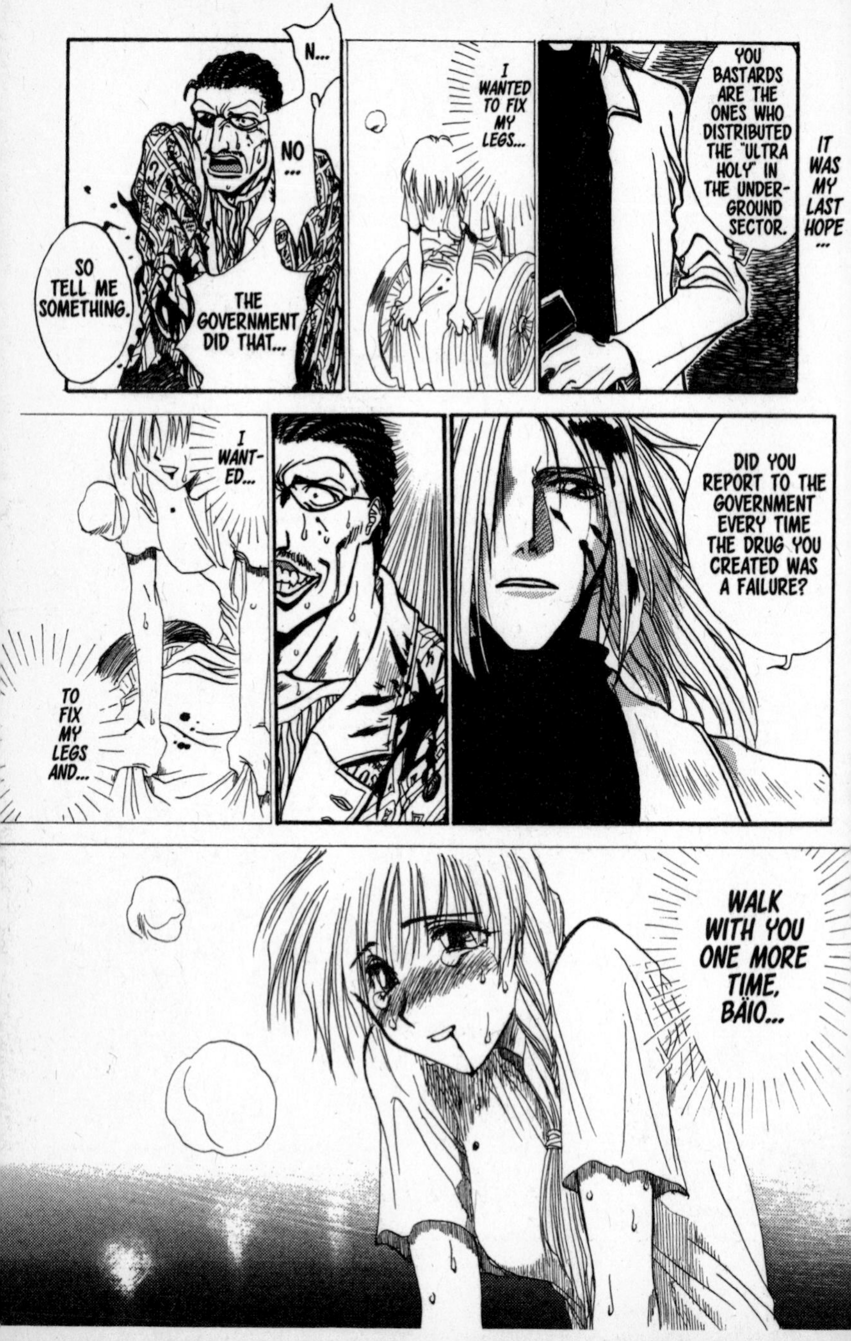
YOU BASTARDS ARE THE ONES WHO DISTRIBUTED THE "ULTRA HOLY" IN THE UNDERGROUND SECTOR.
IT WAS MY LAST HOPE...
I WANTED TO FIX MY LEGS...
N...
NO...
THE GOVERNMENT DID THAT...
SO TELL ME SOMETHING.
DID YOU REPORT TO THE GOVERNMENT EVERY TIME THE DRUG YOU CREATED WAS A FAILURE?
I WANTED...
TO FIX MY LEGS AND...
WALK WITH YOU ONE MORE TIME, BÄIO...

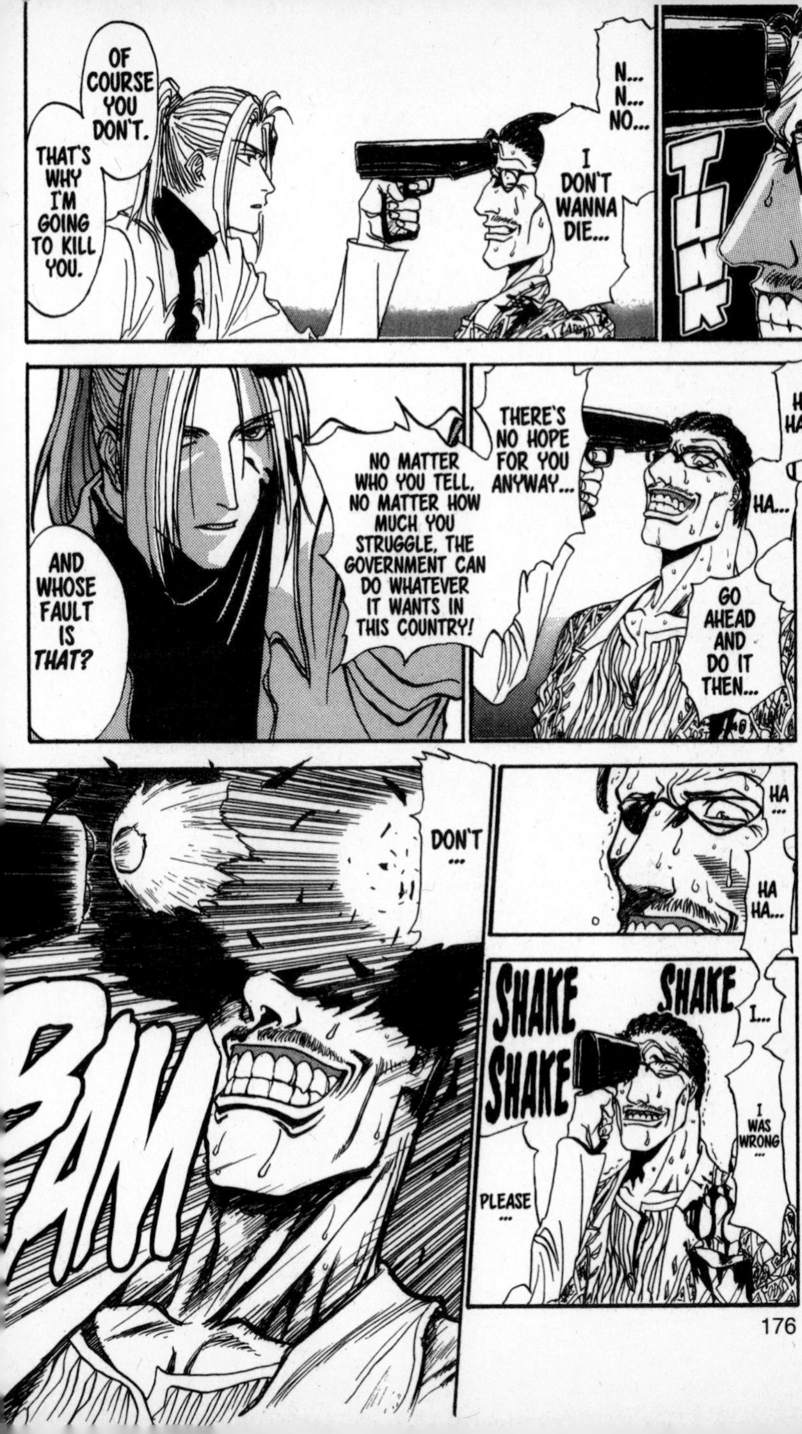
THUNK
N... N... NO...
I DON'T WANNA DIE...
OF COURSE YOU DON'T.
THAT'S WHY I'M GOING TO KILL YOU.
HA HA...
HA...
THERE'S NO HOPE FOR YOU ANYWAY...
NO MATTER WHO YOU TELL, NO MATTER HOW MUCH YOU STRUGGLE, THE GOVERNMENT CAN DO WHATEVER IT WANTS IN THIS COUNTRY!
GO AHEAD AND DO IT THEN...
AND WHOSE FAULT IS *THAT?*
HA...
HA HA...
SHAKE SHAKE
SHAKE SHAKE
I...
I WAS WRONG...
PLEASE...
DON'T...
BAM

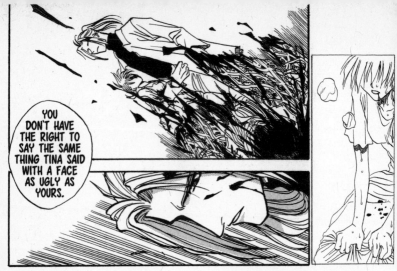

YOU DON'T HAVE THE RIGHT TO SAY THE SAME THING TINA SAID WITH A FACE AS UGLY AS YOURS.

BOOM

OKAY.

LET'S WRAP IT UP, TINATINA.

BAI...

GWOOOOOOOOMM

CAPTAIN !!

177

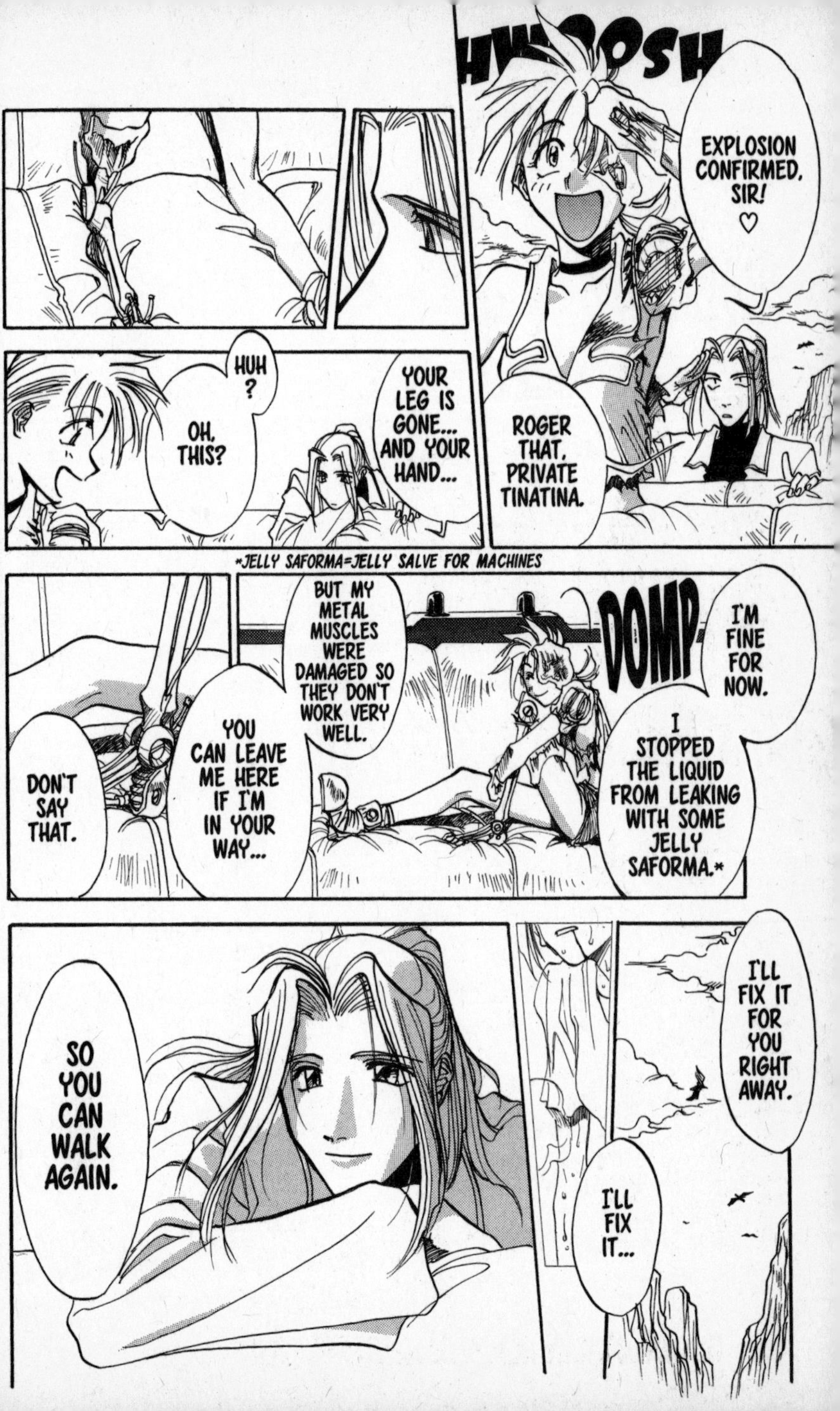
HWOOSH
EXPLOSION CONFIRMED, SIR! ♡
ROGER THAT, PRIVATE TINATINA.
YOUR LEG IS GONE... AND YOUR HAND...
HUH?
OH, THIS?
*JELLY SAFORMA=JELLY SALVE FOR MACHINES
DOMP
I'M FINE FOR NOW.
I STOPPED THE LIQUID FROM LEAKING WITH SOME JELLY SAFORMA.*
BUT MY METAL MUSCLES WERE DAMAGED SO THEY DON'T WORK VERY WELL.
YOU CAN LEAVE ME HERE IF I'M IN YOUR WAY...
DON'T SAY THAT.
I'LL FIX IT FOR YOU RIGHT AWAY.
I'LL FIX IT...
SO YOU CAN WALK AGAIN.

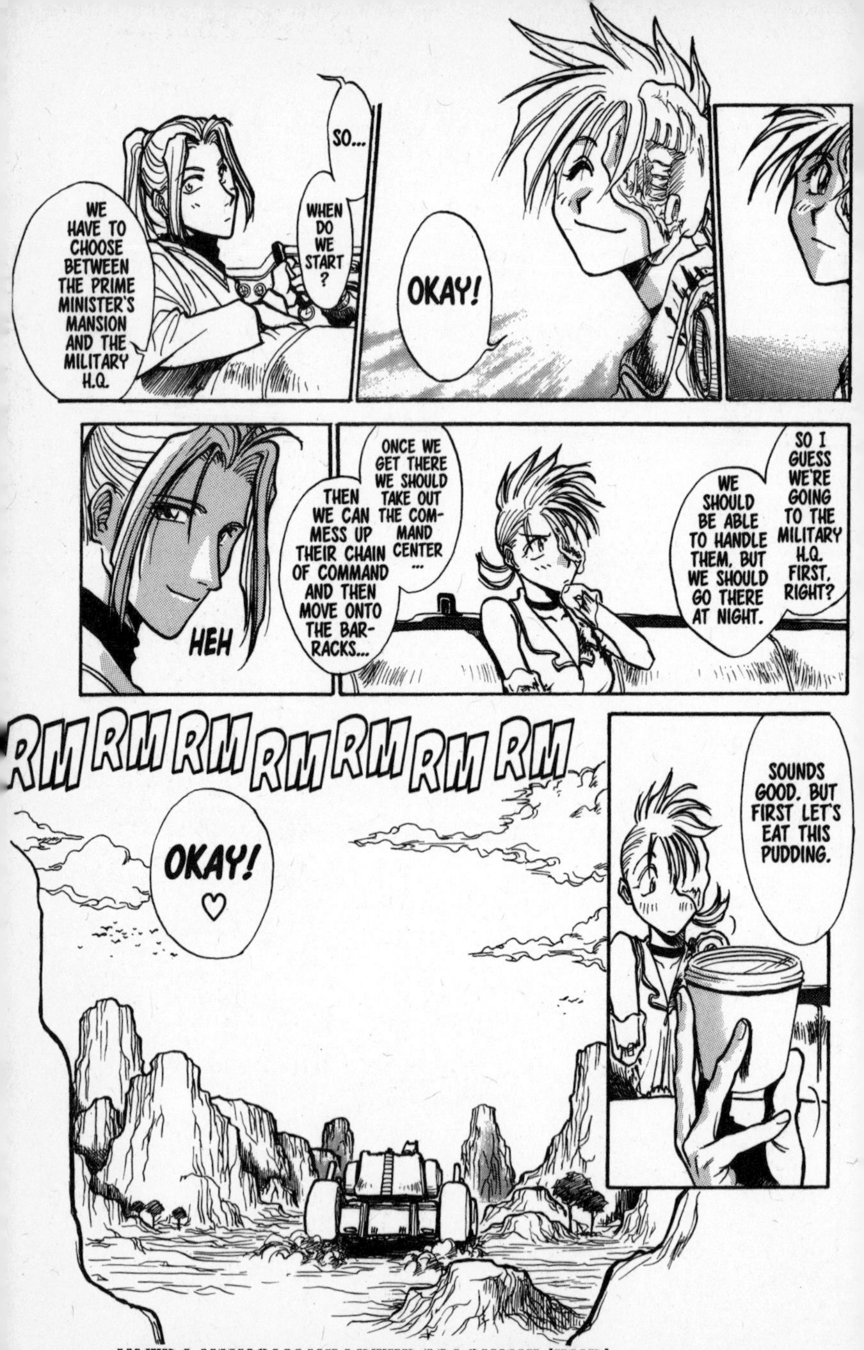
OKAY!
SO...
WHEN DO WE START?
WE HAVE TO CHOOSE BETWEEN THE PRIME MINISTER'S MANSION AND THE MILITARY H.Q.
SO I GUESS WE'RE GOING TO THE MILITARY H.Q. FIRST, RIGHT?
WE SHOULD BE ABLE TO HANDLE THEM, BUT WE SHOULD GO THERE AT NIGHT.
ONCE WE GET THERE WE SHOULD TAKE OUT THE COMMAND CENTER...
THEN WE CAN MESS UP THEIR CHAIN OF COMMAND AND THEN MOVE ONTO THE BARRACKS...
HEH
SOUNDS GOOD. BUT FIRST LET'S EAT THIS PUDDING.
RM RM RM RM RM RM RM RM
OKAY! ♥

ULTRA UNHOLY HEARTED MACHINE (END)

# SPECIAL FEATURE!!
# CHARACTERS' IMAGE MUSIC SOUNDTRACKS

Well, the plan was to release only three volumes of *ZOMBIEPOWDER.*, but we suddenly decided (mostly for myself) to put all my short stories in there too. That's why we had to put out a fourth volume. But when we added a volume, guess where there was some space left over? That's right…at the end of this volume! (Even though it's just three pages.)

In order to deal with this emergency, I asked one of my good friends, "Do you have any good ideas?"

He replied disinterestedly, "You used to get your ideas for your characters from music. Why don't you do something like that?"

So in this section I've decided to list some of the music that helped me to visualize the "image" of each character. There might be some readers that might say "Music that helped you visualize the character's image? What are you talking about?" If you're one of those people, try to think of them as theme songs. By the way, it's image "music," not image "songs." The important thing is the melody and the emotional associations…the lyrics have nothing to do with it.

I wonder if anyone's going to enjoy this section? But I did have fun writing it.

Tite Kubo (DJ. TITE)

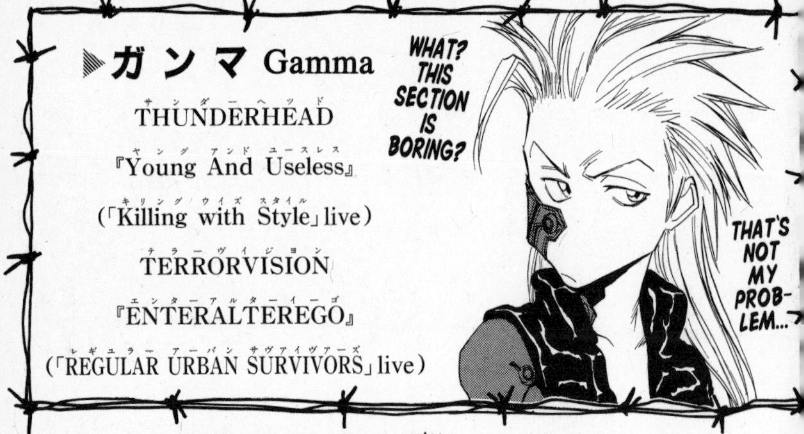
WHAT? THIS SECTION IS BORING?
THAT'S NOT MY PROB-LEM...

### ▶ガンマ Gamma

THUNDERHEAD

『Young And Useless』

(「Killing with Style」live)

TERRORVISION

『ENTERALTEREGO』

(「REGULAR URBAN SURVIVORS」live)

### ▶スミス Smith

PROPELLERHEADS

『History Repeating (Featuring Miss Shirley Bassey)』

(「DECKSANDRUMSANDROCKANDROLL」live)

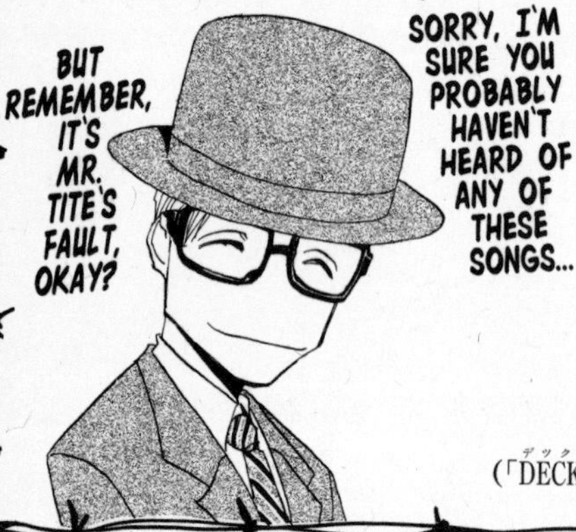
SORRY, I'M SURE YOU PROBABLY HAVEN'T HEARD OF ANY OF THESE SONGS...
BUT REMEMBER, IT'S MR. TITE'S FAULT, OKAY?

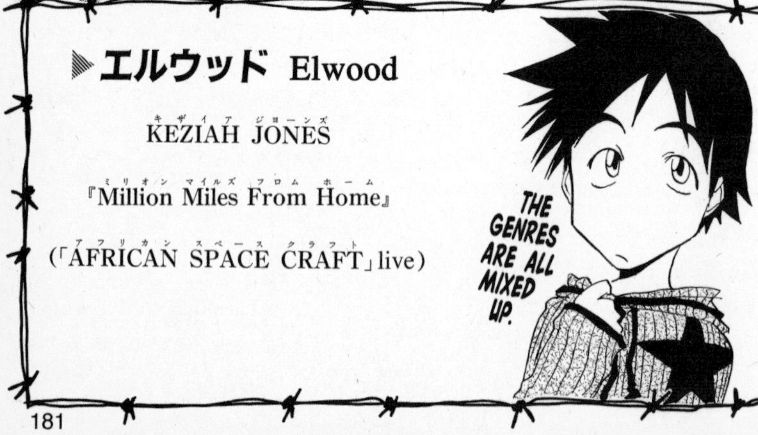
THE GENRES ARE ALL MIXED UP.

### ▶エルウッド Elwood

KEZIAH JONES

『Million Miles From Home』

(「AFRICAN SPACE CRAFT」live)

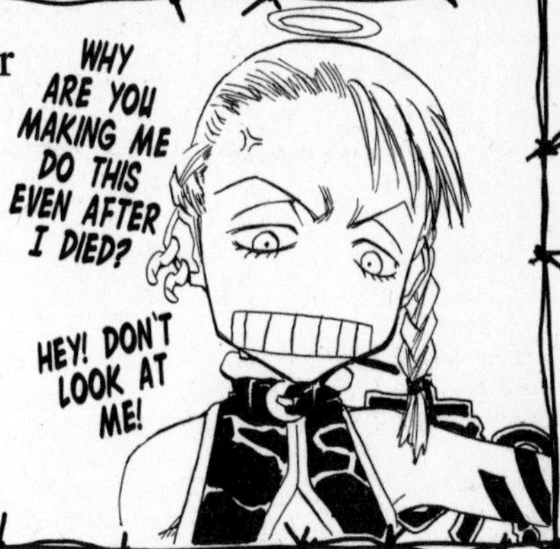
WHY ARE YOU MAKING ME DO THIS EVEN AFTER I DIED?
HEY! DON'T LOOK AT ME!

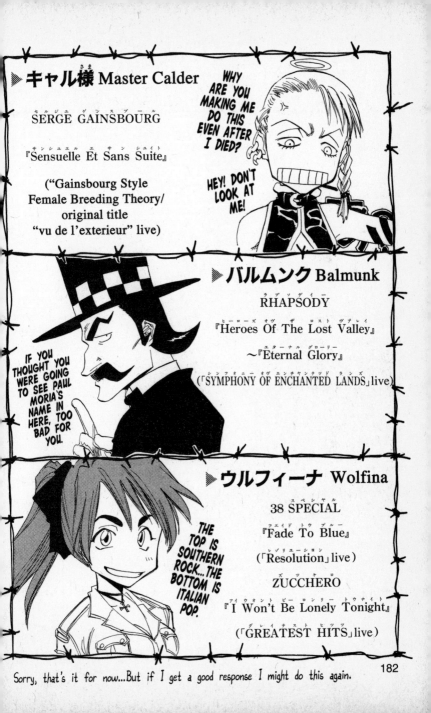

▶キャル様 Master Calder

SERGE GAINSBOURG

『Sensuelle Et Sans Suite』

(“Gainsbourg Style Female Breeding Theory/ original title “vu de l’exterieur” live)

▶バルムンク Balmunk

RHAPSODY

『Heroes Of The Lost Valley』

~『Eternal Glory』

(「SYMPHONY OF ENCHANTED LANDS」live)

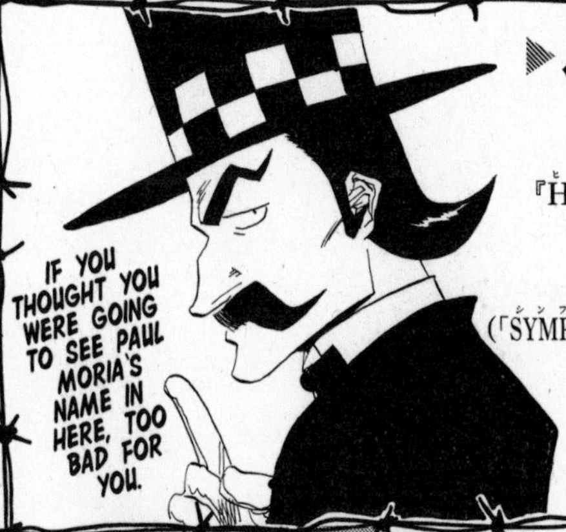
IF YOU THOUGHT YOU WERE GOING TO SEE PAUL MORIA'S NAME IN HERE, TOO BAD FOR YOU.

▶ウルフィーナ Wolfina

38 SPECIAL

『Fade To Blue』

(「Resolution」live)

ZUCCHERO

『I Won’t Be Lonely Tonight』

(「GREATEST HITS」live)

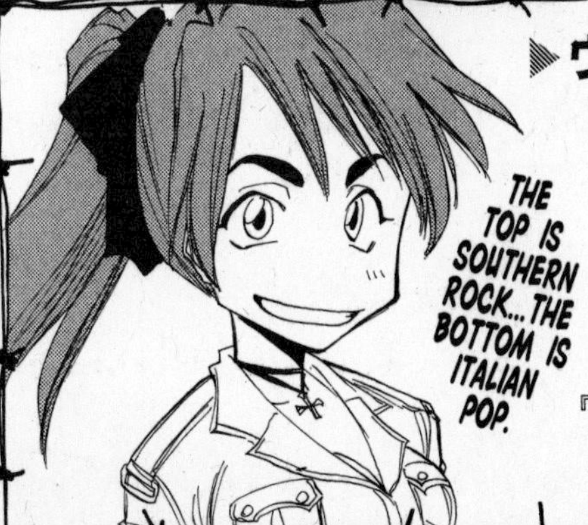
THE TOP IS SOUTHERN ROCK...THE BOTTOM IS ITALIAN POP.



Sorry, that's it for now...But if I get a good response I might do this again.

# IN THE NEXT VOLUME..

The curtain rises on Balmunk's Circus of Death, with three all-star acts of murder! Against deadly knife-throwers, fire-breathers and clowns, have our heroes finally met their match? Meanwhile, the circus train races across the desert, bearing the comatose body of Wolfina's brother. Can Wolfina set him free, or will he be consumed by the ring…and by Balmunk's lust for immortality? Includes another one of Tite Kubo's early stories, "Rune Master Urara"!

## AVAILABLE MARCH 2007!

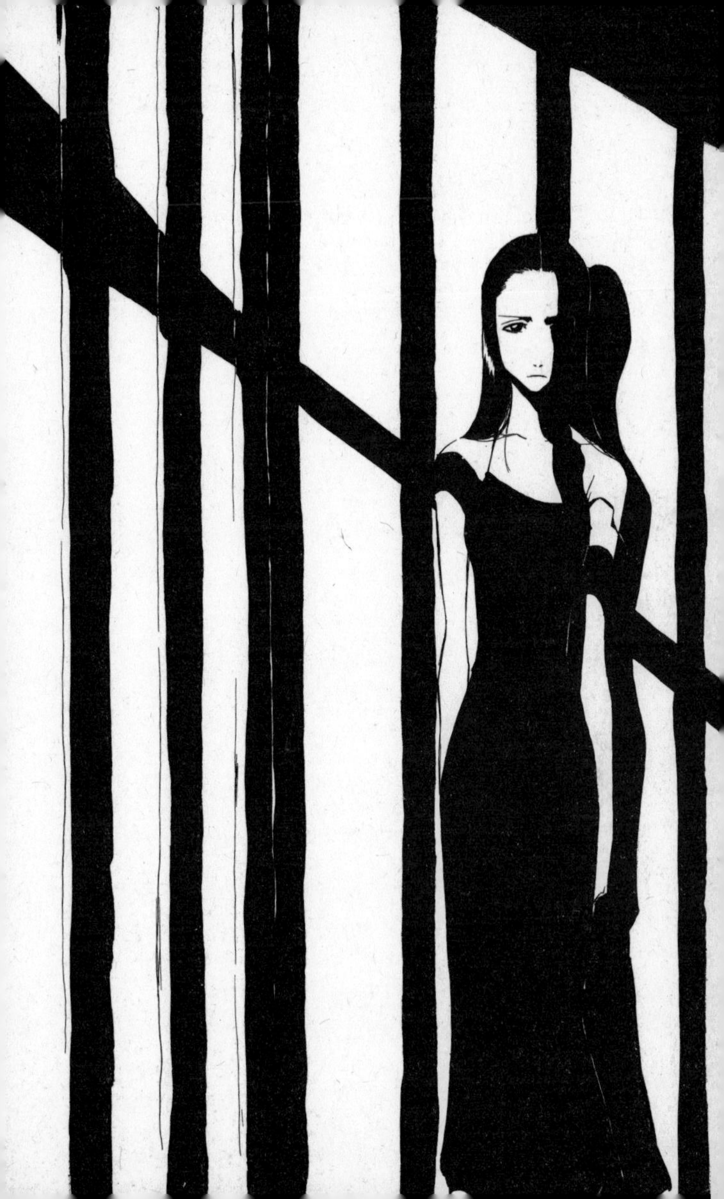

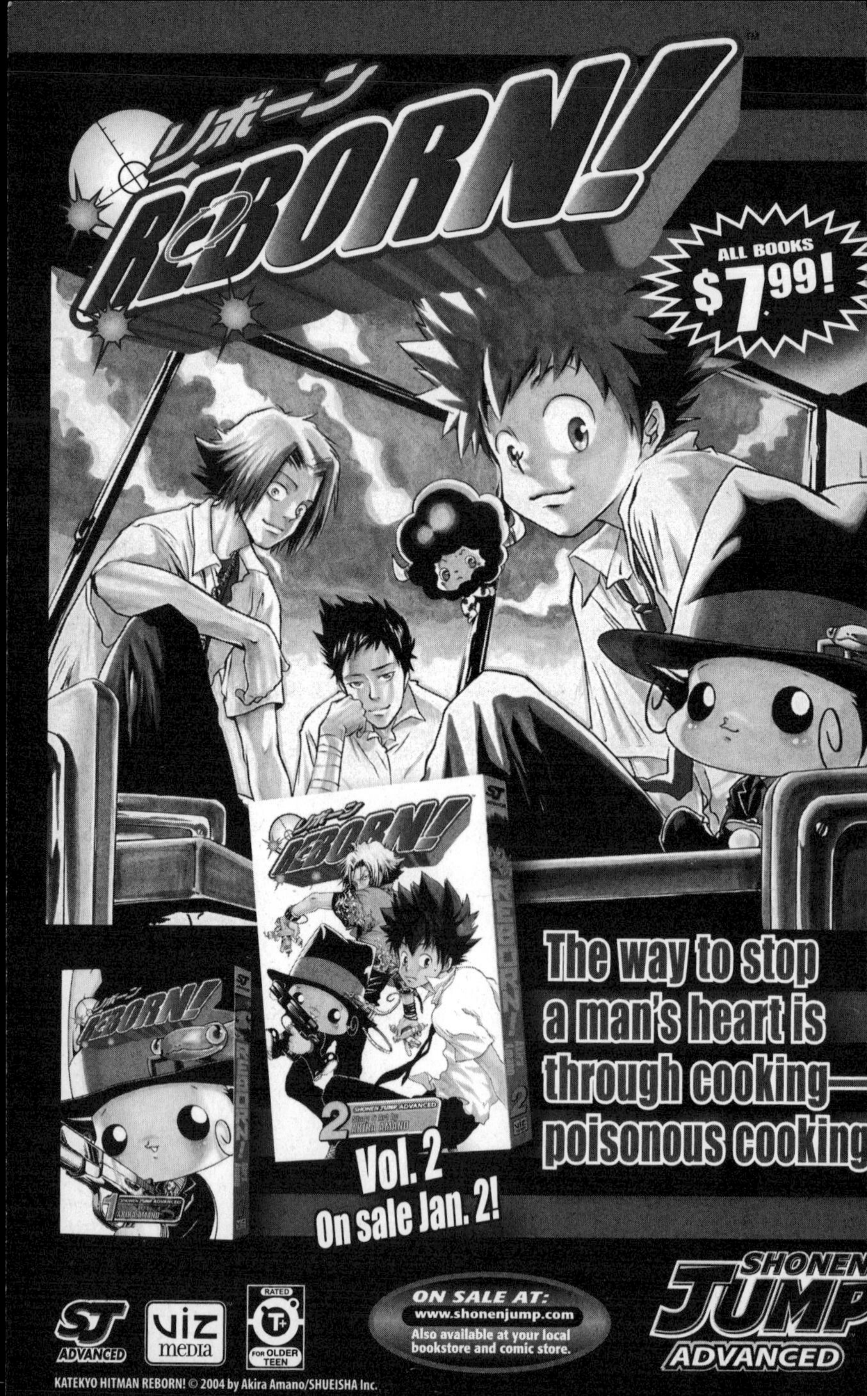
リボーン
REBORN!
ALL BOOKS $7.99!
The way to stop a man's heart is through cooking—poisonous cooking
Vol. 2
On sale Jan. 2!
SHONEN JUMP ADVANCED
ON SALE AT:
www.shonenjump.com
Also available at your local bookstore and comic store.
RATED T+ FOR OLDER TEEN
KATEKYO HITMAN REBORN! © 2004 by Akira Amano/SHUEISHA Inc.

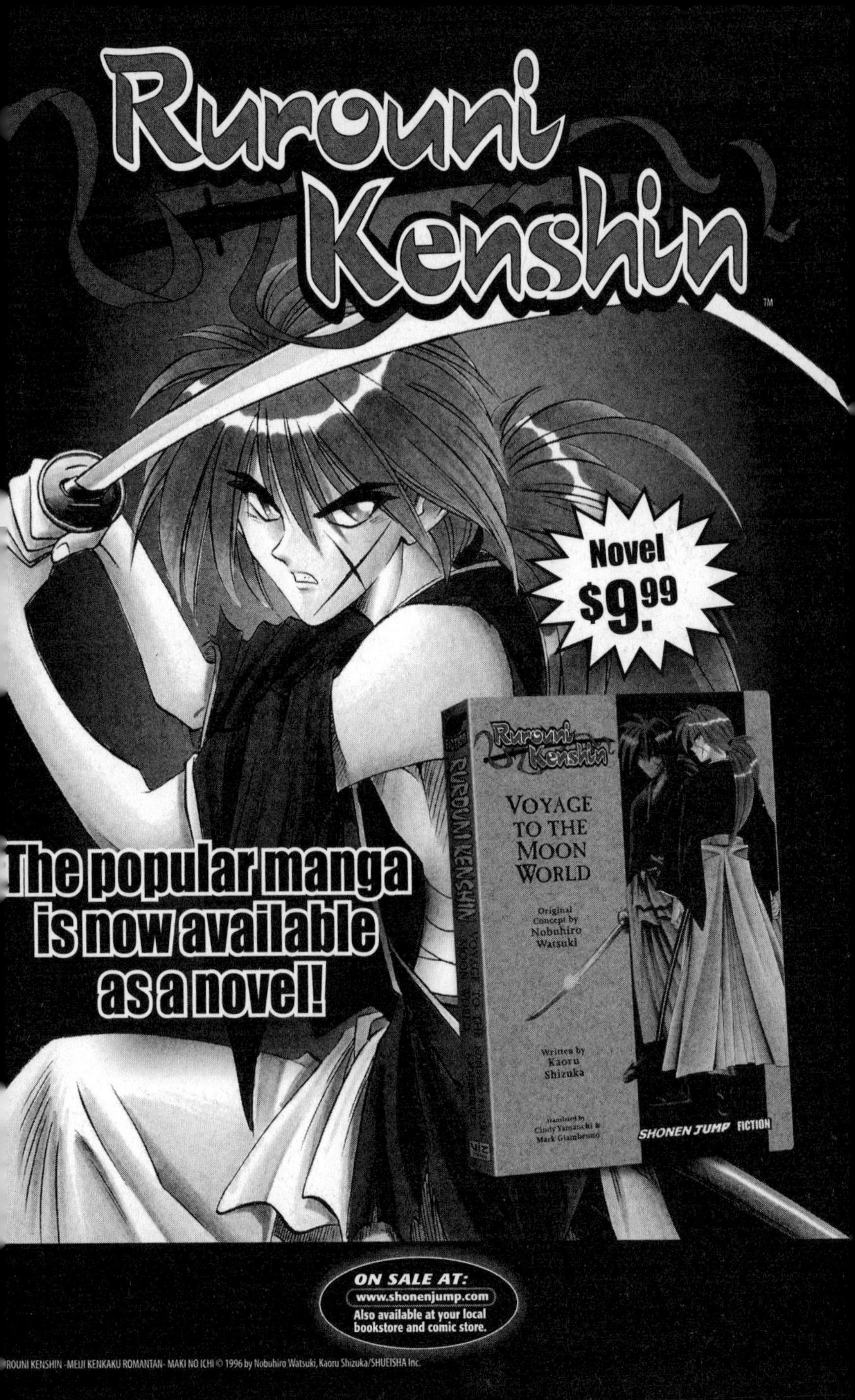

Rurouni Kenshin
™
Novel
$9.99
Rurouni Kenshin
RUROUNI KENSHIN
VOYAGE TO THE MOON WORLD
Original Concept by Nobuhiro Watsuki
Written by Kaoru Shizuka
Translated by Cindy Yamauchi & Mark Giambruno
SHONEN JUMP FICTION
The popular manga is now available as a novel!
ON SALE AT:
www.shonenjump.com
Also available at your local bookstore and comic store.

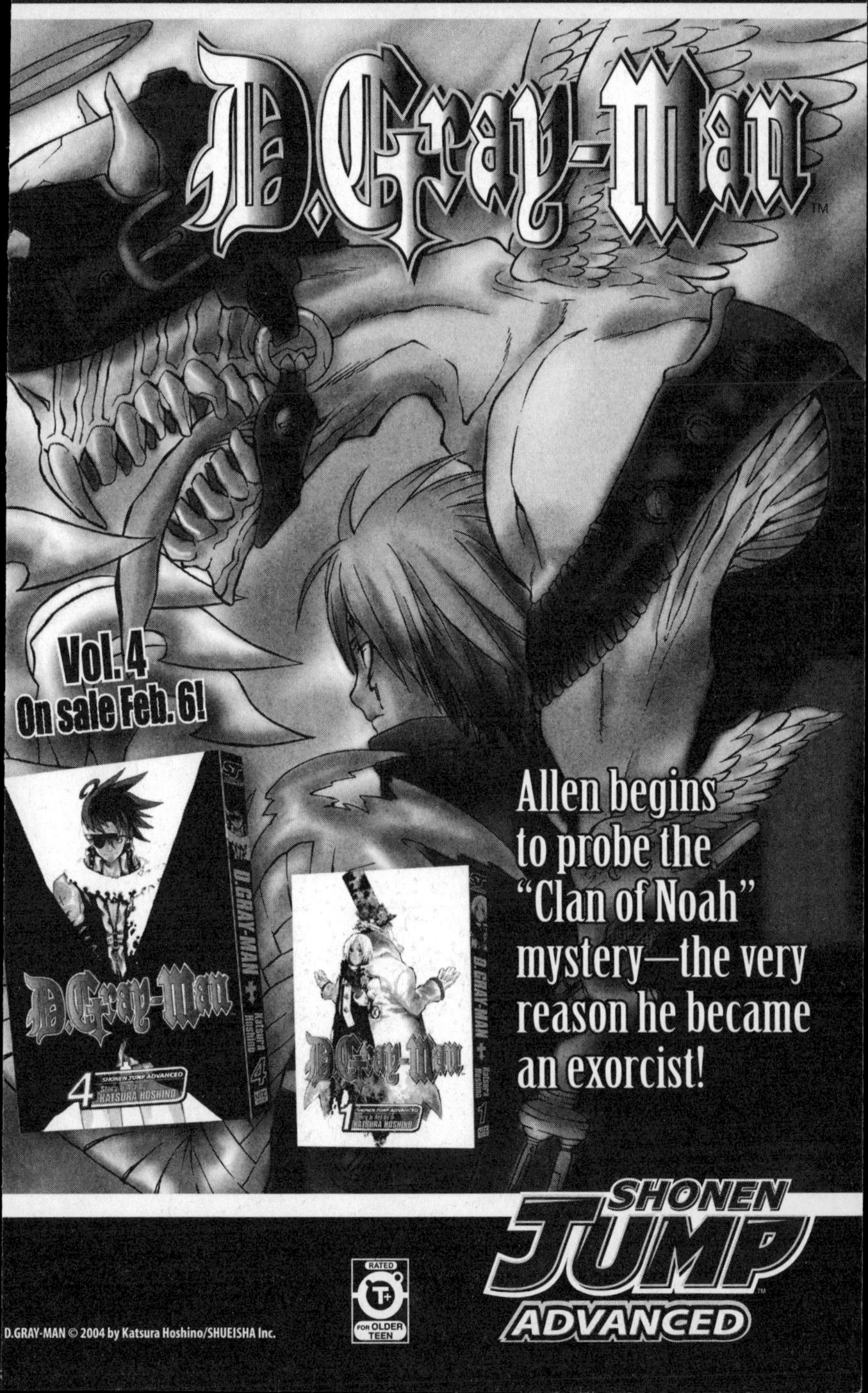
D.Gray-Man™
Vol. 4
On sale Feb. 6!
Allen begins to probe the "Clan of Noah" mystery—the very reason he became an exorcist!
D.Gray-Man
D.GRAY-MAN
4
SHONEN JUMP ADVANCED
KATSURA HOSHINO
1

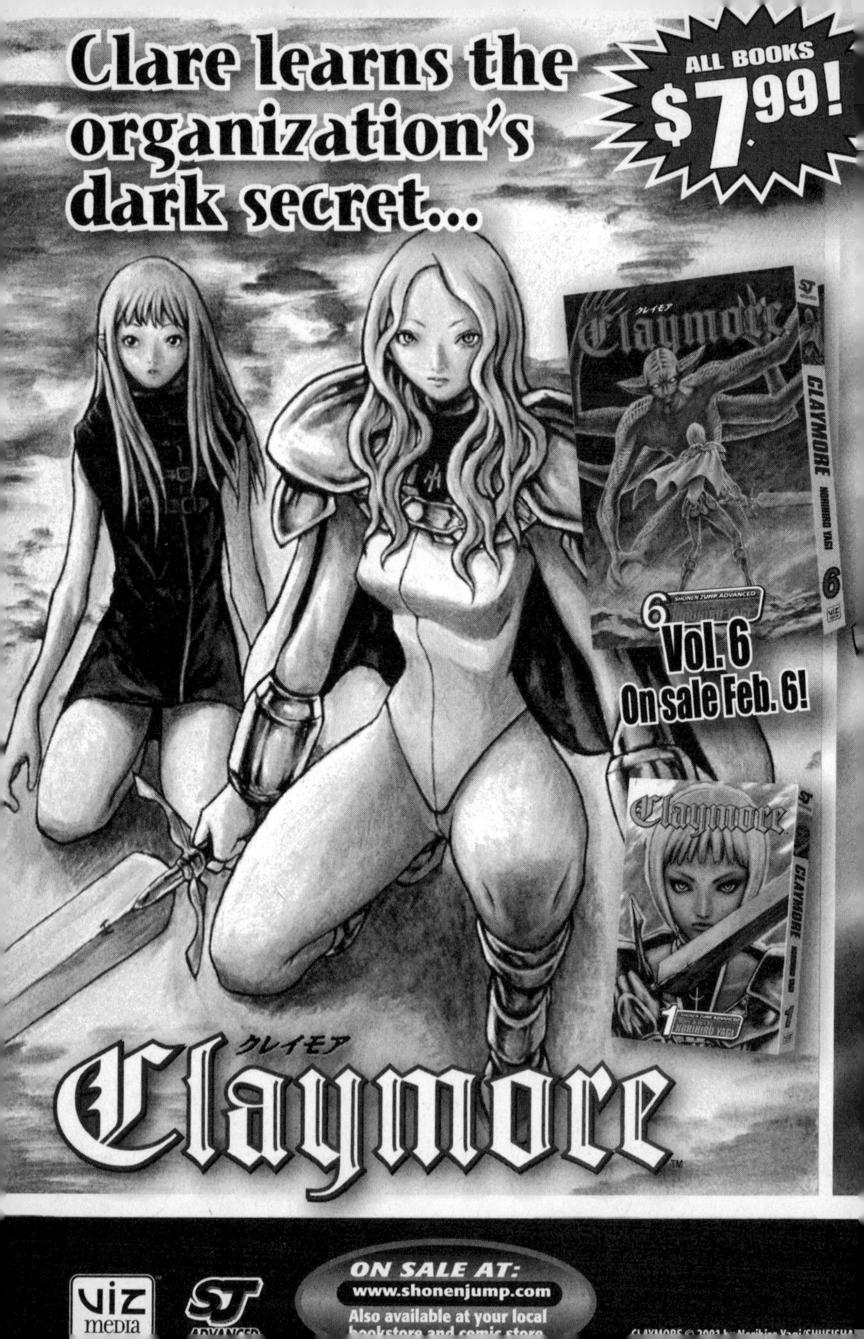

Clare learns the organization's dark secret...
ALL BOOKS $7.99!
クレイモア
Claymore
CLAYMORE
SHONEN JUMP ADVANCED
Vol. 6
On sale Feb. 6!
クレイモア
Claymore™
ON SALE AT:
www.shonenjump.com
Also available at your local

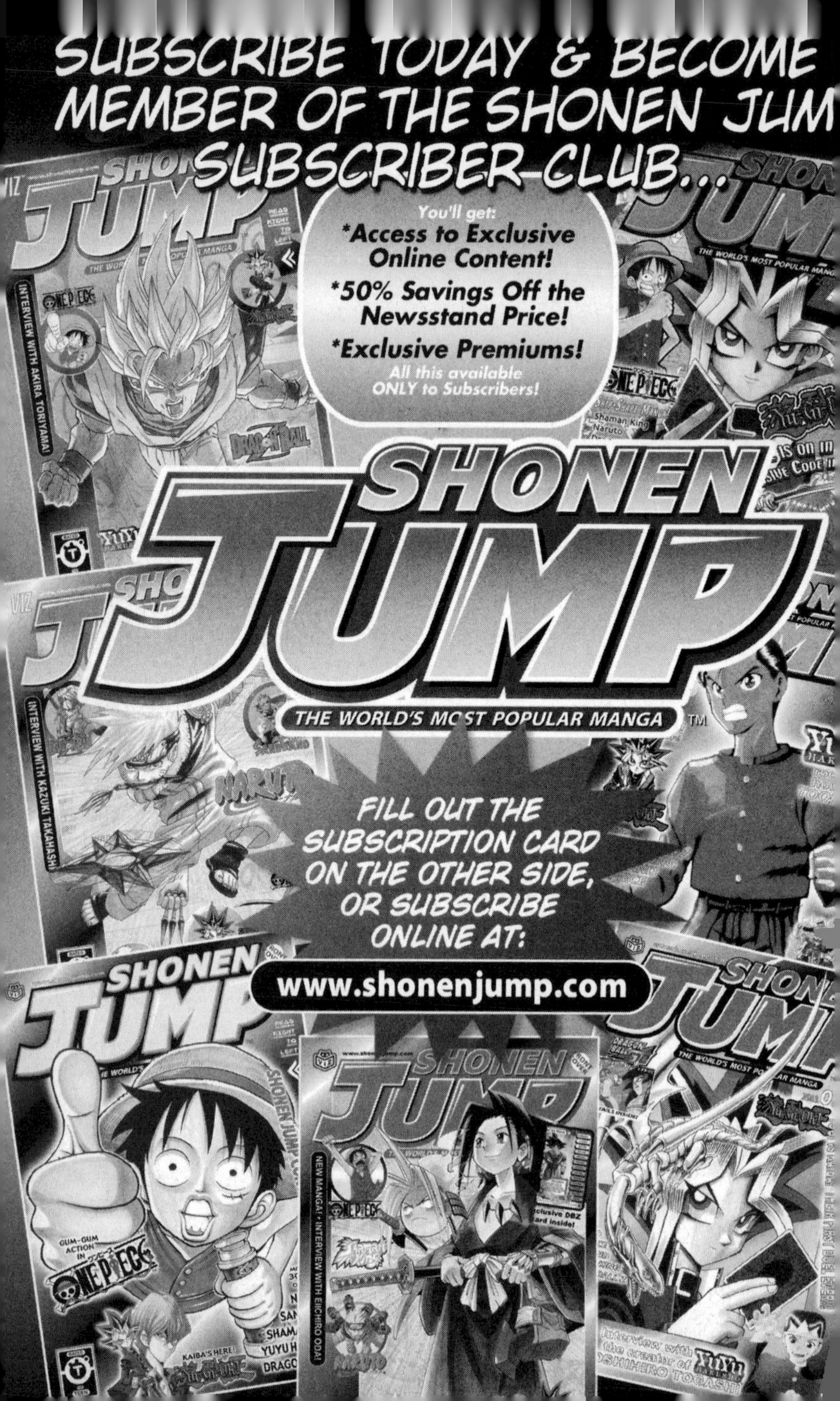

SUBSCRIBE TODAY & BECOME
MEMBER OF THE SHONEN JUM
SUBSCRIBER CLUB...
You'll get:
*Access to Exclusive Online Content!
*50% Savings Off the Newsstand Price!
*Exclusive Premiums!
All this available ONLY to Subscribers!
SHONEN JUMP
THE WORLD'S MOST POPULAR MANGA ™
FILL OUT THE SUBSCRIPTION CARD ON THE OTHER SIDE, OR SUBSCRIBE ONLINE AT:
www.shonenjump.com